PSYCHOTHERAPY:
THE
ANALYTIC
APPROACH

PSYCHOTHERAPY: THE ANALYTIC APPROACH

Edited by

**Morton J. Aronson, M.D., and
Melvin A. Scharfman, M.D.**

JASON ARONSON INC.
*Northvale, New Jersey
London*

Production Editor: Judith D. Cohen

This book was set in Palacio by Lind Graphics of Upper Saddle River, New Jersey, and printed and bound by Haddon Craftsmen of Scranton, Pennsylvania.

The authors gratefully acknowledge the following for permission to reprint material:

Chapter 7, from *Journal of the American Psychoanalytic Association*, 1983, vol. 31, pp. 587–618. Copyright © 1983 by International Universities Press. Reprinted by permission of International Universities Press.

Chapter 12, from *Handbook of Phobia Therapy*, edited by Carol Lindemann, pp. 395–403. Copyright © 1989 by Jason Aronson Inc. Reprinted by permission of Jason Aronson, Inc.

Chapter 13, from *Hysterical Personality Style and the Histrionic Personality Disorder*, edited by Mardi J. Horowitz, pp. 149–191. Copyright © 1991 by Jason Aronson Inc. Reprinted by permission of Jason Aronson, Inc.

Library of Congress Cataloging-in-Publication Data

Psychotherapy : the analytic approach / edited by Morton J. Aronson
  and Melvin A. Scharfman.
     p. cm.
  Includes bibliographical references and index.
  ISBN 0-87668-508-4 (hard cover)
  1. Psychoanalysis. 2. Psychotherapy. I. Aronson, Morton J.
II. Scharfman, Melvin A. 1928-   .
  [DNLM: 1. Mental Disorders—therapy. 2. Psychoanalytic Therapy—
methods. 3. Psychotherapy—methods. WM 460.6 P97474]
RC504.P82 1992
616.89'17—dc20
DNLM/DLC
for Library of Congress   92-10540

Manufactured in the United States of America. Jason Aronson Inc. offers books and cassettes. For information and catalog write to Jason Aronson Inc., 230 Livingston Street, Northvale, New Jersey 07647.

CONTENTS

CONTRIBUTORS

Sander M. Abend, M.D.

Training and Supervising Analyst, The New York Psychoanalytic Institute; Associate Editor, *The Psychoanalytic Quarterly.*

David W. Allen, M.D.

Clinical Professor Emeritus, Psychiatry, University of California, San Francisco.

Jacob A. Arlow, M.D.

Past President, American Psychoanalytic Association; Former Editor-in-Chief, *The Psychoanalytic Quarterly.*

Morton J. Aronson, M.D.

Training and Supervising Analyst, Columbia University Center for Psychoanalytic Training and Research; Assistant Clinical Professor of Psychiatry, College of Physicians and Surgeons, Columbia University.

Isidor Bernstein, M.D.

Training and Supervising Analyst, The New York Psychoanalytic Institute; Training and Supervising Analyst for Child and Adolescent Analysis, The New York Psychoanalytic Institute and The Psychoanalytic Institute, New York University Medical Center; Associate Clinical Professor of Psychiatry, New York University Medical Center.

Harold P. Blum, M.D.

Clinical Professor of Psychiatry and Training and Supervising Analyst, The Psychoanalytic Institute, New York University Medical Center; Executive Director, Sigmund Freud Archives.

Martin H. Blum, M.D.

Faculty, The Psychoanalytic Institute, New York University Medical Center.

Robert M. Chalfin, M.D.

Clinical Associate Professor of Psychiatry, Albert Einstein College of Medicine; Faculty, The Psychoanalytic Institute, New York University Medical Center.

Barbara G. Deutsch, M.D.

Assistant Clinical Professor of Psychiatry, New York University; Faculty, The Psychoanalytic Institute, New York University Medical Center.

Jules Glenn, M.D.

Clinical Professor of Psychiatry and Training and Supervising Analyst in Child and Adult Analysis, The Psychoanalytic Institute, New York University Medical Center; Former president of the Association for Child Psychoanalysis.

Warren H. Goodman, M.D.

Faculty, Departments of Psychiatry, Cornell University Medical College, Albert Einstein College of Medicine of Yeshiva University, and New York University Medical Center.

Stanley Grossman, M.D.

Training and Supervising Analyst and Clinical Professor of Psychiatry, The Psychoanalytic Institute, New York University Medical Center.

Eugene Halpert, M.D.

Training and Supervising Analyst, The Psychoanalytic Institute, New York University Medical Center; Clinical Associate Professor of Psychiatry, New York University Medical Center.

Richard J. Kessler, D.O.

Assistant Clinical Professor of Psychiatry, Albert Einstein College of Medicine; Faculty, The Psychoanalytic Institute, New York University Medical Center.

David Newman, M.D.

Training and Supervising Analyst and Clinical Associate Professor of Psychiatry, The Psychoanalytic Institute, New York University Medical Center.

Melvin A. Scharfman, M.D.

Clinical Professor of Psychiatry, New York University College of Medicine; Training and Supervising Analyst, The Psychoanalytic Institute, New York University Medical Center.

Arthur M. Schwartz, M.D.

Clinical Associate Professor in Psychiatry, Cornell University College of Medicine.

Foreword

Jacob A. Arlow, M.D.

There is a compelling need for a book on psychoanalytically informed psychotherapy. A consistent presentation of the theoretical and practical aspects of this form of treatment has long been overdue. There are many reasons that this is so. In his encyclopedic textbook of psychoanalysis, Fenichel (1950) said that while there are many different kinds of psychotherapy, only psychoanalysis, which constitutes a comprehensive theory of mental functioning, can explain how any form of psychotherapy works. For him and for most members of his generation, classical psychoanalysis, consisting of the psychoanalytic situation, free association, and at least four sessions a week, constituted the definitive testing ground, the laboratory wherein issues of both theory and practice could be confirmed. Fundamentally, this is still true, but in the past forty to fifty years much has changed in psychoanalysis. With the passing of Freud and the generation of his immediate successors, uniformity of viewpoint concerning what constitutes psychoanalysis no longer prevails. Disagreements are so wide that Wallerstein (1988) raised the issue of whether there is no longer one psychoanalysis but perhaps several psychoanalyses. Often enough, I might add, one person's psychoanalysis constitutes another person's psychotherapy.

Broadly viewed, the controversies within psychoanalysis today fall into two categories, that is, issues concerning the nature and function of the psychic apparatus in general and, more specifically, issues concerning the nature of the process of pathogenesis. For example, there are those analysts who minimize or would eliminate the dynamic aspect of psychoanalytic theory by discarding the concept of driving forces. They attempt to base a theory of mental functioning on concepts derived from studies of development, personal interaction, or neurophysiology. The central question is: What motivates mental activity? Tied to these problems are issues that concern theories of pathogenesis. Exactly what is mental illness? How and why do people develop psychological difficulties? For every mental health practitioner using a psychoanalytic orientation, issues of pathogenesis pertain not only to a general theory of mental functioning; they also affect the practical, technical measures that the therapist employs in the treatment of his patients (Arlow 1981, 1986).

These controversies have only compounded what has been a long-standing problem regarding the nature of psychoanalytic psychotherapy. In one of the earlier debates on the subject, one colleague had occasion to lament how "the pure gold of psychoanalysis was being contaminated by the dross of psychotherapy." His ability to make so sharp a separation between the two, however, was not shared by many of his colleagues. On several occasions (1954, 1979) the American Psychoanalytic Association devoted a full panel to the distinction between psychoanalysis and psychoanalytic psychotherapy. Some of the most gifted and articulate analysts contributed to these symposia. No unanimous agreement, no common opinion emerged from these discussions.

As stated earlier, these problems reflect differences analysts have among themselves concerning the nature of the psychoanalytic process and its implications for technique. This poses the question of what the therapist does, and why. For example, there are some analysts who believe that the psychoanalytic experience should be approached purely as scientific inquiry, the counterpart of a laboratory experiment. They believe one should analyze without concern for therapeutic gain. Such technique epitomizes in extreme form Freud's (1912) original advice, that the analyst should serve as nothing more than a reflecting mirror. At the other extreme are those who orient their technique primarily toward making the patient feel better during the treatment experience. They tend to be more active, use techniques they consider empathic, and share knowledge of their affective responses with the patient. With so wide a range of divergent views and approaches to the conduct of standard psychoanalysis, it is not at all surprising that little agreement could be reached on the distinction between psychoanalysis and psychoanalytic psychotherapy. Any book on psychodynamic psychotherapy, accordingly, must consider where to strike a proper balance between these two extremes.

No volume on psychotherapy can deal definitively and comprehensively with issues concerning the individuality of the particular psychotherapist. Every practitioner develops his own style and technique based on what he has been taught and what he has experienced, but, as we know, in a most fundamental way based on the nature of his own personality makeup. The psychotherapist has to be aware of his or her personal foibles and predilections, of the type of patient or problem preferred, and of the characteristic responses to the inevitable challenges and trials that supervene in the course of therapy. These issues are difficult enough to deal with at the more leisurely pace that standard or classical psychoanalysis affords. In fact, dynamic psychotherapy is perhaps even more challenging to the practitioner. One has to be nimble and quick and forever in intimate contact with the derivative manifestations of the patient's conflicts, as well as with the significance of the affective and intellectual responses of the therapist. In dynamic psychotherapy, prolonged silences on the part of the therapist, for example, and excessive periods of free-floating attention are impermissible luxuries. It goes without saying, therefore, that each therapist should have undergone a period of personal analysis and should have benefited from the additional insights about self and style acquired during the experience of supervision. It may be ironic, but it seems that years of work with patients in standard psychoanalysis is perhaps the best preparation for conducting psychoanalytic psychotherapy.

With the foregoing considerations in mind, it is clear that in many respects, the conduct of psychoanalytic psychotherapy makes even greater demands on the skills of the therapist. Accordingly, it behooves each therapist to sharpen his methodology and to be especially mindful of the context, the sequence, and the contiguity of the elements in the patient's productions. The therapist must also be sensitive to the intrusion of unusual or bizarre elements and to the use by the patient of figurative language as manifestations of unconscious conflict. Psychotherapy requires more efficient, more dynamic, and less stilted listening on the part of the therapist.

The fact that the setting of dynamic psychotherapy is more in the nature of communication in terms of ordinary dialogue is, in my opinion, a favorable element, one that assists, rather than hinders, the therapeutic process. All psychotherapy is basically a special form of conversation. In ordinary conversation, communicative dissonance is disruptive of the process of meaningful interaction. Viewing the psychotherapeutic encounter in terms of a conversation makes differences of meaning, lapses of continuity, and intrusive irrelevancies stand out more clearly, thus directing the therapist's attention to the distortions of communication generated by the intrusion of unconscious factors. While all these elements are significant in the conduct of standard psychoanalysis, they become even more important in the course of dynamic psychotherapy.

Finally, there are the practical considerations that influence the nature of psychotherapy in the current American scene. These considerations apply both to standard psychoanalysis and to dynamic psychotherapy. Psychoanalysis and psychotherapy have long since ceased being the special domain of medically trained therapists. Preparation for the practice of medicine nowadays is perforce predominantly and almost exclusively a matter of acquiring vast knowledge of a highly technical nature. Today in medicine there are subspecialties within subspecialties of specialties. Very little of the knowledge acquired in medical school is relevant to the practice of dynamic psychotherapy.

In addition, the influence of economic factors is very important but can hardly be dealt with adequately in a brief introductory essay. For a large percentage, perhaps the majority, of patients in dynamic psychotherapy, the cost of treatment is borne by third-party payers. The original texts or handbooks of psychotherapy were directed primarily toward physicians practicing in an economic world that is now in the distant past. With the increase in the cost of living, fewer patients nowadays are ready to accept the arduous and expensive experience of classical psychoanalysis. Accordingly, while the number of patients in psychoanalysis has been shrinking in the past few years, the number of individuals choosing dynamic psychotherapy has increased enormously. Also, the nature of the patient population and of the therapist population has changed in recent years, and so have the complaints that bring people to psychotherapy. For the reasons enumerated above, in this altered context it is clear that an updated, coherent statement of the principles and practice of dynamic psychotherapy is in order.

Meeting this challenge, the editors of this volume have made a most felicitous choice of contributors. The authors of the individual chapters are all psychoanalysts with many years of experience in the conduct of both psychoanalysis and analytic psychotherapy. As individuals, they were trained in several different psychoanalytic institutes, and they tend to emphasize different aspects of the vast body of psychoanalytic theory and practice. What is unique about this group of contributors, however, is that nearly all of them have worked together in the same geographic area, in an analytic society, in a teaching institute, in study groups, and in joint seminars. During many years of sharp discourse they have honed their understanding of the essentials of the theory and practice of dynamic psychotherapy. They have prepared themselves well for the challenge that a volume of this sort represents.

REFERENCES

Arlow, J. A. (1981). Theories of pathogenesis. *Psychoanalytic Quarterly* 50:488–513.
_____ (1986). The relation of theories of pathogenesis to therapy. In *Psychoanalysis—The Science of Mental Conflict: Essays in Honor of Charles Brenner*, ed. A. Richards and M. Willick, pp. 49–63. Hillsdale, NJ: The Analytic Press.
Fenichel, O. (1950). *Psychoanalytic Theory of Neurosis*. New York: W. W. Norton.
Freud, S. (1912). Recommendations to physicians practicing psychoanalysis. *Standard Edition* 12:111–120.
Wallerstein, R. S. (1988). One psychoanalysis or many. *International Journal of Psycho-Analysis* 69:5–22.

1

Principles of Psychoanalytic Psychotherapy

Morton J. Aronson, M.D.

INTRODUCTION

This book is addressed to the broad spectrum of mental health professionals who practice psychotherapy. The concepts may at times be difficult for those not yet familiar with the psychoanalytic literature and at times be a bit basic for the experienced psychoanalyst. We aim for the broad middle range and hope those at the poles can find enough of value to warrant the reading.

The book grew out of a series of lectures to the mental health community by members of the Long Island Psychoanalytic Society at North Shore University Hospital in 1990. Additional chapters have been included, but all are by members of the American Psychoanalytic Association, all classical in training and in orientation. Despite the commonalities, there will be differences in theoretical points of view and in technical approaches to clinical work. However, all the authors share the basic core concepts of classic psychoanalytic theory, as well as the basic principles of analytic psychotherapy. These are analysts writing about psychoanalytic psychotherapy, not about psychoanalysis.

Psychoanalytic psychotherapy represents the application of the broad spectrum of unified psychoanalytic theory (i.e., classical analytic theory with accretions from developmental, object relations, and self psychology theory) to psychotherapy. Whether in one or five sessions a week, the face-to-face therapy is an effort by the analyst to understand the patient and to help him to understand himself. The basic goal of understanding, comprehending one's unconscious conflicts and how they give rise to neurotic symptoms

1

and troublesome character pathology, differentiates this approach from other therapies that attempt modification of behavior by manipulation or support. Although we understand that change in analytic psychotherapy, as in analysis, is partly the result of such noninterpreted elements as transference gratification, learning in a new object relationship, and identifications in the ego and superego with the benign work ego of the analyst, the primary or overriding principle is emotionally meaningful insight growing out of interpretation of unconscious intrapsychic conflict.

This approach stands in sharp contrast, for example, with the type of therapy employed by many adherents of the self psychology movement. Although self psychology therapists acknowledge the role of interpretation of intrapsychic conflict in the treatment of neurotic patients, they eschew such an approach in patients whose problems reflect primarily narcissistic pathology. With these patients the role of interpretation is confined to fostering the growth-promoting therapeutic relationship. Narcissistic patients, in their view, suffer primarily from developmental deficits that can be repaired by means of a corrective emotional experience in which the therapist provides them with the empathic resonance they failed to receive age appropriately in their early childhood. Kohut (1977) viewed such patients as *tragic man*, as opposed to neurotic patients, so-called *guilty man*. In the treatment of tragic man, there is no role for guilt; his failures are the fault of significant others in his adult life, his parents in childhood, and his therapist in the treatment relationship. As it has occurred throughout the history of psychoanalysis, the problem with the alternate schools is that they tend to exaggerate one particular area of psychoanalytic theory and psychopathology and neglect other large areas of psychoanalytic knowledge, as well as the multiple determinants of neurotic symptoms and character pathology. One gets the impression that virtually all the patients they see turn out to suffer from narcissistic personality disorders, that guilty man no longer exists. Mainstream psychoanalysts recognize that many patients have narcissistic features, but that these exist alongside many other areas of intrapsychic conflict. Furthermore, it is not a case of deficit versus conflict; all patients have some areas of developmental deficit, which then shape the form of preoedipal, oedipal, and postoedipal intrapsychic conflicts.

Let us imagine a case of a patient embroiled in a sadomasochistic marriage who is in therapy because of marital unhappiness. The patient recounts in a given session an episode of abuse by the marital partner. The patient is distraught. The self psychology therapist typically responds with empathic understanding of how hurtful this experience must have been for the patient. Thus the self psychology therapist displays his empathy. The analytic therapist uses his empathy to help him understand the patient. While sympathizing with the patient's distress, he raises the question of whether the patient has considered the possibility that, without being aware of doing so, he might have played a part in provoking the attack. If the data were available, he might also point out that on earlier occasions the patient seemed to be trying to provoke the therapist and that this was similar to experiences in the past when, as a child, the patient witnessed such provocation and attacks between the parents.

In this example, the analytic therapist is exploring the possibility that the patient is enacting an unconscious masochistic fantasy, the meaning of which can then be interpreted dynamically, genetically, and in the transference in terms of the drive, defense, and superego elements that form a compromise that finds expression in the fantasy. Other aspects of the patient's conflicts could be explored as well. The example is chosen only to illustrate the interpretative approach. This approach is unique to analytic psychotherapy and psychoanalysis. Other therapies may be successful in symptom removal, such as behavior modification, sex therapy, and drug therapy; but the usual patient who enters analytic therapy seeks more comprehensive goals and wants to understand why he feels, acts, and suffers as he does.

BASIC TECHNIQUES

Bibring (1954) pointed out that all forms of psychotherapy are defined by their employment of five basic techniques.

Suggestion

On the basis of a primitive form of positive transference in which the therapist is endowed with authority, the therapist is able to induce thoughts, feelings, attitudes, or behaviors in the patient independent of the patient's rational, critical thinking. Therapeutic change based on suggestion tends to be transitory and requires the continuing presence of the primitive transference figure. In a more subtle form, suggestion may enhance the process of therapy by encouraging the patient to explore the reasons for his avoidance of certain topics, feelings, and transference wishes or to produce memories, fantasies, and dreams.

Abreaction

Abreaction refers to the discharge of pent-up, previously warded off affects. This technique goes back to the early days of psychoanalysis, when Freud and Breuer believed that hysterical patients suffered from *reminiscences*, memories of traumatic sexual seductions in childhood that, with their associated effects, were barred from consciousness and found disguised symbolic expression in hysterical symptoms. Recovery of these memories under hypnosis and discharge of their associated affects was thought to be curative. With the abandonment of the seduction theory of neurosogenesis and the discovery of the drives, the defenses, and the superego, as well as with the abandonment of hypnosis and the discovery of the free-association technique, the role of abreaction changed from curative to technical. The technical role of abreaction consists of those measures by which the analyst enables the patient to make contact with, and optimally express, the affects associated with his impulses, fantasies, and memories, conveying a sense of conviction to the insights he achieves. This is what is meant by emotionally meaningful insight as opposed to intellectual, theoretical insight. Emotionally meaningful insight is achieved by abreaction combined with interpretation.

Abreaction as a curative technique continues to be used in the treatment of acute traumatic neuroses, such as traumatic war neuroses, particularly where amnesia is present.

Manipulation

This technique in crude form refers to giving advice, running a patient's life, and has no place in analytic psychotherapy. Bibring (1954) used the term to denote a technical maneuver on the part of the therapist aimed at promoting the treatment or fostering therapeutic change. For example, it would foster the treatment to persuade a phobic patient to expose himself to his fears. Maintaining an equilibrium in the transference between too little and too much activation would be a technical manipulation. Therapeutic manipulation would find expression in "the analyst's accepting attitude, his friendly neutrality and objectivity, his readiness to understand and not to judge, etc. These represent not only technical tools which help the patient to release his self expression, but offer him also the 'new' experience in relation to parental and other images as well as in relation to his own self" (Bibring 1954, p. 763). The use of the term *manipulation* as a technical instrument in psychotherapy and analysis has dropped out of favor in recent years, probably because of its slightly pejorative connotation. The concept is subsumed in such terms as *technical parameters, treatment tactics,* and *analytic attitude.*

Clarification

This term subsumes those efforts of the therapist to make clearer for the patient the nature of his feelings, thoughts, attitudes, and behaviors as they are communicated in the flow of his associations and in his attitudes and behavior toward the therapist. According to Bibring (1954),

> Clarification does not refer to unconscious (repressed or otherwise warded off) material but to conscious and/or preconscious processes, of which the patient is not sufficiently aware, which escape his attention but which he recognizes more or less readily when they are clearly presented to him. Many, if not all, patients are often rather vague about certain feelings, attitudes, thoughts, impulses, behavior or reaction patterns, perceptions, etc. They cannot recognize or differentiate adequately what troubles them, they relate matters which are unrelated, or fail to relate what belongs together, or they do not perceive of or evaluate reality properly but in a distorted fashion under the influence of their emotions or neurotic patterns. In brief, there is a lack of awareness (recognition) where awareness is possible. Clarification in therapy aims at those vague and obscure factors (frequently below the level of verbalization) which are relevant from the viewpoint of treatment: it refers to those techniques and therapeutic processes which assist the patient to reach a higher level of self-awareness, clarity and differentiation of self observation which makes adequate verbalization possible. [p. 755]

Clarification enlists the observing ego of the patient to gain distance from and a degree of objectivity toward his experiencing ego. It is a clarification when the therapist points out to the patient that he, the patient, always talks about terminating the treatment before the therapist's vacations. This clarification lays the groundwork for the interpretation of how the patient unconsciously turns passive into active in order to ward off the pain of rejection.

It is a clarification when a therapist points out to a patient how frequently he seems to feel let down and depressed after a success in one or another competitive activity. It is a further clarification when the therapist explains that the patient's depression is the result of a feeling of guilt over his triumph. These clarifications lay the groundwork for interpretation of the patient's unconscious wishes to castrate and murder his rivals, his brothers, or his father, and the fear of punishment and guilt that these wishes engender.

This usage of clarification comes close to what many analysts call confrontation. For example, "I think you are feeling annoyed with me today," or "You are late for your session as you are late in paying your bill," or "You are resisting today." I prefer to use the term *clarification* to denote all those ways by which the therapist brings feelings, thoughts, and behavior to the attention of the patient. The term *confrontation* has the unfortunate implication of an aggressive act, a challenge to the patient. Clarification for purposes of mutual exploration leading to interpretation is what is meant.

As can be seen from the above examples, clarification and interpretation are intimately related techniques. Clarification precedes interpretation and frequently follows it in the ongoing work of achieving insight in the therapeutic process.

Interpretation

Interpretation is the sine qua non of analytic psychotherapy and psychoanalysis. It is specifically applied to unconscious psychic processes. It is that technique that identifies and gives meaning to unconscious wishes, motives, defenses, fantasies, and so on. Interpretations are informed inferences, hypotheses, and guesses arrived at by the therapist from his knowledge of the patient's mental life and behavior; from the patient's associations, dreams, fantasies, and parapraxes; and from the therapist's theoretical knowledge and knowledge of his own unconscious processes. Of particular importance in arriving at interpretations is the therapist's close scrutiny of the patient's feelings, attitudes, and behavior toward the therapist and the feelings and attitudes about the patient that arise in the therapist. Interpretations are provisional hypotheses and find verification or refutation in the subsequent flow of the material and in the patient's reaction or lack of reaction to them. The therapist makes many interpretations in the course of his work with the patient, but even a single interpretation is not a single act. It is part of an ongoing process called *working through*, in which an interpretation is applied repeatedly to first one and then another example in the patient's present and past mental life.

Suggestion, abreaction, and manipulation may be utilized to produce therapeutic change and to facilitate the therapeutic process, but only clarification and interpretation lead to insight into unconscious psychic conflict.

Interpretation is the subject of several chapters in this book, and examples are given in every essay. It would be redundant to discuss interpretation further at this point. Suffice it to say that clarification and interpretation are the fundamental technical principles of analytic psychotherapy and psychoanalysis.

SIMILARITIES AND DIFFERENCES BETWEEN ANALYTIC PSYCHOTHERAPY AND PSYCHOANALYSIS

Freud's discoveries at the turn of the century, an incredible advance in the history of human thought, created a revolution in psychiatry and reached out to leave their imprint on virtually every aspect of human experience. Psychoanalysis, as a technique of treatment, reached its greatest popularity in the United States after World War II. Physicians in the armed forces were exposed for the first time to psychoanalytically trained military psychiatrists who applied psychoanalytic knowledge to the treatment of combat neuroses with impressive success. Psychoanalytic training institutes thrived, and analysts taught psychiatric residents how to do psychotherapy in programs all over the country. As a result, analytic psychotherapy became the dominant treatment modality for nonpsychotic mental and emotional illness in the United States and in much of the Western world. In the last twenty years the revolution in biological psychiatry has eclipsed the popularity of analytic psychotherapy, particularly in psychiatric residency programs. As a result, more and more young psychiatrists, expert in psychopharmacology, graduated with little interest or training in analytic psychotherapy. The public demand and need for psychotherapy, however, has continued, and the gap provided the opportunity for psychologists and social workers to provide this service. Thus, at present, psychologists and social workers in private practice and in clinics make up a large segment of the mental health professional community who practice analytic psychotherapy. In psychiatry the pendulum is starting to swing back, with more and more calls for balanced training and treatment that include both drugs and psychotherapy. It has been said that prior to the rise of biological psychiatry, psychiatry was a "brainless" science. With the rise of biological psychiatry, it became "mindless."

The close relationship that exists between psychoanalysis and analytic psychotherapy has led to the blurring of the distinction between them and has been the subject of debate in the analytic literature for many years. Psychoanalysis consists of (1) a comprehensive theory of the mind, (2) a means of research utilizing the method of free association, and (3) a technique of treatment that focuses on the analysis of transference, resistance, and unconscious intrapsychic conflict. Analytic psychotherapy shares in all three aspects. Its basic science is psychoanalytic theory, whether experience-near clinical theory or more abstract metapsychological theory. As a method of research, its observational data consist of a form of free association that is similar to but also different from free association in analysis, a difference that will be discussed below.

It is in the realm of technique that the major differences occur. Even though analytic psychotherapy also focuses on transference, resistance, and unconscious intrapsychic conflict, the method of approach is fundamentally different. The failure to understand the essential difference between the analytic situation and the therapy situation not infrequently leads therapists to view therapy as a mini-analysis. In a caricature of analytic technique, the therapist may become too rigid, too silent, and too abstinent. Such an approach to therapy often causes intense dissatisfaction in the patient and may result in disruption of the treatment. One not infrequently sees patients who left a previous therapist because "he never said anything, he just sat there." Although lengthy periods of silent listening to the patient's free associations and to the analyst's associations and feelings are appropriate in psychoanalysis, in the face-to-face therapy situation, which by its nature is interactive, prolonged periods of inactivity by the therapist are unnatural and inappropriate. Therapy is essentially a conversation between patient and therapist, although the burden of the conversation and the selection of topics is largely left up to the patient. Analysis is not a conversation; it is a much more solitary experience for the patient, and the analyst's interventions are confined to clarification and interpretation.

The abstinence rule in psychoanalysis consists of the analyst's efforts to keep at a tolerable minimum the gratification of the patient's infantile instinctual wishes as they emerge toward the analyst. The frustration of these wishes fosters the development of a regressive transference neurosis in which feelings toward and conflicts about the analyst and the analytic situation come to dominate the patient's emotional life. It is through interpretation and working through of the transference neurosis that maximum insight is achieved. The analyst is warm, friendly, and concerned about the patient but nevertheless declines to answer the patient's questions, provide reassurance, support, advice, and so on. For example, if the analyst cancels sessions, he does not explain to the patient that he canceled because he was ill. Such information would close off the opportunity to analyze the patient's fantasies and resentment. The rule of abstinence plays a similar role in the psychotherapy situation but is less rigorously applied. At one end of the continuum, in work with patients whose conflicts are primarily preoedipal and who have significant areas of developmental deficit and poor frustration tolerance, a supportive stance is necessary to keep the treatment process going, particularly in the early stages. At the other end of the continuum, in work with high-functioning patients whose conflicts are primarily oedipal, who have few developmental deficits, and who have a reasonable tolerance for frustration, the therapist's abstinent stance approaches that in the analytic situation. Too much warmth, encouragement, and support tend to produce idealizing, submissive transference. Hostile, negative transferences do not emerge, and the opportunity to identify and resolve important areas of unconscious conflict is lost.

THE THERAPEUTIC RELATIONSHIP

All forms of therapy work in the context of a therapeutic relationship. In psychoanalysis and analytic psychotherapy, the therapeutic relationship consists of (1) the real relationship between therapist and patient, (2) the therapeutic alliance, and (3) the transference and countertransference.

The real relationship refers to the reaction of each participant to the perception of the actual, realistic characteristics of the other. If one is a physically attractive person and the other feels some faint sexual attraction, this is not necessarily a transference. Similarly, if one participant tends to be cold and critical and the other reacts negatively, this is not necessarily a transference reaction. However, in either case, the appropriate realistic reaction may become intertwined with and augmented by transference distortions from previous object relationships. Throughout the course of both forms of treatment, it is an important task of the therapist to determine which of the patient's reactions to him are transference distortions and which are appropriate reactions to his own behavior and actual self. In like manner, he must continually scrutinize his own reactions to the patient and determine which are his transference reactions to the patient or to the patient's transference and which are appropriate reactions to the real behavior and actual self of the patient.

One of the important differences between therapy and analysis is to be found in this area of the work. Despite the therapist's adoption of a physicianlike attitude and neutral stance, many more aspects of his real personality will emerge in the give-and-take of the face-to-face, interactive therapy situation than will be discernible in the analyst's quiet anonymity. As a result, transference distortions in therapy tend to be more subtle and stand out less in bold relief than they do in analysis. Because they are less clearly recognizable, it is more difficult to detect them and to convince the patient of their existence.

The therapeutic alliance, although it has transference roots, refers to the mature, relatively nonneurotic, reasonable rapport the patient has with the therapist. The term was introduced by Zetzel (1956) and is essentially the same concept as the effective transference or rapport of Freud (1913), the rational transference of Fenichel (1941), the mature transference of Stone (1961), and the working alliance of Greenson (1967). This rapport reflects an alliance between the patient's reasonable ego and the analyst's analyzing ego. It represents a partial identification with the therapist's nonjudgmental, exploratory analytic attitude. It is an essential ingredient in the therapeutic relationship that sustains the analytic work and makes it possible for the patient to listen to the analyst's interpretations and give them serious consideration, even when they make him uncomfortable. The development of the alliance is facilitated by the patient's neurotic suffering and the analyst's reliability, empathy, and emphasis on understanding, as well as by the daily frequency of the sessions and the use of the analytic couch (Greenacre 1954). In psychoanalysis no particular activity is required by the analyst to foster the development of the alliance. Interpretation of resistance and the analytic attitude are usually sufficient. In analytic psychotherapy, because of the infrequency of the sessions, the analytic stance and resistance interpretations frequently need to be buttressed by educative measures to enhance the development of the alliance. For example, the therapist might guide the patient in what topics to talk about or explain why he has to pay for a missed session.

Transference

Transference is the unconscious displacement onto a current person of patterns of thought, feeling, and behavior that originated in an important object relationship in childhood. Although it is a feature of all human relationships, it is a technical term for the distortions the patient experiences in the perception of the therapist in the relatively uncontaminated patient–therapist relationship. The development of a full-blown regressive transference neurosis is a central, although not exclusive, feature of psychoanalytic treatment. Its development is fostered by the analytic situation, the neutral abstinent stance of the analyst, and the analyst's interpretations of the patient's resistances to the awareness of the transference. Transference manifestations are usually not interpreted early in analysis; they are allowed to broaden and deepen. They are interpreted when their clarity is unmistakable in the "here and now" of the analytic relationship and in the "there and then" of their genetic origins. In analysis the transference is interpreted and worked through in all of its manifestations, so that it is largely resolved by the time of termination.

Transference interpretation is an important feature of analytic psychotherapy but, in my view, it does not play the central role that it does in psychoanalysis. This is one of the essential differences between psychotherapy and psychoanalysis. In psychotherapy a regressive transference neurosis is deliberately not fostered. Because of the infrequency of the sessions and their face-to-face character, a regressive transference neurosis would disrupt the treatment if it were to occur. Explicit transference manifestations, particularly if they are negative, are interpreted early, both to convey insight and to prevent them from broadening and deepening. Implicit transference manifestations are not made explicit by interpretations unless they will interfere with the work or prove harmful to the patient (such as acting out of transference wishes in displaced form outside the therapy situation). Nonerotic positive transference is not interpreted and thus is not dissipated at termination.

Countertransference

Countertransference refers to the therapist's unconscious reactions to the patient and the patient's transference. These reactions arise from the therapist's unconscious conflicts and, typically, find expression in inappropriate displacements onto the patient of object relationships in the therapist's childhood. In this sense, the countertransference of the therapist parallels the transference of the patient. Countertransference also means that the patient's conflicts and wishes impinge on unresolved problems in the therapist, leading to blind spots or inappropriate responses to the patient's transference love or aggression. Thus, for example, if the therapist is threatened by his own unconscious aggression, it might be difficult for him to detect similar impulses in his patient or to placate him when his resentment is directed at the therapist.

Many analysts, including the editors, consider countertransference as a reference to the analyst's transference to the patient, the patient's material, and the analytic setting, as well as to the analyst's transference to the patient's transference. Some analysts limit the term *countertransference* to the analyst's transference to the patient's transference. At the other extreme are those who view countertransference as the total emotional reaction of the analyst to the patient in the treatment situation. Classical analysts consider the totalist view so broad as to render the term countertransference practically meaningless.

Whether countertransference reactions cause blind spots in the therapist's understanding of the patient, or errors in technique, such as incorrect or ill-timed interpretations, or inappropriate feelings or attitudes about the patient, all constitute serious hindrances to the treatment. Freud (1910) said that "no psychoanalyst goes further than his own complexes and internal resistances permit" (pp. 144–145). For this reason, he recommended that the analyst have a personal analysis of his own and that he conduct a continual self-analysis. Although countertransference reactions are a threat to the treatment, analysts since Freud have increasingly recognized that they exist throughout the treatment and that the analyst's understanding of them can lead to increased insight into processes occurring within the patient.

Countertransference is as important in analytic psychotherapy as it is in psychoanalysis. The analyst's position behind the couch, the daily sessions, and the long periods of quiet reflection make it much more feasible for the analyst to monitor his countertransference feelings and attitudes than is possible in the faster moving, face-to-face, interactive psychotherapy setting. Thus countertransference reactions are less likely to be detected in psychotherapy and pose an even greater threat to the treatment than they do in analysis. For this reason, among others, the analytic psychotherapist should undergo a personal analysis or intensive analytic psychotherapy as part of his training and, in addition, have extensive supervision both during his training and after it.

RESISTANCE

Resistance refers to all the forces within the patient that oppose the work of analysis and interfere with his wishes to gain insight and achieve therapeutic change. Resistance may be conscious or unconscious and may be expressed in thoughts, feelings, fantasies, attitudes, or behavior. Obvious overt expressions of resistance include missed appointments, lateness, failure to pay the bill on time, silence, absence of affect, forgetting of dreams, focus on the past as opposed to the present or vice versa, avoidance of emotionally charged topics, and acting out. More covert examples of resistance include failure of the content of a given session to deepen or the divergence of associations away from areas of conflict rather than converging upon them.

Resistance is the expression in the analytic situation of the defensive aspect of the patient's intrapsychic conflict. As a result, it appears in myriad forms and is present at every step of the treatment. Freud (1912) said, "Every single association, every act of the patient under treatment, must reckon with resistance" (p. 103). Every defense utilized by the patient's ego in his outside life will appear as resistance in the course of his analysis. The motive of defense and resistance is always to avoid a painful affect, such as anxiety, shame, guilt, or depression. The defense is directed against a dangerous instinctual wish, external danger, or self-punitive trend which, if not defended against, would produce the painful affect. Thus instinctual wish, external danger, painful affect, superego-induced guilt, and ego-induced defense are the elements of every conflict. These elements exist in varying proportions, and the relative importance of each varies from one instance to another. Their interaction results in a compromise, and this compromise formation appears in the form of neurotic symptoms, fantasies, dreams, and behavior (Brenner 1976). As Brenner points out, the analysis of resistance and defense is characteristic of modern psychoanalytic technique. It began with the publication of "Inhibitions, Symptoms and Anxiety" (Freud 1926) and was expanded in the works of Anna Freud (1936), Fenichel (1941), Greenson (1967), and many others.

Before the addition of ego analysis, analysts focused on explorations of the id, on bringing repressed infantile wishes into consciousness. Since then, analysts also focus on the anxieties produced by the infantile wishes and on the means of defense employed against them. Because defense, or resistance as the form in which defense appears in treatment, is only one aspect of intrapsychic conflict, it cannot be considered in isolation. It is not sufficient to identify and interpret a resistance or defense without also interpreting what it is defending against and why. It is usually not possible to accomplish this all at once, since it is a task that requires analytic work over a period of time. Furthermore, it is the responsibility of the analyst to help the patient understand how the conflict has been expressed in the analysis, in the patient's outside life, and in his past.

In the early history of psychoanalysis, transference was viewed as the greatest obstacle to the treatment. The patient relived the past experiences instead of remembering them; thus transference functioned as a resistance to the recovery of lost memories, which was the main therapeutic goal of analysis at that time (Aronson 1986). After the abortive analysis of Dora, Freud (1905) realized the significance of transference and said that instead of it being an obstacle to the treatment, it would be its greatest ally. The same is true of the history of resistance. Thus the analysis of transference and resistance are the two pillars on which psychoanalytic treatment rests. Indeed, it is in the arena of the transference that the major resistances in analytic work are encountered. On the one hand, transference itself functions as a resistance, in that the past is relived rather than remembered. On the other hand, transference wishes, particularly when they are intensely sexual or hostile, evoke tenacious resistances to defend against painful anxiety and humiliation were they to be exposed. Also, one set of transference wishes may serve as a resistance to the awareness of another, more threatening set of transference wishes. For example, a competitive, critical, hostile transference may defend against a more anxiety-provoking erotic transference. The identification, interpretation, and working through of transference resistances constitute much of the daily work of analysis.

Most of what has been discussed thus far about the role of resistance in psychoanalysis applies to analytic psychotherapy as well. Some analysts think that all of it does—that a properly conducted analytic psychotherapy is indistinguishable from psychoanalysis, that analysis can be conducted as easily in the chair as on the couch, and that the differences between the two are only quantitative, based on the time available for the work. Editors of this volume, like most classical analysts, do not share this view. Although there are some patients in intensive therapy over a number of years with a skilled psychoanalyst who achieve analytic goals (major resolution of infantile conflicts traced to their genetic dynamic origins, extensive structural change, and reorganization of the personality), this is not true for the vast majority of patients who are treated in analytic psychotherapy. The reason for this is that the two forms of treatment not only are quantitatively different but also are essentially qualitatively different. First of all, the goals of psychotherapy are less ambitious than those for analysis. The goals for most therapy patients are symptom resolution, selected areas of character and behavioral change, and restoration of the pre-illness level of intrapsychic equilibrium—all by means of insight into selected areas of intrapsychic conflict. Second, the process is different. Dewald (Panel 1979) described it as follows:

> Changes occur at a derivative level rather than at core levels; specific conflicts are selected to be the focus; the depth of regressive thinking is limited; conscious and unconscious resistances may be accepted by the therapist and remain uninterpreted; feedback in regard to the therapist's responses is provided; the process of identification with the therapist persists; conscious and unconscious use is made by the patient of the therapist's interventions to provide psychological reinforcement and transference gratification. [p. 130]

Third, the technique of interpretation is different. As Stone (1982) described it,

> Instead of orienting itself to facilitating the spontaneously evolving transference neurosis of the basic psychoanalytic situation, it is usually based on the therapist's conception of what constitutes the major and currently active conflict or conflicts in the patient's presenting illness or disturbed adaptation, and the relationship of such conflict or conflicts to his actual objects. . . . Interpretations, moreover, tend to be holistic, integrative, minimizing the distinctions between defense and impulse, infantile and current, emphasizing large, accessible, and readily intelligible personality dynamisms, except as more detailed elements prevent themselves unequivocally for such understanding. [p. 87]

Fourth, the data available for the therapist's scrutiny are much more limited than is the case in analysis. Rangell (1981) wrote, "The distances between the observational data and the genetic mysteries to which they open doors are generally less in psychoanalysis than in dynamic psychotherapy . . . in therapy the process proceeds via a positive transference, i.e., the basic trust or therapeutic alliance, than by a systematic analysis of the transference and its contents as compared to psychoanalysis" (p. 682).

Analytic psychotherapy is a sector approach in which selected areas of intrapsychic conflict are explored, while others are deliberately left untouched. In contrast to analysis, the therapist guides the process at the rate and depth he considers optimal for a given patient. While in both treatments the therapist functions both as participant and observer, in therapy the participant role is much greater than in analysis at the expense, relatively speaking, of the observer function.

FREE ASSOCIATION

The method of free association was one of Freud's most important discoveries. In Brenner's view (1973), its importance in the exploration of the human psyche was comparable to the microscope in biology and the telescope in astronomy. It is the basic and unique method for communication by the patient in both analysis and analytic psychotherapy. For both analyst and analytic therapist, it is the major avenue to the patient's unconscious conflicts. In analysis the fundamental rule consists of asking the patient to say whatever crosses his mind, whatever he thinks or feels or experiences without choice, direction, or censorship.[1] The intent is to free his associations from conscious control so that their unconscious and preconscious determinants will become discernible to the listening analyst. As the work of analysis continues and the analyst interprets the unconscious resistances to free association, and the patient's insight grows, the associations become progressively freer of unconscious control. This is one of the important indicators of the progress of the analytic process.

The nature of the free-association experience and the data that it yields are substantially different in analysis than they are in therapy. The position on the couch without visual cues from the analyst and the daily sessions promote relaxation of conscious control, emergence of fantasies, and regression toward primary process modes of thinking. For the analyst, the position behind the couch frees him of the need to continually interact with the patient and promotes his relaxed immersion in the continuity of the daily free-association process.

---

[1]Most analysts do not offer the basic rule as a formal instruction on beginning the analysis. However, the sense of it is communicated to the patient in various ways during the opening phase.

In psychotherapy the associations are more influenced by external stimuli. The patient reacts to verbal and nonverbal cues from the therapist more frequently than is the case in analysis. Thoughts emerge at a more fully conscious level and tend to be more rational and reality bound. According to Kris (1982), the less frequent sessions

> usually result in a tendency to diminish the significance of free association. There is a corresponding tendency to substitute formulation for experience, closure for uncertainty. In these circumstance, in order to promote a therapeutic process, the therapist must assist the patient to make formulation and understanding substitute for some of the functions of free association rather than from its content. The experience of satisfaction in free association tends to play a lesser role in psychotherapy. This serves additionally to create a therapeutic process different in quality from the free association process in psychoanalysis. [p. 99]

For these reasons and for the reasons discussed throughout this chapter, less comprehensive data about the richly overdetermined unconscious conflicts become available to the participants in therapy than is the case in analysis. The therapist is obliged to rely on creative guesswork more often than the analyst. As a result, insight into and resolution of even selected areas of conflict tend to be less comprehensive and thorough than in analysis. Thus noninterpretive aspects, such as transference gratification, identification with the therapist, superego modification through identification, and fantasies of gaining strength through contact with the therapist, play a larger role in psychotherapy than they do in analysis.

CONCLUSION

To conclude, I have discussed the principles of analytic therapy and the profound similarities and significant differences between analytic psychotherapy and psychoanalysis. In the analytic community, the status of analytic psychotherapy has come a long way from the early days of its use, when it was regarded as a poor stepchild of psychoanalysis, little more than a form of suggestion, albeit psychoanalytically informed. It has grown into a mature and highly respected scientific discipline, an alternate form of treatment with its own indications and contraindications, but a full partner to its former psychoanalytic parent. Although they continue to be important, the differences between the two forms of treatment have diminished over the last fifty years.[2] The techniques of each have infiltrated the other. As Rangell (1981) noted:

> But just as analysts apply analytic principles freely and copiously to their practice of dynamic psychotherapy, reciprocally and empirically, with ever-increasing complexity and length of psychoanalysis, the opposite also holds. There is no analysis without its share of each of the technical maneuvers noted by Bibring (1954) (i.e., suggestion, abreaction, manipulation, and clarification, along with interpretation), which he also described as occurring in both techniques but which typically one considered to characterize mainly psychotherapy. [p. 670]

Although each form of treatment has its own indications and contraindications, it is a frequent occurrence that a patient who was initially considered unsuitable for analysis becomes suitable after a preliminary period of work in psychotherapy. The reverse is also sometimes true. There are patients who have had a reasonably successful analysis who develop problems later in life that are more suitable for treatment by analytic psychotherapy.

REFERENCES

Aronson, M. (1986). Transference and counter-transference in the treatment of difficult character disorders. In *Between Analyst and Patient*, ed. H. C. Meyers, pp. 13–31. Hillsdale, NJ: The Analytic Press.

Bibring, E. (1954). Psychoanalysis and the dynamic psychotherapies. *Journal of the American Psychoanalytic Association* 2:745–770.

Brenner, C. (1973). *An Elementary Textbook of Psychoanalysis*. New York: International Universities Press.

———— (1976). *Psychoanalytic Technique and Psychic Conflict*. New York: International Universities Press.

Fenichel, O. (1941). *Problem of Psychoanalytic Technique*. Albany, NY: The Psychoanalytic Quarterly.

Freud, A. (1936). *The Ego and the Mechanisms of Defense—The Writings of Anna Freud*, vol. 2. New York: International Universities Press, 1966.

Freud, S. (1905). Fragment of an analysis of a case of hysteria. *Standard Edition* 7:1–122.

---

[2]For a detailed history of the development of psychotherapy and its relationship to psychoanalysis, see R. S. Wallerstein (1989), "Psychoanalysis and Psychotherapy: An Historical Perspective," *International Journal of Psycho-Analysis* 70:563–591.

—————— (1910). The future prospects of psychoanalytic therapy. *Standard Edition* 11:139–151.

—————— (1912). The dynamics of transference. *Standard Edition* 12:97–108.

—————— (1913). On beginning the treatment. *Standard Edition* 12:121–144.

—————— (1926). Inhibitions, symptoms and anxiety. *Standard Edition* 20:75–122.

Greenacre, P. (1954). The role of transference: practical considerations in relation to psychoanalytic therapy. *Journal of the American Psychoanalytic Association* 2:671–684.

Greenson, R. (1967). *The Technique and Practice of Psychoanalysis.* New York: International Universities Press.

Kohut, H. (1977). *The Restoration of the Self.* New York: International Universities Press.

Kris, A. (1982). *Free Association—Method and Process.* New Haven, CT: Yale University Press.

Panel (1979). Conceptualizing the nature of the therapeutic action of psychoanalytic psychotherapy. *Journal of the American Psychoanalytic Association* 27:130.

Rangell, L. (1981). Psychoanalysis and dynamic psychotherapy, similarities and differences twenty-five years later. *Journal of the American Psychoanalytic Association* 50:665–691.

Stone, L. (1961). *The Psychoanalytic Situation.* New York: International Universities Press.

—————— (1982). The influence of the practice and theory of psychotherapy on education in psychoanalysis. In *Psychotherapy: Impact on Psychoanalytic Training,* ed. E. D. Joseph and R. S. Wallerstein, pp. 75–118. New York: International Universities Press.

Zetzel, E. R. (1956). Current concepts of transference. *International Journal of Psycho-Analysis* 37:369–376.

2

The Clinical Assessment of Patients

Melvin A. Scharfman, M.D.

It may seem unnecessary to have a chapter on assessment in a book dedicated to psychoanalytic psychotherapy, but there have been many changing views over the years of what the nature of that assessment should be and what kind of clinical interview best facilitates that assessment. Many current practitioners were trained during an era in which the initial contact emphasized an open-ended, unstructured interview with patients to assess their suitability for treatment. Quite often this was a single interview, on the basis of which a recommendation was made to the patient for exploratory therapy or for psychoanalysis. In the hands of the most experienced clinicians, that was sometimes sufficient. It became clear, however, that for many practitioners this single interview led to inadequate data and sometimes to inappropriate choices of treatment.

In more recent years, partly under the impetus of the increased emphasis on accuracy of diagnosis, there has been a swing in the opposite direction. Largely because of the *Diagnostic and Statistical Manual of Mental Disorders* (currently *DSM-III-R*), there has been a revived effort to acquire specific data, which could only be collected in the context of a very structured interview. The introduction of this kind of structure undoubtedly has refined diagnostic assessment and is particularly oriented toward using that assessment for the appropriate choice of psychopharmacological treatment. Within the manual, there is a section that deals with the evaluation for treatment planning and quite explicit general guidelines for the clinician considering a psychodynamically oriented treatment. Beyond the statement that additional information about the individual being evaluated will invariably be necessary, there is one paragraph devoted to that subject in a volume of almost five hundred pages. That paragraph reads:

> For instance, the clinician considering a psychodynamically-oriented treatment will pay particular attention to the nature of the interaction of the patient with the clinician during the interview, focusing on the particular way the patient molds and distorts the interview situation in order to make it conform to his or her deeply ingrained (usually unconscious) fantasies, attitudes and expectations about interpersonal relationships. The nature of these transference phenomena will be noted in order to predict future behavior in the treatment setting and to shed light on the patient's early developmental experiences and the conflicts that underlie the current disturbance. The clinician will note the patient's ability to reflect upon feelings and fantasies as they are being experienced. The clinician will also monitor his or her own responses to the patient as an indicator of the patient's unconscious conflicts and defensive style. Finally, the clinician will make a psychodynamic diagnostic formulation that is an explanation of the patient's psychopathology in terms of the nature of the unconscious conflicts and defense mechanisms, and the origins of the current behavior in early life experience. [*DSM-III*, p. 11]

There is no doubt that this manual has led to more accurate descriptive assessments and diagnostic categorizations, which was an expressly stated goal. The *DSM-III-R* is atheoretical with regard to etiology and emphasizes categorizations based on a description of the clinical features of the disorders. The lowest order of inference necessary to describe the characteristic features of the disorder are stressed, particularly easily identifiable behavioral signs or symptoms, such as disorientation, mood disturbance, or psychomotor agitation. It is noted that for some disorders, especially the personality disorders, a higher order of inference is necessary, but this is not spelled out in any detail.

While the intention of the many contributors to this manual in formulating categorizations was clearly to aid the clinician, the result has been an emphasis on the descriptive and a deemphasis on the patient's life history and prior functioning, the nature of psychic processes, conflicts, special aptitudes and interests, and a host of other factors that make up each individual. A more specific diagnostic assessment is certainly of use to the clinician, but it is insufficient in evaluating the appropriate choice of treatment, particularly where any form of psychodynamic treatment is under consideration.

This chapter will try to address those factors that need to be included in order to make an appropriate determination of the modality of treatment. It will emphasize an assessment of the nature of the patient's psychic structures and their functioning and the nature of intrapsychic conflicts, particularly those factors that influence the choice of psychotherapeutic approach.

There are a number of basic requirements for patients to be able to engage in exploratory psychotherapy that the therapist must attempt to evaluate. Patients clearly must have sufficient verbal facility to be able to describe their difficulties and something of their life situation. They must demonstrate an adequate degree of intelligence. There must be some degree of distress, either about symptoms that are causing them difficulty, or about ego-alien character traits that they find are interfering with their personal relationships or job function. They must be capable of presenting themselves and their life situation in a sufficiently organized manner so as to be understood by the therapist. In other words, their mental processes should be reasonably logical, goal directed, and organized along secondary process lines without undue intrusions of primary process thinking. They must also be in a life situation that suggests a sufficient degree of stability in their external reality. People who are sufficiently caught up with realistic problems in their lives that appear to be overwhelming are probably not candidates for analytically oriented psychotherapy. This is not to say that a therapist could not engage such patients in a supportive therapy and reevaluate if there is some change in the situation.

Implicit in talking about a sufficient degree of distress is the question of motivation. Will such patients be able to direct themselves to an attempt to understand the nature of their conflicts without excessive pressure from reality problems or from symptomatic distress? At the same time, will they have enough discomfort so that they will wish to change something about themselves. More will be said about this assessment of motivation later on. There are two other basic requirements that need more extensive discussion. One is the patients' capacity for psychological-mindedness, for some degree of introspection in the form of curiosity about themselves or their motivations. The second is these patients' capacity for basic trust in the therapist.

The capacity for psychological-mindedness and for introspection are not the easiest things to assess. We would hope that part of these patients' motivation for treatment was a wish to understand themselves, but this is only occasionally expressed as such. Almost all patients come with some expectation of a magical kind of cure, whether or not that thought is conscious. What the clinician needs to assess is whether, in addition to that expectation, some capacity for seeing themselves as having had a role in creating the difficulties in their life is present. This often means that the clinician needs to consider whether some educative intervention is required or if a limited confrontation might be useful.

This kind of confrontation is to clarify the patients' motivation for change within themselves, but it also touches on the question of psychological-mindedness. One example would be a patient who describes a pattern in which he always withdraws from challenges and seeks a safe position, whether it be in terms of a choice of colleges, the kind of job he winds up taking, or similar situations. The therapist can present the patient with what the patient has told him and inquire whether the patient sees a pattern in this and what he might think about it. Similarly, the patient may come in and complain about his inability to have a satisfactory relationship. He may present a whole series of flawed relationships in which he has obviously chosen inappropriate partners. The therapist may simply point this out to the patient and inquire as to whether he sees this as coincidence or whether he sees himself as having something operating within him that leads him to make such choices. Of course, the therapist cannot expect the patient to say very much about what is operating within him, since that is presumably unconscious. The limited function is to see whether the patient considers such a possibility, becomes curious about it, or even responds, "Gee, I never thought about that before, but it does look that way."

These are obviously rather simple examples, but the major point is that the therapist, according to the patient's presentation and his own style, may use such interventions in any area as part of the assessment procedure. Any of the interventions discussed in the previous chapter, namely, clarification, education, suggestion, confrontation, or interpretation, can be used, although obviously interpretations would be rather limited by virtue of the amount of information available to the therapist. All of this suggests that assessment needs to be a reasonably active procedure on the part of the therapist. However, the baseline still remains that the primary function of the therapist is to listen to the patient and, based on his own clinical insight and training, construct hypotheses about what might be operating in the patient without communicating these to the patient.

With an ideal patient, the therapist may gain sufficient information from this technique with very limited interventions. However, this ideal situation rarely obtains, and a totally unstructured interview is unlikely to provide sufficient information to the clinician to make an informed decision about treatment. In what follows about assessing ego functioning, it will be clear that the more experienced therapist can inventory various structural functions within the context of a relatively unstructured interview. On the other hand, the less experienced therapist may utilize a more active questioning process to obtain some of the information, hopefully always in the context of the patient's spontaneous productions.

Inasmuch as the therapist wishes to do a reasonably complete assessment of the nature and degree of psychic structure within the limits of a consultation, it seems useful to review the various ego functions and their disturbances, as well as to consider the assessment of superego functioning. For this purpose, a relatively condensed and abbreviated outline is presented (Table 2–1), which follows a description originally given by Beres (1956) and subsequently reorganized by Bellak (1955, 1958).

Obviously, such a list is merely an outline of suggestions about some possible disturbances. There have also been contributions in the literature that would suggest additional ego functions, but those are generally functions that are not crucial for the clinical evaluation or not easy to evaluate within the context of the usual interview situation. Rather than attempt any comprehensive discussion of each of the functions and how they might be evaluated, what will be discussed below will be some comments about certain functions or component factors involved with those functions, along with selected examples of disturbances and how they impact on the choice of the form of therapy. It should be stated at the outset that any clinician will expect that there is no patient who will not present some disturbance in one or another of the functions. It is a composite of the disturbances that the clinician must integrate to determine treatment or modifications in technique. One final note: There are obviously overlaps in terms of where a particular function or its disturbance belongs, since some of these components will contribute to various ego functions.

REALITY TESTING

The usual disturbances in reality testing are, of course, familiar to most clinicians. The therapist will certainly look for any distur-

TABLE 2-1. ASSESSMENT OF EGO FUNCTIONING

EGO FUNCTIONS	DISTURBANCES

1. Relation to reality
  a. Adaptation to reality
    1. Differentiation of figure and ground
    2. Role playing
    3. Spontaneity and creativeness: regression in the service of the ego
	1. Disturbances in relation to reality
	  a. Disturbances in adaptive capacity
	    1. Inappropriate behavior with subjective or objective difficulties
	    2. Inability to cope with deviations in normal routine
	    3. Failure in social adaptation; rigidity

b. Reality testing
    1. Accuracy of perception
    2. Soundness of judgment
    3. Orientation in time, place, person
	b. Disturbances in reality testing
	    1. Projection, rationalization, denial, and distortion of reality by hallucinations and delusions

c. Sense of reality
    1. Good "self-boundaries"
    2. Unobtrusiveness of ordinary functioning
	c. Disturbance in sense of reality
	    1. Feelings of estrangement and lack of spontaneity
	    2. Excessive feelings of déjà vu
	    3. Oneirophenia
	    4. Cosmic delusions
	    5. Confused body images
	    6. Intrusion of self as subject or object
	    7. Physiological manifestations

2. Regulation and control of drives
  a. Ability to engage in detour behavior
	2. Disturbances in drive control
	  a. Conduct and habit disorders (temper tantrums, nail biting, etc.)

(continued)

TABLE 2–1 *(continued)*

EGO FUNCTIONS	DISTURBANCES
b. Frustration tolerance (neutralization of drive energy) c. Anxiety tolerance d. Integrated modality e. Tolerance of ambiguity f. Sublimation	b. Accident proneness c. Excessive impulsivity d. Tension states e. Catatonic and manic excitement f. Psychomotor slow up of catatonia and depression g. Lack of or incomplete acquisition of control of excretory functions h. Physiological manifestations

3. Object relations
  a. Capacity to form satisfactory object relations
  b. Object constancy
	3. Disturbance in object relations
	  a. Psychotoxic and psychic deficiency diseases (in infancy)
	  b. Narcissism, autism
	  c. Symbiotic relationships
	  d. Anaclitic relationships
	  e. Hypercathexis of the self; ambivalence, fear of incorporation, sadomasochism

4. Thought process
  a. Selective scanning
  b. Ability to avoid contamination by inappropriate material or drivers
  c. Good memory
  d. Sustained ability to concentrate
  e. Abstracting ability
	4. Disturbances in thought processes
	  a. Thinking organized and compelled by drives
	  b. Preoccupation with instinctual aims
	  c. Autistic logic
	  d. Loose and "nonsensical" types of associative links
	  e. Distortion of reality
	  f. Lack of referents in time and place, anthropomorphism, concretism, symbolism, syncretism, etc.
	  g. Magic thinking

(continued)

TABLE 2–1 *(continued)*

EGO FUNCTIONS	DISTURBANCES

5. Defensive functions
  a. Repression (as a barrier against external and internal stimuli)
  b. Sublimation, reaction formation
  c. Projection
  d. Denial, withdrawal, and other defenses
	5. Disturbance in defensive functions
	  a. Emergence of primary thought process
	  b. Overreactive to stimuli
	  c. Déjà vu experiences
	  d. Lack of drive control
	  e. Frightening hypnagogue phenomena
	  f. Increase in parapraxes
	  g. Impairment in emotional control

6. Autonomous functions
  a. Perception
  b. Intention
  c. Intelligence
  d. Thinking
  e. Language
  f. Productivity
  g. Motor development
	6. Disturbance in autonomous functions
	  a. Corresponding impairment of these ego functions

7. Synthetic function
  a. To unite, organize, bind, and create—the ego's ability to form Gestalten
  b. Neutralization
  c. Sublimation"
  d. Somatic "homeostasis"
	7. Disturbance in synthetic function
	  a. Tendency to dissociation
	  b. Inability to tolerate change or trauma
	  c. Inability to "bind" psychic energy

Adapted from *Schizophrenia: A Review of the Syndrome* by Leopold Bellak. Copyright © 1958 by Logos Press, New York. Used by permission of the author.

bances in the accuracy of perception, such as how the patient interprets external events, whether the patient maintains his orientation in time and place, and whether he is aware of the differences between inner and outer stimuli. The relation to reality gives some broad index of how well the patient has been able to find a place in the world that is compatible with his own potential and how comfortable he is with that role. Judgment is one component of the adaptation to reality in the sense that the clinician tries to assess whether the patient is aware of some of the consequences of his behavior and how it impacts on others. A patient may seem to be aware of the consequences of something he anticipates doing, which may have negative effects on his situation, and yet, in his manifest behavior, seem to ignore those consequences. Such a disparity is a potentially important phenomenon for the clinician to be aware of. Quite clearly it overlaps with the ability to control or regulate the drives.

Disturbances in the sense of reality can occur without there being any disruption in the patient's reality testing per se. Clearly neurotic patients may describe feelings of estrangement or circumscribed feelings of depersonalization. Such phenomena would not be uncommon in many hysterical patients. On the other hand, a lack of spontaneity would be described by many obsessional patients. One area of particular difficulty is sometimes the evaluation of the sense of reality in an obsessional person who is troubled by persistent intrusive thoughts or compulsive acts. Such familiar comments as, "I know it doesn't make any sense, but I can't get the thought out of my head," or "I know it's ridiculous to have to go back and check the lock on the door six times, but each time I'm not sure if I really locked it or just thought about it," indicate a circumscribed disturbance in this area. This must be differentiated from a delusion.

A brief clinical example may illustrate that this is not always easy. A young man of 20 came for consultation during his junior year of college. He had had plastic surgery on his nose the previous summer. He was now totally preoccupied with looking at his nose in the mirror, feeling strange when he saw himself, and wishing to have surgery to restore his nose to its original condition. He was so preoccupied with this that his ability to concentrate and study was seriously interfered with, and he was contemplating leaving school. Dynamically, it became clear during the assessment that his preoccupation with his nose represented a displacement from his genitals and from feelings of inferiority about them. This displacement was very clear when he discussed some of his sexual practices, including the fact that when he performed cunnilingus on a girlfriend, he tried to use his nose to stimulate the clitoris. Inasmuch as his overall functioning had appeared to be reasonably intact, it was quite tempting to consider that he would be a patient who would benefit from exploratory therapy, given some of the obvious dynamics.

However, after beginning such a therapy, it became clear that the patient's preoccupation with his nose was an isolated delusion. He persistently clung to the idea that the surgery had destroyed his feelings about himself and rendered him incapable of functioning. The only solution would be another surgical intervention. Interpretations of conflict on many different levels made no difference in his conviction. This seemingly isolated symptom was the first sign of a more progressive disturbance of a psychotic type. The patient was eventually put on appropriate medication. A more careful initial assessment may have brought the clinician to this conclusion earlier. The patient's sense of reality had clearly been disrupted, as manifested in his saying that he no longer felt like himself, but it is not always easy to determine if such a disturbance is on a neurotic or psychotic basis. The alerted clinician would certainly have been more cautious about the likely success of an exploratory psychotherapy as his sole mode of therapy in such a patient.

REGULATION AND CONTROL OF DRIVES

Disturbances in drive control have considerable significance for the therapist. Disturbances may appear in the control of aggressive drives, for example, in a patient who describes frequent outbursts of fighting at the least provocation or exhibits marked self-destructive behavior. Disturbances and control of sexual impulses can be indicated by marked promiscuity, various forms of sexual acting out, or perversions. The extent to which such disturbances are combined with disturbances in judgment is quite significant. Does the patient ignore potentially dangerous outcomes of his behavior— legal culpability or social censure? This is important in determining the degree of disturbance. Other obvious disturbances in impulse control, such as abuse of alcohol or other substances, or gambling, need to be carefully evaluated in terms of the extent to which they disrupt the patient's reality function or cloud his judgment.

One of the requirements for participation in any exploratory therapy is the ability to tolerate the lack of gratification or even feelings of deprivation that may be present at times. While some difficulties with impulse control appear in many patients, significant impulsive behavior suggests that at best the treatment will be marked by a tendency on the part of the patient to act out. At worst, it suggests that the treatment will be disrupted or broken off because of the difficulty in tolerating any degree of frustration.

THOUGHT PROCESSES

In this area it is fairly clear that the patient should operate, for the most part, with secondary process thinking. Any significant intrusion of primary process thinking, such as that which results in a loosening of associations, would rule out exploratory therapy at that time. The only issue here is that the patient may have a capacity to regress in the service of the ego. Such regressive thinking, however, where it is modulated and well controlled, may be a positive indication in terms of suitability for psychotherapy. An unusual ease in the direction of free association can manifest itself even in a first interview. There is unlikely to be a problem if the overall form and content of the thought processes retain an appropriate degree of structure.

DEFENSIVE FUNCTIONS

In the course of the assessment, the interviewer should be able to delineate those manifestations that indicate which group of defensive functions the patient utilizes. More likely to be evident in the interview situation are those defenses that have not been successful. The failure of what may have been previously adequately functioning defenses is indicated by the degree of anxiety or depression with which the patient presents. The grouping of defenses utilized by the patient is, of course, useful in evaluating the predominant characterological patterns and can give the clinician some idea of the major resistances liable to be encountered in the course of the therapy. The extensive utilization of other defenses, on the other hand, may prove to be indications that the resistance to therapy itself may be quite formidable. At times, even during the assessment, the therapist may wish to call the patient's attention to the operation of such defenses in order to assess the patient's motivation for treatment.

One example is a patient who presents for therapy but spends almost all of the time in the initial sessions complaining about the significant people in his life and wishing they were different. He wishes his spouse, parent, child, boss, and so on, would act in a different manner. Such an externalization raises questions about the patient's motivation for treatment in terms of whether he sees any possibility of himself changing. Here a therapist may wish to present to the patient the observation that the patient sees all difficulties as outside himself and wonder what it is that the patient would wish to change about himself. Can the patient even consider the possibility that his seeing himself as the victim of parent, spouse, employer, and so on, may have something to do with the way he experiences the world? The greater the degree of ego syntonicity of the patient's belief that all problems are outside himself, the less the chance that such a patient will be able to successfully use any exploratory therapy. What the clinician wishes to observe in such an intervention is also whether the patient has some capacity to split the ego that will be involved in self-observation. Can the patient begin to show at least some curiosity about why he sees things as he does? Predominant use of such defenses as externalization and denial can be significant obstacles in therapy. In this initial assessment, of course, no complete inventory of defenses is possible. Greater knowledge of the defensive patterns of the patient will emerge as psychotherapy proceeds. The clinician should be alerted to the presence of those defenses that can influence the choice of therapeutic modality.

A more detailed description of the various ego functions and potential disturbances is not possible within the confines of this chapter. Hartmann (1950, 1958), Bellak (1955, 1958), Beres (1956), Arlow and Brenner (1964), and Rangell (1965), among others, have made pertinent contributions to understanding ego functioning. What is most important is that the clinician obtain an overall index of both ego strengths and deficiencies as part of the assessment of psychic functioning.

ASSESSMENT OF THE SUPEREGO AND EGO AND EGO IDEAL FUNCTIONS

The therapist will want to obtain as much information as possible through an assessment of the operation of the superego and the ego ideal. In broad terms, the clinician wishes to know whether the patient has an excessively harsh and punitive superego, a somewhat rigid superego, a seemingly well-functioning superego, or a superego in which there are evidences of inadequate superego organization. For these purposes, the therapist looks first for indications of the degree of guilt or self-blame. Obvious indications of an overly punitive superego will be self-directed punishment, such as suicidal behavior, marked feelings of being "bad," and extreme self-criticism. The therapist also needs to know whether, for the patient, there seems to be even a core of reality in the sense of guilt or need for self-punishment, but, of course, this will largely indicate the degree of unconscious guilt. Unconscious guilt has great clinical significance and in an extreme form can be a significant obstacle to initiating treatment or maintaining it. This commonly takes the form of a patient who feels he does not deserve to have the chance to feel better through the treatment process. Such a patient commonly presents with a significant degree of depression, with indications of having subverted himself in a variety of situations, while at the same time having very little awareness of his own role in this. He may present any variety of reasons that make it difficult or impossible for him to engage in treatment, such as the time involved, finances, concerns that a family member or spouse will object, or doubts about the recommendation for treatment. Unconscious guilt leads the patient to feel that he does not deserve help. This pattern is quite common in masochistic patients. If the therapist recognizes it, he may wish to confront the patient even during the initial assessment to determine whether he is at all capable of looking at the operation of guilt within himself. Even if treatment is able to be initiated, the therapist will be forewarned about such a patient's tendency to unconsciously undermine the treatment. Such a patient always presents a degree of risk and challenge to the therapist, but there is really no other way, other than exploratory therapy, to attempt to help him become aware of the sources of his guilt and perhaps be able to modify it.

At the other end of the spectrum is the patient who shows defective superego functioning, in the sense that he seems not to have a sufficiently strong superego to assist the ego in modulating control of drive impulses. Such a patient usually gives some indication of the areas in which he bypasses ordinarily expected restrictions on certain impulses. Obviously, indications of lying, cheating, stealing, or any variety of other antisocial actions will be noted by the therapist. Some patients attempt to collude with the therapist in arrangements about the treatment, which may indicate very early their wish to evaluate whether the therapist also has some area of superego deficit. This commonly takes the form of patients who wish to pay cash for their sessions. They are often using unreported income and operate with the assumption that the therapist who accepts cash will also not report that as part of his income. Other patients attempt to collude with the therapist in the area of utilization of third-party payment, sometimes suggesting that the therapist falsify the dates of visits, alter the diagnosis, or otherwise tamper with the truth so that the patient may obtain reimbursement from an insurance company. Such issues need to be engaged by the therapist as early as possible. The therapist will, of course, expect that many patients will show some indications of difficulty with their superego functioning. The obsessional patient, for example, will have an unduly strict superego. While such issues will undoubtedly appear in the treatment of these patients, they in no way preclude an exploratory therapy. Again, it is only in an exploratory therapy or a psychoanalysis that such problems in the operation of psychic structure can be addressed, with a view to seeing what degree of modification is possible.

The therapist will attempt to see if he can begin to understand something about what may have led to the development of distorted superego functioning. Indications in the history of a parent who had such severe difficulties suggest the possibility of an early identification with a defective parental superego. The therapist may or may not begin to get some idea about the source of unconscious guilt. It will be helpful for the therapist to try to evaluate if such guilt seems to operate on the basis of oedipal issues, sibling rivalry, or other dynamics which may present. In my own experience, the more the patient's material gives the therapist some derivatives to begin to form a hypothesis about the sources of such guilt, the better the prognosis for his being able to be engaged in treatment, even though the initial hypothesis will be very tentative and offer very partial understanding.

What the therapist wants to obtain is as much of an overview of superego functioning as possible during the interview, particularly any indications of how intrapsychic conflict involving superego issues play a role in the patient's presenting symptomatology or other dysfunction. For purposes of this presentation, assessment of the ego ideal is included as part of superego assessment, even though it is clear that there is much disagreement about exactly where the ego ideal operates in terms of psychic structure. Evaluation of the ego ideal and the extent to which the patient has been able to approach it plays more of a role with particular kinds of pathology. A narcissistic patient almost always presents with some indications that his ego ideal is the embodiment of perfection. A sense of shame or embarrassment is most closely connected with disparities between the patient's ego ideal and how he sees himself in relation to it. A patient who disparages his intellectual accomplishments, work achievements, and social relationships, in spite of what seem to be reasonable achievements in those areas, is strongly suggestive of intrapsychic conflict involving the nature of his ego ideal. Here again the data available to the clinician in the course of assessment interviews may be relatively limited, but there may be enough indications to at least suggest areas that will undoubtedly come into fuller review and understanding in the course of therapy. The information obtained, however, may alert the clinician to narcissistic patterns that suggest how sensitive the patient will be to what he experiences as critical interventions and may enable the therapist to approach the initiation of treatment in optimal fashion.

ASSESSMENT OF DRIVE ORGANIZATION

The therapist will attempt some understanding of the overall pattern of the patient's drive organization, in particular, looking for whether the patient's conflicts appear to be primarily of an oedipal or preoedipal nature. The clinician will also consider the balance between aggressive and libidinal drives. Does the patient's data suggest adequate areas of gratification for these drive derivatives? Does the patient present indications of excessive breakthroughs of these aggressive or libidinal drive derivatives in such areas as those discussed under disturbances in the ego's regulation of drives? In addition to such symptomatic behaviors, the clinician will note whether there are indications of a predominance of unmodulated expression of aggressive or sexual wishes in the patient's fantasies or dreams.

In all of the above there is no attempt to be comprehensive in describing the patient's psychic structures. This is not a reflection of their relative importance. What is most important is that the therapist attempts to understand as much as possible about the intrapsychic organization and functioning of the particular patient. Since intrapsychic conflict will be the focal point of any exploratory psychotherapy, it is clearly helpful for the clinician to understand as much as he can about the kinds of conflict operating within a given patient.

OBJECT RELATIONS

Object relations can be viewed as either an ego function or as a different order of conceptualization. Whatever the therapist's orientation, it is important that as much information as possible be obtained about the nature and level of the patient's object relationships. Such information is usually obtained by observing how and in what depth the patient discusses the significant people in his life. Clearly, the more detailed the patient is about the people in his life, the more convinced the clinician will be that there are indeed meaningful relationships in the patient's life.

The nature of a prospective patient's object relations affords the clinician one of the most important considerations on the likelihood of successful engagement in psychotherapy. As far as diagnostic considerations are concerned, the lack of enjoyment in close relationships, particularly family relationships, and the lack of close friends or confidants are important considerations in the diagnosis of a schizoid personality disorder, a diagnosis that carries with it the suggestion that exploratory psychotherapy is not likely to be the treatment of choice. Its differentiation from other diagnostic considerations showing limited object relationships, for example, an avoidant personality disorder, can be made not only on the basis of additional criteria, but also on the clinician's response to the patient's contact with them. Other patterns of pathological object relations, such as those seen in the borderline patient, who will describe overidealized objects as well as severely devalued objects in his life, pose technical problems for the psychotherapy. They also offer a better possibility of engaging a patient in treatment. Object relations play a central role in the diagnosis of many other personality disorders and similarly offer some guidelines about the nature of the preferred treatment modality.

Object relations are assessed not only in the patient's descriptions of the important people in his life and his relationship with them, but also in the interview process. The often intuitive feeling that the therapist has that he can relate to the patient, that he can empathize with the patient, or that the patient "comes to life" is a very valuable indicator of the possibility of successful engagement in treatment. While this particular aspect is more difficult to describe, it is no less important than any of the other means by which a clinician can assess a patient. Certainly it offers the best perspective on whether the patient has the capacity to develop a basic transference and can give some clues as to what the initial transference manifestations might be. In point of fact, at least to this clinician, this aspect of the assessment is so central that it may be enough to consider exploratory therapy, even where there are other indications of problems with ego or superego dysfunction.

In addition to the structural assessment considered above, the clinician will make some tentative formulation along psychodynamic terms with full knowledge that this will be incomplete and may be reformulated in the course of the treatment process. The psychodynamic formulation should include not only the nature of the predominant conflicts and possible clues about some of the unconscious factors involved, but also an assessment of motivation for treatment.

MOTIVATION

One of the considerable limitations of the more structured diagnostic interview is that it tells little about a patient's motivation. Many patients who present with acute symptomatology may sound as if they would be suitable patients for an exploratory therapy, but the clinician may find that what they seek is not any understanding of themselves, but simply symptomatic relief. For example, many patients with a panic disorder will be eager to begin treatment. However, within that group of patients, there are some who seek only the relief that the clinician can offer in the form of a psychopharmacological agent and others who would refuse any form of medication. In between there are patients who may or may not feel that they need medication to get some degree of control of their anxiety, but who also want to understand what is happening to them and what has gone wrong in their lives. Manifest anxiety or dysfunction is not a good or sufficient indicator of motivation. Most of us have been taught that ego-dystonic symptoms are more accessible to treatment than ego-syntonic problems. This is not always the case. While a patient obviously has to have some degree of discomfort in order to be willing to engage in treatment, too much distress and too much of an urgency to want some immediate relief may be indications that the patient is less likely to be successfully engaged in any exploratory therapy.

In addition to the degree of distress the patient feels, the clinician will look at the source of distress. There are patients who are in considerable distress, but who, in their description, quickly attribute the source of their distress to people or factors outside themselves. Such patients sometimes indicate that they have indeed sought consultation because of some external pressure, even where that external pressure itself can be a source of considerable anxiety. For example, a man who presents for treatment with any variety of symptoms, including dysfunction at work and in a marital/sexual relationship, may indicate that he has come because his spouse insisted on it and threatened divorce if he didn't seek help. This is a relatively poor prognostic sign for exploratory therapy, although in some cases it is the additional stimulus that the patient has needed to overcome his own fears about the treatment process. Very few patients come prepared for exploratory therapy. Part of the role of the clinician, therefore, is to educate the patient about what treatment is and what it is not. The recommendation for appropriate treatment can only be made based on the patient's motivation and life situation at the time of assessment.

It will certainly be familiar to most therapists that there are certain life situations that, in and of themselves, may be the cause of considerable distress, and yet such situations can be indications that it is not the best time to attempt any exploratory treatment. One familiar example is that of patients in acute mourning. To get over the death of someone close to them or the disruption of a close relationship, such patients will be engaged for a brief period of time in a more supportive therapy. Some will then go on to be sufficiently motivated for exploratory therapy. Patients on the brink of marriage, or others in the midst of a chaotic divorce, may also benefit from exploratory therapy, but an intervening time period before such treatment can be successfully engaged may be needed. Many situations are best handled in the manner just described, namely, that the clinical assessment is tempered by the life situation.

CONCLUSION

All of the above considerations about assessment for psychotherapy are most meaningful when they are combined with the experience and skill of the particular therapist. It is the therapist who must integrate and balance these "objective" considerations with that most difficult to describe factor called clinical intuition. The clinician will consider the nature of any structural disturbance, the nature of the conflicts, the level of object relations, the life situation, and so on, before making a specific recommendation for treatment. What is essential to emphasize is that the diagnostic assessment will not be sufficient to arrive at such a conclusion, and that only by balancing all the factors discussed here can an intelligent, well thought out, and reasonable recommendation for treatment be made.

REFERENCES

Arlow, J., and Brenner, C. (1964). *Psychoanalytic Concepts and the Structural Theory.* New York: International Universities Press.

Bellak, L. (1955). Toward a unified concept of schizophrenia. *Journal of Nervous Mental Diseases* 121:60–66.

_____ (1958). *Schizophrenia: A Review of the Syndrome.* New York: Logos Press.

Beres, D. (1956). Ego deviation and the concept of schizophrenia. In *Psychoanalytic Study of the Child* 11:167–235. New York: International Universities Press.

Diagnostic and Statistical Manual of Mental Disorders (1980). 3rd ed. Washington, DC: American Psychiatric Association.

_____ (1987). 3rd ed.-revised. Washington, DC: American Psychiatric Association.

Hartmann, H. (1950). Comments on the psychoanalytic theory of the ego. *Psychoanalytic Study of the Child* 5:74–96. New York: International Universities Press.

_____ (1958). *Ego Psychology and the Problem of Adaptation.* New York: International Universities Press.

Rangell, L. (1965). Some comments on psychoanalytic nosology: with recommendations for improvement. In *Drives, Affects, Behavior*, vol. 2, ed. M. Schur, pp. 128–160. New York: International Universities Press.

3

Structuring the Psychotherapeutic Situation

Eugene Halpert, M.D.

INTRODUCTION

The rationale for the approach to patients in a psychoanalytically oriented psychotherapy, including the structuring of the therapy, derives from the analytic understanding of the human mind and the principles involved in how it works. Among the most important principles are those of psychic determinism, of a descriptive and dynamic unconscious, and of transference and resistance. In beginning any discussion of the structuring of the psychotherapeutic situation, it is helpful to review one of these most basic concepts on which the rationale for the techniques of structuring rests: psychic determinism.

Psychic determinism holds that everything that takes place in the mind, all psychic events and acts, including the seemingly random and incomprehensible, are both comprehensible and determined by the psychic events, usually unconscious, that precede them and form their context. Both psychoanalysis and psychoanalytically oriented psychotherapy are set up to maximize the chances that both the patient and the therapist will be in a position to observe how the patient's mind works; in particular, how the seemingly irrational, incomprehensible, anxiety-producing mental contents that have caused the patient's suffering are determined by unconscious conflict and fantasy.

STRUCTURING THE TREATMENT SETTING

The structuring of the psychotherapeutic setting covers both formal and informal aspects. Formal aspects include the time and frequency of sessions, the fee, the policies regarding missed sessions or changing times of sessions, as well as the patient's and the therapist's individual roles. Included in the less formal aspects are all those things that the therapist does from the very first moments of contact with the patient that will maximize the possibility that that particular patient will come to trust and be progressively better able to work with the therapist. It is necessary to speak of these less formal actions of the therapist in setting up the structure of a therapeutic situation before speaking of the more formal ones because not only do they come first chronologically, but they reveal a basic attitude toward the patient and the process of therapy that in itself plays a role in the determination of the structure of therapy. A basic attitude that encourages the formation of an optimal structure for an insight-oriented therapy is that each patient is an individual with his own foibles, strengths, expectations, needs, external reality, symptoms, and character structure. Another element in this basic attitude is that the therapist should be open to and listening for the manifestations of these attributes of the patient and responsive to them in such a way that the patient knows that he is being heard. To clarify and understand how one goes about doing this, it is necessary to discuss briefly the technique of the assessment interview or interviews that precede the more formal structuring of psychotherapy.

THE ASSESSMENT PHASE

Attitudes toward and understandings of the structure of treatment will affect not only the specific approach chosen but also the decision of whom the therapist might or might not treat. If one holds that neutrality, objectivity, anonymity, and confidentiality are of importance in providing the best possible structure for psychotherapy, then one would choose not to treat certain patients. Among those patients are one's own friends and relatives, the friends and relatives of current patients, and, in some instances, of past patients. The determination of what is significant to the patient or to the therapist that may compromise the therapist's neutrality or threaten the patient's right to confidentiality is usually easy to make.

Sometimes, however, the possible extratherapeutic connection with the patient may not be discovered until the patient is seen in consultation. For instance, it has happened that a patient has sought treatment with a therapist as the result of the enactment of a particular fantasy involving another patient of the therapist. In one such case, a man came for consultation after having heard a series of talks by the therapist. In the initial interview the patient said only that after hearing the therapist talk, he had felt that the therapist was the sort of person with whom he could work. Since there is generally no threat to neutrality or objectivity in seeing someone who has heard a therapist give a lecture, a second consultation was scheduled. In the next consultation, the patient revealed that he was a very good friend of another current patient of the therapist's who he felt had changed for the better since he had been seeing the therapist. The therapist at this point became aware that the man before him was indeed a very close friend of his current patient (the current patient had never referred to the man in consultation by his full name) and that the two were involved in an intense unconscious homosexual fantasy and rivalry. To have continued seeing the second man beyond the consultations would have set up a therapy in which this fantasy was being lived out and abetted by the therapist and would have led to the first patient's feeling abandoned and betrayed. In addition, the therapist would have been in a position in which his capacity for neutrality would have been strained with both parties and his ability to remember who told him what about whom sorely tested. The latter situation could readily lead to breaches in confidentiality, for example, with the therapist mistakenly telling one patient what the other had said. Or the fear of a breach in confidentiality could lead to a lack of spontaneity or increased stiffness on the part of both the patients and the therapist. In short, seeing the second patient would have put unnecessary and probably untenable burdens on all three parties and created an unworkable structure in both therapies.

The conduct of the assessment interviews makes its own contribution to the ultimate structure of psychotherapy. It follows from the principle of psychic determinism that form is also content and/or a clue to latent content. If the therapist allows the patient to tell his story in his own way, then the pauses, silences, seeming digressions, sequence of content, omissions, and spontaneous corrections that inevitably ensue will yield information about the patient's intrapsychic functioning that is not as readily available from a strict question-and-answer approach. This approach will yield information about the patient's dynamics and conflicts, ego strengths and weaknesses, defensive style, verbal ability, capacity for self-reflection and insight, object-relatedness, affective state, and transference readiness. In this way, the therapist will have additional information on which to base his judgment as to whether insight-oriented psychotherapy is the treatment of choice for the patient. Structuring the assessment interviews by allowing the patient to structure them and having one's comments or questions derive from what the patient has said or done or how he has said or done it also helps set the tone of a therapeutic structure, in which it is more likely that the patient will have the freedom to speak.

It is important to stress that a patient will almost never spontaneously supply all the data (either from form or content) that a therapist needs to come to the dynamic formulations and diagnostic conclusions that are necessary to make a recommendation to the patient vis-à-vis treatment. Rather, the form and content of the patient's spontaneous productions serve in large measure to stimulate tentative formulations, hypotheses, and questions in the mind of the therapist. These tentative formulations and questions may then be pursued via comments and questions to the patient. The form and content of the patient's response to these questions and comments provide additional data that may further clarify the dynamic formulation or diagnosis.

For example, in an initial interview, a man complained of difficulty getting along with his co-workers. He then spoke somewhat ambivalently about both of his parents but made no mention of siblings. The therapist wondered to himself whether the patient was an only child who either could not tolerate the existence of siblings (unconsciously equated with his co-workers) or who felt guilty because he believed that he had killed them off. The therapist also wondered if the patient had siblings but had failed to mention them as a reflection of a wish that they had never existed. When in the second interview the patient again failed to mention whether he had siblings, even though he spoke further about his family, the therapist noted to the patient that he hadn't mentioned any siblings. The patient replied somewhat sheepishly that that was strange, since he was the oldest of four. After a moment of silent reflection, he continued by saying that his omission must be significant because he was consciously aware of resenting them when he was a child. In fact, he said that some of the ambivalence he felt toward his parents was due to what he believed were their greater expectations of him as the oldest child, and, consequently, the greater demands they made on him as compared to his siblings.

The therapist's comment in pursuit of testing a hypothesis not only confirmed one dynamic formulation as opposed to another, but yielded other psychologically relevant material. It suggested that the patient was capable of productively reflecting on threatening conflictual material and of assessing his own defensive maneuvers when confronted with them. It also enabled the therapist to better anticipate the same hostile competitive transference in the therapy that the patient experienced toward his fellow workers.

The number of sessions in the assessment phase depends on the length of time it takes the therapist to form an opinion as to whether treatment is indicated and if it is, what kind would be optimal for the patient at that time. The more formal structuring of a psychotherapeutic situation takes place at the point that the therapist has formed that opinion. It should be remembered that what is being presented about this more formal structuring of the psychotherapy represents only one analyst's approach to the problem. It is presented in the hope that it will help stimulate the reader to think about the various issues involved in the process and to reflect on his own approach. Many other analytic authors, including Knight (1972), Langs (1973), Stone (1951), and Tarachow (1963), have written on the topic, emphasizing or presenting different points than those presented here, although dealing with many of the same issues.

The importance of a recommendation for therapy to a patient and of the discussion of the structure of the therapy suggests that the recommendation and discussion deserve more than a few minutes crammed in at the end of a session. To attempt to discuss them hurriedly limits the possibility of a free and open exchange between the therapist and the patient during which questions, doubts, fears, and any other kinds of feelings and thoughts about therapy that had not as yet emerged might come into the open. Ample time should be allotted.

Another important issue in the formal structuring of an analytically oriented psychotherapy is the attempt to make sure that the patient consciously understands the recommendation and its rationale and agrees with it before proceeding to those parts of the structure that follow from the recommendation. As much as possible, the patient's agreement or disagreement should be based on informed choice. Put another way, one should try to speak to and enlist the aid of the maturer aspects of the patient's ego in the setting up and conduct of the therapy. Proceeding in this manner allows the patient to reflect and question each step of the way before agreeing or disagreeing. If the patient then accepts the therapist's recommendations and conditions, the patient has agreed to a treatment attempt that he consciously understands and has freely chosen.

Most often a patient has his own ideas about the type of treatment he thinks is best suited for him and what he wants. He may come wanting psychoanalysis, psychotherapy, medication, a combination of medication and psychotherapy, sex therapy, or family therapy. These ideas usually emerge during the course of the assessment interviews. Prior experiences in treatment, treatment experiences of friends or relatives, and the patient's assessment of the success or failure of these treatments, as well as what he knows of the various treatment options and his thoughts and feelings about the source of the referral to the therapist all contribute to conscious and unconscious expectations about treatment and its different structures. Even when the patient has already voiced some opinion about the kind of treatment he thinks he needs, he often expresses further feelings about it at the point at which the therapist shares his assessment.

The therapist may agree with the patient's assessment of himself and his ideas of the kind of treatment indicated, or he may have a different opinion and make a different recommendation. In either case, the therapist has the task of conveying his understanding of the nature of the patient's problems and goals and why he has suggested one form of therapy as opposed to another. The patient then has the opportunity to reflect on the therapist's recommendation and to voice whatever thoughts, feelings, or questions he has. He may decide to accept the recommendation, or he may opt not to. He may feel that he needs additional time to make up his mind. He may want the therapist's help in understanding his uncertainty and wish to see him in an ongoing series of appointments without any permanent commitment until he is able to decide, or he may want to make up his mind on his own. Whatever the case may be, the therapist's task is to try to understand the patient's way of going about making a choice, as well as whatever doubts and fears he has about the therapist's recommendation. He must then try to communicate that understanding in such a way as to help the patient make a decision.

If the recommendation is accepted, the next issue to be addressed is with whom the treatment should be. If the recommendation that has been given and accepted is for psychoanalytically oriented psychotherapy, then the patient should be able to say whether or not he feels that he would like to work with the therapist. It is equally important that the therapist feel that he would like to work with the patient and that this be communicated to the patient. If the therapist does not like the patient and after self-reflection still does not feel that he could work with him, then the only resolution may be referral to a suitable colleague.

TIME AND FEE ARRANGEMENTS

After the therapist and the patient have agreed on the need for psychotherapy and on their desire to work with one another, questions of time and money follow naturally. These questions may have been raised by the patient long before this point. Often questions of frequency of sessions and of money come up during the early course of the assessment interviews when a patient recounts prior treatment experiences or the treatment experiences of others. Usually if there is a problem in external reality or the emotional significance of money or time is of unusual importance to the patient, the patient will raise the issue in the initial interview. If the patient immediately asks what the therapist's fee is or presents some special time requirements for sessions that the therapist has not been made aware of either by the patient or the referrer, it may mean that the person who referred the patient either avoided these always important issues or ignored what the patient has told him. Another possibility is that the patient has avoided raising special needs with the referring person or denied what he was told. Whatever the case may turn out to be, the fact that the patient raises these questions immediately is most often an indication that these issues are emotionally loaded and most probably the nidus of significant dynamic issues. However, these questions may also reflect an accurate assessment of a reality that will pose a problem in the undertaking of a psychotherapy. Whatever the determinants of the questions, they merit attention and exploration whenever the patient raises them. To not do so or to ignore the psychic import of the questions with an unempathic response may lead to grief.

For example, a therapist who worked in a low-fee clinic presented the case of a young, married female teacher who came for therapy because certain phobic anxieties had inhibited her to the point where she had been unable to work. Almost immediately she asked the therapist if in the future he could see her after 3:30 P.M. She explained that if she should regain her ability to work, the time at which they were currently meeting would be a problem. The therapist responded that he didn't have any such times available and immediately began asking the patient questions about her presenting symptoms. She responded by telling him of her unhappy marriage to a man she felt was a tyrant, only interested in his own needs, who treated her like a slave. While on the surface she catered to him and complied with his demands, it was apparent in what she said that underneath she seethed with rage and that her conflicts over her sadistic, vengeful fantasies were a determinant of her phobic inhibitions. Although she had come back for a second interview, during which she spoke at great lengths about her mother whom she depicted as abusive, controlling, and belittling of her efforts, she had called after that to say that she was canceling all future sessions.

The therapist was presenting the case because he was perplexed as to why the patient, who had seemed to him to be well motivated, had quit so soon and so abruptly. The therapist had been unable to see that his response to the patient's request about time, a rather curt refusal followed by his turning to other questions, had been interpreted by the patient as meaning that the therapist was a tyrant like her husband and mother, who were not interested in her needs and thoughts. He also had been unable to see that his response had given the patient an external reason to feel that way about him. The patient's request had been an appropriate one. If she was going to get better and be able to work, then she would need a late afternoon time. If the appropriateness of the request had been acknowledged by the therapist and explored further and the patient had been told that when such times became available she would be offered them, it might have been possible to engage the patient's concerns without so intensively activating her unconscious sadomasochistic wishes and fears that caused her to flee.

The questions of fee, frequency of sessions, missed sessions, and changing the time of sessions are other issues of importance in establishing the structure of psychotherapy. While analysts and analytically oriented psychotherapists may agree in general on the principles and issues involved, they may disagree on how these issues should be handled. For example, some therapists may have a set fee for all patients, regardless of the individual patient's circumstances. They feel that to do otherwise increases the possibility of countertransference reactions and compromises neutrality. They caution that the charging of different fees for different patients might already be the expression of such countertransference.

Other therapists may have a scale within a certain range of fees that they will vary according to what they perceive to be the patient's financial reality. A common example of this occurs in the treatment of someone whose financial situation is limited at the time of the initial assessment but who has realistic prospects of earning more in the foreseeable future. A therapist might agree to see the patient at the lower end of the scale, with the understanding that the fee would be increased if and when the patient's financial situation improves. Therapists with this point of view argue that while seeing someone at a lower fee might increase the possibility of countertransference (and transference) reactions, if one is aware of one's own and the patient's feelings and fantasies about the fee and monitors them, there are no greater problems in such a case than in any other. In addition, they say that it spares the patient the pain of being sent away and all the feelings and fantasies attendant on that pain, which might make the patient's further attempts to obtain treatment more difficult.

The frequency of sessions is another element of the structure of the therapy. Generally speaking, the more frequent the sessions, the greater the continuity of content, thought, and feeling expressed. Furthermore, more frequent sessions make it easier for both the patient and the therapist to follow the vicissitudes of unconscious conflict and fantasy as revealed in distorted derivative manifestations. The natural defensive tendency of isolation is more difficult to maintain, and transference feelings tend to become more intense. Consequently, the derivative distorted expressions of transference and of unconscious fantasy become more manifest and more readily recognizable. Some of the factors that have to be considered in trying to arrive at an optimal number of sessions per week for a given patient are the nature of the patient's psychopathology, the patient's goals, and the patient's external reality vis-à-vis work, family, time, and money.

The question of one's attitude toward changing a patient's time or charging or not charging for a missed session is also determined by how the therapist feels about the odds of reaching the goal of a psychotherapeutic structure in which the possibility of introspection leading to insight can be maximized. Most analysts believe that the optimal way to arrange the psychotherapeutic structure is to charge for all missed sessions and to not change the times of sessions upon the patient's request. They feel that to not charge a patient for a missed session or to change a session upon request inevitably involves a transference gratification and that this gratification will increase resistance. In addition, these therapists feel that in patients with certain character structures this resistance would become manifest in increasing numbers of missed sessions or increasing numbers of requests for changes of times. The transference gratification being spoken of might involve heterosexual or homosexual wishes (e.g., my therapist is not charging me for this missed session because he loves or desires me and expects sexual favors in return). The unconscious transference fantasies can also express aggressive wishes (e.g., my therapist is so afraid of my rage if I do not get what I want that he gives in to me).

Those analysts who believe that it is a mistake not to charge for missed sessions or to change times also point out that if a therapist does not always charge or readily changes times, he puts himself in the position of having to evaluate each missed session or request for change of time to try to judge which requests might be more realistically valid and therefore granted and which might more reflect the wish for gratification of unconscious transference wishes and therefore not granted. Most feel that this is an impossible task that wastes the time of therapy and places the therapist in the position of judge.

There are some analysts who feel otherwise. They argue that charging a patient for missed sessions or not changing a patient's time has meanings that may involve unconscious transference gratifications that can lead to the intensification of resistance. As an example of the latter, Silverman (1985) reported a case in which a patient had had a prior analysis in which her analyst had charged her for every missed session and would never change an appointment time, no matter what the circumstances were. Silverman's policy was "to make reasonable appointment changes when possible and to free [the patient] from financial responsibility when I could make alternate use of the canceled time" (p. 183). He reported that what emerged was that the prior therapist's policy of never changing times and always charging had in itself become the vehicle for a sadomasochistic transference interaction and gratification.

CONCLUSION

While the patient has a responsibility for the time and cost of the treatment, the intrapsychic meanings, the mental representations, the structure of the therapy, and the various parts of the structure are what are most important. It is the therapist's understanding of these intrapsychic meanings and mental representations that will determine what he thinks is the structure that will be most beneficial to the patient in the psychotherapeutic situation.

REFERENCES

Knight, R. P. (1972). *Clinician and Therapist: Selected Papers of Robert P. Knight,* ed. S. C. Miller. New York: Basic Books.

Langs, R. (1973). *The Technique of Psychoanalytic Psychotherapy.* Vol. 1. New York: Jason Aronson.

Silverman, M. A. (1985). Countertransference and the myth of the perfectly analyzed analyst. *Psychoanalytic Quarterly* 54:175–199.

Stone, L. (1951). Psychoanalysis and brief psychotherapy. *Psychoanalytic Quarterly* 20:215–236.

Tarachow, S. (1963). *An Introduction to Psychotherapy.* New York: International Universities Press.

4

The Therapeutic Relationship and the Role of Transference

Melvin A. Scharfman, M.D.

The role of transference is central in psychotherapy, in terms of its providing very useful information for access to understanding the patient's conflicts, and its being a major source of interference with the treatment. In any psychotherapy situation there are two participants, the patient and the therapist. In this chapter we will deal primarily with those things that occur within the patient in the course of therapy. However, there will be a number of comments about the therapist's role and technical position. It therefore seems advisable to consider the basic structure of the psychotherapy situation before discussing how transference influences the psychotherapeutic relationship.

THE BASIC STRUCTURE AND THE DEVELOPMENT OF TRANSFERENCE

When people initially seek a therapist, they are likely to be under some degree of emotional stress. They have usually tried for some time to cope with the difficulty they are experiencing, whether that be anxiety, depression, impaired functioning at work, problems in their sexual relationships, marital strains, problems with children, or difficulties in school. Regardless of the manifest nature of the problem, they have usually gotten to the point of feeling they can no longer manage on their own. Patients feel helpless because of their inability to handle the situation and, to varying degrees, regress to a childlike state in which they look for someone to step in and provide relief from their distress.

Most people in such situations have some basic expectation that if they present themselves for help, there will be someone who will be available to help them. They have a basic trust, often mixed with magical expectations, of that potential helping person. Basic trust in the availability of someone to help—that is, a willingness to attribute to another person a degree of confident expectation in his ability to help—is one of the requirements for most psychoanalytically derived psychotherapy. It is the foundation of what is sometimes called basic transference. As we understand it, this capacity depends on the patient as an infant or very young child having had someone available who met its basic needs when it was in distress. In other terms, the patient must have had a "good enough" mother to have been able to establish that degree of trust in the mothering person, so that he will be able to bring to new situations the anticipation of needs being met. As minimal as this requirement may seem, there are patients who present for psychotherapy who have failed to develop this basic expectation of potential help. They are often people whose early childhood had been extremely deprived. They had been neglected, frustrated, or abused, leaving them doubting or firmly not believing that anyone would ever want to help them.

One example would be an extremely paranoid patient who distrusts the therapist from the onset of treatment, expecting that he will be experimented on or poisoned, or that his thoughts are being read and will be used to hurt him. He can in no way trust the therapist. Such a patient is clearly not suitable at this time for exploratory therapy. It is occasionally possible for an accepting therapist who takes pains from the outset to try to correct some of the distortions to help such a patient gradually develop some degree of trust. The patient may then be able to go further from that point. That initial period of therapy, however, would be supportive rather than exploratory. In the more usual psychoanalytically derived psychotherapy, we expect the patient to come to treatment with the capacity for basic trust or basic transference.

When Freud wrote initially about the psychotherapeutic or psychoanalytic situation, he expected that the patient would cooperate with him by trying to say what was on his mind. The patient, in turn, would expect that the analyst would try to be helpful. In terms of what we have just discussed, we could say that the patient had a positive transference that would serve as the basis for entering into a therapeutic relationship with the therapist. This positive transference would be part of what contributes to the development of the therapeutic alliance (Kanzer 1975).

Freud discovered, however, that, despite these conscious wishes of the patient to cooperate, various other intense transference feelings began to develop that interfered with the patient's producing the material that would eventually lead to recovery. Freud called this transference *resistance*. Included under this heading are those feelings that are either manifestly negative or else positive but intensely erotic. Freud understood transference as the desire to fulfill and gratify early childhood wishes originally directed primarily toward the parents, but now directed toward new objects. Each person had a store of such frustrated or forbidden childhood wishes as part of his mental life, but for the most part he was unaware of their existence. That is, the wishes were unconscious. One of the early therapeutic aims was to make the patient aware of these unconscious transference feelings so that the flow of associations could proceed more smoothly. Freud did this by trying to trace those transference feelings to their genetic origin.

Such was the state of his understanding when he first wrote about transference in one of his papers on technique, "The Dynamics of Transference" (1912). Freud, of course, had been aware of transference earlier, having attributed the disruption of the treatment with Dora to her development of a transference of a negative nature. However it came about, partially by trial and error, the psychoanalytic situation evolved in such a manner as to facilitate the development of the transference. In psychoanalysis the patient is in a recumbent position. There is no direct eye contact with the therapist. The therapist does not answer questions about his personal life (which might in any other context be easily answerable) or in many other ways does not respond to the patient's demands that he act like a real person in the patient's life. This tends to turn the patient away from the reality of the therapist to earlier intrapsychic representations. As we now understand it, this is the major reason for the relative anonymity of the analyst. It is necessary, as a technique, to facilitate the patient's turning toward earlier and earlier perceptions that are then projected onto the analyst and that will form the basis for the transference neurosis.

What is essential is that the patient will undergo a controlled regression within the transference. With a suitable patient, the interpretation of defenses, starting with the surface will gradually lead to a deepening transference. All of this requires a patient who can experience the transference distortions while maintaining the ego's capacity to observe them. This is another way of saying that the patient must experience the transference in an "as if" manner, reacting as if the analyst were the mother, father, or other important object in his childhood experience (Freud 1914).

When we turn to psychotherapy, we encounter a different situation. The patient is sitting up and has direct visual contact with the therapist. Both of these tend to limit the development of transference in most patients. In other areas, the therapist has the option of moderating the degree of transference development by the stance he adopts. The more the therapist presents himself as a real person, such as answering questions about himself or his family, the more he will be perceived as a real person and the more restriction there will be on the development of the transference.

In psychoanalytic psychotherapy we tend to take a position somewhere between that of a supportive therapy, where the therapist may very well wish to be seen as real by the patient, and analysis, where the analyst wishes the patient to maximally develop the transference distortions. The psychoanalytically oriented therapist will tend not to answer personal questions because he wants the patient to understand what the inner meanings of those questions might be. He wants the patient to develop a transference because the understanding of some of the patient's transference feelings will be helpful in the treatment. However, the psychotherapist wants the patient to develop a workable transference, one that can be used to facilitate understanding (Greenson 1965). When the transference in psychotherapy becomes overly intense, it takes the form originally described by Freud of serving the resistance, and, in fact, may disrupt the treatment or lead to other extensive acting out. In my own experience based on many years of supervising resident psychiatrists and other psychiatrists, this is probably the most frequent cause for treatment failures in psychoanalytically oriented psychotherapy.

Let us discuss in more detail why transference is such a powerful force, one that will either help the treatment or disrupt it. Transference is a ubiquitous phenomenon in life, and some degree of transference is involved in most object relationships. Clinical transference is that which develops within the treatment situation. The structure of the treatment relationship will, in part, determine the intensity of the transference. All patients inevitably repeat the childhood object relationships they experienced and seek gratification of unfulfilled wishes within those relationships. In treatment, the therapist will become the focus of those unfulfilled wishes. The greater the degree of deprivation of childhood wishes within the treatment situation, the more intense the transference.

Both psychoanalysis and psychoanalytic psychotherapy deprive the patient of the gratification of childhood wishes, but they do so to varying degrees. Classical analysis attempts to maximize depriving the patient of various ways in which he seeks childhood neurotic gratification. The analyst would not answer personal questions about himself, although he may explain why he is doing so. The purpose of not answering is to seek the unconscious meaning underlying those questions. The unconscious wishes and meanings will only become clear when the analyst does not gratify the patient by answering. This goes beyond personal questions into what might seem in other contexts to be ordinary requests. For example, the patient asks, "Can I borrow the magazine from your waiting room? I was in the middle of an article," or "I'm sure you won't mind if I use your telephone. I have to make a call." These, and a host of other similar behaviors on the part of the patient, represent for the analyst attempts to seek some transference gratification. Any and all such behaviors come within the analytic field and are explored as much as possible.

It is the deprivation that leads the patient to turn more forcefully to earlier object relationships when the analyst does not respond. The patient attributes various meanings, based on earlier experiences, to the analyst's behavior, such as, "I'll bet you let the women patients borrow a magazine," or "You don't want me to touch anything because you think I'm a dirty person." These are obviously transference responses at a superficial level. As analysis proceeds, the transference will become intense and the analyst will accumulate more and more data to allow the patient to understand that transference. The analyst sees the patient every day. There is much more access to dreams. It is much easier for the analyst to understand the transference because he has much more specific data available and has the continuity of the analytic situation that provides an outlet for the patient's gradually intensifying feelings.

In psychoanalytic psychotherapy there is a greater range of patients with varying diagnoses. The therapist should vary his technique, to some extent, depending on the specific kind of patient he is treating. With a more neurotic patient or with a personality disorder, the therapeutic stance would be one that would provide some similarity to analysis, in the sense that there would be an attempt to deprive the patient of gratification of transference wishes. The therapist would try to get the patient to look at his behavior in a way similar to what the analyst might attempt, but the patient is much less likely to be able to explore the subject as fully. Less frequent sessions means less opportunity to understand the transference manifestations within the treatment situation.

There is also a greater likelihood that when the transference becomes intense, the patient may have a difficult time during the intervals between sessions. If a patient develops an intense transference, he will be preoccupied with thinking about the therapist much of the time outside the treatment situation. He will have strong feelings about the therapist and very little outlet for them. Much of the time such a situation will lead to an acting out on the part of the patient. If the patient has a negative transference toward the therapist and is not really able to work on it and understand it within the treatment, the patient may go home and fight with his spouse, displacing the transference into an outside relationship. If the patient has an erotized transference, he may become involved in an affair, which is an acting out of a transference (Blum 1973, Swartz 1969). Such occurrences are not uncommon when a patient has intense feelings about the therapist that are not dealt with in the treatment situation.

The treatment situation in psychotherapy is structured so that the therapist has less opportunity to be able to help the patient contain and adequately understand an intense transference. In psychotherapy the therapist often deals more with hunches about the transference. He may make an incomplete interpretation or an inexact interpretation because he does not have enough data to know exactly what the patient is repeating. This difficulty in getting to the specific genetic origin of the transference is what leads to psychotherapy dealing, to a greater degree, with the here and now of the relationship rather than its childhood origins, although those are explored to the extent they are accessible. Even when the therapist understands some of the genetic origins of the transference, he may limit the interpretation of the transference unless it is causing a technical problem in the treatment (Jackel 1966). Rather than transference, defense interpretation and conflict resolution are the major focus.

TRANSFERENCE INTERPRETATION

Transference interpretation usually does not play a predominant role in psychotherapy. As a therapist, you will interpret certain aspects of the transference. You will certainly hope that you can get the patient to see some things that happened earlier in his life and how they are affecting him now. Parallel to that, you are also going to allow the patient to use you as a new kind of object. This has gotten a bad name historically as meaning that the patient is going to use the therapist for a corrective object relationship based upon the therapist's playing a role.

You do not need to play a role when you allow the patient to experience you as a new object. A therapeutic stance that is noncritical, nonjudgmental, and benevolently neutral is sufficient to allow the patient to experience you, the therapist, as unlike anyone else in his life. The patient who is unconsciously seeking to gratify needs from early childhood will experience you as the object of some of these wishes in a different way than he had experienced it in childhood. You allow the patient that new experience. For example, a woman in treatment presents a clinical picture in which she grew up her entire life feeling that she had never had any closeness, warmth, affection, or understanding from her father. She also had difficulties throughout her life with men, and she had come into treatment because of these difficulties. Everything has been unsatisfying for her. Men devalue her, criticize her, put her down. Based on this, what will happen in a transference situation? You as the therapist will become someone who does the same thing to her. She is apt to see you as critical when you are not critical and justify seeing you as devaluing her without your having to say anything. When you interpret the negative transference distortions, you will be fostering the development of a positive transference if the patient has some observing capacity. You will be saying in effect, "That's not what I'm doing. That's essentially what other people did to you earlier in your life, and your reactions to it are such that you're now distorting me into being that kind of person." You will gradually have a patient who begins to entertain the idea that you are not that way. You are not yet a nice person or someone who is trying to understand and help her, but maybe you are not as much of a bastard as she thinks most of the other people have been in her life.

Suppose such a patient begins to have a positive feeling about you? She feels better understood. She feels closer. Maybe there is even a man out there in the world who might not be just like her earlier object relationships were. If that were a patient of mine in psychotherapy, I would have no intention of interfering with the development of those feelings. The patient is going to have this different kind of experience because the therapist is noncritical and maintains a neutral stance, not because he plays a role with her or does anything out of the ordinary. She will use the therapist as a new kind of object. She may go through something from her early development that she never quite experienced before and take that out of the therapy and apply it in her real life.

At the very least, such a patient will use this kind of attachment to the therapist to allow herself to have some greater distance in acknowledging the preoedipal problems in her life. Her inability to attach herself to her own father was inevitably followed by an overly involved ambivalent relationship with her mother. This relationship, as well as many other conflicts that constricted her functioning, is more accessible by virtue of the attachment she has formed to the therapist. If the only mode of therapeutic action were that attachment, this would be more of a supportive therapy rather than an exploratory one. Interpretation of conflict and conscious derivatives is the core of what makes psychotherapy analytically oriented.

What the example illustrates in a relatively simplified manner is that the psychotherapist will interpret the negative transference. This will tend to produce a gradually developing positive transference. However, for the most part positive transference feelings will not be interpreted in psychotherapy, but a relatively benign positive transference will contribute to the therapeutic effect.

There is another technical problem that may arise, namely, the erotized transference. An erotized transference can develop either from the patient or through the therapist's technique. There are a number of factors that may contribute to the development of an erotized transference. A history of early sexual gratification, particularly involving a parent or other member of the household, is certainly one of the most prominent. Patients who have experienced early gratification of their intense childhood sexual wishes will have subsequent difficulties in dealing with the frustration or delay in gratification of those wishes. This overgratification may involve direct sexual contact in the specific sense, or it may involve a more gradual overstimulation and seduction of a child through such means as excessive exposure to primal scene, continued parental nudity, or protracted periods of sharing a parent's bed. If transference wishes become more intense, the patient will press for some form of gratification. That gratification can be sought through an intensifying series of behaviors in which the patient seeks a relationship of greater intimacy with the therapist and some indication that he or she is special.

Such a patient may begin by trying to extend the time of the session or by repetitively requesting additional sessions. The patient may want to deal with the therapist on a first-name basis or may press for answers about the therapist's personal life. With some patients, this leads to much more overt behavior, such as suggesting that it would be far more relaxing if the therapy sessions were held outside the office. The patient would speak more readily if the therapist would only agree to have a drink at a bar that evening. Some proceed to the point of making very explicit sexual overtures.

It may seem unnecessary to point out the dangers of such involvement with a patient, but, unfortunately, it is a not infrequent experience. Many patients are quite expert at pushing the therapist's "buttons"—looking for some area that might make the therapist susceptible to responding to such overtures. The therapist who is lonely or unhappy in his own personal life is obviously more susceptible, as is the therapist who enjoys the patient's flattery and suggestions that an involvement with someone as attractive as the therapist would certainly alleviate any problems. However, an erotized transference can develop even with a therapist who maintains an appropriate therapeutic stance. It is sometimes manifested early in the treatment by a patient's saying, "You remind me so much of my sister," or "You really look a lot like my father." Another indication may be the direct appearance of the therapist in a patient's dream very early in treatment, including an overtly erotic dream. These early indications should alert the therapist to a need to maintain strict neutrality, neither becoming excessively restrictive about nor repetitively encouraging the elaboration of such feelings.

CLINICAL EXAMPLE—EROTIZED TRANSFERENCE

A well-dressed 26-year-old woman sought consultation because of her depression related to a series of unhappy relationships with men and her failure to move ahead in her career. She was quite bright and psychologically minded and brought up during the consultation that she was not sure whether she should be in therapy or in analysis. Just prior to her fourth visit, one during which I told her I would make a recommendation concerning the treatment, she came in and reported that she had had a dream the previous night. In the dream she arrives for an appointment with her mother. When they ring the bell, someone comes out to say that her therapist is not available, but why doesn't she come in anyway for a while since there is a party going on. She agrees and comes into the office, where there are a number of people involved in drinking and social conversation. They eventually drift away and someone who seems to be another therapist says to her, "Why don't you come in and have a drink and we can talk while you lie on the couch." She agrees, and some sexual involvement takes place. Following this, the scene changes and she is now in the lobby of a big office building with the therapist. She kisses the therapist, whereupon her mother, who had apparently been in a nearby phone booth, emerges and says, "I know what you're doing."

The patient said that she was not sure what the dream was about. Perhaps it had to do with the fact that she felt more comfortable during the first few interviews than she had when she consulted a psychiatrist a year and a half earlier who wanted to put her on medication. She found it easier to talk to me. She said that taking a drink always had an effect on her. In fact, her sexual involvements were always preceded by having two drinks and then by being very vague about what subsequently occurred. She also said that she imagined that it might be easier for her to be on the couch. I inquired about the fact that in the dream, I was not available, so another therapist appeared. She laughed and said, "Well, he was younger and he had a full head of hair." I said that she must be very uncertain about exactly what to expect in terms of her therapy situation. She then said that she knew that in the course of therapy, some people fall in love with their therapist, but she really was not worried about that. She was not able to do much more with the dream at that time. Alerted to the fact that there was some rapidly developing transference that I could not really understand at that time, I suggested that it would be best if we continued to meet twice a week, with her sitting up as we had done during the consultation. We could then assess whether analysis would be indicated later. I felt this would modulate the development of an erotized transference in this young woman who was prone to acting out. Analysis began about six weeks later.

Over the next year or so, the patient returned to this dream several times, and its meaning gradually became clearer. She had had an intense, unresolved attachment to her father, who was a dentist. Among many other overstimulating experiences, he did all of her dental work when she was a child. On several occasions he had administered anesthesia so that she would not be uncomfortable during the procedures. She had very clearly intensely erotized her dental procedures, and her drinking was an analogy to the anesthesia. She did not know exactly what happened after she was sleepy from the anesthesia, and she was unable to remember what happened after she took two drinks. It also became clear that the part of the dream where her mother said, "I know what you're doing" when seeing her kissing a therapist had several meanings. One was that her mother had failed to interfere in some of her highly erotic play with her father, such as her having showered with him and having had sleep disturbance as a child, during which she demanded that her father sleep with her.

The scene with the mother was also a reversal relating to her own primal scene fantasies and occasional experience. All of this emerged gradually over that period of time, but only in the context of our developing a more stable therapeutic alliance in helping her to look at her own thoughts and feelings before she acted on them. Despite my precautions, an erotic transference did develop and was at times expressed in acting out with another man. When, on one occasion, it was a resident in psychiatry with whom she became involved, she herself observed that it must be more than a coincidence. Rather than dealing with the fact that the wishes really related to displaced feelings about me or her father, I chose to point out that she was uncomfortable and having doubts about the relationship because she was afraid that those feelings might have something to do with me. At other times, we would deal repetitively with her feeling that the only way a man could be interested in her was sexually. I carefully avoided anything that might tend to intensify the erotized transference, while paying careful attention to the ways in which it sometimes made it difficult for the patient to talk about certain subjects.

This brief example illustrates that the therapist who picks up early indications of the potential development of an erotized transference is usually better prepared to modulate its development. One of the more frequent technical errors, made particularly by inexperienced therapists, is the tendency to focus the transference on the therapist, which only serves to intensify it. Pointing out to such a young woman that the feelings she had in her other relationships with men were really feelings she had about the therapist would be such an intervention. The patient would indeed focus those feelings more strongly on the therapist. One of the problems of the psychotherapy situation is that, given the decreased frequency of sessions and the lesser access to specific genetic material, it would be more difficult to contain such a transference reaction within the treatment. There are also occasions, as indicated earlier, when, despite the best efforts of the therapist, the patient develops such a transference. It is frequently best under such circumstances to refer the patient to another therapist if the therapist's interventions are not successful.

Over the years, one of the more frequent reasons I have been referred a patient by another therapist has been that the patient was involved in such an erotized transference. Within that group of patients, there have been some who developed an erotized transference because of specific qualities of the therapist and others who would develop such transference regardless of the therapist. There were still others who responded to technical errors on the part of the therapist that encouraged transference gratification. Such errors are particularly common among inexperienced therapists. Some of that undoubtedly has to do with the fact that people in training read a good deal of the analytic literature in trying to learn about psychotherapy. It is an error if they try to apply some of what they read about psychoanalysis to psychotherapy, since the basic structures of the techniques are different. People who want to learn about an exploratory therapy are interested in the unconscious, and transference seems to be the ideal area in which to learn about unconscious derivatives. Unfortunately, this is sometimes facilitated by supervisors who, in their wish to have residents gain some conviction about the unconscious, may suggest that they focus their interventions on the transference.

Transference distortions and the so-called real relationship with the therapist fluctuate throughout the course of therapy. Transference interpretation, as indicated earlier, should not be the major focus of psychotherapy.

The positive transference will be one of the factors influencing the degree of therapeutic change that the patient experiences. The extent to which this positive transference allows the patient to experience the therapist as a new object at higher levels of interpersonal relationship than he had previously experienced will vary. In psychoanalysis it will essentially be a silent partner, much as it is in an exploratory therapy, with a relatively intact neurotic patent who develops a modulated transference and has the ego capacity to participate in observing those transference distortions that do occur.

When we turn from the patient who has neurotic symptomatology or a neurotic character to the patient who has less intact levels of personality organization, transference poses different technical problems. We will briefly consider narcissistic personality disturbances and borderline personality organizations as they influence the development of transference. Since there will be specific chapters dealing with the borderline and narcissistic patient in psychotherapy, I will limit myself to some general observations about the nature of their transference responses and their technical handling in the psychotherapy of such patients.

TRANSFERENCE AND THE NARCISSISTIC PATIENT

It is well known that the narcissistic patient who comes for therapy is exquisitely sensitive to anything that he experiences as criticism from the therapist. For this reason, a heightened vigilance on the part of the therapist is required so that interventions be made with great consideration and tact. Much has been written about the role of empathy in the treatment of such patients by self psychologists. Of course, empathy is the central factor in the treatment of any patient. Empathy in this context refers to the therapist's awareness of the extremely tentative nature of the therapeutic alliance. A narcissistic patient has a tendency to react to anything in the way of the usual confrontations or even clarifications as criticism. Most therapists, even of different theoretical persuasions, would agree that a narcissistic patient tends to develop an idealizing transference. Such a patient generally seeks approval and admiration from idealized objects and will do so in the psychotherapeutic situation, provided that the therapist is not experienced as disapproving or critical.

This search for approval from an idealized object was explained by Kohut (1971) as a search for the idealized mother that the patient had not experienced during very early childhood. The child of the late separation-individuation phase seeks approval for a budding ego capacity from the mother. If the mother is less available during that time in the child's life, because of her own narcissistic pathology, major depression, emotional turmoil in the marriage, or birth of a sibling, she may be less than appropriately responsive to the child's search for approval. The theoretical formulation of self psychology is that such patients had less than optimally empathic mothers, particularly during that phase of life, and that they never saw the gleam in their mothers' eyes. Their mothers didn't glow when they ran to show a finger painting or a smearing of mud. As a consequence, the patients have less than adequately internalized good feelings about themselves. They proceed through life looking for the positive response that they missed in their early childhood.

In therapy such a patient tends to exhibit the same kind of behavior, gradually idealizing the therapist and then simply feeling good by virtue of being with that therapist. It is further suggested that the disturbance at that particular time in childhood is one in which the focus is not so much on the other person as an object, but rather on what has been called a self-object. Essentially, that means that such a patient is focused not on the therapist as a person, but rather on something that makes him feel good about himself.

As previously indicated, such a patient is extremely sensitive to any disruptions in the nature of the relationship he has with the therapist. This means that the therapist will have to be aware of any relatively subtle disturbances in the nature of that relationship, since the patient seeks an idealized relationship. The patient will be extremely sensitive to any interruptions in the treatment, feeling that he is not getting the optimal amount of attention or understanding from the therapist or that a particular intervention is experienced as criticism. If the therapist utilizes the understanding that it is not the therapist as such who is being responded to, but rather the therapist being experienced as an idealized self-object, there are subtle changes in approach that may be quite significant. For example, it is generally not technically correct to point out to such a patient, "You are angry with me because I wasn't available over the weekend," or "You felt sad because you missed me over the vacation." Rather, the focus should be on the self-experience: "You found it hard to continue to feel good about yourself when we weren't meeting." Different therapists of different theoretical persuasions will vary in the extent to which such a shift in the approach to patients is necessary or how central a role it has in the treatment of narcissistic patients. For some, it is the most basic aspect of the psychotherapy of such patients. Their formulation is essentially that the therapist, in striving for optimal empathy, will be experienced as an idealized object or self-object by the patient, who will eventually internalize this idealized self in the process of therapy. As a consequence, the patient will achieve a new stability in his own sense of self and self-esteem.

Such a formulation is essentially one that emphasizes the corrective object relationship aspect of the psychotherapy. The therapist is a new object, more empathic than the mother, who will help the patient overcome what is essentially conceptualized as a developmental deficit. The therapist is in the role of someone with whom the patient has the opportunity to correct that deficit. Other therapists, such as myself, would see this as only a part of the therapy of such a patient. We would see the need for more balance in the conceptualization and technical interventions. Narcissistic pathology is not always a developmental deficit. Similar-looking personality patterns can evolve as defensive organizations to conflicts experienced more on the phallic oedipal level. It may well be that some of the theoretical formulations about the narcissistic patient are too generalized, as if they were applicable to all such patients and as if there is a formula that can be universally applied. Most therapists will seek to incorporate some of the understanding of the early disturbances in the development of this particular kind of psychopathology. However, they will give equal attention to disturbances at other levels of development, rather than always conceptualizing the problem as a deficit that has a more or less universal basis.

What I think is central is the balance previously indicated between the different therapeutic factors. The balance in the treatment of the narcissistic patient tilts in the direction of the therapist as a new object, with a major factor in the process of therapeutic change coming from what is essentially a corrective object relationship. In psychotherapy, such a corrective experience for the patient should not be belittled as a factor in the degree of therapeutic change. To repeat, this is not a matter of the therapist playing a role, but rather of the therapist allowing the patient to experience him as a new object. What is essential from the perspective of the transference is that the therapist consider that the nature of the transference responses in the narcissistic patient will be quite different than what might be expected in a neurotic patient. Some technical modifications on the part of the therapist will be required, but within the framework of maintaining a neutral, noncritical, nonjudgmental, yet understanding and empathic position in relationship to the patient. Whether or not someone conceptualizes a treatment in which there is a minimal interpretation of conflict or understanding of unconscious derivatives as psychoanalysis, it is clearly within the range of effective psychotherapy. Understanding the transference in the narcissistic patient in greater depth than can be provided here is an essential factor of any engagement in psychotherapy. However, unless the treatment deals with conflict resolution, I would not call it an exploratory psychoanalytic psychotherapy.

TRANSFERENCE AND THE BORDERLINE PATIENT

Similarly, any understanding of how to deal with transference in borderline patients rests on understanding some of the genetic factors in the development of such psychopathology (Abend et al. 1983). In general, the borderline patient is someone who experienced some developmental failure even earlier than the more integrated narcissistic character. The borderline patient has had partial degrees of failure in a relationship to self-object differentiation and failures in the integration of the "good" and "bad" internalized representations of both self and object (Kernberg 1968). Varying degrees of maternal inconsistency, with alternations between overgratification and frustration, interfere with developing ego autonomy. This is probably one of the most common elements in the early development of such a patient. Whether one conceptualizes it as a defense, which it clearly can be, or as a lag in development, the splitting of these representations interferes with the achievement of object constancy and is one of the core elements in understanding the transference reactions of a borderline patient. The transference reactions are particularly intense and can be extremely rapidly shifting. The therapist is frequently experienced in black-and-white terms as either an "all good" object or a hostile, rejecting, critical object.

Like narcissistic patients, borderline patients begin frequently enough by looking for a perfect object who will gratify all their wishes. However, they have extremely intense wishes, both erotic and aggressive, and very little frustration tolerance when these needs are not met. Transference fluctuations may indeed be quite stormy. Much of this is based on the failure in integration. When the therapist is interested, attentive, and understanding, borderline patients will want more and more of him. Such patients are notoriously reluctant to see a session end, trying various ways to extend the time. They tend to call the therapist between sessions. They present an increasing crescendo of demands for more of the therapist's time. Whenever there is some situation that suggests that the therapist is depriving them, they are easily frustrated and quickly angered. In that sense, the therapist needs to understand that these patients, in the face of their anger, fail to hold on to whatever the previous positive experiences have been. Even between sessions, patients can fail to hold on to any positive pictures of the therapist. Instead of having a stable basic transference, they may vacillate to an extreme degree. One patient said to me, "You know, I never know when I come to a session which Dr. Scharfman is going to be here. Sometimes I think you're friendly, interested, and are trying to help me. Other times I think you despise me and would be happier if I didn't come to a session." This failure in internalized object constancy is most dramatic when there is any kind of interruption in treatment. Borderline patients will call the answering machine over the weekend or between sessions or during a vacation period simply to hear the therapist's voice. Their anger at the interruption is not balanced by any ability to hold on to the previously positive periods of therapeutic work. They forget what has gone on previously and react predominantly to the affect of the moment. One borderline young woman I was treating suddenly took a camera out of her purse during the last session before an interruption and took a picture of me. She said, "I need this to remember what you look like when I'm not seeing you, but who knows—maybe I'll just throw darts at it."

Borderline patients differ considerably in the extent of their psychopathology. Some seem to use this splitting of representations more as a defense used under circumscribed conditions. In others it seems to be much more of a developmental failure. Some of the latter are so unstable in their object relationships that even an exploratory psychotherapy is impossible. Some patients are able to be treated in psychoanalysis, while others must be treated in some combination of supportive and exploratory therapy. Even with those who are approached in an exploratory therapy, the therapist needs to be aware of these rather extreme and fluent shifts within patients and modify the therapeutic stance accordingly.

Most borderline patients find it difficult to deal with the degree of deprivation involved in a psychoanalytic situation. I am not referring to those patients who show some borderline traits within an otherwise more integrated personality organization, but rather to those who present with the full picture of borderline psychopathology. Even in an exploratory psychotherapy, these patients often require more gratification, that is, more supportive treatment, particularly in the early stages of their treatment. For example, if in response to an interruption in the treatment a neurotic patient asks where the therapist is going on vacation, there is no need for the therapist to answer that question. Instead, the therapist can try to get the patient to look at what it is he is really curious about. Who is he imagining the therapist is with on vacation? What is his curiosity about what the therapist is doing? Is he imagining himself with the therapist, or is he feeling neglected and left out? The therapist would obviously try to understand some derivatives of these unconscious fantasies.

With the borderline patient, the approach may be quite different. The patient is threatened by the potential loss of positive feelings about the therapist and may become disorganized in the face of that. He can become so overcome with negative, angry feelings that he feels that the therapist will disappear or abandon him. At some point early in the treatment, the therapist might tell such a patient where he is going to be, recognizing the nature of the fear. The therapist may also be able to get the patient to look at why he wants to know or try to explain what it is that makes him so frightened. Over time the patient will be better able to integrate and synthesize these transference feelings, at which point there would be no need to answer the same kind of question.

For many borderline patients, when the therapist goes away, he disappears. Answering such questions from borderline patients would be in relationship to understanding the specific pathology of those patients. These intense alternations in the transference reactions of borderline patients can also cause intense emotional reactions in the therapist, but that is again something to be discussed in another chapter.

CONCLUSION

Transference is a powerful force. It is the transference that motivates patients to remain in therapy when some of their initial symptomatology has abated. Properly handled, a relatively strong positive transference is one of the factors that makes psychotherapeutic work possible. My main aim in this chapter has been to help the therapist avoid aspects of technique that can complicate the transference picture and, in turn, make psychotherapy difficult or lead to disruptions of the treatment. Understanding transference is important for the therapist, but it is what he does with that understanding that will be most significant for the outcome of any psychotherapy.

REFERENCES

Abend, S., Porder, M., and Willick, M. (1983). *Borderline Patients*. New York: International Universities Press.

Blum, H. (1973). The concept of erotized transference. *Journal of the American Psychoanalytic Association* 21:61–76.

Freud, S. (1912). The dynamics of transference. *Standard Edition* 12:99–108.

———— (1914). Observation on transference-love. *Standard Edition* 12:157–171.

Greenson, R. (1965). The working alliance and the transference. *Psychoanalytic Quarterly* 34:155–181.

Jackel, M. (1966). Transference and psychotherapy. *Psychoanalytic Quarterly* 40:43–58.

Kanzer, M. (1975). The therapeutic and working alliances. *International Journal of Psychoanalytic Psychotherapy* 4:48–76.

Kernberg, O. (1968). The treatment of patients with borderline personality organization. *International Journal of Psycho-Analysis* 49:600–617.

Kohut, H. (1971). *The Analysis of the Self.* New York: International Universities Press.

Swartz, J. (1969). The erotized transference and other transference problems. *Psychoanalytic Forum* 3:307–318.

5

Empathy, Countertransference, and Other Emotional Reactions of the Therapist

Jules Glenn, M.D.

Ideally, the psychotherapist observes his own emotional reactions in order to best use them. His feelings frequently help him to understand his patient, but his emotions, especially if not perceived and understood, can interfere with his therapeutic stance. In this chapter I will discuss empathy, signal reactions, transference, countertransference, and identification.

EMPATHY

Empathy consists of the therapist's transient identification with the patient to help understand the patient's feelings and conflicts (Beres and Arlow 1974, Moore and Fine 1990). Transient projection supplements identification. Thus the therapist puts himself in the patient's place, imagines how the patient is reacting. Reality evaluation must confirm the therapist's imaginative speculation for these to be true empathy and not wild conjectures. Knowledge of psychodynamics will supplement the emotional empathy to further understanding.

Clinical illustration: Mr. F., an immaculately dressed man, neat to the extreme, carefully straightened his tie and then his hair as he entered the consultation room. He apologetically pointed to the dirty pair of galoshes he was wearing, as he asked whether he should remove them.

Dr. L., the therapist, immediately felt that he understood the man. He speculated that his patient was a compulsive person who tried to control his tendency to be messy by excessive orderliness. He saw Mr. F.'s apology for his galoshes as an attempt to control an angry wish to mess. These speculations were confirmed. The man complained of compulsions to straighten out objects. He could not stand it if, when he dined, a fork was not aligned properly on top of a napkin, for instance; the fork had to be exactly in the middle of the napkin. Eventually the therapist learned that his patient, although unaware of his fury, was an intensely angry man, who could express his rage by messing. As he suspected, his patient controlled his anger by keeping it unconscious and by orderliness. (His defenses were repression, isolation, and reaction formation.)

The therapist examined his own feelings to ascertain how he reached the conclusions. He realized that he identified with his patient. Dr. L. recalled that he too was orderly (but not to the degree his patient was). He knew from his own analysis that this trait could defend and had defended against hostility and messiness. His identification was thus supplemented by projection, attributing his own feelings to the patient. But, as we have seen, Dr. L., throughout the treatment, made further observations to determine whether his conjectures were correct. Further, the empathy was supplemented by practical and theoretical knowledge of the dynamics of compulsive personalities. Psychoanalysts have discovered the conflicts and defenses Dr. L. postulated for his patient, thus adding credence to his speculations.

Through the empathy, the therapist not only guesses the patient's dynamics, he also gauges what type of interpretation to make and the dosage and timing of interpretation. Dr. L. wisely decided not to tell the patient all he knew or guessed. He made comments about the surface aspects that his patient could easily accept. Only later, when defense interpretations made drive interpretation acceptable, did he point out the patient's hidden aggression. Throughout the treatment, Dr. L. continued to employ empathy to decide what comments he could effectively make.

Although I have described a particular sequence in understanding patients—empathy preceding the use of theory and clinical knowledge—that need not be the case. Some therapists develop a theoretical understanding and then apply empathy. Many therapists do not employ a fixed sequence, but vary it, often using theoretical and empathic approaches simultaneously.

"SHOWING" EMPATHIC FEELING

Empathy is an inner experience of the therapist. Kohut (1971) has used the term in an additional sense. He postulated that some narcissistic patients need to perceive the therapist's empathy in order to overcome fragmented, incomplete feelings and become integrated or feel cohesive. The therapist cannot simply be "empathic"; he must demonstrate his empathy. In that way, the patient experiences the therapist as a good mother who completes him. Psychopathology is due to the mother's failure to empathize and the resultant rage. According to this theory, treatment consists of correcting this early error of child rearing.

This approach creates certain problems. First, the theoretical premise that defect, not inner conflict, determines pathology may apply to some patients, but it is far from universal. Unfortunately, many people have neglected Kohut's original limitation and applied his concepts indiscriminately to all patients.

Second, when defects do occur they can facilitate the development and poor resolution of conflict between ego and drive.

Third, primary defects are not restricted to failures of empathy. Ego pathology may include failures of integration from other causes; learning disabilities and biological disorders, for instance.

Fourth, *acting* empathic can backfire. The patient will become aware of the insincerity behind the show. Feeling empathic without trying to demonstrate it to the patient will produce a more therapeutic by-product than an intentional attempt to reveal empathy.

Fifth, attempts to replace early failed experiences may fail because the more mature individual misinterprets the therapist's attempts as dangerous seductions rather than as early infantile replacements.

Finally, attempts at correction of earlier experiences may interfere with interpretive activity and its effectiveness. In cases where interpretation and insight do not work, corrective attempts may be justified.

SIGNAL REACTIONS

The therapist also uses his feelings to understand his patient in another way: He observes his own aggressive or affectionate feelings to his patients. Sometimes these responses can be very intense, but optimally they are minimal. Such mild feelings, called *signal emotions*, may alert the therapist to the patient's provocations.

Dr. L., for instance, noted that he felt slight irritation at Mr. F.'s behavior; the patient was actually soiling the carpet. Dr. L. concluded that his patient intentionally but unconsciously was attacking him and that possibly he was trying to get the therapist to attack back. His signal reaction tended to confirm his speculations derived from his empathy. Again, a definitive conclusion about the patient's aggressiveness did not appear for some time. In the treatment, final evidence for the patient's provocativeness (trying to get a rise out of the therapist) never emerged.

Another of Dr. L.'s patients, Mrs. S., a seductive woman in her thirties, wore a low-cut dress. She frequently raised one leg in a teasing manner. Dr. L. noted that he was experiencing a minimal signal sexual excitement. His conclusion that the patient was trying to excite him was confirmed by her continuing coy, teasing behavior. She shyly drew attention to her sexual interests and activities. The patient later revealed that when anxious, she tried to control the people around her by seductiveness.

TRANSFERENCE AND COUNTERTRANSFERENCE

The term *countertransference* is often used to cover all of the therapist's emotional reactions, even empathy and signal reactions (Little 1951). This confusing practice blurs the distinctions among the various reactions and encourages the therapist to be uncertain about what emotion he is experiencing. Following Bernstein and Glenn (1978, 1988), I distinguish empathy and signal reaction from countertransference. I also observe that countertransference is different from transference to a patient.

During the course of treatment a patient can develop transferences toward the therapist. The patient displaces feelings originally felt toward his parents or other significant persons when he was a child.

For instance, as a child, Mrs. A. had spent much more time with her father than with her mother. Her mother was rather reclusive and did not like to go out with her husband. Mrs. A. thus went to the movies with her father and worked with him in his store. The crush she had on her father appeared in her relationship with her therapist. She developed sexual feelings for the therapist as part of her transference to him. The transference also included defenses against forbidden emotions. Thus the patient as a child felt it was wrong to love her father, and so at times her love disappeared and her feelings became neutral. Similarly, she developed blank feelings toward her therapist and denied her affection.

The therapist can develop transferences toward his patients. Dr. T.'s father had died when he was 4 years old. He had loved his father and wished he had rescued him, kept him from dying. Each encounter with a new patient, no matter what the characteristics of that person, evoked memories of losing his parent. He had a strong desire to save his patients from misery and to keep them from leaving him. This led him to be overly comforting to them. His patients felt threatened by his clinging to them. In addition, Dr. T. sometimes threw caution to the wind and made desperate, nonproductive interventions to try to save patients. Often he extended a session past the usual ending time, much to the patient's confusion.

Only through his personal analysis did Dr. T. come to understand these unconscious transferences. He was then able to maintain a helpful and contained therapeutic stance.

Dr. T.'s emotions were not countertransferences. Countertransference, as I define it, consists of transference in response to the patient's transference. This definition is consistent with Freud's (1910, 1915) description. He described an analyst's falling in love with a patient who, through the transference, fell in love with him. The analyst took the patient's affection as unequivocally directed at him, was flattered, and responded inappropriately.

Dr. C., a woman therapist, experienced a true countertransference. Mrs. O., an older woman patient of 60, was very attached to Dr. C., as she had been to her mother when she was a child. The patient spent many sessions pleading to be given things—extra sessions, long, verbose interpretations, even, through a lower fee, money. Dr. C. felt drained by her. The patient was like Dr. C.'s mother, who had wanted Dr. C. to be with her, to comfort her. Dr. C. had responded by wanting to be fed by her mother. In the therapy sessions the therapist would become drowsy and several times fell asleep. Self-analysis revealed that the sleepiness defended against anger at the demanding Mrs. O., who was equated with Dr. C.'s mother. It also represented the sleep that the baby enters after being fed, Dr. C.'s wish which also defended against rage.

Drowsiness is but one symptom that may alert the therapist to the impingement of a countertransference. Others include (1) loss of interest in the patient, (2) inability to understand the patient, (3) inability to make proper interventions even when the patient is understood, (4) anger at the patient, (5) anxiety or depressive affect, (6) inexplicable guilt, (7) sexual feelings toward the patient, and (8) dreams about the patient.

I have emphasized the maladaptive aspects of transferences and countertransferences. Often enough these reactions interfere with the therapist's ability to carry out the treatment. In addition, the reader should be aware that countertransferences and transferences are universal phenomena that, especially if analyzed and understood by the therapist, may not interfere. Spitz (1956) asserted that a maternal countertransference reaction to the patient's infantile preoedipal desires for help is necessary for the proper conduct of analysis (and presumably therapy). Anna Freud (1962) noted that the traits essential for a working alliance are more advanced than those of the preoedipal period. She wrote:

> I think you will not misunderstand me if I say that the therapeutic alliance between analyst and patient is *not* carried by any of these earlier stages of object relationship, although all these earlier stages are "material." The therapeutic alliance is based, I believe, on ego attitudes that go with later stages, namely, on self-observation, insight, give and take in object relationship, the willingness to make sacrifices. It is the oedipal relationship that offers those advantages. [p. 192]

We have observed that rescue fantasies, when too intense and unanalyzed, may interfere with therapeutic ability. Probably, however, rescue fantasies are universal. They may be the basis for normal desires to help people overcome emotional disturbances. Indeed, when rescue fantasies are taboo because of an oedipal meaning, their repression may interfere with treatment.

Sometimes the therapist becomes aware of the patient's transferences only through first noticing his own countertransferences or their maladaptive consequences. This is not the ideal state. The therapist had best be capable of observing the patient's transferences directly or with the help of empathy and signal affects. Nevertheless, the therapist must be aware that the countertransference route exists. To spurn it when it occurs will result in therapeutic failure.

Dr. S. was disturbed that he had to struggle to stay awake as his patient, Mr. E., rambled in a most boring way. He realized that he was barely listening to his patient. He remembered being anesthetized for a tonsillectomy when he was 4 years old. Then Dr. S. realized that every once in a while his patient would mention his own appendectomy at that very age. Dr. S. was responding to his patient's "anesthetizing" him by his droning speech as he had been anesthetized by the physician in his childhood, a physician he equated with his father. After recognizing his own countertransference, Dr. S. realized that Mr. E. had transferred his feelings from the doctor who had put him to sleep and operated on him (a composite in the patient's mind) to the therapist. Feeling victimized by the physician, Mr. E. as a child had wanted to turn the tables and become the active attacker. He wanted to put the doctor to sleep and operate on him. His soporific speech accomplished this goal in fantasy. The therapist became the helpless one. In addition, Mr. E. vented his aggression on the therapist the way he wanted to attack the surgeon of his childhood.

IDENTIFICATION WITH THE PATIENT

We have seen that transient identification is one of the elements of empathy. Identification can be more intense and prolonged. It can interfere with therapeutic acumen or enhance it. Maladaptive identification is sometimes called *overidentification*. The therapist puts himself in the patient's place to an extreme degree, suffers with him, becomes joyful with him, and may become exceedingly anxious with him. The result may be blind spots and paralysis. The patient may recognize the therapist's excessive reaction and may become more frightened with him. Especially when the therapist considers the patient to be an extension of himself, the patient may struggle to break away.

Mr. I. was in a perpetual panic after repeated confrontations with his boss, who intimidated him sadistically. Dr. P. could easily put himself in his patient's place, since he had had similar experiences as a young student. His identification resulted in palpitations and sweating, anxiety so intense that it interfered with his thinking.

An adaptive, long-term identification has been described by Greenson (1967). The therapist develops a changing picture of the patient that he uses to understand him and his reactions. When the therapist gets ready to make interventions, he first uses the model of his patient that he maintains to assess the patient's responses and determine whether the comments will be therapeutic or disruptive.

THE FRIENDLY THERAPIST AND THE
BLAND THERAPIST

Some therapists consciously try to be kind and friendly to their patients in the belief that they will help them overcome feelings that the world is hostile. They also think that their patients will then speak more freely. There is some truth to these expectations. A therapeutic alliance depends on the patient's awareness that the therapist is on his side, intends to help him find relief, and will not reprimand him for outspoken proclamations and feelings that run counter to common morality. The therapist's open friendliness can, however, cause trouble. It may frighten a patient who fears closeness, or it may make it very difficult for a patient to express or even feel hostility. In the latter case, an essential dimension of the patient's personality may be repressed, only to burst forth later directly or in the form of symptoms.

Mr. A. benefited tremendously from his therapy with Dr. K., who was kind, tolerant, and intentionally helpful. Mr. A., with the aid and advice of his therapist, worked out a new relationship with his wife and child, whom he had previously criticized incessantly; he became a sweet, caring husband and a doting father to his son. His hatred disappeared, even though the treatment never uncovered the character and roots of the antagonism. Indeed, during the therapy the patient never felt angry with Dr. K. Dr. K., in turn, never effectively called attention to defenses against hostility. In fact, when the patient showed signs of irritation, he demonstrated how kind he, Dr. K., actually was. Thus, when Mr. A. asserted that Dr. K. was charging too much, Dr. K. lowered the fee without examining the reality of the financial situation or the inner causes of the patient's objections.

The treatment ended successfully and peacefully. Although Mr. A. was pleased with the results, in a few months his symptoms returned. In a second psychotherapy his hidden fury toward Dr. K. emerged, and along with it rage toward his second doctor. Interpretation of the defenses against anger, the anger itself, and its sources led to a more sustained therapeutic success.

Lack of kindness can be as detrimental as excessive kindness. The patient may become furious at the doctor who is never friendly at all and may never get interested in understanding his hostility, which appears based on the actual situation. Stone (1961) suggested that ideally the patient in analysis recognizes that the doctor has to behave in certain neutral ways for the good of the treatment while maintaining a primarily beneficent attitude. This principle applies to therapy as well.

Mrs. B., a borderline woman of 40, could not tolerate the frustrations that most persons can. Her murderous impulses burst forth when the therapist, Dr. C., could not make up a missed session. She felt like throwing bookends at the therapist, and sometimes did. Her outbursts were altered repetitions of earlier feelings when her mother left her in the charge of a housekeeper who did not truly take care of her in her first few years. This woman was convinced that the therapist did not care for her. Dr. C.'s bland, neutral expression confirmed this belief for her. Dr. C., in an imitation or a caricature of a psychoanalytic stance, was inexpressive to the extreme. After evaluation of the patient and self-analysis, the therapist realized that she was hostilely parodying analysis and misapplying her idea of that procedure to the therapeutic situation. She could then relax and be more expressive, enabling the patient to pay attention to her own reactions and put them in perspective.

Incidentally, the therapist's behavior expressed a transference to her own analyst and to the analytic situation rather than to the patient.

PROJECTIVE IDENTIFICATION

Projective identification, a concept originated by Klein (1957), implies the existence of a state similar to that experienced by an infant. The individual identifies with those about him, then projects the characteristics he acquires. Or the individual projects onto his objects the traits he identified with to start with. This implies a fluidity of ego boundaries, a form of symbiosis between self and object or preobject.

Although this usage is prevalent, projective identification in practice often connotes empathy or an awareness that the patient is trying to make the therapist feel the way he feels—usually bad. Thus in usage, the term may describe phenomena similar to the reversal described above; the victim tries to become the perpetrator of injury, the master of the traumatic or disturbing situation.

In a frequent Kleinian interpretation, the analyst will tell the patient that the patient is making the therapist feel sad to show him how the patient feels. This employment of the therapist's feelings is often sound but will lead him astray if he assumes that any emotion of the therapist is necessarily identical with that of the patient. Bion (1963) erroneously justified that position by suggesting that the analyst is a container in which the patient puts his feelings and thoughts. As mentioned with regard to empathy, reality testing must supplement the therapist's awareness of his own feelings.

TRANSFERENCE TO PEOPLE IN THE PATIENT'S LIFE

Jacobs (1983) described his transferences to important persons in adult patients' lives. The therapist may idealize the father of his patient (as the therapist had been awed by his own parent) and thus overlook certain noxious influences and the patient's reaction to these.

Therapists' transferences to parents occur frequently in child analysis and therapy (Glenn et al. 1978). The child therapist often identifies with his patient and may then become hostile to the child's parents, as he himself had been to his own parents. The therapist may view the parents as bad and try to undo their pathogenic influence, ignoring the child's inner conflicts and their resolution. Or the therapist may lean over backward to avoid his conviction that the parents are bad and thus fail to recognize pathogenic external influences. Or the therapist may experience the child's parents as supervisors and thus try to please them. Not infrequently, child therapists feel guilty that they are not doing a good enough job quickly enough.

Idealization of the child's parents may also influence the use of information the parents provide. The therapist may erroneously think that their view of things is the correct one and misjudge the child's state of mind. Clearly, irrational, affectionate, or hostile transferences to patients' parents must be subject to self-analysis.

CONCLUSION

We have seen that the therapist experiences a variety of emotional reactions to his patients that often help his therapeutic work and all too often impede it.

We have described empathy, signal reactions, transference, countertransference, and identification, but there are other reactions as well. The categories examined are not monolithic; they overlap and interweave. The conscientious therapist will monitor his reactions and try to understand himself. Self-analysis will be facilitated by not calling all reactions "countertransference," as is often done. So too will the application of knowledge of the therapist's responses to the understanding of the patient.

REFERENCES

Beres, D., and Arlow, J. A. (1974). Fantasy and identification in empathy. *Psychoanalytic Quarterly* 43:26–50.

Bernstein, I., and Glenn, J. (1978). The child analyst's emotional reactions to his patients. In *Child Analysis and Therapy*, ed. J. Glenn, pp. 375–392. New York: Jason Aronson.

_____ (1988). The child and adolescent analyst's emotional reactions to his patients and their parents. *International Review of Psycho-Analysis* 15:225–241.

Bion, W. R. (1963). *Elements of Psycho-Analysis.* New York: Basic Books.

Freud, A. (1962). The theory of the parent–infant relationship: contribution to the discussion. In *The Writings of Anna Freud*, vol. 5, pp. 187–193. New York: International Universities Press.

Freud, S. (1910). The future prospects of psychoanalytic therapy. *Standard Edition* 11:139–151.

_____ (1915). Observations on transference-love. *Standard Edition* 12:157–173.

Glenn, J., Sabot, L. M., and Bernstein, I. (1978). The role of the parents in child analysis. In *Child Analysis and Therapy*, ed. J. Glenn, pp. 393–426. New York: Jason Aronson.

Greenson, R. R. (1967). *The Technique and Practice of Psychoanalysis.* New York: International Universities Press.

Jacobs, T. J. (1983). The analyst and the patient's object world: notes on an aspect of countertransference. *Journal of the American Psychoanalytic Association* 31:619–642.

Klein, M. (1957). On identification. In *New Directions in Psycho-Analysis*, ed. M. Klein, P. Heimann, and R. Money-Kyrle, pp. 3–22. New York: Basic Books.

Kohut, H. (1971). *The Analysis of the Self.* New York: International Universities Press.

Little, M. (1951). Countertransference and the patient's response to it. *International Journal of Psycho-Analysis* 32:32–40.

Moore, B. E., and Fine, B. D. (1990). *Psychoanalytic Terms and Concepts.* New Haven, CT, and London: The American Psychoanalytic Association and Yale University Press.

Spitz, R. A. (1956). Countertransference: comments on its varying role in the analytic situation. *Journal of the American Psychoanalytic Association* 4:256–265.

Stone, L. (1961). *The Psychoanalytic Situation.* New York: International Universities Press.

6

The Nature of Interpretation

Robert M. Chalfin, M.D.

PSYCHOANALYSIS AND PSYCHOTHERAPY

As most concepts of interpretation arise from the psychoanalytic situation, the similarities and differences between psychotherapy and psychoanalysis need to be clarified as a background for viewing the nature of interpretation in psychoanalytic psychotherapy. There has been a trend toward a narrowing of the differences between psychoanalysis and psychotherapy. In the 1950s and 1960s most observers (Gill 1954, Rangell 1954, Stone 1954) thought of the two treatments as quite distinct, with relatively few areas of overlap. Nowadays there is more agreement on the similarities, although important differences clearly still exist (Rangell 1981). One group of important differences comes from the setup of psychoanalysis: frequency of visits, neutrality of the analyst, use of the couch, and emphasis on free association. Each in one way or another is different in psychotherapy. A central difference of great consequence is the face-to-face situation of psychotherapy, which fosters more interaction than the intrapsychic focus of psychoanalysis. A wider range of conditions is treated in psychotherapy. In addition, there is now a greater body of knowledge about psychotherapy that is now more structured (Friedman 1988, Langs 1982). The face-to-face setup, the greater understanding of psychotherapy, and the wider range of conditions treated has somewhat altered how we look at what goes on in treatment. The shift to a more interactive, interpersonal focus has considerable consequences. This includes an increased awareness of therapeutic factors aside from interpretation and insight.

THERAPEUTIC VS. ANALYTIC FACTORS

There are many noninterpretive interventions that one makes in psychotherapy, as well as in psychoanalysis, and there is a good

deal that goes on in treatment other than the giving of interpretations. This is not simply a consequence of the fact that one is
psychotherapy and one is psychoanalysis. Bibring (1954) divided
interventions into suggestion, manipulation, clarification, confrontation, and interpretation itself. These are arranged in a hierarchical
fashion with the latter seen as analytic. Self psychologists like Basch
(1980) have divided interventions into pacification, unification,
optimal disillusionment, and interpretation. In this view, only
patients with "oedipal neuroses" can utilize interpretation; for most
patients, the proper intervention is one of the first three. An
important aspect of this is the conceptualization of noninterpretive
interventions as therapeutic. A therapeutic intervention helps the
patient feel or function better. The self psychologists have contributed to the recognition of therapeutic factors other than interpretations. This has been especially relevant to understanding psychotherapy. In psychoanalysis the crucial intervention is interpretation
leading to insight as the curative factor. Experience in analytic
psychotherapy with a wider range of patients has helped clarify
how much else is going on and necessary in terms of interventions
(Friedman 1988).

Much controversy exists regarding what is therapeutic action in
psychotherapy and, to some degree, in psychoanalysis (Rothstein
1988). There are verbal and nonverbal influences on the therapeutic
process, with different authors emphasizing different aspects of the
situation. Empathy, identification, "corrective emotional experience," and transference manipulation are all separate but related
concepts attempting to characterize what moves the treatment aside
from interpretation. This leads to the issue of the weighting, of the
impact of the experience with the therapist versus insight in terms
of curative effect. The noninterpretive factors affect the development of the treatment relationship, and are a consequence of the
relationship and rapport between therapist and patient. To do any
kind of effective therapy, a bond between the two participants is
necessary. To do any effective interpretive work, this bond is
imperative. The patient–therapist bond has been conceptualized in
a variety of ways. It has been called the therapeutic alliance by
Zetzel (1958) and the working alliance by Greenson (1967). According to the self psychologists, empathic immersion with the
other leads to this bond (Basch 1988, Kohut 1959, 1971). The concept
of the holding relationship with its dependent transference was
developed by Modell (1976). Jerome Frank (1973) labeled nonspecific

but curative factors in the doctor–patient relationship. Others thought of it simply as transference (Brenner 1982). This necessary bond is therapeutic in itself. The bond serves as the fulcrum and focus for interpretation. To the degree that a treatment can focus on the analysis of this relationship and bond, the treatment can be considered analytic.

In recent years there has developed a viewpoint underlining the centrality of "here and now" interpretations of the transference. Merton Gill (1979) has been the main promulgator of this point of view. The therapist will pick up the hidden allusions to the therapist, which are then clarified to the patient as referring to the therapist and the therapy. "Here and now" transference interpretation has a prominent role in various constructs regarding what happens in treatment and in various issues of technique (Schwaber 1985). A good deal of interpretation in the "here and now" involves a focus on the resistances and fears that the patient has of the intimate or potentially intimate relationship with the therapist (Gitelson 1962). Some writers think as therapeutic the interpreting of patient's fears, which are transference, based on the past, and which interfere with the patient's allowing a relationship to form. The relationship that then develops is seen as somewhat curative and therapeutic in itself. An example would be the fostering of Kohut's (1971) "selfobject" transference, in which "mutative" or "transmuting" interpretations allow the patient to take something in from the therapist. This has been developed by Kohut (1971) into a comprehensive theory of how treatment works.

Also related is the concept of the therapist/analyst as a new object for the patient, which again deals with resistance to the forming of a relationship (Loewald 1960). This is part of psychotherapy and is considered therapeutic. Many therapists see the formation and maintenance of this relationship as sufficient without taking the resistances and fears back to their genetic roots. This kind of "here and now" interpretation can lead to an unanalyzed transference, which is curative, or to a change in the psychic structure of the patient through an identification with a new object (Loewald 1960). An example is psychotherapy with a same-sex therapist leading to what could be thought of either as a homosexual transference consequent to an unanalyzed and unresolved negative oedipal phase or as a development in which the therapist serves as an ego ideal that becomes internalized and made part of the self. Internalization without the analysis of it will be helpful in many cases and will be lasting. Such interchanges and interactions are therapeutic. However, it is not the same as analyzing the genetic roots of unconscious conflict and compromise.

What is being emphasized is the host of interchanges that occur and are useful and, where appropriate, serve as the focus ultimately for interpretation. These can be thought of as transference enactments that lead to lasting improvement or cure. At one time it was thought that improvement based on unanalyzed transferences would be short-lived. This has not turned out to be true. More important, even with interpretation, these factors and effects remain. The impact of the two-person relationship will still be there (Friedman 1988). The degree to which these aspects of the relationship can be analyzed and interpreted determines the degree to which a therapeutic process can become an analytic process.

THE NATURE OF INTERPRETATION

Interpretation in therapy is a process understood only in the context of the treatment situation and relationship. Making interpretations is the central function of the psychoanalyst. Interpretations are those interventions designed to increase the patient's knowledge of himself (Kris 1951, Loewenstein 1951). The aspect of psychotherapy that is analytic is insight as a result of interpretation. It is most effective and useful in the context of a relationship. It should be emphasized that interpretation is not a single act. Interpretation involves a step-by-step process in which the patient's knowledge of himself increases over time and usually slowly. This process has been defined in various ways. In an earlier era, "making the unconscious conscious" was the aim and consequence of interpretation. Later, with ego psychology and structural theory, it became "where id is, ego shall be" (Freud 1923). With Strachey (1934), it became a process that led to "a remolding of the superego" as the therapeutic action or consequence of interpretation.

In recent years Arlow (1979, 1987) and Brenner (1982) have conceptualized the changing of the dynamic equilibrium of forces in conflict as the function of interpretation. There is a delineation of the nature of the forces in conflict, especially unconscious conflict, and the purposes that they serve. It is evenhanded or neutral in that one deals with defenses, impulses, superego functions, reality, transference, extratransference, and so on, depending on the presenting surface. This delineation of forces in conflict is the overall strategy, and to this end the psychoanalytic situation is set up to demonstrate the dynamics of mental functioning as revealed by the patient's free association (Arlow 1979, 1987, Brenner 1982). Our focus on the processes in the patient's mind reveals this dynamic interplay. This viewpoint focuses very strongly on intrapsychic functioning in the psychoanalytic situation. In psychotherapy this can be approached or approximated, but our field of observation is clearly less intrapsychic and more interpersonal. The position from which we view the conflict of forces, our sources of data, is somewhat different. Although we utilize the spontaneous productions or free associations of our patients to the degree possible, the face-to-face situation leads to a shift to the interaction of therapist and patient as the field of study or exploration. The important data one utilizes in making interpretations come more obviously from this interactive, interpersonal field (Langs 1982, Racker 1968).

The strategy is to delineate the nature of the forces in play and the purposes they serve. Although in psychoanalysis we usually think in terms of analysis of resistance and transference, the focus here is more on tactics than on overall strategy. Tactics of interpretation include issues of "here and now" versus "there and then," or the past; transference versus extratransference; defense versus impulse; surface versus depth. These are all different aspects of the treatment process in which interpretations are made. Arlow (1987) emphasizes the moment-to-moment variations in the sequence of thoughts revealed by free association. His methodology emphasizes factors of contiguity, context, and repetition of themes in studying mental life. There is a step-by-step acquisition of insight that promotes mastery by altering the balance of the forces in conflict and that leads to a more adaptive, more functional compromise formation. This healthier adaptation can be achieved by decreasing the impact of the superego, that is, by decreasing guilt and the need to suffer or punish oneself. Or it can be achieved by decreasing the intensity of infantile fears, such as fear of castration or injury, or loss of love or object. It can be realized by increasing acceptance and awareness of one's own urges and the ability to find more adult ways of expressing and gratifying them, or by improving objectification of reality. In general, it is accomplished by decreasing the impact of unconscious fantasy on our sense of reality, on our perception of reality, and on our object relations. Interpretation of the transference, of that object relation, and the accompanying distortions of perceptions of reality can carry the most telling and convincing message that allows the patient to become much more aware of the impact of unconscious fantasies. Interpretations involve overcoming resistances, repeating and remembering, and working through (Freud 1914). This is all part of the interpretive process. It does involve what can be called a preparatory phase; it might involve confrontation, clarification, construction, and reconstruction as part of this process (Kris 1951, Loewenstein 1951). It is not possible or desirable in one intervention to be able to include everything that one could see about a particular conflict, including the present, its relationship to the transference, its relation in the patient's life, and its infantile roots. It comes together, to some degree it is synthesized, but it is basically piece-by-piece analysis leading ultimately to integration and change within the patient.

Interpretation is utilized in the establishment of a therapeutic relationship, at times by the analysis of resistance and fears of entering a relationship. It helps promote in analysis, and to various degrees in psychotherapy, the development of a workable transference, a persistent transference, or transference neurosis (Greenson 1967). It involves clarification of common themes or patterns, the delineation of the dynamic context in which it is occurring, the defensive functions it serves, and ultimately the infantile roots. It gains its greatest immediacy and conviction by interpretation of the transference. It is important in following the process in treatment to recognize that any intervention one makes affects the equilibrium of the balance of forces (Arlow 1987). To assess the impact of an interpretation, we must follow the patient's responses. We cannot make an interpretation and then sit back. We must make an interpretation and look at its effect on the patient, which obviously can be highly variable. The effect can include agreement or disagreement, new material, or the recovery of a new memory. We should observe what occurs, as the response to the interpretation will lead to the next theme. An interpretation is not the end of a process; it is the beginning and continuation of a process that is the work of the treatment and ceases only with termination.

THE FOCUS OF INTERPRETATION

Our attention will shift from the transference to the past or current life. One is not automatically more to be desired than another, since it is a similar unconscious conflict or fantasy seeking expression, whether in the transference or in the history of the patient's life or childhood (Brenner 1982). To have as a strategy a shift away from a focus on the past to a focus on the transference or current life is not useful. The fact of the therapist's participation and involvement with the patient will tilt much of what the patient experiences and feels into the relationship with the therapist and make that important.

An example of this came up with a patient in analysis.

The patient has been in analysis a short time, but some things are relatively clear. He had a distant relationship with his father, who was never really there for him, and has always felt intimidated, threatened, and controlled, first by his mother, later by his wife. He is terrified of his anger. One of his childhood recollections is of the song about Lizzie Borden, who "took an ax and gave her mother forty whacks." One of his aims for treatment is to divorce his wife. He desires to become stronger vis-à-vis women. My role in this is to give him strength.

Among his dreams is one about blue jeans. In the dream, the patient is not fully dressed, but some people are coming. He looks for a pair of pants to put on. His jeans don't quite fit, but he puts them on anyway. His associations lead to me as the clerk selling him the jeans, or the tailor making him the pants. My association was to these jeans not fitting.

I made an interpretation about his dissatisfaction and feeling I wasn't aiding him enough in his struggle with his wife. As I commented, I was aware that I had been relatively quiet in his sessions. I had been quiet for a very good reason, I had thought. But now I was uneasy about it. He had always let himself be controlled by other people, so I felt that my quietness would help him to discover things about himself. Over the sessions he had become much more aware of his feelings—his anger, his fears, and his defenses against affect.

In response to my transference interpretation, he said: "This is the second or third time you said something like this lately. No, no, no, this is going fine, this is going as well as it possibly could for me. I can't tell you what a great relief I had yesterday when I became even more aware of the fact that I was afraid to confront my wife about this." This is something I hadn't told him but he had realized himself. The transference referent is there; it will continue and eventually become important. However, one can't force or allude to it above all others at this stage.

This example is counter to the current emphasis on transference interpretation in the here and now as the sine qua non of a good analytic or therapeutic process (Gill 1979). Here it seems undeserving of priority. Perhaps after a struggle I could convince this man that it is his resistance to experiencing rage and anger with me. But that would not promote the analytic situation. The process here needs more time to unfold. We have to wait for greater, more affective evidence. Of course, my intervention has an impact on the patient. It becomes part of the experience between us that we both reflect upon.

THE GENESIS OF INTERPRETATION

Referring to the processes leading to the formulation of an interpretation, Arlow (1979) has depicted in a most lucid fashion the workings of the analyst's mind as he attempts to gain insight into the patient's mind. Arlow's clarity usefully delineates many constructs utilized in understanding this process.

We attempt to help the patient increase his capacity to both experience and observe himself (Sterba 1934). In the analyst there is a comparable split. By identifying with the patient in a transient, empathic merging, the therapist is receptively listening to, joining with, and experiencing an attunement to the patient. This lasts for a period of time, seconds or minutes usually, until the analyst becomes aware of a fantasy in his own mind. This fantasy isn't necessarily about the patient. It can be about anything, something the analyst has read, something in his own life, something on his mind that seemingly has nothing to do with the patient—a song or joke, for example. This fantasy is an intuitive response to the patient and the situation. It is experienced as a thought, an image, or a memory and then put through a process of introspection. At times it leads to an immediate insight. At other times the therapist becomes aware of a feeling present since the beginning of the hour that seemed unrelated to the patient but now is recognized as part of the response to the patient and his material.

One of the values of an analytic experience for an analyst or therapist is that, in learning about himself, there develops an inner map, an inner sense in which particular associations lead to the awareness of certain issues and conflicts. All this is the therapist's commentary, his associations to the patient's associations. This commentary, now a conjecture in the therapist's mind, does not lead directly to a verbal intervention with the patient (Brenner 1982).

We have described the subjective aspect; there is an objective aspect as well. The therapist must validate any subjective response against the objective data, that is, the data in psychoanalysis of free association, the data in psychotherapy of whatever is close to free association with a greater focus on the interactive. Arlow (1979, 1987) emphasizes contiguity, context, repetition, and commonality of themes in helping the subjective and objective fit together. This fitting together leads to the giving of the interpretation.

The process as described from the point of view of empathy is thought by the self psychologists to be the only analytic methodology (Kohut 1959). Certainly, empathy is a central aspect, but what occurs requires more than empathy. There is a method, some aspect of a science, a way of objectifying what the therapist sees and hears. This interplay between experience and observation, between the subjective and the objective, constitutes a crucial part of the therapeutic process (Beres and Arlow 1974). Hopefully, it goes on for both participants. In psychoanalysis it has to go on for both participants. Sometimes it goes on only for the therapist. If it is not joined by the patient, it is not exploratory psychotherapy. Instead, it is an analytically informed supportive psychotherapy. The patient has to learn this interplay of subjectivity and objectivity, and in so doing become attuned to himself. This is a step toward the development of the self-analytic function, a goal of psychoanalysis more than psychotherapy.

The matching of the patient's and the therapist's subjective experiences is related to the commonality of human experience. It also has to do with the fact that there is a relationship in which each party is almost always partaking of the same experience (Langs 1982). Both the therapist and the patient are adapting to the same issues, albeit from different positions. In the beginning of treatment, the patient is adapting himself to a new relationship, but so is the therapist. There is the tension of a new experience with some discomfort, along with the task of shaping this new relationship into a therapeutic situation. The awareness that both are dealing with the same issue can help the bond or alliance to develop. This shared adaptive context means, for example, that in one session both parties are reacting to the events of the prior session. In weekly psychotherapy it is hard to recall that previous session. Because a lot has usually occurred during the ensuing week, the process becomes extremely difficult to follow. But even in a weekly therapy a therapist can feel the particular relationship with the patient. This is an expression of the bond and one of the reasons we can understand the other. In the above discussion we are describing not only transference but also countertransference. It is an affective experience. This interplay is our data and in psychotherapy substitutes to a degree for the free association of psychoanalysis (Sandler 1978).

Regarding the consequences of interventions, the therapist watches what comes next from the patient. The patient's response— new material, memories, affective discharge, insightful awareness, resistance—indicates the changes in the dynamic equilibrium of his mind.

THE TACTICS OF INTERPRETATION

Another issue is tactics, meaning the choice and timing of interpretations, or the order of interpretation. If one proceeds without too many preconceived ideas, the proper area for intervention will, to some extent, make itself clear.

There are guidelines that have been put forth over time. Many make sense most of the time, but none makes sense all of the time. Keep in mind that they are guides rather than fixed rules to be followed rigidly (Brenner 1969). A first guide is to start on the surface. Interpretation is not discerning the hidden meaning of something that the patient says or does and then revealing it to him. That type of interpretation more often leads to intellectualization or heightened resistance than to insight, even if it may be accurate. Patients may not even pay much attention to comments that are not directed to the current emotional thrust of the material. Determining the point of the interpretation is essential.

A second guide is to follow the affect, which most therapists do most of the time. In fact, it is difficult not to follow the affect as the affect pulls us, compels us almost automatically to follow, unless we have our own resistance to the affect.

A third guide relates to resistance interpretation: to interpret resistance or defense before interpreting the impulse (Fenichel 1941). This intervention is one that points to the resistance, that is, the warding off or avoidance of some issue. This comes before the therapist shows the patient what he does not want to be involved with. The therapist helps the patient become aware that he is keeping away from something; otherwise, the interpretation of the underlying issue is something to which he is not affectively attuned. Here and now before there and then; that is, the therapist should not immediately aim for the genetic interpretation relating the current to the past. By sticking to the here and now and uncovering the affects and responses in this situation, over time the therapist will slowly get back to the antecedents in the past life experience of the patient.

Related to this is the important concept of process over content. Process usually refers to what is going on between the therapist and the patient. The forces that are in conflict invariably manifest themselves in the processes that are involved in the to-and-fro experience between the patient and the therapist. This, of course, is also transference and countertransference (Racker 1968). The process helps the therapist become aware of resistances and defenses that operate to make the contents less specifically available for intervention.

There is also the awareness of the shifting cathexis or intensity or "bouncing ball" of emphasis between the current life situation, the transference, and the past. These are the referents of the material, it is where the affect is. Of course, a focus on one to the exclusion of all others can be in the service of resistance, but that can be discerned especially when the therapist becomes aware that there is no free movement between these different areas. This would mean that the therapist should not overdo the emphasis on interpretation of the transference to the neglect and exclusion of other areas.

Transference as resistance manifests itself in psychotherapy as well as in analysis. The following example of interpretation of transference resistance leading back to its genetic roots is from a case in a weekly psychotherapy, early in the treatment. It demonstrates a role for transference interpretation in psychotherapy, and also the emergence of transference as a consequence of the therapist's freely hovering attention. It is noticeable in this example of a relatively simple intervention that, to gain insight, it is necessary to know a fair amount about the patient's past life, current life, and experience in the treatment thus far. This is partially because as one listens to the material, one finds oneself resonating between these three poles.

The patient comes to me because of problems in settling down with a man. An attractive woman, she is provocative in her dress and manner but has seemingly limited awareness of this. She is a former adherent of Christian Science but has abandoned it to a large degree.

In the seventh session she lets me know in a vague way that she is uncertain about treatment. She also indicates that she has resumed a telephone relationship with a female Christian Science counselor. This woman, with whom she used to speak frequently, lives in a distant city where the patient had lived. Now, after a period of no contact, she has resumed speaking on the telephone with the counselor once or twice a week. This counselor had been helpful to her in the past in some ways, but not in her dealings with men, partially because the patient had been reticent to talk about this with the counselor. That is, she was uncomfortable to reveal what she thinks of as her wild, uninhibited, sexual behavior.

Three sessions later, the patient tells me that she is very upset, very uncomfortable about the fact that she has been seeing me and speaking to this woman, now three times a week. She is feeling so guilty about it that she was up the entire night worrying about it, anxious and uncertain as to what she should do, whether she should be continuing to see me or not. This session had begun with her expressing annoyance over having to come to see me that day. She knew she would have to pay for the session if she missed it. She had been feeling better in general and just didn't have the desire for a session. She was actually quite bothered by what she perceives as my rigidity; that she had to come on a day when she was feeling well. As she tells me this, I become aware that she was a few minutes late. It strikes me that she is usually a few minutes late for our sessions. Later I learned that she is always a few minutes late to work and for many other appointments as well.

She continues with her discomfort about having to be with me. At this point, I recall something she had told me early on: that her parents had divorced when she was quite young and that she had gone with her mother, a Christian Science member, and sisters, leaving her father, who was an "artistic" type but somewhat of a ne'er-do-well. She had always felt torn between the two of them. (She herself is an artist.) This wilder father had been contrasted with her very rigid, moralistic mother, whom she always experienced as disapproving. She had also told me that her mother had remarried and her stepfather, whom she liked, was under her mother's thumb. However, on at least two occasions, he made sexual overtures to her: once in a swimming pool, where he had embraced her, and another time in a hotel room. The first incident had been at age 10; the second at age 16, when he had suggested that they play "mommy and daddy" and had again embraced her. She was uncomfortable both times and resisted.

As she is telling me about her conflict about two therapists, I am recalling this history. I now remember that in an earlier session she had told me about a reunion with her natural father that had occurred a few years ago. She had looked forward tremendously to this meeting. However, it had turned out to be a big failure and a disappointment to her. She had been barely able to tolerate the meeting, which had ended with him once again letting her down regarding something he had promised to help her with.

It was now obvious to me that this incident regarding her natural father had not been an anecdote that she had added incidentally to the initial history, but had arisen as a consequence of the dynamic process of the treatment. It reflected her experience and, of course, expectations in a hidden way, of the growing relationship between us.

At this point, I comment that it is fascinating that she is stuck in choosing between two therapists, just as she had been stuck in choosing between her mother and her father. (This is a succinct genetic interpretation linking the transference to its genetic roots. At the same time, it is a preparatory remark that I am hoping she can grasp and have some understanding of in its relationship to her and her current dilemma.) She immediately understands. I now remind her of what she had told me, which I am vividly recalling, regarding her fears and disappointments in relationship to men; that she had told me about the meeting with her natural father and her feelings about her stepfather's sexual overtures. I indicate that it seems to me that she is very uncomfortable about the idea of being in a relationship with me. She responds that she had come to treatment at the suggestion of one of her sisters who is in therapy, and in two or three sessions she had felt better after talking with me. Now though, she was beginning to feel dragged into a situation, a treatment, in which she did not have any sense of control. She says, "I guess I am scared," adding, "I don't think you are going to do anything sexually with me." After saying that, she calms down and goes on to talk about other issues that are of importance to her, allowing herself to continue in the treatment. A few sessions later, she begins to talk about her sexual difficulties for the first time, although earlier she had indicated that she did not have such problems with men.

All along I had been pointing out her action orientation, her need to act on her feelings and impulses and not leave them at the level of fantasy. Of course, this contributed to her increased capacity to recognize that she was acting once again, this time in the situation with me. This is all in the context of a once-a-week psychotherapy with a particular kind of patient, a woman broadly diagnosed as "hysterical," a patient for whom these kinds of interpretations emphasizing fantasy, enactments, and transference are quite pertinent even early in the therapy.

The above is an example of an interpretation of transference, first as a resistance, then in terms of its genetic roots. It does not point to the patient's problems so much with her mother and father as with the source of her discomfort: her relationship with me as a man. In all of this one can recognize the resonance between the past, the present, and the transference. It is also a demonstration of the interplay between the data of the patient in the session and one's own fantasies and associations to the patient that come as the patient is talking. Further, it is an example of interpretation focusing on a process rather than a specific content, although, as in this situation, process and content frequently come together.

INTERPRETATION AND THE WIDENING SCOPE

The experience over the past three decades with what has been called the "widening scope of psychoanalysis," which includes, along with psychoanalysis, modified analysis and analytic psychotherapy, has led to an increased awareness and focus on the interpersonal, interactive aspect and the interplay between transference and countertransference (Stone 1954). Kernberg (1979, 1987) states that with the borderline patient the "channel of communication" is less in verbal association and much more immediately affective in the relationship between the patient and the therapist. This is a consequence of the psychopathology of the borderline patient. There is a greater tension in relatedness, on the experience of being there together, and on nonverbal aspects of communication. The borderline patient has greater difficulty in forming the bond or therapeutic alliance that allows verbal communication and interpretations to be made. That very bond is more intense and instinctualized, and in and of itself requires almost immediate attention.

Kernberg (1979, 1987) emphasizes how, through the use of such defensive activities as splitting, projective identification, and devaluation, the patient is fostering certain reactions and responses in the therapist on an unconscious level. Through aggression or unresponsiveness to the interventions of the therapist, the patient is forcing or fostering a regression in the therapist. This leads to more powerful emotional responses and defenses in the therapist.

Therapists always have and need emotional responses, but ordinarily they are thought of as being at the level of "signal" affects, alerting the therapist to emotional issues but not overwhelming them via their own emotionality. Therapists' experiences with the stimulation of their emotional responses in the interaction with borderline patients, and the importance of these responses, have sensitized and alerted them to the fact that these are important and sometimes crucial interactions and emotional exchanges that go on in the treatment of all patients in psychotherapy and in psychoanalysis (Racker 1968, Sandler 1978). It underlines how, even in psychotherapy, there is this regressive potential.

This greater awareness of the transference–countertransference paradigms has contributed to a gradual shift in how therapists think about countertransference (Racker 1968). One of the consequences is that therapists have become more comfortable and accepting of their countertransference responses, allowing themselves to utilize them as data, especially with sicker patients, rather than as something to be suppressed or repressed. This does not suggest actualizing countertransferences, only that the awareness can be utilized in the service of insight (Sandler 1978).

INTERPRETATION AND FREQUENCY OF SESSIONS

Especially in psychotherapy of relatively less frequency, interpretation tends to be less complete, precise, and comprehensive than in psychoanalysis or the most intensive psychoanalytic psychotherapy. Because less frequent therapies are the most common forms of practice, some comments about the nature of interpretation in such situations are indicated. In these treatments there is more of a focus on the clarification of patterns of behavior, including the relationship with the therapist. There is less analysis of the infantile childhood roots of the disturbance and less analysis of the transference in those terms. Where reconstructions or constructions of genetic origins or development occur, it is usually at a more intellectual level as an aid in the clarification of current patterns and conflicts. There is usually much less emotional reexperiencing of the regressive trends. Consequently, there tends to be more of a focus on current functioning and coping strategies.

Interpretations in these less intense psychotherapies have been described variously as incomplete, inexact, and upwards (Glover 1931). What is important to convey here is that the emotional impact and intensity remain more at the manifest level. Also, there is often more of a tendency to focus on defenses utilized in various conflict situations and compromise formations than on the other components of conflict. With less complete interpretation of transference, what is usually less focused on is the "nonobjectionable" positive transference that remains at a stabilizing, supportive level (Stein 1981).

CONCLUSION

Clearly, the above is best seen on a continuum, with frequency, type of pathology, and the patient's ego capacity, as well as the goals of therapy, all playing a role in determining the nature of interpretation utilized in psychotherapy. It is important to recognize the range of factors that alter in various degrees the way psychotherapy can approximate psychoanalysis in its mode of therapeutic action and in the nature of interpretation. It is also important to emphasize how these factors help to define psychotherapy as a unique treatment with its own methodology, paradigms, modes of therapeutic action, and therapeutic potency.

REFERENCES

Arlow, J. (1979). Genesis of interpretation. *Journal of the American Psychoanalytic Association* 27:193–207.

———— (1987). The dynamics of interpretations. *Psychoanalytic Quarterly* 56:68–87.

Basch, M. (1980). *Doing Psychotherapy*. New York: Basic Books.

———— (1988). *Understanding Psychotherapy*. New York: Basic Books.

Beres, D., and Arlow, J. (1974). Fantasy and identification in empathy. *Psychoanalytic Quarterly* 43:26–50.

Bibring, E. (1954). Psychoanalysis and the dynamic psychotherapies. *Journal of the American Psychoanalytic Association* 2:745–776.

Brenner, C. (1969). Some comments on technical precepts in psychoanalysis. *Journal of the American Psychoanalytic Association* 17:333–352.

———— (1982). *The Mind in Conflict*. New York: International Universities Press.

Fenichel, O. (1941). *Problems of Psychoanalytic Technique*. Albany, NY: Psychoanalytic Quarterly.

Frank, J. (1973). *Persuasion and Healing: A Comparative Study of Psychotherapy*. Baltimore: Johns Hopkins University Press.

Freud, S. (1914). Remembering, repeating and working through. *Standard Edition* 12:145–156.

———— (1923). The ego and the id. *Standard Edition* 19:12–59.

Friedman, L. (1988). *The Anatomy of Psychotherapy*. Hillsdale, NJ: Analytic Press.

Gill, M. (1954). Psychoanalysis and exploratory psychotherapy. *Journal of the American Psychoanalytic Association* 2:771–797.

———— (1979). The analysis of the transference. *Journal of the American Psychoanalytic Association* 27:263–289.

Gitelson, M. (1962). The curative factors in psychoanalysis: the first phase of psychoanalysis. *International Journal of Psycho-Analysis* 43:194–217.

Glover, E. (1931). The therapeutic effect of inexact interpretation: a contribution to the theory of suggestion. *International Journal of Psycho-Analysis* 12:397–411.

Greenson, R. (1967). *The Technique and Practice of Psychoanalysis*, vol. 1. New York: International Universities Press.

Kernberg, O. (1979). Some implications of object relations theory for psychoanalytic technique. *Journal of the American Psychoanalytic Association* 27:207–239.

———— (1987). An ego psychology–object relations theory approach to the transference. *Psychoanalytic Quarterly* 67:197–222.

Kohut, H. (1959). Introspection, empathy and psychoanalysis. *Journal of the American Psychoanalytic Association* 7:459–483.

———— (1971). *The Analysis of the Self.* New York: International Universities Press.

Kris, E. (1951). Ego psychology and interpretation in psychoanalytic treatment. *Psychoanalytic Quarterly* 20:15–30.

Langs, R. (1982). *Psychotherapy: A Basic Text.* New York: Jason Aronson.

Loewald, H. (1960). On the therapeutic action of psychoanalysis. *International Journal of Psycho-Analysis* 41:16–33.

Loewenstein, R. (1951). The problem of interpretation. *Psychoanalytic Quarterly* 20:1–15.

Modell, A. (1976). The holding environment and the therapeutic action of psychoanalysis. *Journal of the American Psychoanalytic Association* 24:285–307.

Racker, H. (1968). *Transference and Countertransference.* New York: International Universities Press.

Rangell, L. (1954). Similarities and difference between psychoanalysis and dynamic psychotherapy. *Journal of the American Psychoanalytic Association* 2:734–744.

———— (1981). Psychoanalysis and dynamic psychotherapy: similarities and differences twenty-five years later. *Psychoanalytic Quarterly* 50:665–693.

Rothstein, A., ed. (1988). *How Does Treatment Help? On the Modes of Therapeutic Action of Psychoanalytic Psychotherapy.* New York: International Universities Press.

Sandler, J. (1978). Countertransference and role responsiveness. *International Review of Psychoanalysis* 3:43–47.

Schwaber, E., ed. (1985). *The Transference in Psychotherapy: Clinical Management.* New York: International Universities Press.

Stein, M. (1981). The unobjectionable part of the transference. *Journal of the American Psychoanalytic Association* 29:869–892.

Sterba, R. (1934). The fate of the ego in analytic therapy. *International Journal of Psycho-Analysis* 15:117–126.

Stone, L. (1954). The widening scope of indication for psychoanalysis. *Journal of the American Psychoanalytic Association* 2:567–594.

Strachey, J. (1934). The nature of the therapeutic action of psychoanalysis. Reprinted in *International Journal of Psycho-Analysis* 50:275–292.

Zetzel, E. R. (1958). Therapeutic alliance in the analysis of hysteria. In *The Capacity for Emotional Growth*, pp. 182–196. New York: International Universities Press.

7

Extratransference Interpretations

Harold P. Blum, M.D.

INTRODUCTION

Extratransference interpretation in psychoanalysis seems to have been relegated to a psychoanalytic limbo in discussions of the theory and practice of psychoanalysis. The theory of technique has appropriately centered on the transference, and our technical precepts have not, for the most part, explicitly engaged analytic work outside the transference. Numerous panels have been held on the subject of transference and transference neurosis while, to my knowledge, there have been no additional panel discussions of extratransference interpretation. Similarly, in teaching and supervision, the focus is very likely to be on transference and transference resistance, which remain at the heart of psychoanalysis. Little attention is given to distinguishing interventions and interpretive efforts directed outside the orbit of the transference. Books on clinical psychoanalysis and psychoanalytic technique have extensive discussions of transference and transference interpretation but devote scant attention to the special problems of extratransference interpretation. The problems and indications, value and validity of extratransference interpretation have been insufficiently explored.

While this chapter is specifically addressed to the psychoanalytic process, much of what is discussed also applies to psychoanalytic psychotherapy, to therapeutic process. In psychotherapy, the capacity to analyze the transference is diminished, and the transformation of the adult neurosis toward "transference neurosis" is also diminished. Furthermore, the aims and goals of psychotherapy

This is an expanded version of a panel paper presented at the fall meeting of the American Psychoanalytic Association, New York, December 18, 1981. Published in the *Journal of the American Psychoanalytic Association* 31:587–618.

usually deal with sectors of the personality closer to conscious awareness, with more emphasis on the current reality situation and the more superficial derivatives of unconscious conflict. The locus of therapeutic work may be outside the transference for variable periods unless the transference becomes a major resistance. A patient with unconscious hostility to a handicapped child, for instance, may become aware of the hostility through the psychotherapy without the hostility primarily interpreted in the therapeutic transference. It should also be noted that uninterpreted transference expectations may be part of the symptomatic relief and motive force for constructive change in some psychotherapies.

The nontransference sphere of analytic relationship has received increasing attention over the years, particularly with respect to select areas such as the "real relationship" and the analytic pact (Freud 1940) and alliance. However, the understanding of the patient's object relations and reality outside the analytic situation is a very complex part of psychoanalysis. External reality is never entirely objective and absolute; it is jointly and gradually defined and redefined by analysts and patients. The analyst is also a real, new object.

The nontransference sphere, like the patient's conscious history, has also been viewed in terms of defense and personal myth. The patient's history and object relations are subject to defensive distortions, fantasy falsifications, and rationalized revisions. Analysts are careful not to be seduced again by the patient's subjective reports of seduction and victimization. After all, we know the patient through the analytic situation. This is the microcosm from which we build models of the patient's present and past. Analysis was first defined by Freud (1914c) in terms of transference and resistance, and nontransference interpretation might have seemed nonanalytic. To not always deal with the transference might seem to be a technical error or counterresistance. Tacitly, nontransference interpretation might seem to be a poor relation and preparatory, subordinate, and supplementary to transference interpretation.

The transference is paradoxically the carrying vehicle and dynamism of the analytic process, while simultaneously a center of resistance. Clinical psychoanalysis depends essentially on the analytic formation and resolution of an artificial treatment illness, the transference neurosis. However, the analytic process deals with the patient's unconscious intrapsychic conflicts and neurotic problems as they manifest themselves anew in the transference neurosis, but also in extratransference phenomena. Derivatives of unconscious conflict (and their interpretation) are not limited to transference.

Transference analysis can become exclusive, all-inclusive, and over-idealized.

The formulation of the transference neurosis is an ideal construct: "when . . . the treatment has obtained mastery over the patient . . . the whole of his illness's new production is concentrated upon a single point—his relation to the doctor. . . . All the patient's symptoms have abandoned their original meaning and have taken on a new sense which lies in relation to the transference; or only such symptoms have persisted as are capable of undergoing such a transformation" (Freud 1916–1917, p. 444). This ideal construction is quite removed from clinical transference neurosis as it actually appears both alongside and as a transformation of the adult neurosis. Freud abandoned the term "transference neurosis" after 1922, possibly because of the disparity between the ideal construct and the complex nature of transference-neurotic phenomena and continuation of extratransference manifestations of unconscious intrapsychic conflict.

CENTRAL ROLE OF TRANSFERENCE INTERPRETATION

Correlated to the ideal illness of the transference neurosis and preceding the ideal technique of "interpretation only" (Eissler 1953), Strachey (1934) delineated an ideal interpretation, namely, transference interpretation. For Strachey, the only mutative interpretation was a transference interpretation. This meant that only transference interpretation could produce authentic analytic insight leading to structural change and new integration of what was hitherto unavailable to the ego because of defense. Certain tendencies toward idealization (and conversely toward denigration of opposite trends) develop within our formulations and models of psychoanalytic technique. The transference (succeeding the dream) became the "royal road" to clinical interpretation. These developments have great value; they represent the distilled experience of analysts who, along with patients, may have gained their greatest conviction about the significance of unconscious conflict in the human condition in their daily work with transference and countertransference.

At this point, however, a number of problems arise. Concepts of the transference neurosis and its link to the present and to the infantile neurosis have changed over the years (Blum 1971). The nature of the transference as Freud (1937) noted, is determined by the repetition of the past, a "return" of repressed conflicts which are active in the immediate present. Not all conflicts may be expressed in any one transference situation at a given point in the analysis and in the patient's life. Personality structure and intrapsychic conflict may have undergone various developmental transformations. Present events may have special significance, or the present life situation may provide special support or stress which may obscure their full significance from the analyst or which only would be understandable as the contemporary life of the patient is reconstructed in relation to the transference (Kanzer 1953). This is how we understand the current influence of birth and death, success or failure, the onset of postpartum depression or fate neurosis. The reality changes need not be dramatic, and their relation to unconscious fantasy and danger situations may be very subtle and highly disguised.

The manifestations of certain conflicts may appear in transference but may evade analytic understanding based only on transference. Conversely, certain conflicts may be sharply reactivated, as in the case of separation anxiety and depression, during termination of analysis or following a divorce or a death in the family. Relatives may resist or assist the patient's analysis, and familial change may provide secondary gain or mature gratification. Each patient reacts to the significant real events of life in his own particular fashion, based on his total personality, and some ego-syntonic character patterns may remain distant from transference conflict and analysis.

The analytic process reflects the past, repeats the past, and reviews a past that is given new meaning and definition in the present; the transference itself becomes a major vehicle for reconstructing the past. The task of analysis, Freud (1937) stated, is to reconstruct the patient's childhood from its traces, and in analysis we reconstruct a past no longer directly accessible in the immediate present and that never existed in the way it is reconstructed in analysis. We use the technique of extratransference reconstruction to understand the sources and determinants of the transference, to aid in the resolution of the transference, just as we use the transference itself as our main guide to the patient's childhood conflicts and pathogenic patterns. Transference and extratransference interpretation can be complementary and synergistic. In a broad sense, all interpretation involves transference since there is a transference dimension to all analytic process and all analytic data. Without transference attachment, there could be no analytic alliance and acceptance of interpretation.

Transference is omnipresent, and what appears to be extratransference material is nevertheless invested with transference meaning. As with the patient's associations and symptoms, the analyst's interpretations themselves acquire transference meaning. Interpretations may mean feeding, attention, competition with or penetration of the patient. The patient's mode, manner, timing, and content of reported memories and the concomitant feelings themselves are all subject to transference. The transference is probably never missing, only defended against and unrecognized in varying degree.

THE CLINICAL MATERIAL OF EXTRATRANSFERENCE INTERPRETATION

This position should not be used to obscure what it is meant to clarify. All attitudes and reactions are subject to the principle of multiple function. Transference does not subsume object relations, but current objects are misperceived and reacted to in terms of fantasied infantile object relationships. All relationships are admixtures of the new and the old, of transference and reality. Freud (1914a) illustrated this particular point when he showed the close relation between transference love and actual object love in ordinary life. Indeed, Freud (1926) noted that transference occurs outside the analytic situation and could dominate the whole of a patient's relation to the environment. The transference is obscured in ordinary object relations, but not absent. Extratransference interpretation is not necessarily nontransference, but it does not deal with the transference to the analyst. Extratransference interpretation may include transference to objects other than the analyst, the real or new relationship to the analyst or other objects, or may refer to the sphere of external reality rather than the psychic reality of transference fantasy. The extratransference sphere is different from but clinically often amalgamated with the acting out, displacement, and splitting of transference outside the analytic situation. The realities of the patient's life and of the analytic situation are of course invested with transference, but they may also influence the transference. Strictly speaking, transference and reality, past and present, also determine, define, and interpret each other's domain. In addition to concurrent and mutual influences, it is well to consider that all current associations and reactions of the patient are not necessarily primarily transference, that other forms of neurotic repetition coexist with analytic transference, and that transference is not the sole source of analytic insight or locus of analytic work (which includes, e.g., reconstruction of the past).

Analytic patients have some capacity to free-associate. Their associations will, of necessity, include their thoughts, feelings, and fantasies, their interests and activities, so that we will get to know them as people and form a picture of their day-to-day lives as well as their functioning in the analytic situation. Analysis depends not only on free association, but on a capacity to observe, report, test, and adapt to reality, to assimilate interpretation, and other critical ego functions. When patients tell us about their mothers, fathers, and siblings; whether they are married or divorced; the age, number, sex of their children; the basic facts of their family life and work; we expect there to be a certain veridical statement in the framework from which we can begin to detect omissions, distortions, and inconsistencies. These omissions and distortions become part of the work of defense analysis and are eventually seen in connection with the unraveling of the transference resistance. Self and object representations become more coherent, consistent, and realistic. The analyst will point out a variety of contexts in which the patient has denied reality or isolated affect or has been timid and fearful, just as the patient now deals with the analyst. The patient who is dependent on his mother and then his wife may become similarly dependent on the analyst. He wants the analyst to make decisions for him, complains about the frequency of sessions, becomes angry when there are interruptions in treatment. How can such a patient benefit fully from analytic treatment without connecting the dependent transference to the reliance on his wife?

The extratransference interpretation drives home transference interpretation. In addition, the two are often organically connected and deal with different manifestations and localizations of the same unconscious conflict constellations. In addition to the transference interpretation, the analyst clarifies, connects, and interprets past and present real events, life experiences, traumas, symptoms, character traits, screen memories, dreams, daydreams, and so on. Defenses, including denial of reality, are interpreted. The same unconscious conflicts and their derivative manifestations may be found in numerous compromise formations, from parapraxes to symptomatic acts inside and outside the analytic situation. Converging evidence and interpretation from different areas of the transference and complementary, synergistic extratransference

spheres lend conviction to insights. Insight is analytically internalized and also worked through in life. Multiple, interweaving
interpretations from different dimensions promote insightful integration and bridge the patient's conscious, preconscious, and unconscious psyche. Either form of interpretation may support resistance or analytic progress, or may maintain or violate analytic
neutrality. So-called extratransference interpretation should not be a
disguised form of transference manipulation of the patient, directive
therapy, or judgment of the patient's life and love objects.

Although transference is of inestimable value, analytic technique,
as represented in all of Freud's cases, always includes an extratransference dimension. The present and past life, the familial and
cultural background, the social setting, developmental phase, and
constitutional endowments are all taken into account. To further
understand the transference neurosis, to empathize with patients in
all the different areas of their psychological problems and conflicts,
requires continued attention to the interface between fantasy and
reality, past and present, conscious and unconscious, and recall and
repression. The adult neurosis is never entirely within the transference; conflict derivatives and important compromise formations
also appear outside the transference. Elements of the transference
neurosis may be displaced, split off, or enacted outside the analytic
situation, and the blending or condensation of transference and
nontransference derivatives may be exceedingly difficult to disen-
tangle. Consider a patient's fantasy of encroachment of her work
space and crowding of her room. If the analyst chooses to give
priority to analytic transference issues, he will interpret the patient's
fear of intrusion and impregnation in the analytic space. Closer to
this patient's preconscious awareness are her feelings about her
pregnancy and the intruding, aggressively "crowding" fetus in her
body and in her life. She has a transference and "new" object
relationship to her unborn child. Conflicts that are preconscious in
one realm may be less available for interpretation in other spheres,
such as the analytic transference relationship.

Another patient's transference could not be understood without
taking into account the anchoring of the transference fantasy and
current external reality. This patient entered a phase of negative
transference when she began to complain bitterly that the analysis
had become a form of protracted exploitation. She made progress
up to a point; but now that the analysis was stalemated, the analyst
had chosen to recommend the continuation of treatment, even
though it was not for the benefit of the patient or beneficial to the

patient. Rather, it was the analyst's selfish and mercenary attitude, in addition to his subjective convictions about the value of analysis, that led him to continue to recommend the analytic work. The analyst was selfish and avaricious, eager to maintain her treatment for personal financial gain, with only secondary interest in helping the patient to achieve analytic and life goals.

This patient was actually very conflicted about her own altruism and generosity to her family. She had been generous to a fault. Having encouraged the immigration of two close relatives, she now thought they were taking advantage of her hospitality and material support. Her extended family, formally depicted in idealized terms, were unmasked as greedy and demanding, capable of becoming a "bunch of vultures." The newly arrived relatives were not sufficiently appreciative and would probably want to remain in her welfare state. Her feelings about their becoming parasites have been displaced onto the analyst, and she was afraid that these relatives would become addicted to her "handouts." This patient had been a mother's helper in childhood, for which she gained mother's affection, attention, and approval. However, she had also repressed her feelings of being exploited by her mother for her mother's own selfish purposes and her bitterness of having to serve other members of the family whom she felt were less deserving than herself. The analyst transference could not be fully understood without the synergistic interpretation and reconstruction upward of her current external reality with her moral and material support of her immigrant relatives.

Analysts are not immune to idealization, which historically occurred, for example, in the idealization of dream interpretation and the early conceptualization of the transference neurosis in the analytic process. Strachey's (1934) formulation of the "mutative interpretation" was a very valuable, stimulating, and incisive idealization which was, nevertheless, misleading in its sweeping charismatic absolutism. Although Strachey's influence has been pervasive, it should not and probably has not dominated technical theory and practice. "All-transference" analysis with only transference interpretation has probably been more honored in the breach than the observance. It is, in essence, impossible to do analysis purely on the basis of transference without attention to current conflicts and realities and without reconstruction of the past in which the transference is rooted. Transference analysis only is an ideal fiction like the normal ego and would leave the analysis quite isolated from reality, with danger that the reality principle would not be strengthened but, in the long run, undermined. The analysis might be encapsulated without awareness of its severe limitations. Not all patients are able to translate the transference model of their neurosis into their everyday conflicts. Interpretation, as Loewenstein (1957) indicated, usually moves from conflicts expressed in relation to the analyst, to an understanding of conflicts and symptoms in current life, to their derivation from the infantile neurosis. Freud (1905) understood Dora's unconscious identifications in her hysterical symptoms of aphonia and tussis nervosa and her own seduction and collusion with her parents and the K.s. Transference could not be fully understood without elucidation of the whole network of shared fantasies and activities and inferences about her object relations and identifications. Dora's "real" life situation became clear concurrent with the discovery of transference and its genetic sources. Freud later scrutinized the influence of the analyst's own conflicts and interventions on the analytic process, so evident now from the Dora case in his early, rapid interpretation and his prior treatment of Dora's father.

I shall return to the realities of the analytic situation and to the activation and validation, gratification or frustration, clarification or contamination of transference fantasies at a later point. Here I want to emphasize that transference conflicts and fantasies can never be isolated or segregated entirely from other realities and from conflict expression that is not primarily transference.

Strachey's extreme position on "the mutative interpretation" was not directly challenged at the time. Strachey was influenced by the prevailing technical approach of his day, but in his only and major contribution to the psychoanalytic literature he left an enduring influence in an essay which has become a classic. Strachey's views were certainly derived from Freud's early statement that the struggle between doctor and patient is waged in the transference and that "It is on that field that the victory must be won. . . . For when all is said and done, it is impossible to destroy anyone *in absentia* or in *effigie*" (Freud 1912, p. 108). However, in the very same paragraph, what often goes unnoticed is Freud's attention to the entire psychic field and to considerations that utilized the transference and went beyond it. Freud noted that although the patient regarded the products of "the awakening of his unconscious impulses as contemporaneous and real. . . . The doctor tries to compel him to fit these emotional impulses into the nexus of the treatment and of his life-history . . ." (p. 108). Freud (1914b, p. 152) called attention to the importance of the patient coming to grips with his illness so that it is not denied or despised, and so that its true importance for his life can be assayed. It was in connection with the phenomena of illness to which the patient must attend (rather than deny) that he then stated: "one cannot overcome an enemy who is absent." His recommendations included construction of the conditions under which symptoms such as a phobia were precipitated in life. He advised mastery of phobia in the life situation as part of the final process of working through. Rather than relying solely on the transference, Freud suggested that unless the patient confronts the phobic situation in life, "He will never . . . bring into the analysis the material indispensable for a convincing resolution of the phobia" (Freud 1919, pp. 165–166). Surveying the nature of analytic work long after the publication of the technical papers, Freud (1937) referred to the significant material the patient puts at the analyst's disposal, and he included "hints of repetitions of . . . the repressed material to be found in actions performed by the patient . . . both inside and outside the analytic situation" (p. 258). "The analyst . . . has at his disposal material which can have no counterpart in excavations, such as the repetitions of reactions dating from infancy and all that is indicated by the transference in connection with these repetitions" (p. 259). These remarks appeared after Strachey's paper, and Strachey's position was not affirmed by Freud (who particularly emphasized the importance of reconstruction).

In psychoanalysis, the transference has the indispensable value of being immediate and manifest, of what we today call "the here-and-now." Transference interpretation by the object of transference strips transference illusion from that object (Stone 1967) and separates the infantile from current object in a permissive, meaningful experience (cf. Strachey 1934). In psychoanalysis, the here-and-now distortions of the doctor–patient relationship, the regressive personality alterations and symptoms, need to be linked to related patterns in life and traced to their childhood roots by a circuitous route which takes into account developmental changes in both the neurotic and healthy portions of the patient's personality. Genetic interpretation and reconstruction restore and establish connections between past and present, concurrent with finding new solutions to hitherto unresolved infantile pathogenic conflicts. A purely here-and-now approach would become a form of "new encounter," an existential or experiential psychotherapy. This approach would not permit full contact with the childish fantasies and feelings which continue to excessively influence or even dominate the patient's reactions, as in transference. The childhood origin and childish character of transference would remain unexplained (Blum 1980).

Analysis of the patient's central conflicts may be furthered by extratransference interpretation. Not everything in analysis is transference, and the transference is not always the most salient point of interpretation (Leites 1977). This point of view was actually espoused by Stone (1961), who stated that although the most effective interpretations would be related to transference conflicts, "interpretations other than those directly and demonstrably impinging on the transference can be significant and effective" (p. 141n.). Stone (1967) later remarked, "the extra-analytic life of the patient often provides indispensable data for the understanding of detailed complexities of his psychic functioning, because of the sheer variety of its references, some of which cannot be reproduced in the relationship to the analyst . . . extratransference interpretations cannot be set aside or underestimated in importance" (pp. 34–35). The subtle and multiform expressions of the total personality are not always reproduced in the transference and may be altered in the transference regression. Nontransference observations may enlarge and correct analytic transference perspectives.

Brenner (1976, p. 128) also recognized the appropriate use of extratransference interpretation. He observed, "It seems unlikely that it is either correct or useful to take the extreme position that Strachey advocated." He went on to state,

> Transference should be neither ignored nor focused on to the exclusion of all else; it should be neither excluded from the analytic work nor dragged in by the heels. . . . Its influence often is greater even than one assumed it to be. . . . Nevertheless, it remains but one factor among many in any analytic situation. An analyst has always the task of deciding as best he can from the available evidence which factors are the most important at a particular time in the analysis. If his conjecture . . . is that something other than transference is most important at the moment, he will interpret whatever the "something other" may be. [p. 128]

I would emphasize the importance of the appropriate "surface" area of interpretation, not including all material as transference or excluding nontransference considerations.

A "pure transference" position in analytic work will lead to distortions of analytic process and explanation. Such a position of valuing only transference interpretation will tend to become "all transference" and mold or artificially force all material into the transference, leading to inappropriate, excessive transference interpretation. Surveying contemporary issues in the theory of therapy, Rangell (1979) called attention to the fact that transference analysis, though indispensable, has also been overdone. "The analysis of transference over a period of some years and prominently today, is often allowed to obscure all other important and necessary elements of the analytic process. A good thing has become hypertrophied and the source of complications" (p. 84). Rangell noted the era of the transference becoming the end rather than the means, with the result that antecedents and genetic roots not only are out of reach but regarded as unnecessary or of ancillary importance. Rangell referred to Fenichel's earlier position that transference and extra-transference analysis both go on and are necessary, and that patients may comply with what Fenichel called a monomania of the analyst where an exclusive focus of interpretations is utilized for defensive purposes.

Leites (1977) reviewed the literature on "transference interpretations" only, and noted that many authors were critical of such an extreme position but that their objections took the form of very concise, constricted, and inhibited commentary. Anna Freud (1965, p. 37) noted the exclusive role given to the transference as one of the subjects of controversy in psychoanalysis, warning against the analyst's overinvolvement with the transference. Her statement of the controversy was not taken up by her or other authors in relation to her work on defense analysis. In relation to defense, "transference only" may foster isolation of analysis from life, denial of areas of reality, and continuation of infantile amnesia.

Gray (1973) described the analyst's intrapsychic perspective, the need for continual scrutiny of the patient's psychic reality, and the roles in which the events and experiences the patient reports are given unconscious meaning, in the immediacy of the analytic situation. Excessive concern with reality, traditional in the obsessional preoccupation with trivial and insignificant details of life, is a defensive function and may disguise underlying transference fantasies. Put another way, the day residue is a point of attachment for the latent content of the dream, and excessive attention to the day residue may diminish appreciation of the latent unconscious childhood conflicts. Manifest dream and transference fantasy are compromise formations that disguise the return of the repressed past. Gray, I believe, would give transference priority to other considerations; he recommends an analytic focus "to observe data limited essentially to inside the analytic situation" (p. 492). However, this is not necessarily a priority to working from the surface since the surface and "point of urgency" (Strachey 1934) are not always transference. The "point of urgency" may be denial of current illness or failure, genetic interpretation of denial of a parent's alcoholism, reconstruction of a parent's psychosis and the patient's identification with the psychotic parent, and so on.

Psychoanalytic technique has not abandoned the goal of lifting infantile amnesia and recovering childhood memories (Kris 1956). The memories often turn out to be screen memories, and the discrete memories in themselves are of less importance than the transference patterns in which they become imbricated. Nonetheless, as in overeating, there can be too much of a good thing; and an exclusive preoccupation with the transference and analytic relationship may actually lead to the omission of significant material or connections from the patient's life that will diminish and distort rather than enrich and deepen the analysis.

Not all conflicts are represented solely, wholly, or primarily at any one point in the transference; and the transference representation may be diminished in intensity and fragmented when one of the important parts of the configuration is lived out. The living out (or acting out) of fantasies may have occurred before the analysis with the pattern continuing and gradually acquiring transference meaning only as the analysis takes effect. Insight may be gained and consolidated in shared analytic work on extratransference issues, such as the patient's reactions not only to the analyst, but to his spouse and children.

Consider a female analysand with a persistent central fantasy of performing fellatio on the analyst, a fantasy linked to a childhood seduction experience and to unconscious incestuous conflicts (Dewald 1972). This patient was also a new mother, caring for a neonate who barely appears in the associations. The transference paradigm of seduction is also a transference resistance against other very important transference and extratransference considerations. The baby, who is conspicuously absent, probably is partially represented via identification and replacement in the mother's oral demands in the transference. There is a transference to the analyst as a nurturant mother or phallic mother, and the patient is preoccupied with the fantasy of sucking his penis-breast. The patient brings him her infantile suckling self—she is the baby. She has eclipsed and replaced her baby, whom she also wants the analyst to disregard.

She is envious and jealous of a sibling baby that her own baby now represents. She has a sibling transference to her own baby and an infantile demand for exclusive love and nurturance. The fantasy replaces the realities of nurturant motherhood, the demands of her own infant, the patient's need to be nurtured in order to be nurturant. New motherhood has revived the mother's own oral-maternal conflicts and has altered familial relationships and psychic equilibrium. That her associations do not include the emotional investment in her infant, reactions to the baby's sex, appearance, temperament, and so on, whether mother and child are doing well or are up all night, even whether the baby was wanted by both parents, leaves such crucial issues conspicuous by their absence. The transference cannot be understood without knowledge of the nontransference reality spheres and their transference implications. Both transference and extratransference interpretation of her maternal conflicts, envy of and identification with her infant, and so on, would be necessary and complementary. Extratransference interpretation could focus directly on her ambivalent attitudes and feelings toward her infant (rather than on the transference to the analyst), loosening defenses against the unconscious dangers associated with mothering and furthering analytic work and understanding of the patient's conflicts.

Childhood patterns of collusive denial and avoidance of reality tend to be continued in later life. It is necessary to interpret the collusion as a defense as well as a hidden gratification, and the anxiety and guilt associated with a conspiracy of silence. Such collusion may be unwittingly repeated in the analytic situation. In analysis there is a continuous reciprocal understanding of the transference and resistance, current extratransference influences and manifestations of neurotic patterns, and reconstruction of the past. The study of neurotic patterns and of character traits in the transference and in life is an important arena of analytic clarification and of complementary types of interpretation. A patient's pattern of passivity and impotence in life, leading to psychoanalysis, will be related to blocking in free association, fear of transference regression, and eventually to the underlying intrapsychic conflicts related to both the passive character and sexual symptom. Some of the extratransference interpretations may be regarded as confirmations and extensions of the transference; other extratransference interventions are preparatory steps which culminate in a transference interpretation; and extratransference interpretation may be necessary and valuable in its own effect on the analytic process. The transference interpretation may usually be our most valuable tool, but it is supplemented, complemented, and regularly used in conjunction with other technical agents, and with the here-and-now of the patient's life and continuing childish reactions.

PROBLEMS OF EXTRATRANSFERENCE INTERPRETATION

It is true that attention away from the transference may serve resistance, but exclusive transference interpretation will also serve resistance. Nontransference interpretation may pave the way for analyzing resistance and for conviction about the meaning of symptoms (e.g., predisposition, precipitation, anniversary reactions, etc.) before and during analysis (Arlow 1963). A patient's sleep disturbance and depression were precipitated by the anniversary of his father's death. These problems can be correlated with his denial and fetishistic use of pornography, his fears of death and concern for the analyst's health, his need to expiate his guilt by an act of charity while demanding immediate restitution and reparation for loss through fiscal manipulation.

Extratransference interpretation also concerns the repression of real traumatic experience so often seen in anniversary reactions. Traumatic experience tends to be repeated not only in transference, but in dreams, screen memories, symptoms, and neurotic behavior. The anniversary reactions precede analysis and continue during analysis. We are concerned with the patient's intrapsychic experience, the coordination between fantasy and reality, and the effects of the patient's adult and infantile traumata on conflict, structure, and subsequent development. Each patient defends and adapts in his own way. Some patients who abuse, overstimulate, and seduce their children are repeating the aggressive and sexual abuse they experienced with their own parents. These patterns appear in the transference, and the patient may attempt to use the transference in terms of active mastery of the passively experienced childhood traumata. Nonetheless, the behavior of parents (in analysis) with their children is inundated with meaning and has also to be seen in terms of the meaning, not only of the analyst, but of the child for that particular parent. The past is repeated with their own children before and during the analysis. Of course, the analyst cannot represent all transference figures at any one time and represents more than one object because of condensation and overdetermination. The analyst might represent a parent and the child, an ambivalently loved sibling. The adult parent patient has to see the relation between the transference manifestations during the analysis and the repetitive patterns which have gone on during his own childhood and which are now continued in derivative form with his own children. Sometimes what appears to be a revival of infantile object relations in the transference may not be a simple revival at all. Pathological familial patterns may have been continued throughout life with provocations and seductions going on during family contacts and visits, telephone calls, and so on.

If a crucial part of a pathological constellation is acted out, the complete pattern may not be available for analysis. A patient may be defensively masochistic in analysis and a sadistic tyrant at home. Moreover, certain forms of acting out may have serious consequences and sequelae as in the accident-prone patient. With an accident-prone patient, the analyst must understand the form and content of the prior and repeated accidents, what is enacted outside rather than recalled and verbalized in the analytic situation, and the relation between unconscious fantasies of transgression and actual self-punishment. The primal scene may be evoked by transference revival, but may also be stimulated by visits of parents or children, overnight guests, dances, analytic lectures, and publications.

In training analysis, for example, real contacts with the analyst and information about the analyst from the analytic scene in which both analyst and analysand are immersed lead to activation, reinforcement, contamination, and diffusion of certain transference fantasies. The metaphor of the training analysis being conducted in a goldfish bowl applies to the *entire* range of interplay between fantasy and reality and the necessity to ferret out the grains of truth around which transference fantasies (like delusions) tend to crystallize. Reality, transference, and countertransference have to be differentiated in the analysis and professional life of a candidate with recognition that the training analyst may be a real authority for a candidate. The analytic situation is influenced by the complexities of institutionalization, for example, extra-analytic contact and information; the process of selection, progression, and supervision; the goal of graduation. These factors all have transference repercussions. Additionally, the negative transference in training analysis may be less available than extratransference hostility. The candidate's countertransference problems to his own patients are not simply reflections of his transference to his training analyst, but are additional areas of analytic work and potential insight.

What about those times where the transference may be superseded in significance at a given moment by attention to extratransference material? Again, it is not a matter of either transference or extratransference, that is, of either-or, but of balance and of what seems to be the optimal choice. The patient's material is always overdetermined, subject to the principle of multiple function, and there is often a layering of potential interpretations with no easy solutions and no simple technical choices. Consider a mother who manages to be provocative, with behavior inappropriate to her children's needs. Her conscious devotion expresses her love, but it is also a reaction formation occasionally breached by her sadistic impulses. She reported that her child was getting out of the car, when she had failed to bring the car to a full stop. The analyst interpreted this mother's murderous conflicts involving her child, an interpretation that had a very favorable effect on the course of the analysis. Notice that the analyst did not say to the patient that the patient wanted to kill the analyst or that the patient wanted the analyst to throw her out of treatment prematurely, or that the patient was identified with the child and wished to leave impulsively before the hour was over, or any number of other possible transference interpretations. What was meaningful to the patient at this particular moment was in the area of the parent–child relationship. This could then be related to the transference and to the genetic determinants which led to such neurotic attitudes and behavior inside and outside the analysis.[1]

An analysis of this patient's superego would also entail a study of the patient's identifications. Any attempt to understand a patient's superego structure and function will require investigation of the genetic origins of the superego. Superego regression and progression can be clearly seen in dreams and transference, but the understanding also depends on reconstruction of the patient's infantile object relations and crucial identifications with his objects.

Another possible effect of failure of analytic attention to both the patient's current and past experience is to have the analysis in isolation from all else. The analysis is in danger of becoming an empty ritual, an artificial dramatization, or a narcissistic system, the particular configuration depending on the dominant transference.

---

[1] I am indebted to Dr. Jacob A. Arlow for this clinical illustration.

Lampl-de Groot (1976) commented that extreme devotion to analytic transference interpretation could support hidden analytic grandiosity. The analyst could seriously overestimate his importance to the patient. If the analyst pays no attention to reality and to the patient's extratransference relations, the implication is that only the analyst, the analytic process, and the patient as analysand are of importance. Analysis is aggrandized and external life belittled. Analysis could unwittingly become a *folie à deux*. A. Freud (1965) observed that the adult analyst may overemphasize psychic as opposed to external reality. She stated, "If anything he is too eager to see during his therapeutic work all current happenings in terms of transference and of resistance, and thereby to discount their value in reality" (p. 50). It is of historical significance that Fenichel (1942) had noted, "But the patient's life does not consist in transference alone, and often the analyst's resistance is shown in his neglect of the patient's life outside the transference. The patient who responded to a transference interpretation with the words, 'But doctor, you are conceited—everything I say you refer to yourself only!' sometimes may be correct" (p. 31).[2]

The patient's external life is not simply displaced or extended transference. The invaluable formation of the transference neurosis still leaves aspects of character, symptoms, and action not then available in transference in the same form or intensity. Neither the neurosis nor the healthy personality may be completely expressed in the transference in the analytic situation.

CLINICAL EXAMPLES

Exclusive focus on transference with a tendency to belittle external life is an analytic position communicated to the patient. This may have subtle effects on free association; the compliant patient may produce profuse transference fantasies, like the patient who provides dreams for the analyst who especially favors and savors dream work. This is a special form of transference resistance which may also be related to flight into fantasy. Some borderline patients may too readily regress into archaic transference fantasy, and may derive excessive gratification from the analysis compared to their meager gratifications in life. Such patients may attempt to use the analysis to defend against reality disappointments and injuries.

---

[2] I am indebted to Dr. Eugene Halpert for this citation.

Still another problem engendered by the isolation of analysis from external reality concerns the working through of conflicts in life. This occurs in conjunction with working through in analysis and in the wider application of analytic insight in life during and after analysis. I have already alluded to Freud's comments about the necessity of working through phobia in life; similar considerations apply to other symptoms and character disorder. The working through of the denial of a parent's psychosis or alcoholism, the need to see a spouse as distant and unloving in order to defend against incestuously tinged cravings for love, lead to the appreciation of object relations in a more rational and mature perspective. The analytic picture of the patient's life newly being constructed, which transforms the personal and familial mythical distortions (Kris 1956), emerges from the transference analysis, but also from extratransference illustrations which show the patient what is being repeated, how it is a repetition, and what elements of the pattern are not repeated but have been developmentally transformed. Neurotic patterns have often undergone transformations during development. Early separation anxiety, for example, may be manifest in an infantile sleep disturbance, a childhood travel phobia, adult insomnia and fears of death. Patients can then apply insight to their life, and psychologically minded patients will begin to show greater awareness, empathy, and even insight in their personal and familial relationships. Patients should understand their adaptation to the various facets of life. As parents, they should gain insight into neurotic reactions with each other and their children. As patients, their appreciation of the real qualities of the analyst should grow so that at termination the real or nontransference relationship is relatively undistorted by transference-neurotic fantasy (Ticho 1972).

An important by-product of analysis is not only more successful but more insightful adaptation to life.

One patient brought increasingly clear derivatives of primal-scene fantasy and experience into the analysis. She was very shy, socially and sexually inhibited, had rather puritanical attitudes toward life with an emphasis on decorum and propriety in dress, speech, manner, and behavior. She was defending herself against primal-scene excitement and experience extending through her childhood. Her curiosity was inhibited, she was afraid to explore, and was in constant danger of being seen in and outside the analysis as exposed. Dreams and transference fantasies of erotic nudity in the analysis, the public library, the concert hall, and so on, emerged with associated shame and guilt. Her interest in clothes and what was underneath clothes appeared with increasing clarity. The patient then began to discuss how she had dressed her children and the mode of dress and undress within the family. She would want the children, particularly her daughters, to be nicely and neatly dressed and to stand, sit, and carry themselves like ladies. These values did not apply in the same way to her husband, whose own style was what he considered to be relaxed informality at home. He was fond of going into his daughters' room in his underwear, inviting the children into the bedroom when they were partially undressed or in night clothes, and still later, we learned that her husband insisted on keeping the door to the parental bedroom open at night. As the analysis progressed, her husband's behavior led to serious marital discord. He resented her imposing her values on him, unfairly interfering with his lifestyle, and he resented her analysis.

The patient began to understand the implications of the seduction of her own children by their parents in which she was a passive participant. She unconsciously assigned responsibility and guilt to her husband. The primal scene was continued from the past into the present and was actually being enacted in her adult life before and during her analysis. As her own incestuous attachments were clarified, she understood her husband's behavior in an entirely new way and attempted to shift the whole family interaction to what she considered to be a constructive direction. She was able to use the analytic work to show her husband that his discussion of the sexual abuse of patients by dentists and doctors was connected to an unrecognized abuse of his children. Having tried to insist that the door be open during their nocturnal sexual relations, he had, the next day, exploded at their daughter for having gone out of the house into the cold without a coat. She came to understand that he attempted to make the daughter feel guilty about exposure rather than himself, choosing to present himself as offering guidance and concern rather than abuse and exploitation. The mother's resources and strength in being able to confront these conflicts had positive effects on her children's development, and in the long run upon her husband's functioning as well.

Interpretations have multiple appeal which extends beyond the transference situation and personality reorganization to the wider spheres of life. Such effects can be detrimental if extratransference interpretation is abused by patients who then engage in wild analysis of family and friends. Patients may evade self-scrutiny by shifting analytic inquiry to the unconscious motivation of others (Greenacre 1959). Authentic understanding and insight tend to be applied in life as beneficial intrafamilial influences rather than in the service of regression or provocation.

A pure transference position tends to treat extratransference relations as those "objectionable others" (Anthony 1980) who figure so importantly in our patients' lives in adult and child analysis. It would be interesting to know if child analysts are more comfortable, more at ease with extratransference interpretations and if this technical position complements or competes with essential analysis of the transference. Child analysis has helped to elucidate different dimensions of the analytic relationship and to understand the child in his own developmental phase as well as in his family, social, and cultural setting. Current conflicts are introduced into the analytic situation just as revived unconscious conflicts tend to be reenacted with the original objects at home. Past and present meet and interact in the interpretation of transference and in reconstruction. Within the zone of interaction, there is a redefinition of the past as presently understood and of the present shadowed and shaped by the living past. The past may be used as a defense against the present and the present may be used as a defense against the past (Kris 1956).

The relationship of transference to the realities of the analytic situation is significant and of particular contemporary interest. The patient reacts to all features, cues, and communications in the analytic situation and process. I refer here to the realities of the analytic situation and the real attributes, style, and function as well as possible malfunction of the analyst (Blum 1971). This includes the analyst's age, sex, character, attitude, silence, and the whole range of accurate, inexact, and erroneous interpretations. There are scattered references to these issues in the literature. Greenson (1972) explored the nontransference relationship and pointed to the patient's realistic perception of the analyst's style, taste, temperament, and technique. He offered suggestions about the mutual recognition and management of the analyst's technical errors. This is no place to explore, in depth, Greenson's challenging, controversial formulations, but I do not believe that the issues are beyond interpretation. They are beyond pure transference interpretation.

The analyst is a participant observer and not a pure receiving and reflecting mirror. There are transference reactions to his real personality and his unconscious cues and his interventions which should be understood. Gill (1979), giving early and top priority to transference interpretation, emphasizes the "analytic situation residue" as a current stimulus for transference. The analyst's real behavior might make the irrational transference seem plausible, and this should also apply to premature and exclusive transference interpretation. To my mind, if the "analytic situation residue" were truly plausible, it would tend to obscure, contaminate, or validate the transference. Transference repetition of the past would remain confused with the present. Reality inside and outside the analytic situation may provide an important anchor, a "grain of truth," for transference fantasy. Clinic analysis, supervision, insurance payment, and so on, all tend to activate or lend reality to transference fantasy and transference gratifications. The patient consciously and unconsciously perceives the analytic situation realities—which are not transference distortions. These realities may influence the transference and its full analysis. In contrast to transference displacement, these realities may be displaced so that the patient's distortions of other objects may contain accurate referents to the analyst.

These current or "day residue" influences on the activation of the transference are not restricted to analytic situation residues (nor do such residues "explain" transference fantasy or repetition). They can be compared to a dream "from above" (Freud 1923) where the dream is interpreted with the link between the current stimulus and its reinforcement from the unconscious latent content. In analysis, the current stimulus may or may not be of great significance, but the transference issues are always significant (Stone 1981). The transference, however, is not in its core externally or iatrogenically determined, and the patient is responsible for his transference as for his neurosis.

The realities of the analytic situation cannot be "analyzed away," but the linked transference meanings and reactions, rooted in the past, should be ascertained insofar as possible. The transference meanings will be shown to be childish and ultimately reduced to their genetic origins. The effects of countertransference—parameters, errors, supervision—will be present, but may not be fully analyzable. The realities of the analytic situation should not be denied or overlooked in their possible influence on the analytic process. Not all that a patient thinks or feels about his analyst or analysis is due to transference (Heimann 1950).

It does make a difference if the analyst is anxious or angry, humorous or serious. If the analyst tends to be caustic and critical, the patient's fears of disapproval and punishment in the transference cannot be analyzed in depth without recognition of the reality which tends to validate the transference fantasy. The transference may be obscured or "contaminated." The patient's fears of disapproval, criticism, punishment, insofar as they are transference, stem from the past and from his own superego. Each patient reacts to the same analyst in his own way. A sadomasochistic patient might enjoy the opportunity for battle; a guilty patient might exploit the analytic situation for self-punitive purposes.

Reciprocal provocations inside the analytic situation may promote acting out. Some analysts may instigate, encourage, or enjoy the patient's acting-out tendencies. If an analyst forgets to unlock the waiting-room door, leaving the patient locked out of a session, we are not surprised to hear, in the next session, about an insolent waiter who kept the patient waiting for the meal and provided terrible service. The patient vowed never to return to the restaurant but returned to the analytic session, without any direct reference to the lockout. The patient was afraid of her intense disappointment and rage and could not discuss her thoughts of quitting or her fears of being thrown out by the analyst. A different patient might not have so defended her own feelings toward the analyst and might have reacted with overt outrage; yet another patient might have reacted with glee over the analyst's fallibility. This masochistically provocative patient elicited a sadomasochistic countertransference. The patient's final quitting of treatment was overdetermined, but it included an element of acting out of the countertransference fantasy, like a child who tends to act out the unconscious fantasies of the parents. A malignant cycle of unresolved transference–countertransference issues may supervene with mutual negative feedback. The hypercritical analysand may fear, invite, and finally incite analytic criticism. Efforts at mastery of these complicated problems are immeasurably assisted by their clarification and insightful interpretation (Brenner 1976, Kanzer 1953). This requires an understanding of the entire psychic field, including the "reality" inside and outside the analytic situation.

The problem of the analyst who abuses interpretation for shock effect or to compete, criticize, or erotize is not resolved by compounding problems with parameters. The analytic solution is still one of interpretation that has to include the countertransference. We may distinguish here among the analyst's protracted countertransference (e.g., critical of a particular patient; countertransference at a particular point, as in response to a patient's criticism) and the analyst's character (e.g., a generally exacting, critical attitude with all patients). The countertransference belongs to the nontransference sphere and, though they interact, should not be confused with the transference. The transference cannot be analyzed through the countertransference any more than self-analysis can substitute for analysis of the patient.

That the countertransference may be constructively analyzed and utilized for the benefit of both the analyst and the patient (Heimann 1950, Kernberg 1965) does not mean that countertransference will not have its own transference consequences. The patient's unconscious response to the countertransference is likely to be missed (Little 1951). A particular countertransference may obscure, resist, or reinforce certain transference constellations, may provide hidden transference gratifications, and may elicit certain transference reactions. The analyst should be able to recognize his own contribution to the patient's particular transference response; it is now readily noted in case of a change in fee, time, or office situation. Patient and analyst are likely to have exquisitely sensitive transference–countertransference reactions to the analyst's illness (Dewald 1982), injury, bereavement, and so on.

Analytic problems cannot be solved by a blurring of boundaries between psychic and external reality, between transference and nontransference reactions of analyst and patient. In this connection, A. Freud (1954) noted that analyst and patient are of equal adult status in a real personal relationship, and that neglect of this reality may be responsible for hostile reactions from patients that are ascribed only to transference. Reality is usually invoked to avoid recognition of transference, but transference can also be used to evade reality. The sleeping analyst of the sardonic joke, awakened, attributes the patient's negative transference and indignation to the patient's narcissistic need for constant attention.

Compared to countertransference, little has been said about the patient's unconscious response to the analyst's personality. It would be helpful for both analyst and patient to delineate the more subtle transference response to an analyst's ego-syntonic character trends (e.g., his precision of speech and the careful arrangement of his desk and office decor, or tendencies to be sarcastic or witty). The analyst's character and style, his own variations within correct analytic technique, are often overlooked as influencing the analytic process or treated as part of the analytic frame or atmosphere. Because of differences, however subtle, in the patient's reactions to the analyst's age and sex, character, style, and temperament (Blum 1971), each analytic "match" could influence the analytic process. It might make a difference if the analyst is an ordinary clinician or an authority, married or divorced, parent or childless. The patient will react to the candidate's supervision, or to the status of the senior analyst, with fear of murderous aggression against the latter.

Analysts could treat a wide range of patients with similar but not necessarily identical findings and results.

Strachey (1934), toward the end of his paper, tended to retreat from and correct his rather extreme position. He noted that· by giving extratransference interpretations the analyst might prepare for a "mutative interpretation." His concluding comments concerning extratransference interpretation are surprisingly little known:

> It must not be supposed that because I am attributing these special qualities to transference interpretation I am, therefore, maintaining that no others should be made. On the contrary, it is possible that a large majority of our interpretations are outside the transference— though it should be added that it often happens that when one is ostensibly given extratransference interpretation one is implicitly given a transference one. A cake cannot be made of nothing but currants; and, though it is true that extratransference interpretations are not for the most part mutative, and do not themselves bring about the crucial result . . . they are nonetheless essential. If I may take an analogy from trench warfare, the acceptance of the transference interpretation corresponds to the capture of a key position, while extratransference interpretation corresponds to the general advance. . . . An oscillation of this kind between transference and extratransference interpretations will represent the normal course of events in analysis. [p. 125]

What is analytically indicated is a consistent analytic attitude with a balanced, holistic process of interpretation. Transference analysis is central and essential, but extratransference interpretation, including genetic interpretation and reconstruction, is also necessary and complementary. Reconstruction of the past and transference analysis in the "here-and-now" are mutually explanatory, circular, and synergistic. Analysis progresses beyond interpretation of transference distortions of the doctor–patient relationship and requires genetic interpretation to fully differentiate transference and reality, past and present, as Freud (1940) indicated, to show the patient "again and again that what he takes to be new real life is a reflection of the past" (p. 177). Extratransference interpretation is not reducible to resistance, to transference, or a poor relation of and replacement for transference interpretation.

I conclude there is no royal road to analytic interpretation. The transference is the main road but not the only road to mutative interpretation, and we do not analyze just transference or dreams, we analyze the patient.

CONCLUSION

The role of extratransference interpretation in the theory of technique has been insufficiently defined and only tangentially discussed. Extratransference interpretation refers to interpretation that is relatively outside the analytic transference relationship. Although interpretive resolution of the transference neurosis is the central area of analytic work, transference is not the sole or whole focus of interpretation, or the only effective "mutative" interpretation, or always the most significant interpretation. Extratransference interpretation has a position and value which is not simply ancillary, preparatory, and supplementary to transference interpretation. Transference analysis is essential, but extratransference interpretation, including genetic interpretation and reconstruction, is also necessary, complementary, and synergistic. Transference is a repetition that requires analysis of its genetic sources in childhood conflict and fixation. Transference and reality, past and present, are newly defined, understood, and integrated in the analytic process.

Transference fantasy cannot be clarified without understanding the "grains of truth" to which it may be anchored in reality inside and outside the analytic situation. The analyst's real attitudes and attributes may influence the transference and transference analysis. Countertransference also tends to evoke transference reactions which are unique to each patient, so that there are contributions from both parties to the analytic process and the analytic data. Analytic understanding should encompass the overlapping transference and extratransference spheres, fantasy and reality, past and present. A "transference only" position is theoretically untenable and could lead to an artificial reduction of all associations and interpretations into a transference mold and to an idealized *folie à deux*.

REFERENCES

Anthony, E. J. (1980). The family and the psychoanalytic process in children. *Psychoanalytic Study of the Child* 35:3–34. New Haven: Yale University Press.

Arlow, J. A. (1963). Conflict regression and symptom formation. *International Journal of Psycho-Analysis* 44:12–22.

Blum, H. P. (1971). On the conception and development of the transference neurosis. *Journal of the American Psychoanalytic Association* 19:41–53.

_____ (1980). The value of reconstruction in adult psychoanalysis. *International Journal of Psycho-Analysis* 61:39–52.

Brenner, C. (1976). *Psychoanalytic Technique and Psychic Conflict.* New York: International Universities Press.

Dewald, P. (1972). *The Psychoanalytic Process.* New York: Basic Books.

_____ (1982). Serious illness in the analyst: transference, countertransference, and reality responses. *Journal of the American Psychoanalytic Association* 30:347–363.

Eissler, K. R. (1953). The effect of the structure of the ego on psychoanalytic technique. *Journal of the American Psychoanalytic Association* 1:104–143.

Fenichel, O. (1942). Theoretical implications of the didactic analysis. *Annual of Psychoanalysis* 8:21–35, 1980.

Freud, A. (1954). The widening scope of indications for psychoanalysis: discussion. *Journal of the American Psychoanalytic Association* 2:607–620.

_____ (1965). *Normality and Pathology in Childhood: Assessments of Development.* New York: International Universities Press.

Freud, S. (1905). Fragment of an analysis of a case of hysteria. *Standard Edition* 7:1–123.

_____ (1912). The dynamics of transference. *Standard Edition* 12:97–109.

_____ (1914a). Observations on transference love. *Standard Edition* 12:157–172.

_____ (1914b). Remembering, repeating and working-through. *Standard Edition* 12:145–157.

_____ (1914c). On the history of the psychoanalytic movement. *Standard Edition* 14:1–67.

_____ (1916–1917). Introductory lectures on psychoanalysis. *Standard Edition* 15 and 16:13–481.

_____ (1919). Lines of advance in psychoanalytic therapy. *Standard Edition* 17:157–169.

_____ (1923). Remarks on the theory and practice of dream-interpretation. *Standard Edition* 19:109–123.

_____ (1926). An autobiographical study. *Standard Edition* 20:1–75.

_____ (1937). Constructions in analysis. *Standard Edition* 23:255–271.

_____ (1940). An outline of psychoanalysis. *Standard Edition* 23:139–209.

Gill, M. (1979). The analysis of the transference. *Journal of the American Psychoanalytic Association* 27:263–288.

Gray, P. (1973). Psychoanalytic technique and the ego's capacity for viewing intrapsychic activity. *Journal of the American Psychoanalytic Association* 21:474–494.

Greenacre, P. (1959). Certain technical problems in the transference relationship. *Journal of the American Psychoanalytic Association* 7:484–502.

Greenson, R. R. (1972). Beyond transference interpretation. *International Journal of Psycho-Analysis* 53:213–217.

Heimann, P. (1950). On counter-transference. *International Journal of Psycho-Analysis* 31:81–84.

Kanzer, M. (1953). Past and present in the transference. *Journal of the American Psychoanalytic Association* 1:144–154.

Kernberg, O. (1965). Notes on countertransference. *Journal of the American Psychoanalytic Association* 13:38–56.

Kris, E. (1956). The recovery of childhood memories in psychoanalysis. *Psychoanalytic Study of the Child* 11:54–88. New York: International Universities Press.

Lampl-de Groot, J. (1976). Personal experience with psychoanalytic technique and theory during the last half-century. *Psychoanalytic Study of the Child* 31:283–296. New Haven: Yale University Press.

Leites, N. (1977). Transference interpretation only? *International Journal of Psycho-Analysis* 58:275–287.

Little, M. (1951). Counter-transference and the patient's response to it. *International Journal of Psycho-Analysis* 32:32–40.

Loewenstein, R. M. (1957). Some thoughts on interpretation in the theory and practice of psychoanalysis. *Psychoanalytic Study of the Child* 12:127–150. New York: International Universities Press.

Rangell, L. (1979). Contemporary issues in the theory of therapy. *Journal of the American Psychoanalytic Association* 27:81–112.

——— (1981). Psychoanalysis and dynamic psychotherapy: similarities and differences twenty-five years later. *Psychoanalytic Quarterly* 50:665–693.

Stone, L. (1961). *The Psychoanalytic Situation.* New York: International Universities Press.

——— (1967). The psychoanalytic situation and transference: postscript to an earlier communication. *Journal of the American Psychoanalytic Association* 15:3–58.

——— (1981). Some thoughts on the here-and-now in psychoanalytic technique and process. *Psychoanalytic Quarterly* 50:709–733.

Strachey, J. (1934). The nature of the therapeutic action of psychoanalysis. *International Journal of Psycho-Analysis* 50:275–292.

Ticho, E. (1972). Termination of psychoanalysis: treatment goals, life goals. *Psychoanalytic Quarterly* 41:315–333.

8

Tactics in Psychoanalytic Psychotherapy

Morton J. Aronson, M.D.

INTRODUCTION

Psychoanalytic psychotherapy as a technique of treatment has had a tempestuous, conflict-ridden relationship with its parent and basic science—psychoanalysis. Freud (1919) said:

> The large-scale application of our therapy will compel us to ally the pure gold of analysis freely with the copper of direct suggestion; and hypnotic influences, too, might find a place in it again, as it has in the treatment of war neuroses. But whatever form this psychotherapy for the people may take, whatever the elements out of which it is compounded, its most effective and important ingredients will assuredly remain those borrowed from strict and untendentious psychoanalysis. [pp. 167–168]

The development of dynamic psychotherapy, particularly after World War II, threatened to invade the domain of psychoanalytic treatment and blur the distinction between the two. Alexander and French (1946) and Fromm-Reichmann (1954) introduced modifications of psychoanalytic technique, provoking a storm of controversy and leading to serious efforts to assess the points of similarity and difference between psychoanalysis and analytic psychotherapy. Bibring (1954) categorized psychotherapies by their development of five basic techniques: suggestion, abreaction, manipulation, clarification, and interpretation. In psychoanalysis, "insight through interpretation is the supreme agent in the hierarchy of therapeutic principles" (p. 763), and all other techniques, though utilized, have a subordinate place.

Gill (1954) designated psychoanalysis as a technique that analyzes transference and resistance back to their genetic-dynamic roots, and analytic psychotherapy as a technique that recognizes transference and resistance and rationally utilizes this recognition in the therapy. Knight (1952) considered what he called *expressive psychotherapy*, as opposed to suggestive ego-strengthening therapy, to be closely allied to psychoanalysis, but of more limited range and more circumscribed goals. He found it to be conflict-resolving. This was the position of the long-term research project on psychotherapy of the Menninger Foundation (Wallerstein and Robbins 1956). DeWald (1964) sharply distinguished psychoanalysis from analytic psychotherapy in the following respects:

1. Psychotherapy deals with derivative conflicts only and does not lift the infantile amnesia. (Gill believed that derivative conflicts may develop a relative degree of autonomy and exist in a form that permits resolution with psychotherapy techniques, even though the basic conflict was left unsolved.)
2. Psychotherapy does not involve a regressive transference neurosis, as does psychoanalysis.
3. Psychotherapy does not depend on adherence to the basic rule and the free-association method.
4. Psychotherapy is a "sector" or segmental approach that "helps the patient to gain insight and understanding in the resolution of certain conflicts while leaving others deliberately untouched or unexplored" (p. 298).

Psychoanalysis is a leisurely, relatively timeless compact between analyst and analysand to explore the unconscious together. Regrettably, it is a treatment not well suited to the current socioeconomic climate, which fosters short-term goals, impulse gratification via acting out, and alloplastic as opposed to autoplastic solutions to conflict. Few patients are able to afford the considerable financial outlay for analysis. Insurance companies and federal health planners look at this treatment modality from an economic point of view. Despite the widening indications for psychoanalysis (e.g., the technical modifications introduced by Kohut and Kernberg that appear to make narcissistic personalities and borderline states analyzable), there are fewer and fewer analytic patients. As a result, most analysts spend a significant portion of their treatment time in the practice of analytic psychotherapy. This reality, however, is not reflected in the psychoanalytic literature. Although a large psychotherapy literature has developed, psychotherapy papers and case reports appear infrequently in psychoanalytic journals.

The purpose of this chapter is to focus on the adaptation of psychoanalytic techniques of intervention to the tasks of psychotherapy. Illustrative case material will emphasize the use of tactics in psychotherapy interpretation.

TACTICS

What exactly do we mean by *interpretation?* Loewenstein (1951) said, "This term is applied to those explanations given to patients by analysts which add to their knowledge about themselves . . . drawn by the analyst from elements contained and expressed in the patient's own thoughts, feelings, words and behavior" (p. 4). To interpret means to make conscious the unconscious meaning, source, history, mode or cause of a given psychic event. Interpretation is different from reconstruction in that the former explains the meaning of something in mental life, while the latter unearths the existence of forgotten portions of the patient's past. For Freud (1937), interpretation applies to a single element of the material, such as an association or a parapraxis: "It is a construction when one lays before the subject of the analysis a piece of his early history that he has forgotten" (p. 261). The purpose of interpretation is to change through insight the dynamic equilibrium of the forces involved in unconscious conflict, whether they stem from the drives, the particular defenses employed, or the superego elements involved.

Interpretation begins with what is on the surface of the patient's mind, particularly his affects, and with his present situation. The present situation encompasses what is going on in the patient's outside life but refers particularly to conflicts that appear in the treatment relationship. Interpretation of these conflicts inevitably leads back to similar conflicts in the patient's past. In a well-functioning treatment, content and interpretation fluctuate between the transference, the patient's outside life, and the past. Overpreoccupation with any one area indicates resistance, which calls for exploration and interpretation.

"Tactics" refer to the sequence, choice, and timing of interpretations. Regarding sequence, certain interpretations should precede
or follow other types. Priority, for example, is given to resistances or
defenses over id derivatives, or to transference reactions over
material not dealing with the analyst. Analysis of mobile defense
traits is preferable to analysis of rigid characterologic defenses.
Choice of interpretation is expressed as analytic tact by Loewenstein
(1951), "that intuitive evaluation of the patient's problems which
leads the analyst to choose, among many possible interventions or
interpretations, the one [that] is right at a given moment" (p. 8).
Timing concerns the prompt analysis of resistance and transference
and the avoidance of premature interpretation of drive material
entirely outside the patient's awareness. Such premature id interpretations, a feature of "wild analysis," reflect failure to understand
the ego's defensive structure and may have harmful results. The
following case illustration is an example of wild analysis.

THE MISUSE OF INTERPRETATION: THE CASE
OF DR. P. R.

A 49-year-old vascular surgeon came for treatment because of depression,
irritability, startle reactions, and "flashbacks" following an automobile
accident several months earlier. Although unhurt himself, the driver of the
other car, an 18-year-old boy, was badly injured. The patient gave the boy
emergency medical care that relieved an obstructed airway and probably
saved his life. It seemed clear that the accident was caused by the boy's
speeding, yet the patient blamed himself, insisting that the accident would
not have occurred if he had been more vigilant.

The patient was married and had two sons, ages 18 and 21. The
18-year-old suffered from a rare genetic illness that invariably leads to
premature death, in early adulthood at the latest. The family's life had been
dominated by the boy's recurrent health crises, any one of which would
have been fatal had it not been for the parents' alert intervention. The
patient loved this son deeply and was in a chronic state of grief over his
illness and the associated deformities. He felt responsible for having given
his son the fatal gene, although he had not known previously of its
existence. He often wished that he could die in his son's place. At the same
time, he felt that this was such an intolerable illness that, if his older son
had such a child, the patient would smother it in the cradle and face the
consequences.

The patient was aware of a connection in his mind between his worries about his son and the automobile accident. At the time of the accident, when he saw the victim he had the momentary thought that it was his son. In therapy it became apparent that the patient's intense love for and devotion to his impaired son was significantly determined by his unconscious identification with him.

Even though he was an attractive, successful man who was admired for his work and his devotion to his family, the patient constantly reproached and despised himself as physically ugly and emotionally "weak." As a child, he had felt that he was a disappointment to his critical father, who frequently derided and humiliated him because he was overweight and unathletic. The patient loved his son as he wished his father had loved him. Unconsciously, he perceived his son not only as a constant drain and burden on his family but also as the damaged, castrated image of himself, a narcissistic humiliation exposed for all the world to see. His unconscious hatred of his son was powerfully defended against by repression and reaction formation.

It was clear that a lengthy period of work in therapy would be required before it would be possible for the patient to tolerate exposure of his central unconscious conflict. Accordingly, the focus of therapy was exploration, fostering a therapeutic alliance, and interpretive efforts to modify the harshness of his sadistic superego.

The patient became more involved in therapy, and his symptoms began to improve until his insurance carrier, after nine months of treatment, required that he be examined by the company's psychiatrist to see if further treatment for his "post-traumatic stress disorder" was necessary, as I maintained. In the course of this examination, the insurance carrier's psychiatrist told the patient that he was glad he was beginning to feel better and that he was sure that the patient understood why be became ill. When the patient asked what he meant, the doctor said that it was obvious that the accident victim represented his son to the patient and that it appeared that his death wishes for his son had been realized. He was guilty about these wishes and thus became ill. The patient reacted to the interview with shock, outrage, and depression. He refused antidepressant medication for fear it would interfere with his work. A few days later, he made a serious but unsuccessful suicide attempt and was hospitalized in a psychiatric unit.

What happened here is similar to what occurs in a nightmare. In a nightmare, due to the failure of the dream censorship to disguise and obscure the latent dream thoughts, the dreamer recognizes his unacceptable drive wishes and their associated fears and is overwhelmed by anxiety and guilt. The insurance company's psychiatrist made an inappropriate and gratuitous interpretation of the patient's unconscious conflict without

the support of an ongoing therapeutic relationship and without understanding the patient's defensive structure. Because of the fragility of his
defenses and his endowment of the insurance carrier's psychiatrist with
the authority of his own analyst, the patient recognized the truth of the
interpretation and was flooded with overwhelming feelings of guilt, which
he acted out in his suicide attempt.

Further illustrative case material will focus on tactics in the
treatment of two male patients with phallic narcissistic character
neuroses: one entering marriage, the other leaving it.

HOMOSEXUAL PANIC: THE CASE OF MR. M. L.

The patient was a 30-year-old, six-foot-four inch, strikingly handsome film
executive referred by his internist because of an acute anxiety attack. The
attack began after an evening with his fiancée when he passed a gay bar,
looked in, and wondered what it would be like to have a homosexual
experience. He felt revolted and became acutely anxious.

In the following weeks, severe anxiety symptoms continued, partially
alleviated by jogging and Valium. He found it difficult to work. The job had
been a problem before this episode because he hated his Jewish boss, who
was aggressive, ruthless, and always putting him down. He characterized
himself as the "house goy."

The patient denied that he had ever had any previous homosexual
thoughts or interests. He tried to be understanding of homosexuals, but he
could not help feeling contemptuous of them. The idea of homosexuality
was total anathema to his whole image of himself, his life pattern of
interest in sports and masculine pursuits. He had always been a tense,
high-strung person and had experienced initial anxiety symptoms without
homosexual thoughts when his previous engagement to a famous film
actress ended with her development of a psychotic illness. He realized that
he was not in love with this woman, that the important thing was the
enhanced status that engagement to her provided for him. He thought of
how sexually active he was with a large number of women, but he found
this to be an exhausting life and wanted to settle down. He spoke of his
fiancée in glowing terms, said he was in love for the first time in his life and
that she was perfect for him—sensitive, beautiful, successful in her own
right as an illustrator, wealthy, and socially prominent.

The patient had been raised in an exclusive suburb in a family preoccupied with social status. His father, who in college had been a nationally
known football player, was a corporate executive who traveled much of the

time. When home with his son, he would emphasize the importance of manliness and sports. The patient resented his father because he felt that he could never really please him. For many years the father disparaged him by calling him a "showoff." He was also disappointed in his father because he never made it "really big" in the world of business. There was one sibling, a sister, five years younger. The patient was very close to his mother, whom he idealized. The mother died of cancer when the patient was 14 years old. Two years later, the father married an extremely wealthy woman with a son of her own, five years older than the patient. The patient had a superficially good relationship with him but resented his stepson status and tried to outdo his stepbrother. The father was increasingly dominated by his second wife, gave up his job, and was relegated to managing her money.

The patient grew up as a seemingly well-adjusted boy who was particularly interested in sports, but he also considered himself to be a sensitive, creative person, like his mother. He attended an Ivy League college, where his burgeoning football career was terminated when the school forced him to quit the team because of poor grades. He transferred to another college where he did well academically and was approaching football stardom, when he again lost it, this time because of a knee injury.

Upon graduation from college, he enlisted in the Army and was sent as an infantry officer to Vietnam. Because of difficulties with his superior officer and at his own request, he was transferred to Special Forces. He adjusted well to life as a combat soldier and was decorated for bravery on numerous occasions. He enjoyed the camaraderie, the drunken binges and brawls. He recounted one episode in which he felt as if he were acting out a John Wayne movie. He was awakened by a Vietcong grenade, which was dropped in his foxhole in an attack on an American base. When the grenade failed to explode, he jumped out of the foxhole, rallied the defense, and organized his men. At great peril he fought all through the night. When the attack was finally repulsed, he "lost it," ran about repeatedly shooting dead enemy soldiers, until he was dragged away and subdued by his comrades. For his heroism, he was awarded one of the nation's highest decorations.

Upon his return to civilian life, he entered the film industry, where he was determined to reach the top. He was discouraged with the slow progress of his career and felt that he was still in combat, that the business world was a jungle similar to Vietnam.

I proposed to the patient that he enter psychoanalysis, but, as we explored this proposal, he rejected it on the grounds that it would be too expensive, that he needed more immediate help, that business traveling would interfere, and that he was not interested in any long-term exploration. What he wanted was medication to control his anxiety and reassurance that he would not become a homosexual. In the ensuing weeks, as his symptoms continued, I tried to set up ground rules for psychotherapy and tried to meet his demands for concrete help by pointing out that the only real help would come from understanding, not from such Band-Aids as medication and reassurance. My efforts to build a therapeutic alliance kept the process going until the patient provided me with the opportunity to make a tactically meaningful interpretation of one aspect of his unconscious conflict. This opportunity occurred when he told me of his worry about the future stability of his coming marriage, since all his friends were either already divorced or in the process of becoming so. I told him we could now understand the meaning of his anxiety. He was unconsciously terrified that his growing intimacy with and commitment to his fiancée would make him vulnerable to losing her and experiencing the pain he suffered when his mother died. I explained that his homosexual thoughts represented an attempted solution to the problem, a flight to a safer alternative, but this alternative was just as unacceptable and raised his anxiety to a new acute level.

The patient wept in response and recalled the feelings of grief and abandonment in the months after his mother's death. He said he now understood his inability to make any real friends in Vietnam. He was afraid of how he would feel if they were killed. Similarly, he understood why he dated so many women and kept the relationships superficial. This session was followed by marked symptomatic improvement. As the material was worked through in subsequent sessions, the patient made plans to go ahead with his marriage.

The content then shifted to the work situation, and we explored his intense drive for success, his hostile feelings about his boss, and his accompanying fear of him. Interpretive efforts remained at derivative levels of oedipal conflicts. Emerging resistance to continuing treatment was explored and led to the uncovering of hostile fantasies about my being Jewish. These feelings, as well as those toward his boss, were interpreted as displacements from his disappointment in and aggression toward his father. The main theme then centered on his drive for success in order to find acceptance by his father, his stepmother, and his own grandiose ego ideal. His anxieties about the business world, a jungle, reflected his fear of punishment for and projection of his competitive aggressive fantasies about his father and stepbrother. My stance with him consisted of an admixture of clarification and interpretation close to the surface without any attempt to translate the material into explicit oedipal terms. Of particular impact on the patient were interpretations of his unconscious fears of success, of outdoing his father and stepbrother, and how these fears were acted out in football, in Vietnam, and in his provocation toward his boss.

The patient married after six months of twice weekly psychotherapy and shortly thereafter formed a film company of his own. Increased travel made treatment difficult, but he functioned well and was relatively symptom-free. On a few occasions, when he was temporarily impotent, homosexual fears and anxiety symptoms reappeared. They responded to interpretations of his fear of being trapped in marriage and their connection to his now realized resentment toward his wife and his unconscious fear of retaliatory castration. Now he was able to view his character traits of recklessness and combativeness (he would start fistfights with other men at the slightest provocation and at times would carry a gun) as counterphobic defenses against a pervasive underlying fear of injury, weakness, and castration. He recalled that he had masturbated with intense guilt as an adolescent and after his mother's death had used a maid's stocking in the masturbatory act. The stocking was a fetish that functioned both as a transitional object and as a defense against castration anxiety, in which it unconsciously symbolized the female penis.

The tactics throughout treatment involved a focus on intermediate-level derivatives of nuclear oedipal and preoedipal conflicts. Homosexual fears were interpreted via displacement upward as fearful wishes for closeness and warmth with men and reaction formations against his competitive, aggressive wishes. Fears of becoming dependent on me were interpreted away from his passive homosexual longings and toward his fears of object loss.

Treatment was terminated by mutual agreement after eighteen months. Despite considerable gains and clear structural changes, the patient and I agreed that he should enter analysis when his life situation would make it feasible. After termination, the patient returned for single sessions several times a year and continued to maintain his treatment gains. He attained considerable success in the film industry. All went well until five years after termination, when his wife gave birth to their first child. Unfortunately, the baby had gross birth defects and died a few days later. Following this experience and now with growing tensions in the marriage, the patient again developed anxiety symptoms, which were now in the form of feared coronary attacks. Since his wife had entered treatment with me, I referred the patient to a colleague for psychoanalysis.

A FAILED MARRIAGE: THE CASE OF DR. L. B.

The patient was a 50-year-old dentist who was referred because of depression and indecision about his marriage of twenty-five years. Three months prior to our consultation, he had left his wife, telling her that it was a temporary separation to enable him to think things over. The actual reason was an affair of two years' duration with a 30-year-old woman who was herself married with two small children. The affair initially had gone on for one year, but the woman had broken it off because the patient refused to leave his wife. Her wish was that they should both leave their spouses and marry one another. The patient had mild depressive symp-toms for some months after this breakup. One year later, they met again and resumed the relationship. She again insisted that he leave his wife. He decided that it was now or never and moved out.

Since the separation, he had been in an agony of indecision. He felt that he should end the marriage because he had long been dissatisfied with his wife and was in love with his girlfriend, whom he considered to be the ideal woman. On the other hand, he felt guilty toward his wife and did not want to harm her or his two children. He was also convinced that he was too old for this relationship; it might not work out; he might get sick and have no one to take care of him. His wish at this point was to keep his options open. He vacillated between what he felt he should do and what he wanted to do. Although he wanted help from me in making this decision, coming to see a psychiatrist was also an effort to placate his wife. He felt treatment would give him an excuse to remain away from her, because it would mean he was trying to work things out.

History revealed that the patient was an only child whose parents owned and operated a restaurant. Since both parents worked in the restaurant, much of his childhood was spent in the family apartment alone. He recalled how he dreaded coming home from school to the empty apartment and how fond he was of a neighborhood woman who used to invite him in for milk and cookies. His mother was a dominant, controlling person, and he was always very close to her. She was in the habit of depreciating the father and pointing out all his faults. The patient adopted a similar attitude toward his father and never felt close to him. He recounted an early memory from age 3. While playing during his father's nap, he had found a gun under the bed. The father woke up to see the boy pointing the gun at his, the father's, head. The mother talked about the father having an affair, and the parents argued constantly about this, about the restaurant, and about everything else. The patient vowed to himself as a child that, when he married, he would not quarrel with his wife. He said he never did.

As an adolescent, the patient would take the subway into Manhattan and walk along Fifth Avenue, looking at all the rich apartment houses and having fantasies of how he would meet and marry a rich Jewish princess and live an elegant life in a beautiful apartment. He said that he had masturbated compulsively throughout his adolescence and was besieged by chronic fears that he would damage himself in some way as a result of it. He was extremely shy with girls and almost never dated until his last year at college, when he began to feel more confident and began dating and having sexual relationships. When the patient was 18 and his father 52, the father died of a stroke. He recalled feeling pleased and did not mourn. He went to dental school, where he continued his pattern of casual dating. He disapproved of the women for having sex with him. He developed gonorrhea, which was one of the most anxiety-provoking experiences of his life. He was terrified that he would be left with a urethral stricture and went from doctor to doctor for reassurance. He thought that if he developed a stricture, he would kill himself. He recognized this as a recurrent theme in his life.

When he graduated from dental school, his mother advised him that it was time to get married. He usually followed her advice and proposed to the girl he was dating at the time. Although she was rich, one of his requirements, he felt very ambivalent about her. As their engagement went on, he became more ambivalent, finally told her that he had changed his mind, and broke the engagement. When she left for Florida, he felt he could not let her go and, all the while knowing it to be a mistake, pursued her and married her. He promptly felt trapped in the marriage, a feeling that continued through the years.

Although he considered his wife to be a good homemaker and mother to the children, he was dissatisfied with her because she was too inhibited sexually. She would not experiment, refused oral sex, and was sexually boring. Also, she was afraid to fly, so they could not take the vacations he wanted. However, he carried out his childhood promise to himself that he would not have a quarrelsome marriage. He and his wife never argued. For many years the patient felt depressed in the morning and had frequent thoughts that if it got too bad, he could always kill himself. Yet he enjoyed his children and tried to be a good father.

Early in his marriage he developed what he considered to be his hobby, having affairs with other women. He prepared for this hobby when he was a student by his choice of specialty. He chose orthodontia because this specialty would put him into contact with safely married young women, among whom he could choose sexual partners without fear of prosecution for having sex with a patient—they would be the mothers of his child patients. He rented an apartment under an assumed name for this purpose and kept it a secret for twenty years.

He would have a relationship with one woman at a time, sometimes for several years, and would end the relationship when he began losing interest or when the woman became too interested in him. He was careful, however, never to end a relationship with one woman until he had her successor lined up and waiting in the wings. He never became emotionally involved with any of the women until the last one. He felt he had worked out an excellent lifestyle and had no feelings of guilt or remorse. From time to time he had a fleeting feeling that he was wasting his life. While his colleagues were attending professional meetings and seminars, he was at his apartment engaged in his hobby.

As the initial sessions progressed, the patient put more and more pressure on me for help in making the decision to leave his marriage. In reply, I emphasized the need for patience and explained that when he understood himself, he would not find the decision so difficult to make. My answer did not please him. He thought I must know what was best for him. He was dissatisfied with what he took to be my silence. This complaint continued throughout our work together, despite the fact that I adopted what I considered to be an active therapeutic stance. I felt that it was too early to interpret his angry demandingness and his need to control. Instead, I attempted to build a therapeutic alliance, clarified the material he presented, and encouraged him to continue talking about himself.

We began to explore his depressive feelings, which had become troublesome since he left his wife. He was most depressed when he was in his room in his friend's apartment (his girlfriend was still living with her husband). He realized that his greatest fear was of being alone. I connected these feelings with his childhood experiences and pointed out that, when he went back to his room at night, he was reexperiencing the loneliness and unhappiness he had felt as a child when he went home after school to the empty family apartment. Together we began to see the enormity of his fear of helplessness and abandonment. His recurrent thoughts that he could always commit suicide were now understandable as attempts to master these fears by turning passive into active, thereby enabling him to feel in control. I wondered if his extramarital affairs might not serve a similar purpose. At first, he was resistant to my suggestions. He believed that the seduction of beautiful women was a very masculine thing to do, and he was very proud of his success at it. He could not think of a single friend who would not envy him. In fact, he believed that all his friends would leave their wives if they had the courage and if they had a beautiful young woman to go to, as he had. Then he remembered a very important behavior he had not thought to tell me about before. This behavior consisted of a bedtime ritual that he had used for many years whenever he had trouble falling asleep, a frequent occurrence. The ritual consisted of counting the women with whom he had slept, remembering them in order and by name. He said that other people counted sheep to fall asleep; he counted ex-girlfriends. I told him that I thought we could now really understand the meaning of his extramarital affairs. They provided him with the means to enact his long-suppressed angry feelings toward his wife. He was afraid to fight with her, as he had been afraid to fight with his mother, but he could get even with her by cheating. Furthermore, the girlfriends were not really people to him; they were like interchangeable transitional objects, security blankets whose purpose was to allow him to ward off fears of emptiness and loneliness. He had an inexhaustible supply and was in total control, at least until recently. Just as he had tolerated his wife's behavior without protest and remained with her, despite his unhappiness, out of fear of separation from his mother, so he feared the loss of his new idealized mother, one he fantasized would make him young again, give him new life as well as riches. The issue was not which one and what to do; it was these underlying conflicts. The patient was startled and moved and felt that he could now really get into treatment. Our work continued to revolve around these preoedipal issues. Although the oedipal features were quite apparent (these were sexual affairs with married women), I chose not to interpret them.

The patient moved into an apartment of his own. It became apparent that he was a cheater in other areas beside the sexual. He repeatedly stole petty cash in his practice, cheating his partners and the government. Whenever able, he would go through the bridge tolls without paying. With his girlfriend's encouragement, he began to engage in exciting, dangerous behavior. They would have intercourse in daylight in a parked car on a Manhattan street or in the bedding section of a department store. Of more concern was that they began to engage in shoplifting. Interpretations were of his defiant regression to adolescence as an effort to ward off his fear of age and to secure his girlfriend's love. Also interpreted was his continual acting out of his angry, defiant feelings toward his parents and his wife.

These interventions remained at an intermediate derivative level of oedipal conflict without explicit interpretation of the conflict. Increasingly, the patient recognized the truth of these interpretations, and was particularly affected by the realization that he was also unconsciously seeking to be caught and punished because of his guilt over leaving his wife. The acting out stopped, and, as he realized the extent to which his girlfriend was emotionally disturbed, he broke off the relationship. In addition, he divorced his wife. He made a second apparently successful marriage to a woman who was not the mother of a patient, and treatment was terminated after two years. In the ten years since the termination, I have heard from the patient and about the patient that he is getting along very well.

DISCUSSION

These cases are examples of the application of psychoanalytic tactics to the sector approach described by DeWald (1964), in which certain conflicts are interpreted while others are left deliberately unexplored. In particular, the focus has been on a technique that I have found to be successful in engaging resistive patients in analytic psychotherapy. This technique consists of early (opening-phase) interpretation of an important defensive aspect of the patient's intrapsychic conflict. These interpretations must be carefully timed so as to be emotionally meaningful to the patient. They should be accurate and compelling, conveying insight so impressively to the patient that he develops a new interest in learning about himself by participating in the therapeutic process. In the cases described, this technique was clearly effective in producing insight, symptomatic improvement, and motivation for further work. In the case of homosexual panic, the improvement was partially the result of insight as a result of a correct preoedipal interpretation, but it was also partially a result of an implied reassurance that the patient was not homosexual. If his homosexual thoughts represented a defense, then they did not represent a wish; I had helped the patient to strengthen his repressive defenses against his unconscious homosexual impulses. In a similar fashion, in the case of the failed marriage, the preoedipal interpretation, although clearly correct, may have also helped to shift attention away from the patient's positive oedipal conflicts and thus strengthen the repressive defenses against them.

In these cases, oedipal conflicts were of great importance. For example, the sleep ritual in the latter case represented an oedipal transformation of a transitional object, a preoedipal phenomenon. Although the oedipal conflicts were not interpreted in these patients because of the stratification of the material presented in the sessions, in other patients the interpretation of choice might well be at an oedipal level.

The question arises as to whether the changes that clearly occurred in these two patients were the result of correct interpretation and insight or, instead, were nonspecific improvements based on suggestion, any plausible explanation, and positive transference. Neither patient was suggestible; in fact, they were both highly resistant to psychoanalytic concepts. The close fit of the content of the interpretations to their emotional experiences was so compelling that it was clear that insight was the agent of change.

CONCLUSION

Glover (1931) described the therapeutic effects of inexact interpretation. He pointed out that such interpretations strengthen a patient's defenses by offering substitution products, similar to that of the patient who lives up to an inexact interpretation made by himself regarding the sources of his anxiety. In the patients reported here, the interpretations were not inexact; they were incomplete. Incomplete interpretation is acceptable in psychoanalysis only as a temporary step on the way to complete interpretation of all aspects of unconscious conflict. In psychotherapy, where partial resolution of unconscious conflict is the goal, deliberately incomplete interpretation is the correct therapeutic tactic. It should be emphasized that the type of psychotherapy described in this chapter is best suited for patients who are psychologically minded, capable of understanding interpretation and achieving insight; that is, patients who are analyzable but, because of lack of motivation or life circumstances, are not prepared to enter analysis.

Although the treatment resembles analysis in its reliance on psychoanalytic theory, on interpretation and insight as the modalities for change, and on the abstinence and neutrality of the therapist, it is different from analysis in certain important respects. The goals of treatment, that is, the resolution of selected areas of intrapsychic conflict, are more limited than the more ambitious goals of analysis. Even in these areas, working through cannot be as thorough as we expect to achieve in analysis. Because the use of the couch encourages the development of a regressive transference neurosis, which is particularly difficult to work with in psychotherapy due to the infrequency of the sessions, the couch should not be used in psychotherapy. In opposition to analysis, positive, nonerotic transference is not interpreted, and transference is only interpreted when it becomes a resistance. The treatment can serve as an effective preparation for analysis.

REFERENCES

Alexander, F., and French, T. (1946). *Psychoanalytic Therapy*. New York: Ronald Press.

Bibring, E. (1954). Psychoanalysis and the dynamic psychotherapies. *Journal of the American Psychoanalytic Association* 2:745–770.

DeWald, P. A. (1964). *Psychotherapy: A Dynamic Approach*. New York: Basic Books.

Freud, S. (1919). Lines of advance in psycho-analytic therapy. *Standard Edition* 17:157–168.

――― (1937). Construction in analysis. *Standard Edition* 23:255–269.

Fromm-Reichmann, F. (1954). Psychoanalytic and general dynamic conceptions of theory and of therapy. *Journal of the American Psychoanalytic Association* 2:711–721.

Gill, M. M. (1954). Psychoanalysis and exploratory psychotherapy. *Journal of the American Psychoanalytic Association* 2:771–797.

Glover, E. (1931). The therapeutic effect of inexact interpretation: a contribution to the theory of suggestion. *International Journal of Psycho-Analysis* 12:397–411.

Knight, R. P. (1954). An evaluation of psychotherapeutic technique. In *Psychoanalytic Psychiatry and Psychology*, ed. R. P. Knight and C. R. Friedman, pp. 65–76. New York: International Universities Press.

Loewenstein, R. M. (1951). The problem of interpretation. *Psychoanalytic Quarterly* 20:1–14.

Wallerstein, R. S., and Robbins, L. L. (1956). The psychotherapy research project of the Menninger Foundation. *Bulletin of the Menninger Clinic* 20:239–262.

9

Dreams and Acting Out

David Newman, M.D.

INTRODUCTION

Our subject will include a psychoanalytic understanding of dreams and acting out, specifically how they are utilized in a psychotherapy. Both dreams and acting out are particularly valuable since they have concentrated, special meanings compared to much of the ordinary material of a session. They can be applied to both analytic and supportive psychotherapies (Bibring 1954, Blum 1980, Gray 1978). Acting out, however, can be disruptive to an ongoing treatment if it is not properly handled.

There are two similar aspects of dreams and acting out that should be highlighted at this point. First, they are both compromise formations, that is, compromises between instinctual urges and defensive operations. Like other compromise formations, such as symptoms or slips of the tongue and other parapraxes, they have much condensed, important meaning that is helpful to the psychotherapy (S. Freud 1900, 1911, 1923, Yazmajian 1968). In fact, a link between the various compromise formations can be illustrated by the clinical observation that a patient in treatment can show an increase in slips of the tongue as a prelude to a period of acting out. This sequence often indicates that there has been a shift in the homeostatic balance between instinct and defense with an eruption of instinctual pressure, which first requires one, then another compromise formation to modulate the situation.

The second noteworthy similarity between dreams and acting out is that they are both highly communicative kinds of material in a psychotherapy. One of the unconscious motives in their formation by the patient is almost always to convey certain important meanings and information to the therapist (Kanzer 1955, 1959, Myers 1987).

At this point, a brief clinical example of an instance of acting out would be helpful. A psychotherapy patient, who will be described in greater detail later, rushed into his session in a distraught manner and informed me that he had just earned his third speeding ticket while driving to his session. He now had to appear before a magistrate and insisted that I furnish him with a letter excusing his behavior. Otherwise his license would be revoked, thus interfering with his business and his treatment.

How should one handle this difficult and pressuring piece of acting out, which, incidentally, could more properly be called acting in, an enactment of an aspect of the transference? Without disapproving or complying, in other words, with a neutral attitude, we would try to explore the meanings of the enactment with the patient, with the further goal of attempting to interpret some aspect of the acting out. Most nonpsychotic psychotherapy patients can handle this quite well, and in the long run benefit much more from this approach. It is certainly better than having the therapist enter into the enactment by writing the letter or performing some other action, thus gratifying the patient's unconscious wishes, which would then remain unconscious and continue to generate problems (Abt and Weissman 1976, A. Freud 1968, Rangell 1968).

In this particular example of acting in, exploration and knowledge of the patient revealed his defensive use of rationalization and his seductive use of suffering to persuade me to gratify his intense wish for a nurturing parental person, something for which he desperately searched. Also, he wished me to condone or approve of his speeding tickets, something that represented much serious "speeding" and unethical behavior in his business life and personal relationships. These themes will become clear as this patient is described more fully later on.

A brief review of definitions and current terminology, which might tend to become confusing, is in order at this point. Thus far, *acting out* has been used in its broader sense to include behavior representing a compromise formation between unconscious defensive operations and instinctual wishes that a patient in treatment demonstrates. Where the behavior in question is linked by the patient to the therapist or treatment situation, it includes a transference aspect. Acting in, of course, is such behavior occurring completely within the confines of the sessions. Freud's (1914) original definition of acting out in "Remembering, Repeating, and

Working Through" was narrower than the current one, for it did not include acting out of transference elements outside the sessions; that is, it was confined to acting in. His definition emphasized mainly forgotten childhood memories of events that the action expressed. It also tended to neglect other transference elements. The current, broader definition of acting out, however, does not include all neurotic action or behavior that is independent of treatment and, therefore, of transference to the therapist.

Other terminology should be noted. *Enactment,* for example, is an elegant current term that is used to mean acting out, usually acting in, but that thus far lacks a pejorative connotation. *Reenactments,* of course, are repetitive enactments. *Reliving* is acting out, usually acting in, that includes intense affect with the behavior, while *actualization* is acting out in which the patient tries to experience the unconscious wishes in the behavior as more gratified. Much of the current terminology attempts to emphasize one or another aspect of the concept of acting out thereby sharpening the ideas (Boesky 1982, Roughton 1989).

CLINICAL EXAMPLES OF THE USE OF DREAMS AND ACTING OUT IN PSYCHOTHERAPY

Patient 1

The patient, K. B., is a 42-year-old attorney and businessman who is married and has three children.[1] He was trained as an attorney but has never practiced law. Instead, he went into a fast-moving business, which was much more in tune with his impulsive, action-oriented style. (This is the patient I had referred to earlier who rushed into my office requesting a letter for the judge, after receiving his third speeding ticket.)

K. B. originally entered treatment because he felt thoroughly overinvolved in his business, was becoming progressively estranged from his wife and children, and was experiencing increasing frustration and depression. There was much neurotic action in his life, particularly in his business, where he attended to numerous, simultaneous "deals," often frustrating other people, and in turn was frequently taken advantage of and hurt himself. Moreover, he had a stormy, intermittent affair with a woman half his age. Needless to say, there was not much time or interest to pursue a reasonable sexual life with his wife.

---

[1]All biographical and identifying data concerning the clinical examples in this chapter are thoroughly disguised.

Diagnostically, he can be described as having a masochistic character disorder with narcissistic features, impulsivity, and some depression. His treatment consisted of twice-a-week psychotherapy, mainly exploratory or analytic in type, for about four years, with considerable clinical improvement and resolution of some conflictual issues. Because of his impulsivity, as well as a predominance of preoedipal defenses and instinctual elements, analysis was not suitable. This is a typical situation in which an analytic psychotherapy with certain supportive features is the treatment of choice.

An important theme that emerged in the therapy involved the patient's mother. She was a partner herself in a large company and, consequently, was extremely busy and unavailable. For example, K. B. recalled from his latency years many lonely hours waiting in front of his house after school, hoping his mother would arrive as she had promised. However, she was caught up in too many "business deals." On one occasion at age 7 or 8, he remembered that his mother had him wait for her on a certain street corner. She arrived several hours late. He felt lost, terrified, could not hold his urine, and felt full of rage. On the other hand, when his mother was around, she tried to be overly available and solicitous to her son to compensate for her neglectful behavior. This effort miscarried somewhat, since part of the compensatory behavior included having her son in the bathroom and bedroom with her during most of her dressing, undressing, and toilet activities. K. B.'s father was a loving man but was much too passive to have much influence over his wife. His own pathology contributed to his son's problems.

One method K. B. utilized to master the frustration, deprivation, rage, and overstimulation at the hands of his mother was to identify with her. Such an identification was an important part in his becoming overinvolved with his own business, thus frustrating and partially abandoning his own family. Similarly, he frustrated and partially deprived some of his clients and colleagues in business.

For the first year in treatment, K. B. only wanted to talk about his business, defensively denying and avoiding personal material and problems. His wife, family, and sexual life were hardly mentioned. In addition, he reported no dreams. During this year therapeutic interventions dealt mainly with his neurotic behavior in business, and the flurry of neurotic action slowed a bit. Interpretations aimed at his use of denial in regard to his personal problems and his use of projection in attributing the motives and causes of his difficulties to others helped in the process of slowing the hectic pace of neurotic action.

After one year K. B. reported his first dream: He was looking at clothing in an open dresser drawer—women's panties in bright, vivid colors, red, black, orange. He felt uneasy, closed the drawer, and walked away. He then felt better. The associations to the dream went in a particular direction. He spoke briefly about the vividness of the colors of the panties, laughed a bit nervously, and quickly moved on to various business deals, dismissing the dream as unimportant. I interpreted to him that for the past year thoughts about women seemed to make him uneasy. He avoided talking about them by focusing on business; that is, he "closed the drawer" on them, just as he did in the dream of the colorful panties. He was jolted a bit and thought my comment was one of those different ideas he never agreed with. In the following week, however, he began to talk about his wife, his mistress, and his sexual life for the first time in the treatment. Over subsequent months several other dreams appeared (Alexander 1925), his acting out diminished somewhat, and he began to engage the relationship with his wife in earnest for the first time in his treatment.

We can sometimes observe this reciprocal relationship between dreams and acting out in an ongoing treatment. When the compromise formation of dreams emerges more frequently because of some advance in the patient's conscious understanding, other compromise formations, such as acting out, or symptoms can become less necessary for defensive purposes and diminish (Grinberg 1987, Stein 1987, Sterba 1946).

The above illustration demonstrates how helpful dreams are in psychotherapy. They are usually quite meaningful to patients, despite protestations to the contrary, and they often lead to a beneficial sense of conviction for the patient if they are used interpretively. In this case, the dream was used for the selective interpretation of one particular element, K. B.'s defensive avoidance of an important area of his conflicts and life (Goldberger 1989). This is the typical way dreams are handled in a psychotherapy, to focus on and perhaps interpret selected areas or particular segments of the patient's psychopathology. It is generally not possible and even is contraindicated to try to explore and interpret a dream completely in psychotherapy. In a psychoanalysis with free association, greater therapeutic time, continuity, and a patient different from K. B., dreams would be dealt with much more extensively (Altman 1969, Myers 1989a,b, Natterson 1980). For example, K. B.'s dream was in color, a phenomenon that sometimes relates to childhood fantasies or even direct recollections of parental genitals (Blum 1964, Yazmajian 1983). We would infer that this is probably accurate in K. B.'s case, since there is a history of his mother trying to include him in her bathroom and bedroom activities. Nevertheless, it would have been destructive pseudoanalysis to pursue such material with this particular patient, in a psychotherapy at this phase in his treatment (Isakower 1938, Eisnitz 1961).

We will continue our study of special areas in psychotherapy with an example of a commonly encountered kind of acting out, or more properly acting in, that K. B. provides us with.

For more than half of his four-year therapy, K. B. was frequently and outrageously late, often missing half or three-quarters of a session, and sometimes not showing up at all. In such instances, he would usually, but not always, call after the missed session and leave a rationalization as a message. As long as I maintained a neutral, nonjudgmental attitude, it was usually relatively easy to interpret those transference enactments as K. B.'s wish to frustrate me, as his mother had done to him. Often the rage in the lateness was apparent and could be interpreted as K. B.'s wish to take revenge on me as a transference figure, mainly representing his mother. Sometimes fury at his father also surfaced, for keeping him waiting in a way different from his mother. That is, his father kept him waiting for a more active, masculine parent.

Following much interpretive work with the transference enactments of lateness and missed sessions, the patient gradually recalled much about his childhood relationships with his parents, especially his mother. Some of these recollections have been mentioned. In addition, he recalled that during one instance of his frequent, lonely vigils for his mother outside the family home, he was especially terrified when he was menaced by several stray dogs. He broke some of the glass on the front door in an effort to get to safety. He did not gain entry to the house, but fortunately the noise frightened away the dogs. However, when his mother finally returned, he was promptly punished for his "misdeeds." Gradually, K. B. was able to achieve genuine insight into how he acted out his frustration and rage toward his mother with me in the transference by constantly keeping me waiting. He was then able to understand how and why he kept many of his clients and business colleagues waiting for deliveries, for payment, and especially for himself when he was frequently late for various meetings and appointments. Interestingly, he was rarely late paying his therapy bills, which, of course, had to include his missed sessions.

With these insights K. B. was able to modify an especially serious kind of symptomatic behavior. Needless to say, he kept most of the commercial banks capitalizing his business waiting for loan payments. However, he sometimes rolled one loan into another, coming dangerously close to defaulting, something that would have been especially harmful to his kind of business. The neurotic character of this behavior was underscored by the fact that his business always had enough profits so that loans could be repaid in a timely fashion. Incidentally, it was such behavior that he unconsciously wished to have condoned near the beginning of treatment, when he requested a letter for the judge to relieve him of three speeding tickets.

During the later stages of his psychotherapy, K. B. was able to end his affair with his young employee because of further insights based on earlier work, some of which were outlined above. He came to realize he was really playing the role of a very good parent, mainly maternal, to his dependent paramour, who was half his age. Thus he gradually understood that the rage at his mother was directed at his wife, whom he usually "kept waiting" while he gratified his young lover in a parental way, something he wished would have been his childhood experience.

Toward the end of treatment K. B.'s marriage was getting better, his business life was improving, and he was no longer acting out by being late or missing sessions. He was then able to put together an insight that partially derived from the earlier interpretations of his lateness behavior in the transference. He realized that when he was the sole supplier of a particular item in business, that is, when he had a complete monopoly on that product or service, he kept clients purchasing that particular item waiting longer. He concluded that he made them wait for him since he was "the only one in the world with that item," just like he yearned for his mother, who was "the only mother in the world" for him.

To review briefly, the technical handling of the acting-out behavior in question in this patient was first approached with a neutral, nonjudgmental, inquiring attitude. Care was taken not to be seduced into participating in the patient's enactments, for example, by writing the letter to the judge or by changing the times of sessions to "prevent his lateness," something that he defensively wished to be done. Instead, it was best to explore and interpret what was most available (Blum 1976, Rexford 1978).

It should be emphasized that in a psychotherapy, the acting out is selectively interpreted. That is, we would usually interpret particular segments or areas of the conflictual material, unlike a psychoanalysis, where we would try to deal with all major areas (Greenacre 1968, Kanzer 1968). The interpretations used with K. B.'s acting out most often involved preoedipal issues in the mother–child relationship. Oedipal material was present, of course, but was less available for use. For example, the patient would sometimes offer competitive, rivalrous fantasies about me and be interested in one or another female patient of mine. Therefore, some oedipal material, usually in derivative form, could be interpreted.

As described, K. B. recalled a good deal about the early relation-ship with his mother involving her neglecting and partially aban-doning him, but he remembered less about her overstimulating and exhibitionistic behavior. However, with this patient, it was best to use a selective approach and not push for more direct oedipal interventions. With this method, there was a significant clinical improvement and even some limited characterologic change over the course of the psychotherapy.

Patient 2

This is a second example of a dream and its use in a psychotherapy. Unlike Patient 1, though, this individual was able to utilize the dream far more extensively.

The dreamer was in a room with a large, misshapen beehive structure near the ceiling. There were huge insects sticking out of the hive, a worm, an ugly bug with a fish's tail, and a third nondescript insect. The "bugfish" was flapping its tail against the wall; the mood was awful and disgusting. Also, the distorted hive was made of white stucco. Immediately, we can see that this dream has more detailed imagery and affect than the previous dream example (Silber 1973, Stein 1989). An initial discussion of this dream, using only the manifest content and not knowing anything else, usually results in the following speculations (Pulver 1987). The patient is a woman, and the themes of low self-esteem and some fearfulness are apparent. These speculations are accurate.

A description of the patient is now in order. S. L. is an unmarried 28-year-old woman. A CPA, she works for a very large accounting firm, where she is "only one of the workers in a very large hive." Her initial symptoms were a pervasive lack of confidence in most areas of life, some anxiety, and difficulties in her relationships with men, particularly with her current boyfriend, which included apprehensiveness whenever the rela-tionship would become very close. Sexually, her anxiety usually interfered with her enjoyment, although on the few occasions when she was calmer, she was able to be orgastic. Her attitude toward her symptomatology was determined and perseverant, and she pushed herself to be involved whenever she could. Because of her fearfulness, she was able to start psychotherapy only once a week, but after about six months she relaxed enough to be able to make it twice a week. At the time of the dream, she was in treatment about two years and the psychotherapy was mainly analytic or exploratory in nature, with the patient working well. With additional psychotherapeutic work and a further reduction in her anxiety and inhibition, a patient such as this could convert the psychotherapy to a psychoanalysis, where the goals would include more extensive character-ologic changes. Diagnostically, S. L. is neurotic, with inhibitions, anxiety symptoms, masochistic features, and narcissistic elements.

To return to the dream, we should consider the day residue. The evening before the dream, while eating some dried fruit, S. L. discovered a white worm, a larva, and was relieved that she did not "eat it." The associations following the dream began with her feeling deficient and substandard about her professional work at the large accounting firm, something that was her own perception about herself, since she was recently promoted and praised for her performance. It was true, however, that she was working below her potential. Following this, her thoughts went to her brother and sister. I offered the interpretation that the dream could represent her thoughts and feelings about herself and her two siblings. That is, the three insects represented her feelings of defectiveness about herself, her brother, and her sister.

S. L. had an immediate recollection from her latency years of watching her two younger siblings, alone in their house, unsupervised, and feeling worried and like a failure because everyone was fighting. "It was becoming dirty, messy, and ugly, like the insects in the dream" she said. She further recalled that on one such babysitting occasion, she was tickling her younger brother, touching his genitals. She might have even put his penis in her mouth. The day residue of the dream and this memory were related.

While remembering these events, S. L. felt extremely guilty and anxious, and felt like running from the room. I was able to interpret that this anxiety and discomfort associated with her childhood sexuality are often what she feels during sexual activity with her boyfriend. She commented that during sex she often feels like running out of the bedroom. After this confirmation, she felt angry at her parents for going off together and leaving the three children unsupervised and alone, to behave in such ways that they became frightened and felt worthless.

Later on in the session there was some derivative material about masturbation, which may have related to the flapping fish in the manifest of the dream. Also, since my office is in a building that includes some white stucco, I asked for S. L.'s associations to the white stucco in the dream. Her thoughts did not produce any transference reference. Instead, she recalled the stucco walls of her parents' bedroom in her childhood home. However, there were no associations concerning parental sexuality or primal scene.

This case demonstrates how advantageous a dream can be in a psychotherapy. In this instance, repressed childhood material was recovered. Moreover, some of the origins of the patient's feelings of guilt and low self-esteem were elaborated. Current symptomatology, such as her sexual inhibitions and anxiety, were understood better (Potomianou 1990, Renik 1981). A special advantage for utilizing dream material in a psychotherapy can be seen in this case because it adds significantly to the patient's sense of conviction. S. L. said that she would always remember the image of the bugfish and what it represents to her. Insights such as this and others derived from the work with this dream gradually led to some clinical improvement.

In the technical handling of this dream, the concept of dealing with selected areas or segments of the material in a psychotherapy is again demonstrated. Therapeutic interventions were made about some of the patient's current symptomatology, such as her lowered self-esteem and sexual anxiety, and their connection to some of the childhood material (Glenn 1978). The derivatives of masturbation and primal scene were not pursued at all. Moreover, it was unnecessary to deal with the transference in this instance. In a psychoanalysis, working with this same dream would probably result in these areas emerging in a more utilizable manner, and they could then be pursued to the patient's advantage.

In addition, it should be stated that some of the recent work in the neurophysiologic and biologic aspects of dreaming is beginning to support and augment the psychoanalytic understanding and use of dreams (Fisher 1965, Fisher et al. 1965, Laberge, Levitan, and Dement 1986, Madow and Snow 1970, Winson, 1991).

Patient 3

This patient illustrates a massive type of symptomatic sexual behavior, which was treated in an analytic psychotherapy. The treatment included a particular kind of acting out by the patient, which was very much related to her symptomatic behavior.

K. C. is a 38-year-old married woman with three children, and with a good position in publishing and writing. After fifteen years of marriage there was some discord, but basically she felt that the marriage was successful. However, for the past seven or eight years she has had extramarital affairs. For the three years prior to seeking help, her affairs had become so numerous and were of such a nature that she was gradually becoming alarmed by her own behavior. In the year prior to therapy she had almost two dozen affairs. Many of them were one-time encounters with strange men; none were longer than several weeks. More recently, by being especially provocative, she had managed to get herself slapped and punched. Parenthetically, it should be noted that the psychotherapy of this patient goes back some twenty years, clearly in the pre-AIDS days. In addition to being alarmed and worried about her behavior, during the year prior to seeking treatment K. C. had become depressed. For short periods of time she felt lonely and worthless, and on occasion she would feel estranged.

Because of the intense driven quality of her sexual acting out, or more correctly her symptomatic sexual behavior, her feelings of estrangement, and a marked use of projection and denial as defensive operations, psychotherapy and not psychoanalysis appeared to be the treatment of choice. Her treatment was twice a week for about four and a half years, was mainly analytic psychotherapy, which became more supportive for a few short periods of time during certain regressive episodes, and led to a good clinical result. Diagnostically, K. C. demonstrated hysterical features, but preoedipal and narcissistic issues were very predominant.

As her treatment progressed, several important themes emerged. Partial object loss and loneliness were important childhood elements. Both parents were engaged in a business and were frequently away, with child care being erratic. Moreover, the business utilized large, commercial-sized laundry baskets made of heavy canvas. During childhood the patient was often brought to the business, but was placed in one of these baskets to keep her safe from certain machinery. K. C. recalled not being able to see out of the container and often feeling lonely and frightened for what seemed to be hours. Also, she remembered sometimes being hungry and wet. Toward the end of treatment she was able to utilize some humor about these experiences and described herself as a participant in a "sensory-deprivation experiment of childhood." It is safe to speculate that this patient would not have done well in the traditional analytic situation, where she would not see the analyst and where sensory input would be somewhat diminished. The object-hunger, which resulted from all of her childhood deprivations, was one of the major determinants of her intense sexual activity.

Another theme that emerged revolved around her brother, who was three years older, was also relatively unsupervised, and was intermittently cruel and sadistic to her. He was often her babysitter. Throughout her latency years, K. C. remembered that her brother would sometimes be protective and loving, but at other times would hit her, tease her, and sexually touch her, including her genitals. When her brother was a preadolescent and early adolescent, several friends joined him and matters became worse. For example, she recalled being forced to undress, get down on the floor on all fours, and bark like a dog while the group inserted candles or other objects into her vagina or rectum. Finally, when K. C. became an adolescent herself, she began to fight back. Throughout her adolescent years she became the aggressive, dominant, and sometimes hostile partner in her relationships with boys.

In her later extramarital affairs she was usually the aggressive seductress, often teasing and humiliating her partners. She identified with the aggressor, her brother, and by doing so was able to take revenge by treating men in the same way her brother had treated her. Insights such as these and others were gradually achieved in her therapy, and after about three years of treatment she was able to stop her affairs.

An interesting and elaborate kind of acting out, or more properly, acting in, was quite helpful in working toward some of the insights described above. Initially, K. C. treated me as an idealized parental figure, usually maternal. Gradually, however, she began to subtly "seduce" me by spinning out elaborate stories, which were fabricated. After I was taken in, she would reveal that she had been lying. She would then become hostile and derisive, sarcastically informing me what a fool I had been and hoping I felt humiliated. Many interpretations were offered pointing out her identification with her brother and her wish to treat me as he had dealt with her. It was through interpretations of her acting out that K. C. was able to recall some of the significant childhood abuse at the hands of her brother and achieve some insight into the motives behind her dangerous symptomatic sexual behavior. On occasion in the transference she would attempt to become directly seductive by opening a button or two, with the intent of worrying and intimidating me. This type of acting out was relatively rare.

As K. C.'s psychotherapy progressed, material emerged that helped to explain why her extramarital affairs began when they did, that is, seven or eight years prior to starting treatment and after a number of years of successful marriage. At that time, her husband's career began to progress rapidly and he took on new responsibilities, which entailed more time and some traveling. The relative loss of him was enough to mobilize her childhood deprivations with her parents and lead to a state of discomfort and object-hunger. It was in this context that she began her affairs.

In considering the technical handling of K. C.'s acting out by fabricating stories, it should be emphasized that nonjudgmental neutrality was especially important and had to be borne in mind, since her acting out could become quite hostile and abusive. It would have been an easy matter to become provoked. In the context of neutrality, various aspects of her acting out in the transference could then be interpreted and some of her childhood conflicts reconstructed (Willock 1990). In this case, it should be noted that even though some important issues were interpreted in the transference, as illustrated, the majority of the interpretive work was done extratransferentially, utilizing mainly current symptomatology and genetic material from the patient's childhood and adolescence. This is often typical of deprived, preoedipal, object-needy patients in psychotherapy because such individuals maintain an idealized transference for large portions of the treatment and such a transference can often function smoothly, remaining in the background, and not need much direct interpretive work. In fact, in a psychotherapy we might deliberately leave such a transference uninterpreted, while in a psychoanalysis we would usually try to interpret it as fully as possible.

The importance of therapeutic neutrality in handling K. C.'s acting out in the transference has already been commented on, but neutrality was also especially important in dealing with her main behavioral symptomatology, her many extramarital affairs. A judgmental or prohibiting attitude would have precluded the ability to interpret her behavior, and probably would have made it worse. It is especially important to keep this in mind in the current climate of AIDS infection, when one might be tempted to intervene in a prohibiting fashion. Extensive sexual behavioral symptomatology should be neutrally interpreted. Today's therapy might include interpreting the suicidal component in such behavior.

A REVIEW OF TECHNICAL CONCEPTS

The general idea that dreams and acting out are valuable kinds of material for interpretation in a psychotherapy should be reemphasized. They usually contain within them more concentrated meanings and issues when compared to the ordinary material of a session and therefore usually warrant special therapeutic and interpretive activity. Moreover, when either a dream or a piece of acting-out behavior is utilized in a psychotherapy, the therapeutic intervention should be aimed at a selected area or segment of the conflictual material. Only in a psychoanalysis would there be an attempt to deal with as many issues as possible. For example, in the dream of Patient 1, the closing of the drawerful of colored panties, the interpretation was designed to deal only with the defense of avoidance. When interpreted in this manner in a psychotherapy, both dreams and acting out can add to a patient's insight and conviction in a way that is difficult to duplicate with ordinary material. In fact, in certain instances the impact and conviction can be so great that years after a psychotherapy is completed, the patient will remember a particular dream or piece of acting-out behavior, together with the insights derived from this understanding.

There are some technical ideas that pertain specifically to acting out that should also be reemphasized. The maintenance of neutrality is of special importance for the therapist. Often episodes of acting out are difficult or provocative for all therapists, but an attitude of disapproval or annoyance can seriously interfere with therapeutic utilization of the material or even stimulate the patient to greater acting out. Another technical guideline for dealing with acting out is to try not to get pressured or seduced into joining the acting out when it appears as an acting in, or more precisely, as an enactment of the transference. For example, it was better not to write a letter to the judge for Patient 1, and instead explore and interpret the entire event.

Finally, a current problem in the technique of handling enactments of the transference should be mentioned. With today's ever-widening scope of patients in outpatient psychotherapy, including the more regressive narcissistic and borderline conditions, special attention is being given, as it should be, to issues of a patient's narcissistic frustration, to problems of more severe early deficits and deprivations, to self-esteem difficulties, and to all the self or selfobject disorders requiring a proper "holding environment." As a result, today's psychotherapist may feel under greater pressure to gratify patients and thus become involved in a patient's enactment of the transference. This is usually a technical error. Even in many wider-scope patients in psychotherapy, more progress can be made with acting in by being tactfully neutral, exploratory, and carefully interpretive. One can always move in the direction of a more supportive and gratifying psychotherapy if clinically indicated, but it is much more difficult to move in the opposite direction.

CONCLUSION

The importance and advantages of utilizing both dreams and acting out in psychotherapy are discussed. The similarities between dreams and acting out as different types of compromise formations are elaborated. The major portion of the chapter deals with several detailed clinical examples of dreams and acting out in three patients in psychotherapies that are mainly analytic. In addition, technical concepts involved in utilizing dreams and acting out in psychotherapy are emphasized.

REFERENCES

Abt, L., and Weissman, S., eds. (1976). *Acting Out*, 2nd ed. New York: Jason Aronson.

Alexander, F. (1925). Dreams in pairs and series. *International Journal of Psycho-Analysis* 6:446–452.

Altman, L. (1969). *The Dream in Psychoanalysis*. New York: International Universities Press.

Bibring, E. (1954). Psychoanalysis and the dynamic psychotherapies. *Journal of the American Psychoanalytic Association* 2:745–770.

Blum, H. (1964). Colour in dreams. *International Journal of Psycho-Analysis* 45:519–529.

–––––– (1976). Acting out, the psychoanalytic process, and interpretation. *The Annual of Psychoanalysis* 4:163–184.

––––––, ed. (1980). *Psychoanalytic Explorations of Technique: Discourse on the Theory of Therapy*. New York: International Universities Press.

Boesky, D. (1982). Acting out: a reconsideration of the concept. *International Journal of Psycho-Analysis* 63:39–55.

Eisnitz, A. (1961). Mirror dreams. *Journal of the American Psychoanalytic Association* 9:461–479.

Fisher, C. (1965). Psychoanalytic implications of recent research on sleep and dreaming. *Journal of the American Psychoanalytic Association* 13:197–303.

Fisher, C., Gross, J., and Zuch, J. (1965). Cycle of penile erection synchronous with dreaming (REM) sleep. *Archives of General Psychiatry* 12:29–45.

Freud, A. (1968). Acting out. *International Journal of Psycho-Analysis* 49:167–170.

Freud, S. (1900). The interpretation of dreams. *Standard Edition* 4:1–338, 5:339–626.

–––––– (1911). Handling of dream interpretation in psychoanalysis. *Standard Edition* 12:91–96.

–––––– (1914). Remembering, repeating, and working-through. *Standard Edition* 12:145–156.

–––––– (1923). Remarks on the theory and practice of dream interpretation. *Standard Edition* 19:109–121.

Glenn, J. (1978). Dream analysis in child analysis. In *Child Analysis and Therapy*, pp. 355–374. New York: Jason Aronson.

Goldberger, M. (1989). On the analysis of defenses in dreams. *Psychoanalytic Quarterly* 58:396–418.

Gray, S. H. (1978). Brief psychotherapy: a developmental approach. *Journal Philadelphia Association of Psychoanalysis* 5:29.

Greenacre, P. (1968). Symposium: acting out and its role in the psychoanalytic process. *International Journal of Psycho-Analysis* 49:211–218.

Grinberg, L. (1987). Dreams and acting out. *Psychoanalytic Quarterly* 56:155–176.

Isakower, O. (1938). A contribution to the pathopsychology of phenomena associated with falling asleep. *International Journal of Psycho-Analysis* 19:331–345.

Kanzer, M. (1955). The communicative function of the dream. *International Journal of Psycho-Analysis* 36:260–266.

_____ (1959). The recollection of the forgotten dream. *Journal of Hillside Hospital* 8:74–85.

_____ (1968). Ego alteration and acting out. *International Journal of Psycho-Analysis* 49:431–435.

Laberge, S., Levitan, L., and Dement, W. (1986). Lucid dreaming: physiologic correlates of consciousness during REM sleep. *Journal of Mind and Behavior* 7:251–258.

Madow, L., and Snow, L. H., eds. (1970). *The Psychodynamic Implications of the Physiological Studies on Dreams.* Springfield, IL: Thomas.

Myers, W. A. (1987). Actions speak louder. *Psychoanalytic Quarterly* 56:645–666.

_____ (1989a). The traumatic element in the typical dream of feeling embarrassed at being naked. *Journal of the American Psychoanalytic Association* 37:117–130.

_____ (1989b). Dream frequency and treatment outcome in psychoanalysis and psychoanalytic psychotherapy. *Journal of the American Psychoanalytic Association* 37:714–725, and 1123–1124.

Natterson, J. M. (1980). *The Dream in Clinical Practice.* New York: Jason Aronson.

Potamianou, A. (1990). Somatization and dream work. *Psychoanalytic Study of the Child,* 45:273–292. New Haven, CT: Yale University Press.

Pulver, S. E. (1987). The manifest dream in psychoanalysis: a clarification. *Journal of the American Psychoanalytic Association* 35:99–118.

Rangell, L. (1968). A point of view on acting out. *International Journal of Psycho-Analysis* 49:195–201.

Renik, O. (1981). Typical examination dreams, "superego dreams," and traumatic dreams. *Psychoanalytic Quarterly* 50:159–189.

Rexford, E., ed. (1978). *A Developmental Approach to Problems of Acting Out.* rev. ed. New York: International Universities Press.

Roughton, R. (1989). *Useful aspects of acting out: enactment, reliving, and actualization.* Paper presented at the fall meeting of the American Psychoanalytic Association, New York, December.

Silber, A. (1973). Secondary revision, secondary elaboration, and ego synthesis. *International Journal of Psycho-Analysis* 54:161–168.

Stein, M. H. (1987). The clinical significance of dream interpretation in the analysis of acting out. In *The Interpretation of Dreams in Clinical Work,* ed. A. Rothstein, pp. 57–68. Madison, CT: International Universities Press.

_____ (1989). How dreams are told: secondary revision—the critic, the editor, and the plagiarist. *Journal of the American Psychoanalytic Association* 37:65–88.

Sterba, R. (1946). Dreams and Acting Out. *Psychoanalytic Quarterly* 15:175–179.

Willock, B. (1990). From acting out to interactive play. *International Journal of Psycho-Analysis* 71:321–334.

Winson, J. (1991). *The function of REM sleep and the meaning of dreams.* Presented to joint meeting of the Long Island Psychoanalytic Society and the Nassau Psychiatric Society, Manhasset, NY: January.

Yazmajian, R. V. (1968). Slips of the tongue in dreams. *Psychoanalytic Quarterly* 37:588–595.

_____ (1983). The use of color for the secondary elaboration of the dream. *Psychoanalytic Quarterly* 52:225–236.

10

Medication and Psychotherapy

Richard J. Kessler, D.O.

The inclusion of a chapter on medication in a book about psychoanalytic therapy symbolizes the ongoing and enlarging effort to
reconcile the findings of biologic psychiatry with psychoanalysis. It
also represents recognition of psychiatry's enormous strides in
diagnostic reliability and the development of powerful pharmacologic agents with specific indications for use. At a time of burgeoning specialization, a treatment integrating psychoanalytic psychotherapy and psychopharmacotherapy offers wide applicability,
lasting efficacy, and completeness.

Employing psychotherapeutic techniques, which have undergone continuous refinement as the result of decades of theoretical
discovery and clinical experience and experimentation, psychoanalysts have traditionally viewed proposed variations in technique
with great skepticism. Their opposition to early "organic" therapies
was therefore understandable. Practitioners were often seen as
demonstrating various personality limitations such as impatience,
sadism, and the need to control (Mandell 1968). Moreover, prior to
the revolutionary changes in psychopharmacology of the 1950s,
psychotropic drugs were "relatively unpotent" (Group for the
Advancement of Psychiatry 1975, p. 365), their efficacy undocumented, and clear rationales for their use lacking. The introduction
of specific antianxiety agents, phenothiazine antipsychotics and
tricyclic antidepressants, however, heralded the emergence of pharmacotherapy as a major influence in the treatment of mental illness.

Early on, a few psychoanalysts, most notably Sarwer-Foner (1957,
1960a,b, 1964), Azima (1959, Azima, Cramer-Azima, and DeVerteuil
1956, 1959, Azima, Cramer-Azima, and Durost 1959) and Ostow
(1960a,b, 1962, 1966) began publishing on the utility of psychotropic
drugs and their interaction with the psychotherapeutic process.

They also offered psychodynamic explanations of the actions of the drugs and saw the potential for using them as investigative tools. Bellak and Chasan (1964), Lesse (1956, 1966), and Modell (1966) also reported cases of successful combination of psychoanalytic therapy and pharmacotherapy. Most analysts, however, remained reluctant to endorse the use of psychotropic agents, focusing on their potential for contamination of the transference and disruption of the patient's motivation to seek insight. However, a study by Hayman (1967) indicated that analysts were using psychotropic drugs more frequently than they were prepared to admit.

Nevertheless, out of this struggle between two very different treatment approaches, opportunities and needs for synthesis began to emerge. This was no doubt driven by documentation of the effectiveness of psychotropic agents for the treatment and prevention of psychotic disorders, affective illnesses, and severe anxiety states. In addition, psychoanalysts' experiences with more disturbed patients, the so-called widening scope of psychoanalytic treatment (Stone 1954), began to dictate a change in attitude. Not coincidentally, the several psychoanalysts cited above were often reporting work with more severely disturbed patients. Deriving from work with just such patients, Kernberg (1971) suggested criteria for the uses and guidelines for the management of psychotropic medication in the treatment of patients with a borderline personality organization.

What is often forgotten in the debate about the use of medication in psychoanalytic therapy is that when medication is most clearly indicated, exploratory work is either impossible or contraindicated. A psychotic patient, a patient with a severe depression, or one consumed with acute obsessive-compulsive symptoms or panic is rarely able to pursue the task of exploration because the need for symptom relief is too consuming to permit self-reflection. Furthermore, since the less rigorous and intense techniques of psychoanalytic psychotherapy, as compared to those of psychoanalysis, demand more active intervention and improvising, a less ambivalent use of psychotropic medication can be encouraged. Concerns about their effect on the transference and the exploratory process should and do remain, but the use of drugs can be viewed as therapeutic not only in its own right, but also as an intervention that might allow the exploratory work to proceed.

The goals of exploratory psychotherapy and pharmacotherapy are certainly disparate. The attempt to achieve greater acceptance of derivatives of conflicting, infantile wishful aspects of oneself

(Sandler and Sandler 1983) is quite different from symptom suppression induced by biochemical alterations in cerebral machinery. Van Praag (1979) has suggested that psychotherapy focuses on etiology (psychological dysfunction and perhaps biological predisposition) and pharmacotherapy on pathophysiology (biological state dysfunction). Most important, however, is that these treatments can be combined in ways that are both additive and synergistic. Medication can help restore a therapeutic alliance, along with the patient's ability and motivation for self-reflection, by alleviating serious regression, severe affective disturbance, overwhelming anxiety, and cognitive disorganization. It can encourage the use of verbal expression by enhancing memory, by reducing vegetative disturbance and distractibility (Klerman 1975), and by limiting impulsive action. Moreover, the rich and complex awareness of the patient's mental life, revealed in a psychoanalytic psychotherapy, offers the possibility of highly personalized and fine-tuned utilization of psychotropic agents.

BIMODAL RELATEDNESS—THE THERAPIST'S ATTITUDE

The clinician with expertise in psychodynamic psychotherapy and psychopharmacology has been described as a "split-brain" preparation, reasonably comfortable within either frame of reference, but faced with confusion when both competing hemispheres are required for more complex tasks (Group for the Advancement of Psychiatry 1975). Some clinicians have even suggested that it is extremely stressful to attempt the maintenance of a balance between the two perspectives and that this leads predictably to efforts to simplify matters (Docherty et al. 1977). The making of a psychiatric diagnosis, decisions regarding pharmacotherapy, and active inquiries regarding side effects and symptom change invariably encourage a view of the patient and his symptomatology quite different from the one assumed during a dynamic psychotherapy. The patient is perceived as "having a disease" as opposed to "being the disease," and the structure of symptoms assumes more importance than their content, meaning, or purpose. One's mode of relating to the patient becomes more "subject–object" than "subject–subject" (Docherty et al. 1977), thereby promoting the condolence, agreement, and pity of sympathy (Beres and Arlow 1974) rather than the trial identification of empathy. The psychotherapeutic relationship itself contains this same tension; that between listening to material, which informs the therapist about the workings of a patient's mind, and reacting to the patient as a person recounting the events of his life. In fact, an important theme in the evolution of psychoanalytic technique is the attempt to achieve an optimum balance between the early views of "the patient as cadaver" (Lewin 1946, p. 195) and the more recent emphasis on interaction. Therefore, a successful blending of psychotherapy and pharmacotherapy requires the ability to "shift between these two modes gracefully yet stay attuned to the impact of the shift on the patient" (Gabbard 1990, p. 120).

If medication is prescribed in the beginning of treatment for an acute regressive breakdown, psychotherapeutic goals can be conceived of primarily as the facilitation of the drug therapy by establishing and exploiting a positive transference, by encouraging tolerance of side effects, and by educating as to the benefits and limitations of the medication (Ostow 1983). Even in such circumstances, the effectiveness of the treatment can be significantly enhanced by psychodynamic understanding of the patient's fears regarding drugs and initial reactions to taking them or to their being prescribed.

A woman was brought in by her husband for treatment after close to a year of unremitting psychotic symptoms. Several treatment attempts had already failed because of her mistrust and refusal to take medication. She had become psychotic several months after a close friend had died of cancer and near the two-year anniversary of the birth of her second child, who had cerebral palsy. She was very reluctant to speak, showed labile and inappropriate affect, avoided eye contact, and made repeated accusations about my "hypnotizing" her. Through her sometimes grossly disorganized speech, I was able to detect somatic delusions about someone "twisting" her inner organs and persecutory delusions concerning her neighbors, which had transformed her into a veritable recluse. Mention of the need for medication only served to heighten her suspiciousness.

Midway through this first visit, she suddenly caught a glimpse of a Freud first edition on a bookshelf and commented happily that Freud was an expert on cerebral palsy. She then mentioned the neighbors who had betrayed her and asked me if I was Japanese. Noting to myself that this was Pearl Harbor Day, I told her that I thought that she wanted to trust me and let me help her, but that she was afraid that I would betray her as she felt her neighbors had. She seemed to nod in agreement and shortly thereafter accepted antipsychotic medication, which produced a stable remission of her psychosis within several weeks.

In less acute situations, the ability to place the initial prescribing of medication in a psychodynamic context establishes an important precedent for the inclusion of medication-related issues in the ongoing exploratory process.

A patient with mild depressive symptoms, panic attacks, and various somatic complaints, including abdominal pain, was verbal, well motivated, and seemed to have established a good rapport with her psychiatrist. She was quite enthusiastic about taking antidepressant medication but discontinued the drug after a few doses, complaining of abdominal discomfort and increased anxiety. Despite reassurance regarding the medication, she became intermittently silent. She did report that her new boyfriend had remarked that she doesn't talk enough and that she had responded by telling him that it takes her time to trust. She mentioned that she has become skeptical of this new boyfriend despite an initial good impression.

A suggestion to her that difficulties with the medication might have made her a bit wary of her new treatment could establish the beginning of the integration of her pharmacotherapy and psychotherapy. Such an intervention would point out a relationship between her response to the medication and her silence, and possibly her feelings about her doctor. In addition, this might lead to a realization that the side effects she experienced were similar to her presenting symptoms, indicating that despite (and because of) her enthusiasm about the drug, she may have some anxiety about taking it. Such difficulties with medication were, in fact, presaged by her tendency to somatization, guilt over her conviction that she had caused her son's learning disability by her use of a drug, and childhood preoccupation with fantasies about illness and death.

THE FRAMEWORK OF COMBINED TREATMENT

As the previous examples imply, even when medication is part of the initial treatment plan, the ability to maintain a psychodynamic focus helps pave the way for future exploratory work. In addition, to ensure the most adaptive integration of the patient's experience of being ill, no matter the severity of the symptomatology, one should seek to convey to the patient that his communications (including overt symptoms) are meaningful, that precipitating incidents are relevant, and that his subjective experience is of central importance. Such an attitude is critical in encouraging the patient's necessary participation in the exploratory process, in particular because it suggests a psychodynamic responsibility for his symptomatology.

An analogous activity regarding patient responsibility in pharmacotherapy can be established when the prescriber resists the temptation to revert to the subject–object mode of relating. Instead of assuming an authoritarian posture, which demands a passive-dependent stance in the patient and a viewing of the doctor as having sole responsibility for clinical improvement (Hoge and Gutheil 1989), "participant prescribing," a special version of the therapeutic alliance, can be invoked (Gutheil 1977). In sharing with patients the rationale for the use of the medication, its effects and possible side effects, and the uncertainty of treatment, their collaboration, as well as a share of responsibility for the outcome of the pharmacologic treatment, is enlisted. Patients are less likely to withhold important questions about the medication or reports of symptom change and possible adverse reactions. Moreover, they are more likely to do so spontaneously, which then makes such questions and reports more available as psychotherapy process than if simply stimulated by direct questioning.

Educating the patient regarding the need for and use of medication can be compared to setting the ground rules in the psychotherapy, such as the confidentiality of the treatment, the fundamental rule of free association, the setting of regular hours and payment of fees, and the responsibility for missed sessions. "The patient's conceptions of, and response to, the ground rules sometimes become the vehicle for important resistances, transference fantasies, and reactions, and realistic responses to the therapist" (Langs 1973, p. 89). Similarly, providing the patient with specific information regarding the target symptoms of the pharmacologic treatment, the necessity for laboratory studies, and the expected nature of the treatment regimen, such as the titration of the therapeutic dose, maintenance doses, or need for prophylaxis, represents the framework for the pharmacologic treatment and a working agreement between the patient and doctor. This may serve as a background for the patient's fantasies regarding the medication and its prescriber, idiosyncratic reactions, and possible acting out through its misuse.

A 35-year-old Jewish religious leader and salesman had rigidly divided his life among religious activities, high-powered and intensely competitive business tactics, and reckless gambling. After many years in his father's community and synagogue, he moved to a larger, more well-to-do neighborhood. His gambling began to escalate sharply and within one year he had accumulated enormous debts. He began to worry that the government would begin to pursue him for tax evasion and that his much beloved mentor-boss at work was plotting against him. Within a few weeks he suffered a full-blown psychotic depression that required involuntary hospitalization.

A stable remission of overt symptoms was obtained on a combination of antidepressant and antipsychotic medication. The patient was now back at work for over eighteen months and was taking maintenance doses of each medication. During a weeklong vacation from work, he engaged in an intense episode of gambling and reported at the next session his determination to increase his antidepressant to combat his depression. This desire to eradicate his sense of shame and failure was revealed as similar in structure to the lifelong use of gambling as a way of supplementing the repression of his sense of shame at being "a weak, faggy Jew." In addition, his thoughts about "disappointing" me and yet wanting my "miracle" drug led to exploration of the dynamics of the competition and identification with his father in his religious activities.

One of the tasks of the first several psychotherapy hours is to detect early and sometimes serious resistances to the therapy process, since working with these resistances may prevent premature withdrawal from treatment (Langs 1973). In addition, the nature of these resistances can provide clues to important transference themes, to the patient's characteristic defensive style, and to the conflicts underlying the patient's symptomatology. This is no less true with a patient's difficulties in accepting medication.

A 32-year-old man sought treatment because of moderately severe depressive symptomatology with prominent somatic complaints, chiefly focused on his stomach. He was unable to identify any precipitating circumstances except possibly some financial burdens. During the consultation hour, I noted his numerous references to experiences in the military and his strength and fearlessness. At the end of the second session, he was given a prescription for antidepressant medication, which he failed to fill. In explaining to me his reluctance to take the medication, he again made reference to "masculine" qualities that he felt should obviate the need for medication. When I pointed out to him that he seemed to experience his depression and the taking of medication as a threat to his sense of manliness, he remembered a question he wanted to ask me: "Could having sex make you weak?" Several days ago, he had had intercourse with his wife for the first time in many weeks and had awakened feeling particularly fatigued. I wondered aloud whether he indeed had some sexual concerns, despite his rigorous denial in the first hour. At this point, he revealed that his symptoms had begun during the last trimester of his wife's recent pregnancy and during an extramarital affair. Moreover, when he had first become ill, he had feared that his symptoms were due to AIDS, which he had imagined he had contracted from his paramour.

TRANSFERENCE

Implicit in the previous vignettes is that the prescribing of medication can provoke intense, personal psychological reactions, quite independent of the pharmacokinetic action of the drug. The most obvious demonstration of this is the well-established placebo effect (Benson and Epstein 1975), which can account for as much as 50 percent of a drug's effectiveness in the treatment of anxiety and depressive conditions (O'Connell 1988). Reactions to medication may be strongly determined by fantasy, displacement, and symbolization (Hoge and Gutheil 1989). Patients may react to the shape, color, taste, or markings of a pill, the schedule and form of its administration, even its name. Medication can serve as a "relationship equivalent" (Hoge and Gutheil 1989) or as a nonthreatening connectedness like a transitional object (Gabbard 1990). For some patients, the medication need not be consumed, just carried on their person as a talisman.

Most important is the patient's reaction to the prescriber of the medication, the personal meaning that the patient assigns to the physician who offers or fails to offer drug treatment. "The psychiatrist prescribing medication is no less a transference figure than the psychotherapist" (Gabbard 1990, p. 114). The prescribing of medication, like any action of the analyst, will be seized upon and worked over by the patient's unconscious wishes (Ostow 1979) and therefore, even when appropriate, invariably gratifies important transference wishes. This actualizing of these wishes may impair the patient's ability to distinguish reality from fantasy in the transference and promote acting out as opposed to intrapsychic experience. In addition, defensive and superego aspects of transference will also be manifest in patients' reactions to medication.

Childhood experiences with illness and even previous drug treatment may play a part in the transference to drug giving (Strain 1980). Being given medication may be experienced as "good" (i.e., loved, fed, or freed from responsibility) or "bad" (i.e., deprived, punished, rejected, or deficient). "Paradoxically, the good meanings may be interpreted as bad and vice versa" (Thompson and Brodie 1981, p. 243). Many authors have noted how the prescribing of medication can intensify conflicts over fellatio and oral impregnation fantasies and fears of loss of control and passivity (Ostow 1979). Some patients will begin to attribute everything to the effect of the medication and therefore resist acknowledging the transference. Nonetheless, in the context of a psychoanalytic psychotherapy, the opportunity exists to explore the rich and affectively charged fantasies that underly the transference reactions to drug prescribing, so as to reduce their interference with the pharmacologic benefit of the medication and promote change through insight. The act of medication prescribing may crystallize important transference themes and bring nearer to the surface significant psychodynamic material contained in patients' fantasies about the action of the medication. These fantasies often provide clues to the inner conflicts determining the patients' symptomatology.

Ms. A. presented with panic attacks, complicated by a compulsion to vomit, high levels of generalized anxiety, crying jags, and temper tantrums. This collection of symptoms had first appeared in her early teens, when she had discovered that her father's second wife was pregnant. They had now reemerged with great intensity when her mother's second husband left the home. The patient was unable to continue in college, could sleep only in her mother's bed, avoided her boyfriend, and cried hysterically for her father. In addition, as was invariably the case, she attempted to prevent her anxiety and vomiting by not eating, avoiding any "excitement," and removing all jewelry and makeup.

The patient's parents had separated when she was 5 years old. Attempts by her parents to deceive her about the status of the marriage and their active dating served as a source of great stimulation, as well as a model for her own defensive activity. On weekends, the patient would often stay with her father and his fiancée. She recalls vomiting at night, which necessitated her sleeping with her father, effectively separating him from his fiancée. She often fantasized that she would have been spared her problems if her father had never left home. She imagined that his strictness and conservatism would have prevented many of the "wild things" that had happened in her childhood, such as her own early sexual activity, fights with her brother, and her mother's casual and exhibitionistic sexual attitudes.

Ms. A. had serious conflicts over her sexuality. Although sexually active, she denied ever having masturbated, rarely had any interest in sex except to "prevent a boyfriend from cheating," and was pathologically jealous. She even became anxious at seeing a passionate kiss on the movie screen, although she would attribute this to a concern that her boyfriend might become excited. During intercourse, she was tremendously inhibited and was repulsed at the feeling of having a penis inside her, a feeling she reported as identical to that which compelled her to vomit. The threat of losing a boyfriend often provoked active fantasizing about telling him she was pregnant. One time, after her boyfriend left the house during an argument, she experienced a mysterious "itch" in her genitals, which she imagined was due to an injury or disease.

The panic attacks and generalized anxiety responded well to antidepressant and antianxiety agents. In addition, the patient was seen three times a week in psychoanalytic psychotherapy. Her acute regressive behavior remitted, and she was able to return to school and gradually expand her range of activities, which had been quite restricted for several years. She occasionally still vomited after excitement and felt numbness in her hands. Within the first year of treatment the antianxiety drug was discontinued.

The patient's feelings about me were dominated by idealization. She reported great comfort in my "seriousness and formality." If my therapeutic techniques frustrated her, she felt it must be for the best. She imagined that I was different with my other patients, more friendly and revealing about my personal life. She thought that it would "terrify" her if I were to behave similarly with her.

The patient was instructed to reduce her antidepressant medication by a small amount, with the idea of gradually reaching a maintenance dose. The following session, she reported that after reducing the dose, she had awakened in the middle of the night in a panic and with the need to vomit. She was desperate to see me and felt numbness in her hands on the way to the session. Primarily, she thought her reaction to the medication reduction was physiologic, but she also thought that I must be thinking she was getting well and that she would eventually be able to stop treatment. I suggested that she must have been thinking about how it would be not to see me anymore. She then remembered a dream she had that night: "I came an hour early to the appointment. You weren't here. You were in the bathroom. Then you looked at your watch and said you had another patient coming in. I told you I had an attack. You told me you wouldn't keep me waiting and the other patient left. Then your daughter walked in and said, 'Hi, Dad.' You were mad, but you didn't lose control."

The patient's thoughts about the dream included her idea that if she were sick I would keep seeing her, how I didn't lose control, and her notions about the closeness I have with other patients. I told her that she was afraid of the feelings she has for me and that these had intensified when she had been thinking about the end of treatment. She imagined that the medication controlled these feelings. Also, when she was sick like a child these feelings seemed less threatening. The patient compared this with her longings for her father's strictness and then mentioned how she had been trying not to get close to her mother's boyfriend in case he would leave. She was visiting her father on the weekend and was nauseous. Her father had said that she had looked better than ever, gorgeous and sexy, and he had wanted to show her off. She had thought that this surely would make her sick. The next day she found out that her friend was pregnant and wanted Ms. A. to accompany her to the abortion clinic.

The following session, another dream was reported: "The doors are open. I'm the only patient here, and you come in with shorts and a T-shirt." (These were the same clothes her father had worn that weekend.) "You ask if I am supposed to have a session that day. I start to throw up." I pointed out the recurring theme, as in the previous dream, of her getting rid of her rivals, my other patients and my daughter. Her conscious approval of my closeness to other patients and my formality with her guarded against frightening competitive wishes, resentment toward me for not favoring her, and wishes for closeness with me. She imagined that the medication kept these very feelings in check, but at the same time, also gratified some of the wishes for a special relationship with me. As the weeks went on, the wishes for informality were more clearly defined as sexual urges, the vomiting an undoing of a fantasied pregnancy that would compensate for separation, and the numbness in her hands a conversion symptom related to her struggles with masturbatory impulses.

At this point in treatment, the taking of the medication primarily symbolized the gratification of forbidden aggressive and sexual oedipal wishes and impregnation fantasies, as well as a defense against these wishes, by providing disguised representation and supporting the displacement from genitals to mouth, inherent in her symptomatology. In addition, the patient's fantasies about the action of the medication paralleled the transference superego attitudes about sexual excitement and masturbation, competitive wishes, and rage at being abandoned.

COUNTERTRANSFERENCE

"The prescribing of medication is just as likely as any other treatment intervention to be contaminated with countertransference" (Gabbard 1990, p. 116). It is possible for the analyst to assign any of the varied unconscious meanings to this activity that the patient does. In the worst of circumstances, these unconscious determinants of drug giving can distort or override the rationale for the use of psychotropic medication, just as a countertransference reaction in a purely verbal therapy can serve as a conduit for errors in psychotherapy technique. On the other hand, the self-examination of countertransference in psychotherapy can help to avoid technical errors and provide important clues to patient psychodynamics, in particular, the state of the transference. Similarly, examination of one's feelings about a patient and one's motives for prescribing or not prescribing can short-circuit incorrect or inappropriate drug giving and reveal important information about the patient's conflicts.

A psychiatrist fearing closeness with a patient may prescribe drugs to maintain a formal, interpersonal distance, while unrealistic expectations of drug therapy may be associated with an inattention to psychological issues and result in repeated unsuccessful drug trials and drug combinations (Thompson and Brodie 1981). However, a failure to prescribe a necessary drug may arise from a concern that the exchange of a prescription represents the fulfilling of forbidden wishes for intimacy or indicates a failure of psychotherapeutic intervention (Gabbard 1990). In psychoanalytic psychotherapy with schizophrenic patients, Levy (1977) described the countertransference use of drugs to establish interpersonal boundaries, to treat the therapist's own anxiety, and to both renounce and express hostile, rejecting wishes and forbidden, regressive pleasures. Likewise, in treating the sicker patient, medication is sometimes offered prophylactically in the face of difficult external pressures or changes. Such a practice might express a therapist's unconscious wish to maintain a patient's dependency and is likely to undermine a patient's sense of mastery over his emotional life.

In addition, medication may be prescribed because of a psychiatrist's fear of a patient's feelings and impulses, the implication being that such feelings are too dangerous to be expressed in the therapy. This is especially true with patients and therapists who have difficulty with aggression. For example, a psychiatrist may refuse to set limits on a patient's requests for medication in the hope of barring hostility from the therapeutic relationship (Gabbard 1990). In such circumstances, the countertransference prescribing encourages acting out because it suggests that the feelings targeted by the medication should not be known or expressed verbally.

Prior to the first vacation interruption of therapy, Ms. A. had requested a small supply of antianxiety drugs, "just in case." Since she had been in psychotherapy for less than a year, had shown a tremendous propensity for dramatic regressions, and had experienced remission of her panic attacks for only a few months, I felt that this was a clinically appropriate request. However, her failure to attend the last session before the vacation and her declaring the uselessness of talking about her feelings on the matter, because "I would leave her no matter what she said," had made me wonder whether this medication prescribing had represented a forfeiture of a psychotherapy opportunity.

In fact, despite steady progress in her psychotherapy and an intense positive transference, her curiosity about me had steadily waned. Moreover, despite the crucial importance of separations in intensifying her pathogenic intrapsychic conflicts, interruptions in treatment more and more produced an inattention to her feelings, a scheduling of substitute activities, and a focus on the value of her medication.

In the fourth year of treatment, Ms. A. again made a request for a supply of anxiolytics prior to a two-week interruption of treatment. I again found myself mentally agreeing with her argument that she needed the medication. She was about to face a variety of phobic situations and had had an anxiety-ridden past few months, due to her reaction to her stepmother's pregnancy. When I did not immediately reply to her request, she began to talk about how she had felt, early on in treatment, whenever she had telephoned me. She had always imagined me in my office, no matter the day or hour, purposely not answering her call as some special technique to help her with her desperate feelings. As usual, she claimed to be appreciative of such handling of her emotional storms.

I found myself annoyed at her ingratiating picture of what I imagined she felt was my sadistic mistreatment of her. Then, with palpable anxiety, I remembered the raging temper tantrums of her early months in treatment. It seemed clear to me that I was frightened at the anger that lurked menacingly beneath her idealization, and I wanted to treat this anger with the medication. The patient could only imagine me in my office because her wishes to interrupt me at home provoked too much guilt. Just as her parents had felt compelled to lie to her about their dating activities in order to stem her temper tantrums, my giving her medication during a separation would support her view of me as only existing in my office and mean that she wasn't really abandoned and didn't need to be angry. Interpretations about her need for the medication to repress the anger, instigated by a sense of loss and betrayal, led to further material concerning her need to see both her father and me as idealized men, that is, men who never have sex or look at other women.

SIDE EFFECTS, DENIAL, AND COMPLIANCE

In the same manner that they produce placebo-driven symptom amelioration, a patient's fantasies about the taking of medication can produce significant nonphysiologic side effects that often lead to poor medication compliance. A glance through the side-effect profile of any psychotropic drug will reveal significant reports of adverse reactions to placebo, particularly referable to the central nervous system, gastrointestinal tract, and cardiovascular system. This seems to be particularly true for anxious patients (Shapiro et al. 1974) and patients with paranoid trends (Book 1987). Careful psychodynamic listening can offer a means of distinguishing such reactions from side effects and thus produce effective interpretations rather than numerous, unnecessary medication changes.

A 22-year-old schizophrenic man had been in a stable remission for several years but had complained intermittently of "staring" episodes. Assuming this was an effect of the medication on his extraocular muscles, several clinicians, including myself, had made numerous changes in antipsychotic and anti-Parkinson drugs, without benefit.

After about a year of psychotherapy, I noticed that this "staring" usually occurred around the time the patient would go out with friends to meet women. I told the patient that he seemed to experience this problem when he was "looking for women" and that possibly it was caused by anxiety and not by the medication. He then revealed a theretofore unknown detail of the symptom. He would become transfixed on a blemish on a person's face and then feel confused about what he was looking at. In other words, the patient really was "staring"! As the conflicted sexual wishes behind this conversion symptom became more available, the patient began having the attacks after sessions.

Within several weeks, he remembered being taken to bathhouses by his mother during his childhood and being repeatedly exposed to women's genitals "at eye level" in the locker room. Exploration of the relationship between his "staring" symptom and the excitement, anger, and anxiety aroused in the bathhouses led to a disappearance of the symptom.

In addition, patients may have highly personalized reactions to actual physiologic side effects, including decompensation (Van Putten, Mutalipassi, and Malkin 1974), suicide (Drake and Ehrlich 1985), and psychotic interpretation (Vaughn, Oquendo, and Horwath 1991). Clearly, such reactions can threaten a drug treatment, but when less severe they can also provide an opportunity for exploratory work.

A 19-year-old man was seen in the early stages of his first schizophrenic decompensation. After improvement on gradually elevating doses of an antipsychotic, he became increasingly anxious, referential, and tearful. He attributed this to the recent increase in dosage and wanted to stop the medication. As he described this new emotional state, he spoke of some vague changes in his body image, concerns that he was being "looked at from behind," and a return of "voices" calling him a "fag."

After suggesting to the patient that he seemed to feel the medication had changed his body in some way, he began to describe that a stiff feeling in his legs had made him concerned that he was walking like a woman. This reminded him of his being teased, in a childhood summer camp, about the way he walked and his concerns about the size of his penis. The patient's reaction to a mild extrapyramidal side effect had resembled a further decompensation, but psychodynamic exploration and clarification of the symptom helped to avert discontinuation or an unnecessary increase in the medication.

Even when medication has been clearly effective and has produced no significant side effects, compliance can remain a problem. Nevins (1977) described how even beneficial responses to antipsychotics can be disruptive of schizophrenic functioning by the effect they might have on defenses, object relations, psychotic restitution, use of external reality, and body image. In schizophrenic and manic patients, Van Putten (1974, 1975, 1976) found that "the wish to be crazy," the wish to restore grandiose delusions, was an important determinant of chronic medication noncompliance. To the psychoanalyst, such findings would fall under the familiar heading of resistance, the preference of illness to health (Gabbard 1990). Since a symptom represents an adaptation, albeit a misguided one, to a patient's psychic reality, it is not so easily relinquished. A related phenomenon, the denial of illness, is highly correlated with noncompliance and typical of patients who "seal over" rather than integrate their psychotic experience with their pre- and postpsychotic mental life (D'Angelo and Wolowitz 1986).

A psychodynamic view of psychotic regression and recovery reveals the ongoing effort of the patient to resolve inner conflict, through compromise formations of wish and defense. Conceptualizing ego operations in dynamic terms rather than simply defective, automatic, or mechanistic permits insight into the personal nature of the psychotic experience, of precipitating events, and of childhood traumata, and therefore into the need to resist symptom change and deny illness. This allows an easy transition from theory to therapeutic work (Levy, McGlashan, and Carpenter 1975). Exploration of denial and resistance in psychotic illness is often long and painstaking, but it can lead not only to acceptance of effective, prophylactic medication, but also to a reduction in the restrictiveness of defensive structure and a beneficial integration of psychotic symptoms into a continuous life experience.

A 25-year-old factory worker was seen after his first schizophrenic decompensation. He had been living at home with his elderly parents, had few friends, and had never had a serious girlfriend. Three times in his first five years of psychotherapy he stopped taking his highly effective antipsychotic medication, interrupted his psychotherapy, and decompensated. He continued to deny his illness, despite these decompensations, which had a typical course. Initially, his love for a particular female rock star would develop into an erotomanic delusion and he would become uncharacteristically confident, would excel at work, and would actively seek out and meet women. Without medication, however, this state would deteriorate into one characterized by rage at this rock star, a variety of persecutory delusions, autistic withdrawal, and bizarre ritualistic behavior.

After several months of weekly psychotherapy following his fourth decompensation, he began to reveal the painful loneliness and frustration of his nonpsychotic state and his sense of hopeless inadequacy in social-sexual matters. His psychotherapy demonstrated how such feelings might lead him to prefer the psychotic state and how his denial of illness and medication noncompliance achieved that state. The patient began to accept his illness, and his medication became a valued ally as he sought changes in the outside world to bolster his self-esteem rather than retreat into fantasy.

When a relationship with a woman in a distant city failed to materialize as he had hoped, he spontaneously suggested that his unrealistic expectations in this relationship bore similarities to his delusion about the rock star. He began to wonder why he was so inhibited with women who were more accessible. Subsequent exploratory work on his homosexual fears eventually led to his establishment of a relationship with a "real girlfriend."

CONCLUSION

The opportunity to conduct a treatment that combines psychoanalytic psychotherapy with psychopharmacotherapy poses special challenges and opportunities for the psychoanalyst. The availability of drug therapy requires a stressful split in the analyst's attention. "When we serve our patients best, our minds are partly on the mind–body question, but then our minds are not fully on matters of mind" (Kramer 1986, p. 17). In addition, drug therapy is a readily available tool for countertransference acting out, easily rationalized as an attempt to cure. It may significantly reduce a patient's motivation to engage in psychotherapy and reinforce the assigning of responsibility for symptomatology to forces external to the mind. Moreover, access to important unconscious material may be forever lost to the extent that drug taking reinforces maladaptive resolution of inner conflict, gratifies transference wishes, and encourages action as opposed to verbal expression.

On the other hand, the ability to prescribe medication may allow the psychoanalyst to extend his treatment efforts to a wide range of patients and to develop unique prescribing skills, anchored in great wealths of patient information and an intimate awareness of the subtleties of patient–drug prescriber interaction. Although the complexity of dealing with data of great quantity and variety can be daunting, it does avoid the considerable problems associated with the splitting of treatment between prescriber and therapist. In addition, combining treatments means that patients who require medication need not be deprived of opportunities to gain mastery through insight of their emotional problems, a mastery that, in some cases, can eventually replace the drug therapy.

Finally, at a time when technological innovation continues to erode the interpersonal aspects of medical care, the combination of psychoanalytic psychotherapy and psychopharmacotherapy promotes a unique melding of therapeutic art and science and a collaboration of patient and physician seen only too rarely today.

REFERENCES

Azima, H. (1959). Psychodynamic alterations concomitant with tofranil administration. *Journal of the Canadian Psychiatric Association* 4:172–176.

Azima, H., Cramer-Azima, F., and DeVerteuil, R. (1956). A comparative behavioral and psychodynamic study of the effect of reserpine and raudixin in schizophrenia. *Monograph on Therapy* 2:10–13.

———— (1959). Effects of rauwolfia derivatives on psychodynamic structure. *Psychiatric Quarterly* 33:623–635.

Azima, H., Cramer-Azima, F., and Durost, H. B. (1959). Psychoanalytic formulations of effects of reserpine on schizophrenic organization. *Archives of General Psychiatry* 1:622–670.

Bellak, L., and Chasan, J. B. (1964). An approach to the evaluation of drug effect during psychotherapy: a double blind study of a single case. *Journal of Nervous and Mental Diseases* 139:20–30.

Benson, H., and Epstein, M. D. (1975). The placebo effect. *Journal of the American Medical Association* 232:1223–1227.

Beres, D., and Arlow, J. A. (1974). Fantasy and identification in empathy. *Psychoanalytic Quarterly* 43:26–50.

Book, H. E. (1987). Some psychodynamics of non-compliance. *Canadian Journal of Psychiatry* 32:115–117.

D'Angelo, E. J., and Wolowitz, H. M. (1986). Defensive constellation and styles of recovery from schizophrenic episodes. *Hillside Journal of Clinical Psychiatry* 8:3–14.

Docherty, J. P., Marder, S. R., Van Kammen, D. P., et al. (1977). Psychotherapy and pharmacotherapy: conceptual issues. *American Journal of Psychiatry* 134:529–533.

Drake, R. E., and Erlich, J. (1985). Suicide attempts associated with akathesia. *American Journal of Psychiatry* 142:499–501.

Gabbard, G. O. (1990). *Psychodynamic Psychiatry in Clinical Practice.* Washington, DC: American Psychiatric Association Press.

Group for the Advancement of Psychiatry (1975). *Pharmacotherapy and Psychotherapy: Paradoxes, Problems and Progress,* Report 93. New York: Group for the Advancement of Psychiatry.

Gutheil, T. G. (1977). Psychodynamics in drug prescribing. *Drug Therapy* 2:35–40.

Hayman, M. (1967). Drugs and the psychoanalyst. *American Journal of Psychotherapy* 21:644–654.

Hoge, S. K., and Gutheil, T. G. (1989). Psychology of psychopharmacology. In *Outpatient Psychiatry,* ed. A. Lazare, pp. 690–694. Baltimore: Williams & Wilkins.

Kernberg, O. (1971). Prognostic considerations regarding the borderline personality organization. *Journal of the American Psychoanalytic Association* 19:595–635.

Klerman, G. L. (1975). Combining drugs and psychotherapy in the treatment of depression. In *Drugs in Combination with Other Therapies,* ed. M. Greenblatt, pp. 67–82. New York: Grune & Stratton.

Kramer, P. (1986). The mind-mind-body-problem problem. *Psychiatric Times,* January, pp. 3, 17.

Langs, R. (1973). *The Technique of Psychoanalytic Psychotherapy.* New York: Jason Aronson.

Lesse, S. (1956). Psychotherapy and ataractics: some observations on combined psychotherapy and chlorpromazine therapy. *American Journal of Psychotherapy* 10:448–459.

———— (1966). Psychotherapy plus drugs in depression–technique. *Comprehensive Psychiatry* 7:224–231.

Levy, S. T. (1977). Countertransference aspects of the pharmacotherapy of schizophrenics. *International Journal of Psychoanalytic Psychotherapy* 6:15–30.

Levy, S. T., McGlashan, T. H., and Carpenter, W. T., Jr. (1975). Integration and sealing over as recovery styles from acute psychosis: metapsychological and dynamic concepts. *Journal of Nervous and Mental Diseases* 161:307–312.

Lewin, B. D. (1946). Counter-transference in the technique of medical practice. *Psychosomatic Medicine* 8:195–199.

Mandell, A. J. (1968). Psychoanalysis and psychopharmacology. In *Modern Psychoanalysis*, ed. J. Marmor, pp. 274–290. New York: Basic Books.

Modell, A. H. (1966). Psychotherapy plus drugs in severe depressions—technique. *Comprehensive Psychiatry* 7:224–231.

Nevins, D. A. (1977). Adverse response to neuroleptics in schizophrenia. *International Journal of Psychoanalytic Psychotherapy* 6:227–242.

O'Connell, R. A. (1988). Psychological and social aspects of psychopharmacologic treatment. In *Psychobiology and Psychopharmacology*, ed. F. Flach, pp. 1–11. New York: W. W. Norton.

Ostow, M. (1960a). The effects of the newer neuroleptic and stimulating drugs on psychic function. In *The Dynamics of Psychiatric Drug Therapy*, ed. G. Sarwer-Foner, pp. 172–192. Springfield, IL: Charles C Thomas.

—————— (1960b). The use of drugs to overcome technical difficulties in psychoanalysis. In *The Dynamics of Psychiatric Drug Therapy*, ed. G. Sarwer-Foner, pp. 443–463. Springfield, IL: Charles C Thomas.

—————— (1962). *Drugs in Psychoanalysis and Psychotherapy*. New York: Basic Books.

—————— (1966). The complementary roles of psychoanalysis and drug therapy. In *Psychiatric Drugs*, ed. P. Solomon, pp. 91–111. New York: Grune & Stratton.

—————— (1979). *The Psychodynamic Approach to Drug Therapy*. New York: The Psychoanalytic Research and Development Fund.

—————— (1983). Letter to the editor. *American Journal of Psychiatry* 140:371–372.

Sandler, J., and Sandler, A. M. (1983). The past unconscious, the present unconscious and the interpretation of the transference. *Psychoanalytic Inquiry* 4:367–400.

Sarwer-Foner, G. (1957). Psychoanalytic theories of activity–passivity conflicts and of the continuum of ego defenses. *Archives of Neurology and Psychiatry* 78:413–421.

—————— (1960a). *The Dynamics of Drug Therapy*. Springfield, IL: Charles C Thomas.

—————— (1960b). The role of neuroleptic medication in psychotherapeutic interaction. *Comprehensive Psychiatry* 1:291–300.

—————— (1964). On the mechanisms of action of neuroleptic drugs: a theoretical psychodynamic explanation. In *Advances in Biological Psychiatry*, vol. 6, ed. J. Wortis, pp. 217–232. New York: Plenum.

Shapiro, A. K., Chassan, J., Morris, L. A., et al. (1974). Placebo-induced side effects. *Journal of Operational Psychiatry* 6:43–46.

Stone, L. (1954). The widening scope of indications for psychoanalysis. *Journal of the American Psychoanalytic Association* 2:567–594.

Strain, J. J. (1980). Meaning of medication. *Art Medication* 1:19–24.

Thompson, E. M., and Brodie, H. K. H. (1981). The psychodynamics of drug therapy. In *Current Psychiatric Therapies*, vol. 21, ed. J. H. Masserman, pp. 239–251. New York: Grune & Stratton.

Van Praag, H. M. (1979). Tablets and talking—a spurious contrast in psychiatry. *Comprehensive Psychiatry* 20:502–510.

Van Putten, T. (1974). Why do schizophrenic patients refuse to take their drugs? *Archives of General Psychiatry* 31:67–72.

_____ (1975). Why do patients with manic-depressive illness stop their lithium? *Comprehensive Psychiatry* 16:179–183.

_____ (1976). Drug refusal in schizophrenia and the wish to be crazy. *Archives of General Psychiatry* 33:1443–1446.

Van Putten, T., Multalipassi, L. R., and Malkin, M. D. (1974). Phenothiazine induced decompensation. *Archives of General Psychiatry* 30:102–105.

Vaughn, S., Oquendo, M., and Horwath, E. (1991). Letters to the editor. *American Journal of Psychiatry* 148:393–394.

11

Women in Psychotherapy

Barbara G. Deutsch, M.D.

Gender issues are ubiquitous in our daily work with patients. Any serious consideration of these factors, often referred to as gender bias, must include both our traditional cultural attitudes and a variety of fantasy elaborations. In this chapter, I will be concerned with how issues relating to gender may affect the therapeutic situation from the perspective of the patient and the therapist. I believe that a heightened awareness of gender issues is of vital importance in all psychotherapeutic work.

Freud said in his 1933 paper "Femininity," "When you meet a human being, the first distinction you make is male or female" (p. 113). He thus acknowledged the importance of gender. In the same paper, he suggested that female analysts were in a better position (than he or fellow male analysts) to learn about the preoedipal phase of development from their women patients. While we may now disagree with this formulation,[1] it clearly demonstrates the influence of gender attitudes on Freud's thinking.

Gender attitudes, both conscious and unconscious, pervade all aspects of the psychotherapeutic situation. They can be the crucial factor that influences a patient's choice of therapist. I will suggest some answers to the intriguing question of why so many women today choose female therapists. Gender attitudes are reflected in both the reality-based and irrational aspects of transference. They inform countertransference attitudes as well. I think that an assertion that issues regarding gender can be neutralized in a well-

---

[1]According to Helen Meyers (1986), "Theoretically, in a well-conducted analysis as a whole, the analyst's gender, like all other reality issues, should have little effect, since all transference paradigms are eventually established and worked through" (p. 159).

conducted psychotherapy is questionable. It denies the rich nuances that careful attention to the subtleties of gender can bring to the treatment situation.

Familiarity with current views of female development is an important basis for an appreciation of our own attitudes about gender in work with both male and female patients. Therefore, I will begin with a brief summary of some of the important revisions of Freud's theories about female development.

REVISIONS OF FREUDIAN THEORY

Women in general and feminists specifically, have found Freudian theory concerning female development an anathema. Freud was never fully satisfied with these hypotheses himself. He believed that the girl's development was more or less identical to the boy's until the discovery of the difference between the sexes. After that, he considered that female development was essentially derivative. It emerged as a reaction to a series of disappointing events in a girl's life. For example, he did not believe that the wish for a baby was a feminine instinctual wish and/or a value within the female superego based on a positive identification with the mother. He considered this wish to be derived from, and a result of, frustrated penis envy. According to Blum (1976b):

> What was emphasized [in Freud's theory] was the little girl's disappointments, her fears and her deprivation. She was deprived of a penis, disappointed in her oedipal strivings for father's love, penis and child. She was defeated by her oedipal rival, her ambivalently loved mother. These major disappointments and feelings of damage led her to need to accept her feelings of bodily and personal inferiority. Her feelings of bodily injury and loss and the influence of castration fantasies produced resentment and penis envy as well as compensatory restitutional longing for a child. [p. 160]
>
> The female was viewed as having a diminished and constrained libido, a weaker and masochistic sexual constitution, an ego with an incapacity to sublimate and a tendency toward early arrest and rigidity, a relatively defective superego and incomplete oedipal and postoedipal development. [p. 169]

Chasseguet-Smirgel (1976), a French analyst, succinctly stated these early formulations:

Female sexuality [according to Freud] was a series of lacks, the lack of vagina,[2] lack of a penis, lack of an adequate erotic object and finally the lacks which are implied by [the girl's] being devoid of any intrinsic feminine qualities which she could cathect directly and by her being forced to give up the clitoris. We can add the relative lack of a superego and the capacity for sublimation. [p. 281]

We now know that female development is not derivative, but complex and separate. The task of revising these early concepts about female development is ongoing. Our new knowledge has been acquired from the direct observation of infants and children, from psychoanalytic and feminist theoreticians, and out of therapeutic work with adults and children.

Our earliest ideas about gender are included in the concept of core gender identity. This has been defined by Stoller (1976) as the sense we have of our sex, of maleness in males and femaleness in females. It is made up of a series of influences that include biological forces in fetal life (e.g., genetic and hormonal), the sex assignment at birth, and parental attitudes about the infant's sex, both conscious and unconscious. This is firmly established by 18 months to 3 years of age.

According to Stoller (1975), both boys and girls experience a primary phase of protofemininity as a result of the original symbiosis and identification with the mother. He agrees with Greenson that developing a masculine identity is a secondary process that requires a traumatic repudiation of the original intimacy with the mother, a "disidentification."[3] Because this repudiation is conflictual, there remains in a man the fear that his sense of maleness and masculinity are in danger and that he must build into character structure ever-vigilant defenses against succumbing to the pull of merging again with mother.

The little girl's process of separation is more gradual and, some feel, never completely accomplished. She has the complicated task of changing her erotic object, separating from mother, and managing her competitive feelings, while at the same time maintaining a positive feminine identification.

One of the most controversial Freudian concepts is penis envy. We now understand this as a normal developmental phenomenon that may be reworked at each developmental period. Penis envy is not bedrock, as once believed, but can reflect and defend against

---

[2]Freud believed that a girl had no awareness of her vagina until puberty.
[3]Disidentification is a term originally used by Greenson (1968, p. 371).

earlier conflicts such as narcissistic issues, object loss, and breast envy (Grossman and Stewart 1976). According to Chasseguet-Smirgel (1976), "Freud attributed to man a natural scorn for women. This scorn originated in the fact of their lack of a penis. My experience has shown me that underlying this scorn one always finds a powerful maternal imago, envied and terrifying" (p. 283). Her hypothesis is that "the wish to break away from the primal mother drives children of both sexes to project her power on to the father and his penis and to more or less decathect specifically maternal qualities and organs" (p. 283).

Freud believed that the lack of castration anxiety resulted in a superego in women that was deficient. Blum (1976b) asserted that "the different motives for oedipal renunciation do not predict the final superego identifications or its strength" (p. 174). In addition, he emphasized the importance of the maternal ego ideal within the feminine superego.

With respect to values within the superego, we can take a detour from analytic developmental theorists and consider the work of Gilligan (1982), a social psychologist. She reasoned that values in women and men cannot be judged with the same scale.[4] Using the model of the decision making over abortion as her index dilemma, she demonstrated that throughout moral development, a woman views herself as evolving and growing in relationship to others. Female decisions are made with others in mind. Therefore, a woman's view of moral failure and success involves avoiding hurt and providing care, while a woman's definition of a moral problem most often involves a conflict of responsibilities rather than rights. Gilligan believed that the female and the male orientations predispose women toward interest in human relations and men toward individual achievement. These orientations are different rather than one's being inferior to the other.

GENDER ATTITUDES FROM THE PATIENT'S PERSPECTIVE

The Wish for a Female Therapist

Many patients regard the sex of the therapist as *the* critical variable. At one time, a majority of women sought male therapists, perhaps

---

[4]On the original scales created to study values in males, women consistently had lower scores. This seemed to confirm Freud's original ideas of the deficient female superego.

with the latent or manifest belief that they represented professional authority (Person 1986). Today more women preferentially seek women therapists. This certainly seems to represent a gender bias. How can this be understood?

The question of the therapist's gender involves the effect of the real object on the therapeutic process. Modern analysts (see footnote 1) have favored the proposition that, in the well-conducted analysis, the analyst's gender, like all other reality issues, should have little effect, since all transference paradigms are eventually established and worked through with an analyst of either sex. Meyers (1986) further stated that she found that the gender of the analyst only affects the sequence, intensity, and inescapability of certain transference paradigms in therapy and analysis, that is, issues specific to women, such as pregnancy in the patient or analyst.

In the face-to-face psychotherapies, which are less intensive and more oriented to symptom alleviation, the sex of the therapist seems to be a more significant issue than in traditional psychoanalysis with a neurotic patient, according to a review by Mogul (1982). Chasseguet-Smirgel (in Meyers 1986) thought that the effect of gender is probably greater with more regressed patients, who have a less secure sense of identity and are not sure of their sexual identity and who need, therefore, to cling more concretely to the reality of the sex of the therapist.

Person (1986) states, and I agree, that "the effects of gender are more subtle in analysis than in the other psychotherapies but may well be just as pervasive" (p. 196). She notes that Goz (1973) suggested that the reason for selecting a female therapist was the woman's wish to rework the relationship with the mother. But Person correctly argues that the mother problem has always existed and therefore cannot explain this new trend. She lists four reasons to account for it:

1. Fear that men will hold to sexist values.

2. The belief that it is too easy and tempting to fool a male therapist and thereby avoid problem areas. These are often women who have been disappointed with their first treatment experience with a male therapist.

3. The wish to avoid an erotic transference or countertransference. Here too, this may be a result of a previous unhappy experience with a male therapist or as a defense against strong oedipal wishes.

4. The explicit desire to have a strong, competent woman as a role model (Person 1986, p. 195).

Person feels that women are concerned about possible gender bias in the psychotherapeutic situation. She states that "there is evidence to suggest that the therapies of women, whatever the sex of the therapist, have suffered contamination by gender bias." She believes that analysts and therapists of different persuasions encounter the same data of observation: symbols, dream contents, and fantasies. When a bias occurs, it does not usually take the form of a misperception of these. "In other words, the therapists are working with the same basic information. The bias is most commonly reflected in the way the data are understood and interpreted" (p. 196).

Person (p. 197) presents a clinical vignette to illustrate her point.

Mrs. B., a 30-year-old mother of two, had reached an impasse four years into a psychotherapy. She was withdrawn, felt isolated, and was unable to form intimate ties with her children, despite loving feelings and her ability to provide good physical care. Her marriage was deteriorating. She decided to return to work, at which she had been successful, in the hope of restoring self-esteem that would allow her to be more functional at home.

She had previously had good rapport with her male therapist, but she fell into a silent rage when he interpreted her intention to return to work as acting out, as a defense against closeness with her children, and as a wish to abandon them.

Person was asked by the therapist to consult with the patient. She found that the patient appeared to be in the throes of a "negative identification" with her own mother that was precipitated by staying at home, as her mother had done. She felt that the decision to return to work was a symbolic attempt to break that identification. Person notes that the therapist's incorrect (or inexact) interpretation and interdiction derailed attention from the actual conflict. It confirmed the patient's conviction that she was no good and unable to give, just as her mother had been, and led to more depression, guilt, and withdrawal. It intensified her masochistic stance, which was itself a defensive posture. She was unable to express her rage and was obsessed about whether the therapist was correct, so she withdrew from the therapy. The therapist began to perceive the patient as schizoid.

Person feels that the treatment was salvaged because "the therapist was able to see that he had made a serious countertransference error stemming from his own values" (p. 197).

This vignette illustrates a common form of countertransference that involves gender attitudes. Both the therapist and Person saw Mrs. B.'s problem in essentially the same way. "By virtue of her own childhood experiences, motherhood and the care of small children seemed to threaten Mrs. B. with a loss of autonomy and symbiotic regression viewed as threatening to her integrity, her children's, or both" (p. 197). The difference was in the way the decision to return to work was perceived. Mrs. B.'s therapist viewed it as symptomatic, whereas Person viewed it as an adaptive maneuver. Neither seems to be concerned that Mrs. B. is attempting to resolve inner conflict through action.

Each of these therapists brings his or her own value system, including gender attitudes, to the interpretation of the clinical data. The male therapist made an interpretation that had a negative valence (i.e., that it is "bad" for a woman to leave small children to return to work). Indeed, this may be a countertransference error based on his individual bias or gender values. It could also represent an accurate analysis of this situation prematurely interpreted to the patient. But what about Person? It is true that her interpretation was friendlier and more ego-syntonic for the patient, but doesn't it reflect a bias based on a different set of gender attitudes? Would it be more difficult for Person to conclude from the data that this patient in fact had the unconscious motives as suggested by her male therapist? Without the patient's evidence, I don't think we can assert that we know what the psychological truth is. However, our goal is to try to discover this truth while not being caught in the gender-biased countertransference.

Grossman and Stewart (1976) describe two women patients they had seen for reanalysis. In both cases, the interpretation of penis envy as "bedrock" was close enough to the data for each woman to accept in the first analytic experience. One patient terminated her first analysis with plans to marry a "respectable man of her own class." This seemed to please both her analyst and her parents, and, at the time, herself. It seems they shared a common gender bias concerning normality in women. However, the marriage subsequently proved empty, and the patient became depressed. She returned to her original analyst and was referred to one of the authors because the original analyst had no time. (The patient herself didn't recognize the problems with her original treatment.) The original analyst had accepted penis envy as a bedrock issue, requiring no further analysis. The authors describe how they found, because they looked for it, that these patients used intense penis envy to defend against other important conflicts (narcissism, separation, etc.) that had not been analyzed.

Sexist interpretations and values are not restricted to male therapists. We need to acknowledge the goal of value-free therapy as an ideal rather than as a reality and to maintain vigilance about possible value contaminants in our work with patients. We can deal only with what we can hear, and what we hear is informed by our own theoretical stance and training, as well as by bias and character. Men and women both have gender bias and must seek to recognize and deal with it in the treatment situation.

Person (1986) observes that some women fear that they will be able to fool a male therapist. Either they will beguile him with feminine wiles and thus avoid dealing with problems, or they will be too ashamed to reveal themselves and will keep secrets. This can be a reason to choose a woman therapist, or alternately a reason to avoid one. Some women fear that they will be tempted to revert to a defensive femininity if confronted with difficult material and/or unpleasant truths. In addition, many women do not believe that any male, even a well-trained therapist, will be able to tolerate their anger, confrontation, or wish for equality. Person adds that women trust other women to know about female deviousness and to challenge them when they use the mask of femininity as an avoidance and defense. This represents an idealization of women therapists and conversely a defensive devaluation of male therapists.

Secrecy is often used by women in an attempt to gain approval. This is often related to their need for love. The need to pretend in order to please others leads to a subjective sense of inauthenticity, lack of autonomy, and denial of the inner self. This subjective sense emerges in very different areas, which include the fears of some successful women that they are fraudulent, about to be found out and exposed. According to Person, dissembling and ingratiation in the transference engender unconscious rage, which can express itself as contempt for the therapist whom the patient has successfully deceived. The two patients described by Grossman and Stewart (1976) clearly demonstrate this formulation. They are exposing their first analysts to the second, a derivative of their unanalyzed rage.

I don't agree with Person when she departs from analytic observation to political/social concerns. She states, for example, that the need to dissemble is not derived from shame generated from penis envy. She regards dissembling as reinforced by a social tradition in which woman is the other, whose worth is validated by her status as an erotic object and who must consequently please man in order to be chosen. I believe Gilligan (1991) is closer to the mark with her findings. She has fascinating research data that demonstrate that preadolescent girls move from a state of openness to one of inhibition or secrecy about their thoughts and feelings. Her hypothesis includes the need to please, to preserve, or to maintain relationships out of desperate fears of aloneness and/or abandonment. I believe that in our zeal to rid ourselves of past inaccuracies about female development, we may be throwing out the baby with the bathwater. Penis envy is still a useful concept with important explanatory power. We cannot summarily dismiss it simply because it is unpopular. Women of all ages still describe powerful feelings of defect, worthlessness, or unlovability based on the fantasy of genital inferiority. We now understand that we need to work with these fantasies and explore their earlier origins.

To illustrate the power of secrecy in the mental life of women, the following example is taken from an analytic therapy.

Mrs. A., a 32-year-old married mother of two, was in analysis because of severe anxiety and hypochondriasis. She was an attractive woman who wore very prominent eye makeup but no lipstick. She had lost all her teeth at age 18 after a series of agonizing dental procedures. Her makeup was carefully arranged to draw attention away from her mouth. She slept every night with her false teeth in her mouth. Her husband had never seen her without them.

Mrs. A. considered herself ugly, defective, and therefore unlovable. This narcissistic vulnerability led her to hide the evidence of her defectiveness. This was reflected in the transference when she consciously withheld fantasies while suffering painful anxiety. I interpreted to her fear of exposing her defects to me. Gradually, I was able to show her that hiding from me allowed her to deny or hide painful thoughts and feelings from herself.

As the analysis progressed, she let me know about some of her other "secrets:" She had been found to have a heart murmur as an infant, and her parents had been told she would not live. (She had been underweight as a child but had otherwise been asymptomatic.) Now she lived in fear of this cardiac pathology but was so terrified that she had been unable to see a cardiologist to find out her real status. The anxiety and worry about numerous other ailments detoured her attention from this crucial issue. As she became aware of her need to "hide" from me and from herself, she was able to follow through on a cardiac workup that diagnosed her condition. Her relief at knowing was considerable. Material that reflected her pervasive feelings of damage and defect, defended against by her secrecy, reemerged throughout the analysis.

Some women seek female therapists because of their fear of heterosexual fantasies and/or of their own propensity to act them out. Women worry about their potential ability to seduce their male therapists. Some women feel that they may be too prone to "crushes" or erotic fantasy to enter treatment with a man, fearing they will be sidetracked with romantic fantasies. While many women have had successful treatment with male therapists, some therapist–patient dyads have had difficulty around erotic transference–countertransference issues. Person (1986) observes that the stickier the erotic transference is, the more it is empowered by other than simple oedipal dynamics. The father transference may be a screen for the preoedipal attachment to the mother. Eroticism can mask dependency needs.

In her series of cases, Person found that where the erotic transference was acted out by a female patient–male therapist dyad, prognosis for future treatment positively correlated with how much responsibility the woman took for what had happened. This certainly did not condone the male therapist's behavior, but stressed female motive and complicity. Seductive intent on the part of the female patient was invariably intermixed with the need for control and hostility. Sexuality was used as a vehicle to discredit the male therapist. (Therapists who act out with patients are often reenacting problems within their own treatment experience, much as parents who abuse their children.)

There does not seem to be the same kind of problem for men with female therapists. Sexual acting out has not been reported in the therapies of men treated by women with the same frequency as it occurs with the male therapist–female patient. Women do have sexual fantasies about male patients, but they seem not as likely to act on them. This parallels the incidence in our society. Incest in our society is more frequently father–daughter. Mother–son is less commonly reported and reflects more primitive pathology.

Women today often verbalize their explicit desire to have a strong competent woman with whom to make a positive identification.

This seems borne out in some short-term therapies. Patients develop a positive transference that leads to positive identification, better performance, and increased self-esteem (reported by Zetzel 1966).[5] Yet as Person observes, changes in female identification can take place in the context of treatment with a man. Why does the role model have to be the therapist? Even if a female role model is required, why can't it be some admired woman in the patient's life?

Person reasons that the active ingredient is not just identification but the permission that the female patient gets from the woman therapist to compete, to succeed, to enjoy her life. In psychoanalysis, the woman's wish for a therapist as a role model may be a component of an idealization that in part defends against competitive and/or homosexual wishes. The female therapist is sought not only to be a role model, but to represent mother as well. In this role, it is her permission to achieve that is wished for. Yet Person's earlier argument serves here as well. A male therapist can be experienced in the transference as the mother who gives permission for the realization of feminine aspirations.

Women patients turn to women therapists for a variety of reasons. Little girls and women have long shared their secrets preferentially with their mothers, sisters, and best girl friends. This involves building intimate relationships, offering safety from heterosexuality (and its reciprocal denial of oedipal interests), and providing the freedom to reveal defects and vulnerabilities. Women fear the explicit and implicit dangerous sexual fantasies and potential for acting out that threatens them in the situation where they interact with men. They may choose the lesser dangers of the preoedipal mother or of possible homosexual excitation in the female–female dyad. Other women, disappointed with men because of negative experiences, turn to women to "undo" or make reparation for the past. Still other women, out of intense shame and conflict over narcissistic issues, penis envy included, choose women because they feel that these affects might somehow be mitigated with a woman or that they would feel less ashamed with a female analyst.

Some women fear sexual bias on the part of male therapists. They maintain the fantasy that a male therapist cannot possibly understand or appreciate a woman's suffering. They believe that female therapists are especially knowledgeable about women. Some women may have the fantasy that male therapists still believe in the

---

[5]Zetzel regarded them as transference cures.

"unfriendly" early Freudian views of female development. In addition, the expanding opportunities for women have led to a greater possibility of choice for women, whatever their inner motives are, to select and work with women therapists.

The Wish for a Male Therapist

Liebert (1986) notes that the current cultural milieu has not changed the devaluing and derogatory attitudes that some women have for other women, attitudes formed early in life at home and by the institutions of our culture, and, I would add, derived from penis envy. He notes that a woman may have the fantasy that she can avoid an anxiety-laden confrontation over the inner representation of her mother, her sisters, and herself by seeing a male therapist. Entering treatment with a man may thus seem safer to these women.

Liebert observes that while many prospective patients are drawn to the female–female therapeutic dyad, others seem to be too frightened at the prospect of the maternal transference with a woman. This could carry with it the rageful reproaches, contempt, and dread of retaliatory attitudes from the female therapist (mother in the transference). The initial presentation of these women to their male therapists may involve an attempt at collusion to quickly establish an erotic transference. This itself may be a defense against the expression of rage that would accompany the uncovering and working through of the frightening internal representations of the bad mother.

Liebert suggests that women who have had this kind of therapeutic experience often return for a second analysis as the achievements from the first begin to lose hold: "The unmodified inner representation of the mother continues to exact her toll" (p. 231). The patient labors on with her unconscious sense of herself as inadequate. Her anger is expressed in a low-grade, chronic depression. The following material is an illustration of this situation.

Mrs. C., a librarian married to a prominent lawyer, had had a first analysis with a male analyst that seemed successful. However, years later she began to be depressed and started to abuse alcohol and tranquilizers. An intense preoedipal rage at her mother emerged in the transference to me. There was abundant material that demonstrated that this rage had been avoided in her first analysis. Mrs. C. experienced such profound rage with me that she temporarily lost the "as if" quality of the transference. The intensity of her rage was terrifying to her. She sought consultation with a well-known male analyst, who, on hearing her vitriolic attack on me, recommended that she change therapists. My subsequent interpretation of her action as an attempt to discredit (destroy) me allowed her to deal with her rage within the treatment situation. We learned that she was not only trying to destroy me but also to protect me from her anger by seeking outside help. She was able to verbalize her fears and went on to terminate the treatment successfully.

It would seem that many patients have gender attitudes that, for complex reasons, lead them to choose male or female therapists. Many women choose women therapists and some prefer male therapists. I feel strongly that these wishes should be honored for all patients, whenever possible. Respect for these early attitudes toward the gender of the therapist can ease the opening phase of treatment. Patients intuitively sense their own most vulnerable issues. While these issues do eventually emerge in the transference in any competent treatment, the stage at which they become manifest is of enormous importance. The gender of the analyst may afford protection to the patient from powerful regressive feelings early in the treatment. For example, female child therapists working intensively with girls may get entangled in a particularly thorny transference–countertransference situation.

E. was 8 years old when she entered analysis for social isolation, general stubbornness, and difficulty sleeping. During the first year of treatment, typical oedipal fantasies emerged and were analyzed. However, early in the second year there was a prominent regression in which E. kicked, screamed, threw books, attempted to cut me with scissors, and was generally "impossible." This behavior continued unabated until E. left for summer camp. During this time, she was clearly much improved outside the analytic situation.

Many female child analysts have reported similar behavior in their work with their female patients. The female–female dyad seems to foster the rapid development of an intense sadomasochistic maternal transference. This behavior is seen much less often by our male colleagues. Little girls seem to behave better with their male therapists, even when they are dealing with these intense preoedipal maternal transferences. These girls have the real experience with their male therapists to balance the tempestuous feelings recreated in the early maternal transference. They tend not to lose the "as if" quality of the transference that preserves the alliance during these intense transference manifestations. Tyson (1980) felt that the presence of the positive oedipal situation made real by the gender of the analyst tempers the intensity of the preoedipal transference reaction. She further considered that in the female–female dyad, the therapist's own preoedipal development was stirred and added to the conceptual mix. In this situation, an appreciation of how gender affects the way the transference develops and how it is enacted is of considerable value. It should be noted that in the course of a thorough treatment, all gender attitudes should be subjected to investigation and interpretation.

GENDER BIAS FROM THE THERAPIST'S PERSPECTIVE

Do gender role differences affect how we, as male and female analysts, experience our work role? It would seem that they must. As Gilligan's (1982) work suggests, female development emphasizes empathic attachment to others, while male development leads to separation from modes of feeling and experience and focuses on objective values and aims. As Schachtel (1986) notes, for girls, the process of identity formation is based more on attachment and awareness of others' feelings than it is with boys. Boys separate from mother with a lessening of their sense of an empathic tie with her. They become more individuated in the process, their ego boundaries firmly established. In this sense, masculine identity is defined by separation and is threatened by intimacy, while female identity is threatened by separation. This leads us to expect that male and female therapists would have different gender attitudes with which to deal.

The therapeutic relationship is often experienced as a balance between an interaction with the father, described as the other, the outpost of reality, and the intimacy and dependency first experienced with the mother (Mahler, Pine, and Bergman 1975). Different associations to men and women may reflect the different roles that mothers and fathers play in the process of separation-individuation. Men and women as therapists negotiate this balance from different positions, as well as from different childhood experiences (Gronick 1986).

Therapists are asked to meet in an intimate situation with male and female patients and to be viewed as variously male/female objects of love, hate, and so on. This requires considerable resilience, as well as a sturdy sexual identity formation. Blum and Blum (1986) observed that "the capacity for analytic neutrality and analytic work depends on the analyst's awareness and integration of his or her own bisexuality, the resolution of positive and negative oedipal complex and the ability to use bisexuality for empathy (female or male) and comprehension of universal bisexual conflict in people" (p. 183).

Liebert (1986) suggests that analysis is not the same in the female patient–male analyst dyad as in the female–female dyad. For example, upon meeting her therapist a woman has the accurate perception of his gender and with that, a specific set of socialized as well as uniquely private psychological responses. There are constellations of organized fantasies, associated affect, and styles of behavior that are remarkably constant. They are recurrent in encounters with men who are of potential importance to her. "In the beginning of the treatment, a woman conveys to her male analyst that she regards and responds to him as a male. It is also true that the therapist has a similar set of responses, which include his typical response to the gender of the prospective patient. This would seem to be true for all therapeutic dyads" (p. 232).

Schachtel (1986) asserts that "for a woman to be in the analytic, therapeutic role, she must evoke for herself and for her patient all that is associated with the female gender role—preoedipal experience, the gender expectation of maternal or female caretaking, female sexuality, conception, and so on—with the result that the level of experience evoked may be more regressed. The female analyst is faced with a need to monitor a lifelong gender role, experience countertransferential issues in a more ongoing and pressured way than male analysts might. The female analyst may feel pressure to 'make it better' when that really is not the task. For example, a patient's anger and resistance in the face of nonnurturance may evoke in the female therapist feelings of being bad and of not understanding. This is certainly possible with male therapists too. For a woman therapist, abstinence in her role refers to withholding her almost innate drive to provide nurturance and to relieve pain, in gender-role fashion as opposed to analytic working through" (pp. 248–249).

Women therapists may need to deal with greater fears of regression in both male and female patients. The fear of regression may be further intensified for male patients because it threatens masculine identity. Women therapists commonly deal with their patients' primitive wishes for reunion with the preoedipal mother and fears of engulfment or abandonment by the mother. In the beginning of treatment, intense negative maternal transference may precede the development of a working alliance. Both therapist and patient may fear that the treatment will get out of control. The course of any given treatment may mirror developmental history with preoedipal material emerging first. However, this transference paradigm may be difficult to manage whenever it takes center stage.

Dr. D., a 32-year-old unmarried woman physician, had suffered at the hands of a psychotic mother. Particularly terrifying and life threatening had been an enema given when she had acute appendicitis. Her father had been kind and nurturing but involved with business and unable to protect her. In the first two years of the analysis, the patient made steady progress. When the intense preoedipal maternal transference began to emerge as a central issue, she abruptly interrupted the analysis. Several years later, I met her and was surprised to learn that she had married, had a child, and had advanced specialty training.

I believe that Dr. D.'s flight from the treatment was overdetermined. As with the previous case of E., she lost the "as if" quality of the transference in the female–female analytic dyad. She was unwilling or unable to reexperience the terrifying affects connected with the memories of her psychotic mother. However, her leaving also represented an attempt to preserve the image of me as the good and loving mother. She was able to sustain this image during the years that followed the abrupt ending of the treatment.

Mothering and nurturing aspects of doing psychotherapy may be among the central unconscious fantasies that inform the ambition to be a psychoanalyst. Achievement of secure male sexual identity involves a complicated process of disidentification from mother. Working with a maternal transference may encourage powerful preoedipal regression, which the male analyst may therefore resist experiencing. It may be more difficult for the male psychoanalyst to acknowledge comfortably that he is perceived and reacted to as if he were a woman. Renick (1990) has recently described how difficult it can be for a male analyst to experience himself as the female, homosexual (negative oedipal object) within the transference in work with female patients.

It has been suggested by Goldberg (1979) that the nonresponsive style of psychoanalytically oriented treatment is more consonant with the traditional male role. However, it is dissonant with patients' expectations concerning female therapists. Women are expected to be nurturing and emotionally expressive, and frustrated expectations on the part of patients may stir strong aggressive responses. Male therapists may be less conflicted as they deal with the management of fees and absences because they are less wary of negative transference reactions. They feel less pulled by the gender experience of giving and providing than do female therapists, though each gender may try to fight the pull.

Gornick (1986) asserts that

> In our culture it is still assumed that men will be in positions of authority over women. A woman therapist working with a male patient reverses the expected structure. All illness evokes feelings of humiliation, and both men and women experience shame at having to be in psychological treatment and at having to reveal to another person thoughts that are deemed unacceptable to the self. For the male patient, seeing a woman as a therapist can be doubly shaming, the shame of being a patient and of being in a subordinate position to a woman. [p. 269]

She also states that "the powerful man is perceived as sexually desirable, and being sexually desirable both reflects and enhances his sense of power. In contrast, for women the relationship between power and sexuality is more complicated. For women, sexuality is often equated with being the object of desire, that is, of someone else's agency. To be powerful means to reject a receptive position and refuse to be regarded as a sexual object" (p. 265).

It seems evident that when a women assumes a professional role she removes herself from the position of sexual object. At the same time, paradoxically, her patients are asked to reveal their innermost fantasies to her. This must include intense sexual feelings expressed in the transference where she is experienced as a sexual object.

Because power and sexuality have different meanings for women and men and because the erotic transference may serve a different function for male and female patients, we should expect significant differences between the experience of male and female therapists in working with sexual material. The recent literature suggests how difficult it has been for therapists to identify these cross-gender transferences in their patients. As noted above, it may be difficult for men to allow themselves to be experienced within the transference as female. Similarly, it may be difficult for women to acknowledge and work with negative oedipal, homosexual transferences in their male patients. The difficulty in recognizing ourselves as the "other sex" involves unconscious resistances that may blind us to these transferences. However it seems that once their existence is recognized, they do not present inordinate difficulties to the therapist (Goldberger 1990).

Until quite recently little was written about the erotic oedipal transferences of women therapists with male patients. Lester (1985) described her experience of mild, transient, muted, erotic oedipal transference with male patients. She observed that the working through of pregenital struggles with the vengeful, overpowering phallic mother is played out over dominance–submission or sadistic–masochistic issues. These overshadow erotic genital impulses toward the oedipal mother. Because the preoedipal material is worked through first, the oedipal material comes at a more advanced stage of the analysis and is therefore less potent. The passivity and receptive stance engendered by regression in the male patient will be dystonic to his active male sexual role.

Goldberger and Evans (1985) disagree with this formulation. They describe active erotic transference in several male patients. The implication in their work is that these transferences are common. It remains an intriguing question as to why they have not been identified more easily. In the past they have usually been described as experienced through displacement figures outside the treatment situation.

Gornick (1986) states that "Because of the deeply rooted meaning of sexuality in our culture as an expression of male dominance, the erotic transference of male patients to their female therapists can serve to turn the tables, functioning as a defense against feelings of humiliation evoked by the therapy situation. It can also defend against the threat to masculinity spurred by the regressive pull of the preoedipal transference" (p. 275).

Gornick acknowledges that Freud (1915) recognized the hostile wishes that can exist behind the erotic feelings—to put the analyst in an awkward position or to destroy the therapist's authority by bringing him/her down to the level of a lover. Wishes to defeat, undermine, and ridicule the would-be helper are common. Schafer (1983) suggested that the hostile transference is unavoidable, since attempting to understand the patient is in itself disorganizing and can easily be experienced as an attack on the analysand's stability. What does it mean for a man to have hostile feelings toward a woman? Where hostile feelings by a male patient toward a male therapist may revive castration anxiety and other fears of retaliation, the hostile transference of a male patient to his female therapist has its own dangers. Hating a maternal figure can raise fears of the destruction of the source of basic needs. There is the problem of violence. Irrespective of the realities of physical strength, it is assumed that a male patient could actually physically harm his female therapist.

A male patient may worry that he will lose control and hurt the female therapist. He may be concerned that even the verbal expression of his violent sexual thoughts might harm her. A female therapist may act as a stimulus for a male patient's hostile erotic feelings, in part as a defense against more regressive and threatening material. The fact that it is a woman to whom the male patient is talking may inhibit direct expression of these feelings. (Gornick 1986.)

CONCLUSION

Gender issues, therefore, can dramatically affect the transference–countertransference interplay. To be aware is to be armed to acknowledge the influence our gender has on all aspects of our therapeutic life. Our aim should not be to deny the importance of gender but to use our knowledge to deal better with patients and with these attitudes in ourselves.

REFERENCES

Blum, H. (1976a). Masochism, the ego ideal, and the psychology of women. *Journal of the American Psychoanalytic Association* 24:157–189.

_____ (1976b). Freud and female sexuality: the consideration of some blind spots in the exploration of the dark continent. *International Journal of Psycho-Analysis* 57:275–287.

_____ (1986). On transference love in the male. In *Between Analyst and Patient*, ed. H. Meyers, pp. 177–192. Hillsdale, NJ: Analytic Press.

Blum, H. P., and Blum, E. J. (1986). Reflections of transference and countertransference in the treatment of women. In *Between Analyst and Patient*, ed. H. Meyers, pp. 177–192. Hillsdale, NJ: Analytic Press.

Chasseguet-Smirgel, J. (1976). Freud and female sexuality. *International Journal of Psycho-Analysis* 57:275–287.

Freud, S. (1915). Observations on transference love. *Standard Edition* 12:157–171.

_____ (1933). Femininity. *Standard Edition* 22:112–133.

Gilligan, C. (1982). *In a Different Voice*. Cambridge, MA: Harvard University Press.

_____ (1991). *Joining the resistance: psychology, politics, girls and women*. Paper presented at Hunter Conference, Hunter College, NY, November.

Goldberg, J. (1979). Aggression and the female therapist. *Modern Psychoanalysis* 4:209–222.

Goldberger, M. (1990). Workshop on the influence of the analyst's gender on transference. American Psychoanalytic Association meeting, December.

Goldberger, M., and Evans, D. (1985). On transference manifestations in male patients with female analysts. *International Journal of Psycho-Analysis* 66:295–309.

Gornick, L. K. (1986). Developing a new narrative: the woman therapist and the male patient. In *Psychoanalysis and Women, Contemporary Reappraisals,* ed. J. L. Alpert, pp. 257–283. Hillsdale, NJ: Analytic Press.

Goz, R. (1973). Women patients and women therapists: some issues that come up in psychotherapy. *International Journal of Psychoanalytic Psychotherapy* 2:298–319.

Greenson, R. (1968). Dis-identifying with the mother: its special importance for the boy. *International Journal of Psycho-Analysis* 49:370–374.

Grossman, W. I., and Stewart, W. A. (1976). Penis envy: from childhood wish to developmental metaphor. *Journal of the American Psychoanalytic Association* 24:193–212.

Lester, E. (1985). The female analyst and the erotized transference. *International Journal of Psycho-Analysis* 66:283–293.

Liebert, R. S. (1986). Transference and countertransference issues in treatment of women by a male analyst. In *Between Analyst and Patient,* ed. H. Meyers, pp. 229–236. Hillsdale, NJ: Analytic Press.

Mahler, M., Pine, F., and Bergman, A. (1975). *The Psychological Birth of the Human Infant.* New York: Basic Books.

Meyers, H. (1986). Analytic work by and with women: the complexity and the challenge. *Between Analyst and Patient,* ed. H. Meyers, pp. 159–176. Hillsdale, NJ: Analytic Press.

Mogul, K. M. (1982). Overview: the sex of the therapist. *American Journal of Psychiatry* 139:1–11.

Person, E. (1986). Women in therapy: therapist gender as a variable. In *Between Analyst and Patient,* ed. Helen Meyers, pp. 193–212. Hillsdale, NJ: Analytic Press.

Renik, O. (1990). Analysis of a woman's homosexual strivings by a male analyst. *Psychoanalytic Quarterly* 59:41–53.

Schachtel, Z. (1986). The impossible profession considered from a gender perspective. In *Psychoanalysis and Women,* ed. J. Alpert, pp. 237–255. Hillsdale, NJ: Analytic Press.

Schafer, R. (1983). *The Analytic Attitude.* New York: Basic Books.

Stoller, R. (1975). *Perversion.* New York: Pantheon.

——— (1976). Primary femininity. *Journal of the American Psychoanalytic Association* 24:59–77.

Tyson, P. (1980). The gender of the analyst: in relation to transference and countertransference manifestations in prelatency children. *Psychoanalytic Study of the Child* 35:321–338. New Haven, CT: Yale University Press.

Zetzel, E. R. (1966). The doctor–patient relationship in psychiatry. In *The Capacity for Emotional Growth,* pp. 139–155. New York: International Universities Press.

12

Phobic Patients

Sander M. Abend, M.D.

The treatment of phobias by psychoanalysis, or by psychodynamic psychotherapies derived from psychoanalysis, rests on the assumption that all phobias are defensively altered representations of underlying unconscious conflicts. The essence of the treatment consists in the uncovering and working through of these unconscious determinants; if successfully accomplished, this can alleviate their surface manifestations, the phobic symptoms themselves.

Thus, just as the analytic therapies regard the contents of dreams reported in a session as a perfect point of departure for analytic investigation, the surface texts of phobic concerns are similarly understood as the starting points for exploration of unconscious concerns and the fantasies that express them. Often, to begin with at least, the suffering patient may have no awareness of the existence of these underlying conflicts, much less of their relationship to the phobic symptoms to which they have given rise. The resolution of these unconscious stresses will often result in the disappearance of the phobia to which they are related.

FREUD'S EARLY VIEWS: THE CASE OF "LITTLE HANS"

Perhaps the best-known case of phobia ever reported in the psychoanalytic literature was that of "Little Hans," a 5-year-old boy who developed a paralyzing fear of horses. The monograph in which the unraveling of his phobias is described, entitled *Analysis of a Phobia in a Five-Year-Old Boy* (1909), is one of five famous lengthy clinical reports published by Sigmund Freud. Psychoanalytic theory and practice have evolved since the case of Little Hans first

appeared in print, hence some of Freud's observations and explanations have been superseded by later findings and modifications.
For our present purposes two points are worthy of note: (1) Freud
classified phobias as closely related to what he called at the time
anxiety hysteria, noting that the little boy's phobia only began some
time after a more generalized anxiety state had made its appearance.
(2) The "phobia" was not a single consistent fear of horses, but
instead turned out to be a set of different, rather specific, ideas, all
involving horses, that frightened the little boy. These included (a)
that a horse would bite him, (b) that only a big white horse was
likely to bite him, (c) that a horse would fall down dead in the street,
(d) that a horse would enter his room at night, and (e) that horses
were to be feared only if they were pulling heavily laden carts or
wagons. These individual variations, or refinements, of the patient's
fears gradually came to light as the treatment progressed.

Freud did not conduct Little Hans's treatment himself. The boy
was "analyzed," after a fashion, by his own father, with some help
from Freud, at a time when no organized technique for psychoanalysis or psychotherapy of children had yet been developed, and
when even the treatment of adults by psychoanalysis was at a very
early stage of development. Even so, the material of the case led
Freud to state with some confidence that many layers of unconscious meaning were all *condensed,* thus contributing in conjunction
to the form of the phobic symptoms, and that in phobias the fearful
situation was *projected* outside the individual's mind and onto an
aspect of the environment that could then be avoided, thus enabling
the patient to substitute a degree of constriction of life for what
might otherwise be an intolerable and unavoidable subjective state
of psychic discomfort. Although he did not use the precise term
displacement at that time to explain the formation of the phobic
symptoms, it is clear from his clinical descriptions that the horses,
wagons, and so forth all stood for other persons or objects associated with them only by unconscious connections.

Freud's explanatory formulations in the Little Hans case stressed
childhood sexual wishes and the conflicts stemming from them. His
main purpose in writing up and publishing the case, however, was
to lend support to his thesis about the potential pathogenic significance of infantile sexual concerns and theories. One can find, in the
detailed clinical descriptions, hints of what analytic theory would
only much later incorporate more explicitly: the role played by
aggressive wishes and conflicts in phobia formation. One may also
detect, in the explication of the case material, evidence of the

contribution of preoedipal constellations and issues, of unconscious need for punishment, and of the secondary gains obtainable by manipulation of persons in the patient's environment.

It is also important to keep in mind that Freud's first theory of anxiety held sway when this report was written. At that time, anxiety was believed to be the end product of some quasi-biological alteration in the libido, conceived of rather concretely as if it were a physical substance. The transformation of libido into anxiety was somehow caused by the repression of the forbidden sexual wishes that were thought to be energized by this mysterious libido. Since anxiety was thought to be produced by repression, treatment was aimed at restoring health through the lifting of the repressions, which was gradually to be achieved by the psychoanalytic work.

CURRENT VIEWS OF DYNAMIC CONSIDERATIONS

Although theories and schools of psychoanalytic thought have multiplied since Freud's day, any statement of the current psychoanalytic understanding of the treatment of phobias would certainly include the principle that the symptom itself is overdetermined — that is to say, that a number of levels of meaning are likely to be found in the course of its successful unraveling. Accordingly, no matter what general description of a phobia is obtained at the outset of treatment from a patient, analytic therapists expect that it will be revised in the course of treatment into several, perhaps even many, more specific subtexts, each of which will be related to some aspect or aspects of the unconscious significance of the symptom.

The assumption that phobic symptoms all do have unconscious underpinnings still characterizes the psychoanalytic theory of phobias. In pursuit of the sources of specific phobias analytic therapists are likely to seek associative evidence indicating the nature of their linkage to the unconscious wishes, fears, and fantasies they have come to represent, rather than to pursue a cognitive elaboration of the reality situation that obtained when the symptoms first appeared. It would be anticipated, as a matter of course, that sexual and aggressive wishes and their associated conflicts, stemming from all developmental levels, invariably including certain manifestations of guilt such as restitution or punishment, will combine to contribute to the establishment and maintenance of any phobia.

It is often stated that separation anxiety is likely to play an important role in phobia. It should be realized that *separation anxiety* does not refer merely to the real or imagined loss of an attachment. It is instead a kind of shorthand term for anxiety associated with a whole variety of real or fantasied losses. The complexity of unconscious mental activity is such that any perceived or dreaded loss may represent symbolically any or all the varieties of childhood danger situations and is not to be understood invariably to refer to loss of the mother or other primary caretaker.

As is well known, the therapeutic emphasis on discovering the unconscious meanings behind the surface phobic symptoms leads to a specific technical posture on the part of the analytic therapist. Efforts are directed toward uncovering the unconscious conflicts that give rise to the phobic concerns, rather than focusing primarily on the manifest descriptions and consequences of the phobias themselves or on efforts at reassuring, educating, or otherwise encouraging patients to combat or overcome their problems. It is no longer even considered appropriate analytic technique to urge patients to enter the avoided phobic situations, although that was at one time accepted practice, even among psychoanalysts of the most traditional stripe. The change in technique reflects strongly the accumulated and more accurate understanding arrived at in the recent period of psychoanalytic theory, which holds that the patients' defenses, manifested in treatment as resistance to progress, cannot merely be swept aside or overpowered. Resistance, too, like the forbidden wishes for sexual or aggressive gratification, and like the multiple influences of the patient's internalized moral system, must all receive equal and careful attention from the therapist in order to determine their respective roles in the symptoms and other aspects of the patient's psychological functioning.

In summary then, psychoanalytic therapists regard symptoms as providing a variety of manifest texts that one must attempt to understand and interpret. Treatment consists of as thorough an uncovering of their unconscious significance as is possible to achieve. The hidden significance will in all cases turn out to be complex; many levels of conflict, elaborated into unconscious fantasies, are likely to be incorporated into the formulation of phobic symptoms.

Perhaps the clearest and most comprehensive way to understand matters is to think of the phobias as compromise formations. This means the symptoms are the psychological result of the interplay among (1) certain sexual and aggressive wishes of childhood mental life; (2) the anxiety to which these give rise; (3) various expressions of superego reaction to these forbidden wishes, in the forms of punishment, undoing, restitution, and placation of the internalized moral authority; and (4) a panoply of defenses that may be mobilized against either the forbidden wishes, the anxiety, the superego influences, or some combination of all these forces in concert.

Among the ego mechanisms that are used defensively, those most commonly associated with the formation of phobic symptoms are condensation, displacement, and projection, but many other aspects of psychological functioning can also serve defensive ends.

The tracing out of these unconscious elements and their interrelationships is likely to take many months, even years, and if the effort is successful, the potential benefits of the treatment usually go far beyond the relief of the specific phobia or other symptoms. Patients today generally recognize both the longer time frame and the broader goals of psychoanalysis and psychoanalytic psychotherapy, so it would be unusual for a patient to seek such treatment or accept a recommendation for it, solely for the relief of even the most troublesome phobia. These days, the analytic understanding of phobic symptoms most often comes about during the course of a treatment that was initially undertaken for other reasons, or at least for reasons in addition to the phobic complaints themselves. Conversely, patients who are solely interested in the relief of a specific phobia, and who have no apparent awareness of other coexistent problems, as a rule do not seek psychoanalytically oriented treatment.

Only therapists with a thorough grounding in psychoanalytic conceptualization and techniques are likely to utilize this therapeutic approach to the treatment of patients' phobias. Such therapists and their patients will be prepared for the possibility that, even in successful therapies, improvement may come very slowly and gradually. This is not invariable, however, and in some cases improvement may be quite rapid. It is impossible to predict the rate and degree of change in a given symptom at the outset of analytic treatment, especially since the unconscious determinants of the problems often cannot be guessed at, nor can the patient's genuine motivation for change be accurately assayed from what he or she says to the therapist at the beginning of therapy.

CASE REPORT: A PHOBIC WOMAN IN PSYCHOTHERAPY

The following brief clinical vignette will serve to illustrate some of the points mentioned.

A divorced woman in her early thirties, a successful junior executive in a multinational corporate enterprise, sought treatment because a flying phobia threatened to limit her career advancement. She revealed to the consultant who evaluated her that she had also had a bout of severe anxiety associated with flying some years earlier; this had subsided in the course of a limited psychotherapy that was a mixture of support and exploration. The symptoms had returned about a year ago, but this time a brief course of treatment similar to her earlier, successful, limited-goal therapy did not bring relief. If anything, the anxiety associated with flying seemed to be worsening. The patient added that she had an ongoing relationship with a man she valued highly; she wanted some help to try to assure that problems of hers that she thought had contributed to her previous marital failure did not spoil her present prospects for happiness. Both the patient and the consultant thought that a more intensive psychoanalytically oriented therapy was indicated at this time.

Despite many difficulties in immersing herself freely in the treatment, the patient's persistent and conscientious work gradually permitted a progressive unfolding of the many levels of meaning of her phobia about flying, accompanied by relief to the point of full recovery. (Certain other dimensions of her treatment were also successful but will not be described in the context of this illustration.)

The first level of understanding to emerge was that the patient used her anxiety before and during flights as a way of tormenting and punishing herself unmercifully. This punishment came to be seen as related to her career ambitions, which she imagined would necessarily involve intense and deadly competition, especially with men. As this configuration became clearer, the patient became able to report a more precise description of her anxiety about flying. She was terrified that in the course of a flight her discomfort would grow so intense that she would lose control of herself and become hysterical. Such an outburst would be intensely humiliating to her, especially if it were to occur in the company of a male co-worker. Eventually, she was able to elaborate her view that such a hysterical loss of control as she imagined and dreaded would characterize her as a weak, contemptible female, destroying the image of the competent, firm, rational, and composed person (qualities she attributed to men) that she wished to present to the world. This disgrace would be a fit punishment for her ruthlessly defeating the males she competed with, which she imagined humiliated them terribly. In time it also became clear how these conflicts resonated with issues in her childhood relationship to her father, a successful businessman.

After this was worked out, she was able to recall that the current outbreak of flying phobia had commenced after a particular flight during which a male co-worker accompanying her party had regaled them with "war stories," consisting of harrowing tales of his heroism while in military service as a flyer. She had responded to his boasting with a mixture of inner fury, envy, and the conviction that she would not have been able to stand such experiences.

By this time in the therapy she was able to fly without experiencing much, if any, anxiety, but she still had considerable anticipatory dread. She noted the dread was much worse before flights home than it was when going elsewhere on business or vacation. This observation ushered in an elaboration of a new level of meaning of her phobic anxiety. She now had thoughts of panic and loss of control as a consequence of being confined within the plane with no way to get out, even if she became upset. Claustrophobic feelings led to a fuller exploration of her ambivalent relationship with her mother and to rivalrous feelings toward siblings of both sexes. In one session she described a fantasy that the airplane she was in might break apart, spilling her to her death. This led to associations about pregnancy, delivery, and abortion.

These subjects were also on her mind as she was considering alternatives to her business career, since she and her boyfriend were contemplating marriage. In the course of exploring these issues she revealed she had long held a conviction that her mother had come to wish she had aborted the patient, who had been a troublesome and difficult child. This idea about her mother, which was never confirmed, was expressed symbolically in the patient's fear that the plane would open up, dropping her to her death. With this reconstruction, the flying phobia improved still more.

One last level remained to be clarified. It came up in the course of the patient's description of her preflight ritual. Whenever she noted stirrings of anxiety, she thought of the therapist and usually experienced immediate relief. When she was asked why she thought she needed to evoke his image, since she had obviously done much of the work of overcoming her problem herself, she became flustered and angry. She revealed that she believed she would always need treatment, and she berated her therapist for seeming to take away her comfort and undermining her peace of mind. It took some further time to clarify that she liked the idea of not being alone, especially when she felt possible danger to be present. This meant to her that the therapist had assumed the role of the wished-for benevolent and protective mother, in place of her real mother, with whom she had so unsatisfactory a relationship. When the therapist questioned her need for this fantasy relationship, the patient experienced this questioning as tantamount to rejecting her. The thought of ever ending treatment also carried that connotation. After a mild and brief regression, however, her phobic symptoms again disappeared as work toward termination proceeded.

CONCLUSION

The foregoing case demonstrates a number of features described in the introductory material. Several different specific versions of fear were incorporated in this woman's flying phobia. Various conflicts contributed to it, and these could only gradually be teased out of the material as treatment progressed. The transference dimension of her phobic structure came to light at the last, but it was clearly essential to be included in the treatment, or else the potential for another serious relapse in the future, after termination, would obviously have been much greater.

It should be added that this patient at all times considered her phobia to be irrational, and she clearly remembered her earlier success in overcoming it. Only in retrospect could she see that her lack of confidence in being able to maintain mastery over her symptoms on her own was itself a symptom, having a specific unconscious meaning, and one that had to be worked through in its turn. Only then could she begin to see the future more optimistically, with some sense that she now possessed the capability for mastering her phobia herself.

13

Hysterical Patients and the Obsessive-Compulsive Personality

David W. Allen, M.D.

The initial phase of treatment in an average treatable case of hysterical personality is often one that is an urgent appeal for attention. This phase is followed quickly, once a therapeutic attachment is established, by a period of regression in which unresolved conflicts and childhood fixations of the patient are manifested within the therapeutic relationship itself. Ideally, this second phase overlaps with a period of working through, the therapeutic antidote to the multiply determined nature of the patient's state at onset of treatment. Finally, termination of treatment encompasses the difficult task of separation, itself a phase of important work on self development for the hysterical personality.

This chapter focuses on major themes during these phases, especially on initial problems. Hysterical symptoms are not synonymous with hysterical personality. Nonetheless, persons who do fall within this typology often present for treatment with a conversion or dissociative symptom, and so treatment of such complaints will be included.

The techniques of psychotherapy cover such a wide gamut that any discussion must be circumscribed by boundaries. The approach here is that of brief or extended treatment guided by psychoanalytic theory, using the basic ground rules of psychodynamic psycho-

This chapter was prepared originally with the assistance of Sarah Peelle and the editorial help of JoAnn diLorenzo.

therapy (Abse 1974). The main patient type under consideration is the hysterical or histrionic personality who has developed a separated, although conflicted, self-representation and who has advanced, in capacity for relationship, to at least the beginning of genital aims and conflict configurations. For the more severely impaired hysterical personality, who has not advanced developmentally from pregenital levels of character formation, the addition of techniques for treatment of narcissistic and borderline character disorders would be appropriate (Giovacchini 1975, Kernberg 1970, 1974, Kohut 1971).

MOST COMMON TREATMENT THEMES

Running through the chronicle of hysteria treatment are several colorful themes. One is that the nature of symptom onset, and even the cure, may be quite dramatic. The course is often variable and associated with difficulties in differential diagnosis. Another important theme, although often expressed only vaguely or intuitively, is that sexual and aggressive impulses were repressed and yet returned in a distorted expression through somatic or behavioral symptoms. Finally, there is the theme of the conflicting emotions aroused by hysterics in those who treat them. These themes are illustrated in the following case example.

Case History of an Athetoid Teenager

A young psychiatric resident was called in consultation to see a pretty 16-year-old farm girl who had been referred to the university hospital with the diagnosis of a possible rheumatic fever athetosis. About two weeks prior to admission, she had developed a rhythmic, slow, writhing movement of her right shoulder that continued in spasms almost unabated day and night. Since the onset the patient had hardly slept and had had very little to eat or drink. When the resident first saw her, she was lying in bed, and every few seconds her right shoulder made a twitching shrug. In spite of this symptom and the fact that she looked rather dehydrated and pale, her demeanor was bland and calm. The history was of a sudden onset without apparent cause. There was no history of fever or cardiac symptoms other than somewhat elevated pulse rate, and no history of joint pain.

The past medical history was not remarkable and neither was the initial family history, except for the fact that her family belonged to a strict fundamentalist Protestant sect. Mental status examination indicated no loss of contact with reality or other evidence of psychosis. Except for the symptom as described, neither her physical examination and a careful neurologic examination nor routine lab work and a sedimentation rate test revealed any abnormalities. The resident, proud of his neurologic and medical acumen, was troubled that, despite repeated questioning, the patient, although apparently cooperative, was totally unable to recall any possible traumatic emotional situation connected with the onset.

The resident presented the case to his superior, a psychoanalyst, who insisted that in addition to the motor symptoms without evidence of physical lesion, and despite the patient's calm mental attitude, the resident should be able to demonstrate other positive psychological findings before diagnosing a conversion reaction. The psychoanalyst also said that there should be a stress of onset, with efforts to ward off some unacceptable impulse and a fantasy that had partially escaped repression and returned to the consciousness in the form of the symptom. The psychoanalyst insisted that the writhing and twitching of the patient's shoulder in some way symbolized the conflict, and that the patient's inability to relate the symptom to any emotional stress was evidence of the resistance in her own mind — the manifestation of a defense against anxiety.

When plagued by the resident for more tangible help, the analyst said that undoubtedly through hypnosis or Amytal interviews not only could the patient's symptom be relieved temporarily but relevant history obtained. However, he suggested that it would be more therapeutic to enlist the patient's conscious cooperation in recovering the memory and fantasy, and that this could be done from available clues. Her shrugging might represent, for example, he said, a warding off of a wished-for and feared incestuous impulse such as a caress from her father. She might have been sleeping in the same bed with him with her shoulder up, imagining his hand on her shoulder.

The resident thought his consultant's hypothesis almost bizarre. But he returned to the patient and asked her to describe the sleeping arrangements in her home. Without hesitation she said that her grandparents had come to visit shortly before the onset of her symptoms and that she had had to move into the bedroom with her parents. Further questioning quickly elicited the fact that she had slept next to her father, facing the wall, on her left side, with her right shoulder up. During the night she had had to crawl over her father to get out of bed in order to visit the outhouse. And it was upon her return to bed, just as she was starting to fall asleep, that the uncontrollable twitching of her right shoulder had begun.

I shall not go into further detail on this case except to say that I was the resident, not the psychoanalyst. And the very day the patient talked about being in bed with her parents and next to her father, her shoulder twitching began to diminish, and in another day or two she was completely free of it.

INITIAL PHASE

Approaching the Presenting Symptoms

The hysterical symptom should not be assaulted by direct interpretation. One of Freud's (1913) early cases is instructive on this point.

> In one particular case the mother of a hysterical girl had confided to me the homosexual experience which had greatly contributed to the fixation of the girl's attacks. The mother had herself surprised the scene; but the patient had completely forgotten it though it had occurred when she was already approaching puberty. [p. 141]

Freud learned then that "every time I repeated her mother's story to the girl she reacted with a hysterical attack, and after this she forgot the story once more" (p. 141). Clearly, the patient's resistance stiffened against knowledge being forced upon her. The patient finally simulated feeblemindedness and developed a complete loss of memory in order to protect herself against the conscious knowledge of the incident (pp. 141–142).

While perhaps extreme in demonstrating the forcefulness of resistances, this case of Freud's is certainly not atypical of the ineffectiveness of an attempted direct attack on a firmly placed symptom, especially when the symptom has a strong function in the patient's psychic economy. Any attempt to remove a patient's hysterical symptom by direct reasoning tends to produce a negative result. It is just as futile to attempt to rid the hysteric of a symptom by explaining the functional nature of the reaction as it is to attempt to reason away the paranoid's delusions. To approach treatment along the expected lines of layman logic only strengthens the patient's symptoms and intensifies the patient's negative feelings toward therapy and the therapist. The patient's defensive system is a reaction to inner anxiety, and anxiety is heightened and defenses further excited by threats of external attack. Resistances are stiffened even if the patient is able to agree with the therapist's evidence and reasoning. The patient's symptom is impregnable from the front, as it were, and only a well-prepared and well-timed flank attack or encirclement will relieve it.

The usefulness and effectiveness of the oblique approach is more apparent in long-term therapy, but to a degree it applies in even the briefest psychotherapy, as the following case illustrates. In even an hour's time, information was collected and rapport developed; interpretation did not directly assault the symptom but dealt with it gently through the roots of the underlying dilemma. This is not to say that there need be any concealment of the therapist's intent to try to understand the patient, nor concealment of the therapist's wish to have the patient's active cooperation in the process—quite the contrary. Nor is it to say that the therapist may not ask appropriate questions, request clarifications, or juxtapose meaningful information.

Case History of a Premedical Student

A premedical student appeared in the emergency room with a history of acute onset of feelings of a mass in his throat, sensations of gagging, and uncontrolled vomiting for forty-eight hours. He was given parenteral thorazine, and the retching stopped, but he continued to complain of the feeling of the mass in his throat, and he experienced distressing gagging sensations.

In consultation I discovered that the onset of symptoms began a few hours after he had been to the dental clinic, where a male friend of his, a few years older, had done the dental work on him, his hands and instruments in the patient's mouth. A brief review of the patient's background revealed that since childhood he had been highly industrious, helping a competent mother run a family business. The father was affectionate but passive and ineffectual. The patient felt that he himself carried the family aspirations. I asked the patient to describe the mass in his throat. He said that it was a greasy mass and indicated with his hand that its dimensions were about 6 inches long and 1 ½ inches in diameter. My tentative formulation to myself was that the young man defended against passive tendencies and oral-dependent longings by his characteristic independence and industriousness. Further, I felt that the patient had probably had difficulty in attaining a comfortable masculine identification. In childhood he might have wished for a closer relationship with a strong and capable father. All of these factors probably conspired to produce a latent homosexual conflict that became acute at the time of his oral-physical contact with his friend the dentist.

What should the psychiatrist's intervention be? Should he reassure the patient? Prescribe more thorazine? Tell him that he needs

long-term psychiatric treatment? Offer him a genetic-dynamic formulation of his case? Or interpret the phallic symbolism of the mass
in his throat by suddenly thrusting a large hot dog in his face, as
Lionel Blitzsten is once alleged to have done with a woman opera
singer with aphonia? Blitzsten caused the singer to scream and
thereby relieved her loss of voice (Orr 1961, p. 46). She developed
this hysterical symptom shortly after her first experience with
fellatio, and Blitzsten's rather dramatic action interpretation was an
attempt to relieve her acute aphonia a few hours before she was
scheduled to sing an important role. Blitzsten's dramatic action
interpretation had the advantage of surprise in connection with an
acute symptom in which the symbolic meaning seemed almost
flagrantly preconscious and easily relatable to the recent memory of
fellatio. While Blitzsten's action interpretation might seem to run
counter to the rule that a hysterical symptom should not be frontally
assaulted, it should be remembered that this symptom was a fresh
one that had not become fixed or chronic. But it was a gimmicky
treatment, and while it may have a place in the technique of certain
peculiarly gifted therapists such as Blitzsten presumably was, it was
risky and is generally to be avoided.

The problem with the premedical student was to do neither too
little nor too much within the context of the rapport the psychiatrist
had built up in the hour of the interview. I said to the patient, "It
sounds as if you've always been a pretty independent guy, and it's
difficult for you to accept help even from a friend and colleague." In
my opinion, this statement touched on the essential issues, and at
any rate it was acceptable to the patient, who smiled and agreed
and, in a short while, announced that the lump in his throat was
beginning to go away. If at some subsequent time he required
further psychotherapy, he had at least had a helpful, nonthreatening introduction to it.

Since direct assault on symptoms is often contraindicated, it
follows that one must work on underlying causes. In such an
approach, the relationship established between patient and therapist becomes a key concern for alteration of the pathological
situation. For in the transference phenomena that usually emerge,
the core problems that underlie symptom formation and characteristic maladaptations can be gradually explored.

Transference

Hysterical patients make contact immediately, and it is a reparative
contact they seek. Their anxiety and acting out against deeper

involvements derive from fears and fixations going back to earliest object relations. The narcissism of the hysterical personality bespeaks an impairment in the earliest experiences of loving and being loved and in the conditioned expectations arising out of these body experiences with self and others. These early impairments interfere with normal gender-identity development and result in compensatory, intensified pseudosexuality.

For the beginning therapist, hysterical patients give the clearest and most accessible evidence of transference. The dynamics are less obscure than in most other kinds of patients. The crux of the treatment of the hysterical personality *is* the transference. If we give wrong interpretations, we can correct them in the light of later information. If we miss opportunities to interpret, they will occur again and again. But if we mishandle the transference, the treatment is in trouble. *Mishandling the transference or failing to establish a therapeutic alliance is almost the only vital mistake,* and it is exceedingly difficult to repair. The history of handling the transference is virtually the history of the evolvement of the treatment of hysteria, which became systematically understandable only with the advent of psychoanalysis.

Transference was a stumbling block for Freud's colleague Breuer and a stepping-stone for Freud (Jones 1953). When Breuer treated Anna O., she had developed a museum of symptoms—paralyses, contractures, anesthesias—after much physical contact in nursing her dying father. A highly intelligent and attractive young woman, she first pointed out the value of cathartic talking, but she became very attached to Breuer, and his consuming interest in her began to make Mrs. Breuer jealous. When the patient developed a phantom pregnancy, Breuer was profoundly shocked, but managed to calm her and then fled in a cold sweat. The patient's accusation that he was the father of the child was too much for Breuer. He broke off treatment and left the next morning with his wife for Venice. Ten years later, when he called on Freud in consultation on a case of hysteria, and Freud pointed out evidence of a developing pregnancy fantasy by the patient, Breuer, without saying a word, picked up his hat and cane and left the house.

In reviewing the history of the treatment of hysteria, certain principles—approaching the symptom through its underlying causes and attending to the proper management of the transference—become clear. An adequate theoretical basis for consistent, understandable, repeatable, and teachable application of the therapeutic principles became possible with Freud. Prior to that, treatment results were more a matter of chance and the personality of the therapist.

Countertransference

Now, with nearly a century of psychoanalytic treatment of hysteria behind us, we have little excuse for not knowing the principles of treating hysteria and for not knowing the limitations of the method. Practical experiences of many analysts and therapists are available to supplement the personal practical experience of the individual therapist.

In the treatment of hysterical personality, the therapist should not avoid the eroticized transference. He or she should allow it to develop, and in time, like the hostile transference, the therapist should analyze it. But the therapist must guard against possible eroticized and hostile countertransferences.

Beginning Treatment and the Emergence of the Transference

The general principles of psychotherapy apply in the treatment of the patient with a hysterical personality, but clinical experience teaches us that there are a number of rather predictable kinds of therapeutic difficulty and opportunity that are likely to be encountered in various phases of treatment. It is important during the initial phase that the therapist not act in ways that will make the resolution of the later phases of treatment more difficult or impossible. Freud's (1912) advice on this is still most pertinent:

> Young and eager psycho-analysts will no doubt be tempted to bring their own individuality freely into the discussion, in order to carry the patient along with them and lift him over the barriers of his own narrow personality. . . . The doctor should be opaque to his patients and, like a mirror, should show them nothing but what is shown to him. [pp. 117–118]

This advice has too often been misinterpreted to mean coldness and passivity. Its meaning is more simple and direct: it is not useful in overcoming patient resistance to give glimpses of one's own problems or intimate information about one's life, for it is the patient with a hysterical personality who is most likely to demand and provoke a therapist to reveal her or his own problems. The patient may feel alone in exposing her or his thoughts in treatment, find it unfair, and feel that trust in the intimacy calls for similar revelations by the therapist. This feeling of unfairness is further evidence of the working of the unconscious resistances to understanding by the patient and of anxiety about regression into conflictual areas of childhood thought and feeling. The patient feels vulnerable, but exactly to what the patient does not know.

If the therapist adopts a familiar attitude with the patient, it may induce earlier revelations of certain consciously suppressed information, but the initial gain is lost later a thousandfold in the impediments the familiarity places in the way of the development of a clearly delineated transference that can be seen and felt by the therapist and interpreted and made conscious to the patient. If the therapist is to find the role the patient tends to project on to the therapist and use it to clarify the patient's reaction, then the therapist must not interfere with the process of the patient's attributions by bringing the therapist's own life into the patient's treatment.

The therapist stands at the interface of the patient's unconscious fantasy world and the real world. The therapist needs to be able to demonstrate that what the patient attaches to the therapist is the last part of a long thread winding back through the patient's life to childhood.

Sometimes, out of anxiety about self-revelation, the patient seeks to reverse the roles of patient and therapist. The patient wants to know all about the therapist's thoughts and life as a prerequisite to revealing herself or himself, or because the patient thinks the therapist more interesting, or because the patient thinks of the therapist as a model to pattern after. Often, indeed, such patients feel they had a defective parent model in childhood. That attitude, then, is already a forcible manifestation of the transference as the patient seeks to reexperience and remake her or his childhood and past. The patient is already searching for the defects in the therapist, which *the patient knows* must be there as the patient seeks to recreate the relationship with the parent imago.

In analysis and in extensive uncovering psychoanalytic psychotherapy, an attitude by the therapist that is too intimate and self-revealing is incorrect technique. In psychotherapy, however, the therapist has more leeway for self-revelation when the goal is for limited and immediate symptom relief, and the therapist does not contemplate more extensive working through of character defenses and cognitive style. More than ever in such instances, the therapist must know what he or she is doing and what is being sacrificed for an immediate gain.

The Therapeutic Alliance

Establishing a relationship with the patient, collecting information about the patient, organizing the information, and using it to communicate what may be useful to the patient are appropriate tasks for the therapist. The establishment of the therapeutic role within the relationship is a matter of utmost priority. The therapist asks herself or himself—and in various ways the therapist asks the patient—what's wrong, why now, and how did it come about? The therapist attempts to understand those critical areas of human life having to do with stress reactions and character development: the patient's object relations, past and present; the patient's relationship to the patient's body and self-image and identity; and the patient's concepts and values and how they are experienced.

As clinical data begins to accumulate, answers will reveal that the hysterical (histrionic) personality has strong narcissistic needs and seeks constant reassurance of worth, admiration, and love. And the hysteric is exquisitely sensitive to even the faintest sign of rejection. In part, the hysterical personality seems to need constant narcissistic gratification in order to maintain ego integrity and to reduce the anxiety constantly generated by a gender-identity confusion underlying the compensatory pseudosexuality.

Lacking constant narcissistic supplies and a sense of connectedness with the therapist, hysterics or patients with hysterical personality experience anxiety, frustration, and anger. They become demanding, ashamed, and guilty. In turn, confidence in their own integrity and worth diminishes. They then seek reassurance that by destructive impulses and global rage they have not harmed the therapist as a potential supplier for their narcissistic needs. Patients may then increase demands for favors and special recognition. They require extra time at the end of the session or on the telephone, or they may ask for prescriptions for sedatives or tranquilizers.

Reacting sexually or aggressively in an attempt to define gender identity, hysterics try to force the therapist to have more "real" contact with them. They thereby hope to gratify and counteract unconscious fantasies of omnipotence and helplessness. These inward dilemmas of omnipotence and helplessness and longings for merging and separateness manifest themselves in the relationship with the therapist, often in the form of demanding total gratification or nothing. It is as if the patient is saying, "Either you give me everything or I break off treatment; and if you give me everything it will destroy us." And now there is a dilemma and an opportunity for the therapist. In fact, the therapist knows the dilemma is coming and waits for it to develop so that the therapist can make an emotionally meaningful interpretation.

If therapists attempt to gratify patients' demands, the demands become endless. Then patients' feelings of omnipotence increase, they manipulate the therapist at will and feel guilty and frightened of loss of control. Any effective therapy ends. Many a beginning therapist has been usefully if painfully instructed by the experience of going this destructive route with a patient. On the other hand, if the therapist takes a harsh stand or a punitive or critical attitude and refuses any concession, the patient may not be able to tolerate the deprivation or rejection and the resulting engulfing anxiety and rage. The patient may be unable to continue in treatment and will break off or react with stubborn uncooperativeness or an ultimatum. And the same new therapist who was painfully instructed about permissiveness often fills out her or his experience in this opposite direction.

The splitting tendency of the patient—manifesting and externalizing itself in the relationship with the therapist—is the therapist's opportunity. The therapist's only way out is also the way out for the patient. The therapist must maintain a neutral, steady therapeutic attitude without either indulgent gratification or retaliation. The therapist reminds the patient of the therapeutic task and focuses on the patient's feelings of frustration, anxiety, and anger. As the patient is able to express these feelings verbally, it becomes possible to examine and interpret the patient's underlying fantasies of power and impotence, belief in the power to destroy and rescue, feelings of worthlessness, and need to be rescued. Often the female hysteric, whom we do see more commonly in treatment than the male hysteric, seems to be demanding rescue by a magic, powerful parent figure.

The therapist must avoid being drawn into the patient's cycle of acting out, gratification, shame or guilt, self-punishment, suffering, guilt relief, and more acting out to obtain gratification. The therapist must avoid participating in the cycle while helping the patient examine and understand it. In so doing, the therapist helps the patient to have a learning experience of delaying action and of tolerating some deprivation and frustration, and thus finding better forms of gratification.

A word is in order here about how the patient comes to treatment or the manner in which the patient is referred, since these events make the beginning and the continuation of treatment more or less difficult. Sometimes a patient has been evaluated by a good psychiatrist or psychoanalyst, has been thought to be analyzable, and has been prepared for analysis or intensive psychotherapy through consultation with the referring doctor. In such a case, the patient has a general knowledge of what to expect in terms of time, frequency, continuity, cost, and the nature of the treatment. I usually take this patient, at least on a trial basis, right into analysis or psychoanalytic psychotherapy. I do this even if the patient has a history of repeated and intense but rather superficial personal relationships outside of therapy and even if the patient has seen a number of previous therapists and at some point has broken off treatment with them.

If the patient does not come to me referred in the most appropriate manner, however, or is self-referred but has a history of brief and broken-off relationships, including disrupted therapy with previous therapists, I generally undertake a kind of transitional therapy. I do this either for the purpose of making an adequate referral to another therapist for more definitive work or with the idea of possibly preparing the patient for more extensive therapy with me. Either way, I probably tell the patient something like the following: "Well, this pattern of your breaking off relationships at some point seems to be pretty clear, and I suppose the same thing will, in time, threaten to happen to us if we are going to be working together. You understand, of course, that either of us will be free to discontinue treatment at any time. But I want to call to your attention that it might be important to understand, if we can, what it is that drives you to that pattern of repeatedly breaking off your relationships, why it's necessary for you to do that. Anyway, I just want you to know that in time, the pattern is almost certain to come into the treatment here. And when it does, do you think you might wish to consider taking the opportunity to see what the breaking off could be guarding against, rather than just automatically or reflexively reenacting the same pattern?" Some such statement, made initially, may help later to gain the patient's conscious cooperation when the dilemma of the transference develops.

MIDDLE PHASE

Work on Gender Identification

In time, it can become possible to examine the patient's sense of gender-identity confusion, the absence of inner certainty and integrity, and the core fantasies of merging and destruction, of being destroyed or made whole or perfect by some sort of unification and splitting or rebirth experience. The manifestations of all these fantasies in the treatment relationship and other relationships need to be examined and related to their beginnings in early object experiences. Then the patient can be helped to see what kinds and degrees of gratification are realistically possible and what is realistically possible in therapy.

During this phase a romantic or erotic transference may develop. The patient believes he or she is in love with the therapist and as a resistance to working this through may insist on a "real" relationship with the therapist. If the patient resists interpretations and tests the therapist with threats to quit, it may be necessary to confront the threats quite directly. For example, the therapist may say: "Here we are again at the breaking-off point. We can see that we are on the horns of a dilemma. You say that you love me and that it is real. But if we were to have a romantic relationship, however gratifying it might be, it would certainly go the way of previous relationships in your life and you would be no better off than before. On the other hand, if I don't go along with you on such a 'real relationship,' and if I insist that we need to analyze what's happening, you can always feel hurt or angry and use that to break off treatment. That, too, will defeat us. We can see that it's a damned-either-way thing unless we manage to understand it and work it through."

These situations occur in both gender-matched and gender-opposite pairings of patients to therapists. For example, a male patient with an essentially hysterical character makeup, including hypermasculinity or pseudomasculinity, will also have a pattern of moving on in personal and occupational relationships when intimacy-stirred tensions build up. In some ways male hysterics are more difficult to treat when the therapist is a man. The patient may not only be frightened off by the welling up of homosexual undertones in the relationship with a male therapist but by the intensely threatening dependency aspect of the relationship. He feels a strength in making demands but a weakness in asking for help or even in accepting it. The male stereotype calls for independence, assertiveness, and concealment of tenderness with other males— hence the urge to flee treatment if these threatening feelings begin to arise with a therapist. Dependency and sentiment are more acceptable in the female stereotype and do not so sharply threaten the early treatment relationship.

Society, incidentally, tends to treat men who have a hysterical personality differently from the way it treats women with this style of behavior, particularly if the acting out tends to infringe on legal constraints. Society is more punitive to the male hysteric. An attractive young woman hysteric who runs up charge accounts or bounces checks is never held as accountable nor is her social reputation as damaged as the male hysteric who may rather rapidly become embroiled in legal entanglements that further impair his social adaptation and that may even result in his being labeled sociopathic.

Review of Treatment Guidelines

Let us pause to reconsider four treatment guidelines. First, don't make an initial interpretative attack directly on the patient's symptom. Second, cultivate a good working alliance with the patient, a positive relationship, before making interpretations. Third, allow clinical data to accumulate until conclusions seem almost obvious, before even tentatively pointing them out. It would follow that usually no attempt should be made to deprive the patient of secondary gain attending a symptom or behavior pattern until there is enough understanding of the primary gain, that is, the forces that initially converged to produce the symptom or character trait. When this is understood, it is sometimes possible in the context of psychotherapy to suggest better and more direct gratification of conflicting needs. And finally, the fourth rule, a rule that is simpler to state than to apply, is to establish and maintain the relationship with the patient and the manner of working so as to maximize analyzing throughout the whole treatment and to minimize any reality basis for the patient's conscious expectations of any other form of gratification, such as acting out together with the therapist.

Tailoring Treatment to the Hysteric's Thinking Style

The bland affect of the hysteric in the acute conversion reaction is one indication of the effectiveness with which the mental mechanism of repression can work: repression blanks out anxiety and the anxiety-producing ideas. In the hysterical or histrionic personality, there seems to be an excess of affect; but it is also pseudo-affect, an as-if feeling, which in part functions to screen out the intensity of the threatening feeling. This pseudo-affect may counterphobically permit partial gratification.

With the obsessional, in contrast, small amounts of anxiety are permitted into consciousness but are kept within manageable limits by the mechanisms of isolation of affect, doing and undoing, reversal, reaction formation, and regression. In contrast with the narcissism, sensitivity, and emotionality of the hysterical personality, the obsessive-compulsive seems emotionally blunted. In the obsessive, the forgetting or repressing is mostly limited to dissolving the feeling connections between memories and ideas, leaving the ideas isolated but conscious. Conclusions with appropriate feeling tone, however, may not be drawn even though anxiety and other distressing affects are avoided. The obsessive-compulsive consciousness focuses on, dwells on, certain thoughts and lines of thinking, and in so doing excludes certain feelings and other thoughts leading to threatening or unbearable feelings.

In short, the hysteric has repressed or dissolved the ideational connections between *feelings* to defend against certain affects; the obsessive-compulsive has repressed or dissolved the feeling connections between *ideas* to defend against certain threatening affects. Curiously, these two styles of thinking, though in a sense opposites, are not mutually exclusive and to some extent can coexist in the same person. There is a sense in which the obsessive-compulsive and hysteric are similar in that the obsessive-compulsive dwells on the *thought* content without appropriate conclusion of thought and feelings, and the hysterical or histrionic personality dwells on *feeling* without appropriate conclusions of feeling and thought.

In the anxiety-hysteric or phobic person, anxiety may be intense, but it is limited to the phobic situation or stimulus. The phobic is to an extent intermediate between the hysteric and the obsessive-compulsive and shows some elements of the thinking styles of both the hysteric and the obsessive.

Shapiro (1965) wrote of the factual memories of obsessive-compulsives. He believed the obsessive's thinking provides material on which the recollection must be drawn. He contrasted the obsessive's thinking style to the hysteric's thinking style in terms of apperception, apprehension, data gathering, and recall:

[The hysteric's thinking is] global, relatively diffuse, and lacking in sharpness, particularly in sharp detail. In a word, it is *impressionistic*. In contrast to the active, intense, and sharply focused attention of the obsessive-compulsive, hysterical cognition seems relatively lacking in sharp focus of attention; in contrast to the compulsive's active and prolonged searching for detail, the hysterical person tends cognitively to respond quickly and is highly susceptible to what is immediately impressive, striking, or merely obvious. [pp. 111–112]

Shapiro believed that the lack of detail and definition in hysterical cognition is neither the result of the mental mechanism of repression nor of the exclusion of specific ideational or emotional contents from consciousness; rather, he thought that it is a form of cognition in itself, a form that results in vagueness or diffuseness rather than explicit exclusion. Some of both the hysteric's and the obsessive-compulsive's symptomatologies suggest a physiological substrate in the central nervous system's ability to focus attention—as in sight, hearing, and feeling—that goes awry in excess.

We can look at the hysteric's lack of sharp definition and thought content in another way, one that has implications for therapy. To the extent that the hysteric still unconsciously seeks to reestablish the nurturant child–mother relationship, there is an expectation, an unconscious demand, for an intuitive, primarily nonverbal, global understanding from others. Hysterics seem forever surprised at not being understood; they seem to feel that, of course, others know what they are feeling, and they seem to feel that if their needs are misinterpreted or not met, it is out of some sort of lack of love, rejection, or even hostile perversity by the others. When, for instance, a female hysteric and male obsessive-compulsive are in a close relationship like marriage, the hysteric often seems amazed and offended at the failure of her husband to apprehend her feeling state. The obsessive-compulsive in that marriage just as often seems astonished at the wife's failure to comprehend what seems to him logically obvious in his linear style of thinking.

One of the frequently experienced misunderstandings with hysterics is that manifestations of need for elements of preverbal closeness, such as the wish to be held or cuddled, are reacted to by the other person as an overture for genital sexuality. "I just want to be held and kissed, but my husband always gets turned on and wants to have sex," a female hysteric may complain.

Comment on the Right and Left Cerebral Hemispheres

Of theoretical interest, and tending to support contrasting thinking styles for the hysteric and the obsessive-compulsive, are the studies of the right and left cerebral hemisphere functions (Galin 1974). It would seem that the thinking styles described for the hysteric and for the obsessive-compulsive in many ways correspond, respectively, to the thinking functions of the right and left cerebral hemispheres of the brain that have been reported by investigators. When the corpus callosum, the great tract connecting the two cerebral hemispheres, is transected, it becomes possible to demonstrate the separate functions of each hemisphere: the right is global, holistic, impressionistic, and aesthetic in its apperception; the left deals in details, verbal memory, logic, discrete recall, linearity, and time sequence (Callaway 1975). Both these left–right hemisphere modes of functioning have obvious adaptive value, and each complements the other. One is tempted to speculate that when a clearly defined hysteric or obsessive-compulsive style of thinking exists, it may have resulted from a suppression or repression of the functions of the complementary cerebral hemisphere or that the functions of the complementing hemisphere were not fully activated at some critical time in a specific maturational period.

Among hysterics and obsessive-compulsives of comparable levels of intelligence, it seems to me more common to find the hysteric lacking in mathematical ability and the obsessive-compulsive more able in mathematics (at least in arithmetic calculations). Obsessive-compulsives may be good at bridge and routine money matters; the hysteric, rarely. But the hysteric is often better at such activities as acting, art, and interior decorating.

Thinking Style

The so-called vagueness or emptiness of the hysteric's thinking is apparent but is not the whole story by any means. For example, I treated a very creative woman artist who had a hysterical style in talking, dressing, and behavior. And she clearly had a degree of gender-identity confusion. For this patient, making art forms equaled remaking her body image. She had even had a plastic surgeon remodel her breasts, making them smaller to fulfill an unconscious wish to be more like her brother. In her usual talk, this artist reacted in global terms, often impressionistically, or with seeming vagueness. But in fact she had much specific information and ability to deal with detail both visual and otherwise.

As repressions are lifted in the course of therapy with hysterics, it is often even more apparent that details of events do indeed register with the patient but are immediately pushed from consciousness with only a kind of blurred afterimage available in symbolic outline.

Consider the following familiar example. A therapist is a couple of minutes late in starting an appointment. The patient shows a definite negative response. She is uncharacteristically silent or slow to start talking. She reports feeling "down," but she does not consciously relate her reaction to the narcissistic hurt of the therapist's lateness. Asked if she were possibly reacting to the therapist's lateness, she says that she did not notice he was late. Almost always she gives a large real-life reason for her depressed mood or asserts she doesn't know why she feels down. But in any event, she implies that the therapist is not as important a part of her life as might be inferred from his question about her reaction to his lateness. While her denial or lack of awareness can be either a narcissistic protection or a counterstrike at the therapist or both, it is clear that the detail registers and the patient reacts, albeit in a rather totalistic way, as though the therapist's lateness constituted a major rejection.

To better to understand how you treat the hysteric, it may be helpful to recognize both the contrast and the similarity between the hysteric and the obsessive-compulsive.

I oversimplify to assert that we teach the hysteric to think and the obsessive to feel. To put it another way, the obsessive-compulsive has to rediscover the feeling links between thoughts, and the hysteric needs to relearn the thought connections between feelings. In treatment, the obsessive-compulsive tends to intellectualize without feeling and the hysteric seems to emotionalize without thinking clearly. The hysteric is in a sense phobic about thinking and the compulsive phobic about feeling. But I wish to emphasize that with the hysteric and the obsessive-compulsive what is ultimately being defended against—by their mental mechanisms and by their styles—is feeling. The therapist must treat the feeling part, must help the patients work through the defenses and reexperience the warded-off ideas. In treating hysterics, however, you first have to point out that they really do not feel as much as they seem to be feeling. The woman hysteric may be frigid and not feel sexually, but in other areas she also does not feel as much as she seems to be feeling, or she has by quick and premature expression of feeling aborted the intensity of its full development. Just as her sexuality is a kind of acted sexuality, a role-played sexuality, her anger is often a kind of acted anger. The problem with this patient is to help her learn how to think better about certain situations. To do this, the therapist might first point out that her anger is a kind of as-if feeling. It is a pseudofeeling, an acted feeling, and that is one of the reasons this patient is called histrionic or theatrical—because she is acting and not fully feeling what seems to be felt. In the acting there is a defense against the very feeling that is portrayed, and that defense is what the therapist must first point out. The therapist directs attention toward what the hysteric is having trouble feeling.

The obsessive-compulsive—for example, a male obsessive-compulsive—who seems to think so logically and linearly, up to a point, and has such a good factual and technical memory, is also having trouble with feelings and is defending against feeling. He has trouble making decisions and yet may be dogmatic in defense against his uncertainties. He constantly reverses and undoes things he says. He will, for example, compliment the therapist and then immediately have to take it back or revise it. Or he attacks the therapist and says something derogatory and then must take it back: "Sometimes I think you're full of crap. But most of the time what you say makes sense." You see the immediate reversal and taking back. The reason for this reversal is that the obsessive-compulsive defends against certain feelings that he senses would evolve if he continued that line of thinking. This reversing mechanism serves to let through only a little anxiety, a little feeling, and maintains a control with which he is constantly struggling. He is both afraid of losing control and yet wishes to let go.

With the obsessive-compulsive you bring the patient's attention to this mental mechanism of defense, of doing and undoing; you invite the patient to continue the line of thinking he or she is prone to shut off. You direct attention first to what the patient is having trouble thinking. If the patient is attacking and you have called this mechanism to the patient's attention, you may be able to say, "Now, at any moment, you are automatically going to feel like taking all that back." To some extent this nudges the patient to go a bit further than usual. The patient begins to loosen up the constricted switching back and forth and goes further in each direction. As he goes back and forth further and further, the patient *feels* a bit more of what he or she has been guarding against.

So en route to teaching the hysteric to think and the obsessive-compulsive to feel, the therapist first teaches the hysteric to *feel more* and the obsessive-compulsive to *think further.*

To summarize, both the hysteric and the obsessive-compulsive defend against feeling by the use of their characteristic mental mechanisms of defense and thinking styles. The therapist must help the patients work through the defenses and reexperience the warded-off feelings before their styles of perceiving and thinking can change.

The hysteric and the obsessive-compulsive deal with words differently. If the hysteric says something about being "irritated" and you reply with the word "anger" it will not bother her or him. An obsessive-compulsive, on the other hand, often makes excessively sharp distinctions between related words and is sometimes pedantic about it. For example, I have a patient who says, "I didn't say *angry*. I said I was *irritated*."

I say, "Aren't these things pretty closely connected?"

"No," he says, "they're very different. I certainly was not angry. I was irritated, not angry," he emphasizes.

"Well, granted there's a difference between irritated and angry, and you've emphasized the difference, isn't it mainly a difference of degree? Aren't they related—at least second cousins maybe?"

If the patient's resistances are so strong that he or she treats all this with grim seriousness, further irritation, or intellectualizing, you generally let it go and press no further on the connection at this time. And here the therapist must bear in mind that it is in communicating with the patient through the patient's cognitive style that the therapist can be most effective. It is of little use to ask the hysteric at the outset to think in a manner almost utterly foreign to her or him. And it's just as useless to ask the obsessive-compulsive to feel feelings he or she cannot sense.

Therefore, the first therapeutic step, as I've mentioned before, is for the hysteric to feel more fully and for the obsessive-compulsive to think more logically. The initial interpretations are in these directions. To the hysteric, for example, you may say, "Perhaps you are really not feeling that so intensely." To the obsessive-compulsive, you may say, "If you extend that line of thinking without taking it back or counterbalancing it, where might it lead?" Patients are usually unconscious of their thinking styles without an outside observer to help them be aware of it. It works the same way with characteristics of culture—members of the culture are unconscious of their lifestyles when a basis for comparison is lacking.

TERMINATION PHASE

By the termination phase, patients will have worked through many of their core neurotic conflicts and reduced their anxieties in the context of the transference, in the examination and alteration of their current interpersonal relationships, and in the review of their life stories. Because of their need for attention, they will have tested the therapeutic situation in many different ways and will have experienced turbulent emotional episodes: unconscious aims to recapitulate the past and obtain "this time" a more satisfactory outcome will have been frustrated and analyzed. But they will have found some gratification in the treatment situation itself, in the undivided attention and concern of the therapist, in finding that they have not been misused by the therapist, and in the pleasure of insight.

As separation from the therapist and the therapy situation is contemplated, there will be repetition of many of the earlier themes in the context of giving up the gratification of being in treatment. At this point, the hysterical personality will often reveal aspects of fantasies of rescue and nurture that have remained previously veiled. Especially prominent may be fantasies of relationships beyond the treatment conclusion. Only during this phase may residual symptoms be relinquished, especially symptoms that were maintained because of the fantasy of a particular kind of secondary gain. The patient may have a covert wish for indefinite continuation of treatment, for example, and only in the termination phase is it possible to examine and resolve the desperate need for an enduring sustaining relationship.

All the dilemmas of how to relate to other persons, to gain attention, to fulfill an authentic sexual role will be reviewed in the termination phase in connection with the important issues of separation and the transience of all human relationships. The patient may wish to continue a transference as a defense against the risks of a real relationship outside of the therapeutic situation, as illustrated in the following case example of a course of treatment (for further details of this case see Allen 1974, pp. 93–97).

Case History of a Student Nurse

An intelligent, attractive, foreign-born student nurse sought psychiatric treatment near the end of her training. She complained of feeling mixed-up, depressed, anxious, and a compulsion to overeat and then to gag herself to vomit. These symptoms had begun several months before when she was kissed by a young doctor, at which time instead of feeling pleasurably aroused sexually, she felt as if she were going to be smothered. She felt gagging and nausea. These symptoms had occurred repeatedly after that when kissed by other men. She was a virgin and felt herself unable to work out a relationship with a man. The patient also felt threatened by a demanding, older nurse supervisor. Although this patient's immediate presenting symptom was hysterical gagging, she also had phobic and obsessive-compulsive traits; her personality pattern, however, most nearly fitted that of the hysterical personality.

An only child, the patient's past history revealed many personality resources and adaptive strengths, including the ability to develop enduring friendships. In latency, her parents had divorced after a marriage stormy with physical and verbal fighting. The principal traumas for the patient appeared to have been in the oedipal period. There were overdetermining factors regarding things oral and anal: early feeding problems, struggle with the mother about food, the mother angrily trying to cram homework papers into the patient's mouth on one occasion, and a tonsillectomy without anesthesia as a small child. The patient had been given laxatives and enemas, and she feared assault from both ends. Her father was an artist and fencer. In childhood, she had a disturbing fantasy, later repressed, of his raping her anally.

The patient was taken into traditional psychoanalysis, and over a period of about three years she worked through anxieties about her relationships with men and women and became entirely free of symptoms. She was able to experience sexual feelings directly in appropriate situations and angry feelings in situations calling for anger without, in either case, being overwhelmed by anxiety or anxiety-induced symptoms. She has remained free of symptoms for many years and is married and the mother of two children.

One of the chief problems in the course of a somewhat stormy transference neurosis was not only the interweaving of attempts to fence or fight with the analyst and seduce him, but the patient's use of the transference relationship as a resistance to working out any real-life relationship with men, even though to do so had been her purpose in entering analysis. For example, she would say, "Oh, I know we can't get married now. I know your rules. But after analysis. . . ." This attitude required repeated interpretation of her defense against the real-life relationship with a suitable man.

There are defenses against defenses and reversals against reversals, and these days when many patients in analysis or analytically oriented psychotherapy know something of analytic theory, they are also quick to interpret their reactions to the therapist as transference reactions, and they seek to *dismiss* them on that account. When the patient dismisses a reaction to the therapist as transference, interpretation must be upward rather than downward: that is, the therapist must remind the patient that to call the reaction to the therapist "transference" is to avert anxiety about real and immediate feelings toward the therapist. After adequate working through, the underlying true transference feelings can become apparent and interpretable.

The student nurse went through just this sequence of getting to the underlying transference feelings. As erotic feelings toward the analyst began to develop, she was quick to discount them as transference feelings. She seemed never, however, to doubt the validity of whatever negative feelings occurred in the course of treatment. But in time it became easy to demonstrate to the patient the childhood paradigms for her anger. When it finally became clear to the patient that there would be no real-life romantic relationship with the analyst, she felt betrayed by him as she had felt betrayed by both of her parents. For a time she then attempted to defer working out her relationships with men on the grounds that the analyst was a perfect example of how no man could ever be trusted.

During the middle phase of the analysis these themes were worked through, with gains in her concept of self and in her repertoire of possible relationships with others. They were to repeat themselves later when, with improvement, the theme of completing the treatment contract occurred.

During the final phase of the analysis the transference theme of needing the analyst for a real relationship intensified, and the content of the patient's associations became heavily oral. Thoughts of food and intellectual imbibing were common. She went through rapidly shifting periods of a sort of sweet verbal sucking at me and wishing to prolong a kind of dreamy hanging on to the analytic nipple, and bitter, biting comments at me as though I were an ungiving dried-up breast. There were fantasies of suckling at my penis. Sometimes, too, there was a kind of spitting back of unwanted interpretations as if thrusting away an intrusive nipple, an overfeeding mother.

These periods were experienced with less of a peremptory and needy quality as the termination point approached. She reproached herself for these wishes, but in a mild manner, and exhorted herself to become independent of analysis and the analyst. She expressed realistic satisfaction with the progress she had made, sadness that fantastic goals had not been achieved, and nostalgia that analysis could not become a way of life.

CONCLUSION

If characterologic substrata are to be worked with to any worthwhile extent, it may be important *not* to attempt to relieve the symptom or presenting complaint promptly, since it is the patient's disturbance that is at first the prime motivation for continuing treatment. Premature interpretations, however correct, of the meaning of a symptom may strengthen the defenses and drive the patient from treatment, and to the extent that such premature interpretations also may produce some immediate symptom relief they deprive the patient of motivation for more fundamental working through.

Perhaps because of changes in our society, including more widespread understanding of some kinds of symptoms as stress reactions as well as more liberal and informed attitudes toward sexuality, the kinds of hysterical symptoms have shifted over the years. The acute, naive, symbolizing conversion symptom is rarely seen nowadays except in the lower socioeconomic and less educated groups and among religious groups that are both constrictive and intensely emotional. But the hysterical character or histrionic personality has continued to be prominent. This too will undoubtedly change in manifestation with the times.

In a sense, the hysterical style *is* the symptom. Nowadays it is often very close to being the presenting symptom itself. More often, though, the presenting symptom is still a result of some immediate effect of the patient's cognitive and behavioral style. Not infrequently the patient comes to treatment acutely depressed or acutely anxious *and* with a more global complaint of an ungratifying, distressing life that the patient has begun to see falls into repetitive patterns despite conscious attempts to avert them.

It is small wonder that the patient can by voluntary effort alone so slightly modify her or his behavior when we consider the cumulative conditioning of a lifetime, the more or less fixed forms of imprintlike learning in the early years of psychosexual maturation, and underlying gender-identity confusion. Similarly, it may seem folly for the therapist to attempt to help the patient toward a massive reordering of thinking style. Indeed, massive reordering cannot be an immediate goal and gratification for either therapist or patient in the day-to-day work of psychotherapy.

Instead, gratifications for the therapist lie in the easy use of curiosity, in understanding, and in the craftsmanship of finding and freeing from automaticity what might be called the patient's learned reflexes—reactions just below consciousness that can be made conscious with the help of the therapist. Apart from any symptom relief there is also gratification for the patient in the process of therapy itself, in satisfying her or his curiosity, in the enjoyment of self-understanding, and in increased self-esteem.

An essential part of the craftsmanship in therapy is to communicate within the cognitive style of the patient with full respect for the patient's feelings and values. The hysterical thinking style is not inferior as far as it goes, but the hysterical style needs the complementary advantages of detailed, linear, "left-hemisphere thinking" as well. In a sense, the hysteric does need to learn how to think and what to connect in thinking, just as the obsessive-compulsive needs to learn how to feel and what to connect in feeling. The therapist has to start from where the patient is, not from where the therapist or others think the patient should be; and if this is not done the patient will shut off cooperative disclosure and therapy will be thwarted. Therapy is a special threat to the patient when her or his thinking style is considered the symptom because the style is identified with the self, and to change the style, as it were, threatens annihilation of the self rather than removal of an ego-alien symptom.

No one wants to lose a sense of self, yet that is, in fact, what a change of cognitive style threatens. Because losing something can be so threatening, it is useful and indeed more accurate for both the therapist and the patient to be aware that analyzing and understanding a conflict or a complex does not necessarily mean giving it up or losing it, but rather being able through understanding to make the involved forces work for the person instead of working unconsciously to her or his detriment. A sense of mastery can replace the threat of loss.

Irrespective of a voiced wish for sudden "cure," people do not like a sudden leaving of familiar experience. A patient once said to me, "A vicious circle is a kind of structure—and if it's a familiar one it can become a kind of home—like a project or a cause or a good workout. . . . I guess I can always count on my neurosis." Faced with change, people often need a transitional object and time for the transitional experience. They need a psychologic bridge from the old to the new. And sometimes they need a companion and a chance to try out the new on a small scale and retreat again and again to familiar psychologic territory before separation from the old and before individuation into a newly extended self. Sometimes, almost as a rule, new ways of reacting involve resuming old interrupted ways of reacting.

Reformation in thought and feeling, and an affirmative yielding to change, or at least a passive acceptance of change, precede new actions. Just to take the steps and make the choices of what to talk about without direction from the therapist seems frightening to many patients. Thus, early in treatment I may have to tell the patient: "I think you will find that you can trust your thoughts to lead us to whatever we need to know. I hope to demonstrate that to you. In this sort of work we can't always tell in advance what may be most important to know. And, anyway, it's not up to either you or me to decide in advance. We just have to accept what comes and let it fit itself into the picture. In time, something will begin to repeat and connect, and if you just talk frankly about whatever comes to mind while you're here, sooner or later the important things will become clear to us." Dogma or authoritative direction provides instant familiarity or a kind of portable comforting something. But in the end, dogma is the enemy of human freedom, flexibility, change, and growth. And it is death to the intellect.

In conclusion, I would like to emphasize that while one obviously must fit the treatment to the patient, it is generally helpful to adopt the attitude that, so far as possible, the patient must be a coequal investigator with the therapist. The therapist, generally, should avoid giving advice and should arouse the patient's own powers of initiative. The therapist should be wary of overidentifying with the patient. The therapist should give the patient ample opportunity to tell her or his own story unimpeded by interruptions, and the therapist should not be hasty to interpret. In fact, the therapist will be most effective in focusing on the patient's difficulties in full disclosure and waiting to interpret the patient's dilemmas of contradictory and conflicted feelings.

And most effective of all are the interpretations of transference that can meaningfully be made only in waiting for dilemmas to be felt in the damned-either-way responses the patient unconsciously tends to evoke in the therapist. Under these conditions, the abreactive effect is greatest. The patient does the maximum and optimal mastering work for himself, and the transference manifestations and the transference neurosis become the most illuminating. Therapeutic interventions become both easier and more cogent.

Under the conditions of waiting for the damned-either-way response, the therapist can best find the roles he or she is playing in the patient's projections. The therapist can best demonstrate to the patient that the patient is actively reliving her or his past in the treatment and in present-day conflicts of id, ego, superego, and external reality. Figuratively, the therapist holds the string at the juncture of the real world and the labyrinthine world of the patient's unconscious and past. The therapist allows the patient to unwind that Ariadnean string regressively throughout its long length into earliest childhood. And when the patient comes forward again the therapist gives back the string and map of the patient's personal labyrinth. Generally, no effort should be made to force the pace of the regressive unwinding. The patient needs to explore in her or his own time and pace in order to master. And the patient's feeling forced to yield to the therapist does not usually bring a sense of inner freedom. Only when the patient is stuck does the therapist need to clear the way a little with interpretation or give a little push with an inquiry.

When an attractive young hysterical female patient suddenly turns over on the couch and says, "But that's enough about me, Doctor; let's talk about you," the male analyst has an opportunity to interpret. The patient has a right to keep the analytic situation and the analyst free for fantasy, and it is the analyst's responsibility to guard that right. He should interpret her wish to know about him as a fear of having him know about her and a fear of knowing more about herself. Thus to the patient he might well say, "I think you'll agree that my life doesn't belong in your treatment. But perhaps you're anxious about having us *both* know *your* thoughts."

The therapeutic situation offers ample opportunity for mobilizing scopophilic-exhibitionistic anxiety for both the patient and the therapist, especially with hysterical patients. Nowhere else in life does anyone tell another *all* of his thoughts. Years of work in supervising psychiatrists-in-training convinces me that one of the sources of the beginning therapist's anxieties is an inhibited scopophilia. The doctor's need to act—to advise, to prescribe, to do something, to tell about herself or himself—is often a kind of exhibitionistic and narcissistic defense against anxieties associated with quiet and thorough reflective observation. The ability to defer action in favor of benign curiosity is, however, a necessary prerequisite for real diagnostic understanding in depth.

Finally, in all of the therapist's interventions with the patient the therapist must bear in mind that the patient too has a difficult task and is in a situation of particular vulnerability to intensifications of shame and guilt. Whatever is said to the patient, the therapist should phrase tactfully in a way to cause the least injury to self-esteem while doing the necessary therapeutic work. Hopefully, the patient can get to the point of realizing that hiding is unnecessary and of discovering a wish no longer to hide.

REFERENCES

Abse, D. W. (1974). Hysterical conversion and dissociative syndromes and the hysterical character. In *American Handbook of Psychiatry*, vol. 3, ed. S. Arieti and E. B. Brody, pp. 155–194. New York: Basic Books.

Allen, D. W. (1974). *The Fear of Looking: Scopophilic-Exhibitionistic Conflicts*. Charlottesville: University Press of Virginia.

Allen, D. W., and Houston, M. (1959). The management of hysteroid acting-out patients in a training clinic. *Psychiatry* 22:41–49.

Callaway, E. (1975). Psychiatry today. *The Western Journal of Medicine* 122:349–354.

Freud, S. (1912). Recommendations to physicians practicing psychoanalysis. *Standard Edition* 12:109–120.

——— (1913). On beginning the treatment. *Standard Edition* 12:121–144.

Galin, D. (1974). Implications for psychiatry of left and right cerebral specialization. *Archives of General Psychiatry* 31:572–583.

Giovacchini, P. (1975). *Psychoanalysis of Character Disorders.* New York: Jason Aronson.

Jones, E. (1953). *The Life and Work of Sigmund Freud,* vol. 1. New York: Basic Books.

Kernberg, O. (1970). Factors in the psychoanalytic treatment of narcissistic personalities. *Journal of the American Psychoanalytic Association* 18:51–85.

——— (1974). Further contributions to the treatment of narcissistic personalities. *International Journal of Psycho-Analysis* 55:215–240.

Kohut, H. (1971). *The Analysis of the Self.* New York: International Universities Press.

Orr, D. W. (1961). Lionel Blitzsten, the teacher. In *N. Lionel Blitzsten, M.D.: Psychoanalyst, Teacher, Friend 1893–1952.* New York: International Universities Press (private distribution only).

Schneck, J. M. (1963). Historical notes: William Osler, S. Weir Mitchell, and the origin of the "rest cure." *American Journal of Psychiatry* 119:894–895.

Shapiro, D. (1965). *Neurotic Styles.* New York: Basic Books.

Veith, I. (1970). *Hysteria: The History of a Disease.* Chicago: University of Chicago Press.

14

Panic Disorder and Agoraphobia

Richard J. Kessler, D.O.

Psychoanalytic interest in panic disorder is as old as psychoanalysis itself. Freud's (1895b) definition of anxiety neurosis is nearly identical to that of panic disorder in *DSM-III-R*. Psychoanalytic conceptualizations of the ontogenesis of anxiety from its phylogenetic origins to its character and function in the newborn, and ultimately to its function as a signal of inner danger, represent important interfaces with biological and developmental constructs. Moreover, these conceptualizations contain attempts to distinguish anxiety as a motivated state (signal) and a sign of failed adaptation (symptom) from traumatic anxiety (panic). Such endeavors are relevant to current diagnostic distinctions among anxiety disorders and crucial to the integration of psychodynamic, neurophysiologic, and cognitive-behavioral theories of anxiety disorders (Kandel 1983). There exists a rich clinical psychoanalytic literature that maps out the complex overdetermination of both panic attacks and agoraphobia and includes detailed case histories of successful treatments.

However, systematic demonstration of brief, highly effective pharmacologic and cognitive-behavioral treatments for the acute symptoms of panic have tended to overshadow psychoanalytic findings and apparently diminish the need for exploratory treatments. In fact, popular biological models that declare panic attacks to be nonpsychological, contentless states of biological dysregulation (Gorman et al. 1989, Klein 1981a, Sheehan and Sheehan 1983) or cognitive models that posit panic to result from cognitive misattribution of normal somatic events (Beck and Emery 1985, Hibbert 1984) find little role for the intrapsychic processes that would be explored in a dynamic psychotherapy.

THE NEED FOR A COMPREHENSIVE APPROACH

Nonetheless, even without reference to psychoanalytic data, a body of psychiatric research has steadily accumulated that demonstrates the inadequacy of these simplistic, linear models of causality (Barlow 1990) and the limitations of symptomatic treatment, while suggesting that the many important unanswered questions about the etiology of panic, as well as the significant remaining treatment problems, may be answered by a psychoanalytic approach (Busch et al. 1991). Contrary to the expectations of biological psychiatrists, panic disorder has proven not to be a discrete biologic dysfunction (Barlow 1990) that suddenly strikes otherwise healthy individuals and whose onset and course are largely devoid of depth psychological determinants. Panic disorder is a symptomatic expression of long-standing emotional disturbance and vulnerability; is frequently co-morbid with other anxiety disorders, somatization disorder, major depression, and personality disorder; and even after relief of acute symptoms and their associated impairment often shows itself to be a chronic disorder demanding long-term treatment (Noyes et al. 1990, Pollack et al. 1990). Moreover, in addition to response to antipanic agents, panic attacks and even their neurophysiologic correlates are amenable to a large variety of psychological interventions (Barlow 1990, Busch et al. 1991). It is in these larger contexts that psychoanalytic approaches offer unique understanding and treatment efficacy.

Except for Freud's (1895b) attempts to define anxiety neurosis (panic disorder) as an "actual" neurosis and to separate it from other anxiety disorders by virtue of its supposed biological-sexual etiology, the psychoanalytic literature does not reflect attempts to differentiate among panic attacks, panic disorder, and agoraphobia. Therefore, panic attacks and agoraphobia are both seen as occurring in a psychodynamic context and are each afforded primary relevance. This view contrasts with current biological-behavioral models in which panic onset is "spontaneous" and agoraphobia emerges as a consequence of panic attacks by a matter of simple conditioning. In this scheme, panic does not require meaningful unconscious conflict (Cooper 1985, Klein 1981b) and agoraphobia does not represent the externalization of that conflict, but simply a realistic fear of another panic attack (Klein 1981a).

Nevertheless, for both panic and agoraphobia, psychiatric research increasingly suggests the importance of a psychodynamic view, with its emphasis on the influence of the individual, his life history, and his psychic reality on the onset, nature, and course of these disorders. It has been established that in the year before and particularly in the one- to three-month period prior to the first panic, patients experience more "life events" (Barlow 1988, Faravelli 1985, Finlay-Jones and Brown 1981, Roy-Byrne, Geraci, and Uhde 1986). In addition, they are clearly more threatened by these events, viewing them negatively, feeling less in control, and experiencing extreme lowering of their self-esteem (Roy-Byrne et al. 1986). Panic attacks do not emerge out of the blue. Prodromal symptoms, including depression, generalized anxiety, and hypochondriasis, are clearly the norm (Breier, Charney, and Henninger 1984, Fava, Grandi, and Canestrari 1988, Lelliot et al. 1989). Panic patients have also been found to have pervasively unassertive, fearful, and dependent premorbid personalities (Busch et al. 1991). Precipitants, occurring in more current time frames, days, or hours, have also been consistently discovered (Brehony and Geller 1981, Mathews, Gelder, and Johnston 1981, Raskin et al. 1982), while Hibbert (1984) and Beck and Emery (1985) have found that panic patients report conscious thoughts and/or visual fantasies of danger, often highly personal and of a traumatic nature, immediately prior to or concomitant with panic.

Even patients who sometimes report "spontaneous" panic attacks are often actually in classically phobic situations, whether or not they ever develop agoraphobia (Margraf et al. 1987). In fact, the first panic occurs 95 percent of the time in public places (Lelliot and Marks 1988), which present a surfeit of excitatory cues (Hallam 1985). The development of agoraphobia after panic onset is not related to any characteristics of the panic attack, as a conditioning model would predict, but is correlated with the presence of a history of childhood anxiety disorders (Aronson and Logue 1987) and co-morbid with depression and either avoidant, obsessive-compulsive, passive-aggressive, or dependent personality disorders (Pollack et al. 1990). In addition, agoraphobia is reported as occurring in significant percentages prior to the first panic attack (Fava et al. 1988, Lelliot et al. 1989) and even without panic attacks (Eaton and Keyl 1990, Weissman and Merikangas 1986). A finding from long-term exploratory treatments is that phobic avoidance is often present for many years prior to the onset of panic but has been disguised or hidden by the effects of rationalization, denial, and the availability of a phobic partner.

THE PSYCHOANALYTIC VIEW

Traditional psychoanalytic explanations of the mental events that precede panic attacks designate pathological unconscious conflict as a necessary specific cause. A failure of defense or specifically a miscarriage of the signal function of anxiety is often cited as the immediate antecedent of the panic attack. The anxiety signal represents acknowledgment by the ego of an instinctual danger and provides the impetus for defense so that the traumatic anxiety of original childhood danger situations is not repeated. Thus any degree of pathological anxiety represents a failure of defense. In the panic attack, the anxiety signal sets off the traumatic state, "like a match in a barrel of gunpowder" (Fenichel 1934, p. 476), instead of mobilizing defenses to prevent the traumatic state or any milder expression of anxiety. The development of agoraphobia, on the other hand, is seen as an effort to prevent fresh outbreaks of panic by the avoidance of situations that symbolically represent and therefore intensify dangerous instinctual wishes.

Although anxiety is a reaction to inner danger, it can also constitute a danger itself when it reaches the proportion of panic. The patient becomes afraid not only of the danger of instinctual demands, but also of the ego regression entailed in the "uncontrolled anxiety" of the panic attack (Schur 1971). The experience of the regressive alteration of the ego, the sense of helplessness, the disturbance in experience of the self, and the sense of reality, as well as the experience of the resomatization of anxiety itself, subsequently come to represent a danger. Anxiety over the manifestations of panic, the so-called fear of fear, continues to express the original concern over instinctual danger (Freud 1926), but also represents new meanings associated with the experience of the panic attack. This secondary anxiety corresponds to what is now referred to as anticipatory anxiety. It contributes to the self-perpetuation of anxiety reactions, providing fresh evidence to the patient of the reality of the danger situation that precipitated the original panic (Schur 1953).

Early on, Freud (1895b) noted the connection between panic and phobias: "In the case of agoraphobia, etc., we often find the recollection of an anxiety attack; and what the patient actually fears is the occurrence of such an attack under the special conditions in which he believes he cannot escape it" (p. 81). He described the pathological unconscious conflicts in agoraphobia, as in other phobias, as those involving the erotic wishes of the Oedipus complex.

Many analysts confirmed and elaborated on Freud's findings, but they also found significant conflicts over aggression, especially toward mother. Differences between some severe cases of agoraphobia and "classical" phobias were detected by Deutsch (1929) and Glover (1949), who found that pregenital fixations and early pathological identifications had definitive etiologic roles, and Schur (1971), who noted the presence of early sexual stimulation and seduction in most published cases. Defects in the structure of the ego and superego and in the earliest object relationships were seen as accounting for the failures of defense and signal anxiety in panic and for the urgent necessity of phobic avoidance in agoraphobia. Greenacre (1960) suggested that the unrelieved tension of a stressful early environment could compromise ego functioning and lead to a predisposition to anxiety, which is indistinguishable from genetic or constitutional factors. The child in such an environment is easily overwhelmed by instinctual demands. Conflicts are intensified at each developmental stage, and the ego's organizing and integrating capacities are compromised or produce a precocious but fragile mastery. In such an individual, Tyson (1988) notes, "anxiety rather than functioning to signal, organize and protect becomes a readily generated affect," leading to "repetition rather than the avoidance of the experience of helplessness" (p. 90).

The work of Abraham (1913), Deutsch (1929), and Weiss (1935) presaged object relations and self psychology perspectives. Weiss reported frequent histories of parental loss and noted the significance of steps toward independence as precipitants in bringing the germinating agoraphobia to the surface. Abraham and Deutsch described the phobic partner as both the object of intense aggressive and sexual wishes and an auxiliary ego or superego enlisted to aid in the control over these wishes, which are aroused in the "agora." In keeping with this view, Rhead (1969) characterized a patient's attachment to mother as a defense of symbiotic relatedness regressively reactivated to protect against the dangers of exhibitionistic and sadomasochistic impulses.

In contrast, other psychoanalysts have highlighted the ongoing attachment to home and mother as representing failed development in separation-individuation. In other words, the agoraphobic symptoms are considered more a reflection of fixation than regression and serve both primary and secondary gain. Thus in discussing school phobia, a not infrequent antecedent for adult panic and agoraphobia, Johnson (1941) viewed the agoraphobia as the dependent child's reaction to mother's fear of being alone, while Rappaport (1959) described separation from the "phobogenic" mother as being the central disturbance. Frances and Dunn (1975) carried these observations, plus Bowlby's and Mahler's work, to a logical conclusion in their description of the importance of the autonomy–attachment conflict in agoraphobia, in which the real or symbolic loss of the phobic partner is experienced as a loss of part of the self.

Self psychology contributions are closely related to object relations perspectives. Rappaport (1959) noted the wish to maintain the self as an extension of the idealized parent, and the agoraphobia as the attempt to prevent the loss of objects and therefore of ego functions. Similarly, Reich (1960) described, as an aspect of pathologic self-esteem regulation, the vulnerability to panic because of the effect of early trauma in promoting narcissistic attachment, preventing the binding of anxieties and the formation of defenses. Eventually, Kohut (1971, 1977) speculated that panic states were associated with childhood failures in selfobject merger preceding the firm establishment of the self. Inadequate internalization of anxiety-controlling mechanisms due to empathic failure was seen as interfering with the process of self-consolidation. This led to a vulnerability to the self-fragmentation seen in panic and the need for an external object to compensate for inner regulatory defects (Tolpin 1971). In accordance with this view, Fishman (1989) emphasizes how parental provisions of holding and affirmation are essential for the later capacity to bear and resolve the anxiety of neurotic conflict, so that a compromised capacity for intimacy is a regular accompaniment of panic disorder.

All these interdependent psychoanalytic perspectives would seem to provide a framework for understanding the manner by which a failure in signal anxiety function might come about and contribute to a predisposition to panic disorder. For example, Tyson's (1988) consideration of the ability to regard and utilize affective signals as an indicator of libidinal object constancy is a linking, internally consistent, and testable hypothesis. In addition, failed signal anxiety is a concept clearly parallel to the notion of inappropriate alarm reactions utilized in biological and behavioral models and therefore can serve as a bridge to areas of psychiatric research. Likewise, a psychoanalytic understanding of how depressive affects also serve a signal function (Brenner 1982) can be correlated with the finding of a high incidence of depressive illness in panic patients (Breier et al. 1984, Garvey and Tuason 1984). A syndrome of behavioral inhibition and autonomic arousal (Kagan et al. 1990) in children who develop anxiety disorders might be a constitutional factor that would challenge parenting capabilities and strain the developmental sequences necessary to internalize anxiety regulation. Interestingly, many observers have found panic patients having internal representations of their parents as more controlling and critical and less caring and warm than controls (Arrindell et al. 1983, Parker 1979, Silove 1986).

CONFLICT OR DEVELOPMENTAL FAILURE

Not unexpectedly, psychoanalytic controversies about the etiology of panic and agoraphobia continue to revolve around questions of the primacy of developmental failure or inner conflict. Clinical and developmental realities, however, demand a balanced view of these factors. According to Anna Freud (1964):

> It would be convenient to take the point of view that success or failure of the developmental lines primarily shapes the personalities which became secondarily involved in inner conflict. But any statement of this kind would be a gross falsification once the infant ceases to be an undifferentiated, unstructured being. It would ignore the temporal relations between the two processes which occur simultaneously, but not subsequent to each other. Progress on the lines is interfered with constantly by conflict, repression and consequent regression, while the conflicts themselves and quite especially the methods available for their solution are wholly dependent on the shape and level of personal development which has been reached. However different in origin the two types of psychopathology are, in the clinical picture they are totally intertwined, a fact which accounts for their being treated as one. [pp. 114–115]

Although it might be said that a patient who panics at a time of separation has problems in object constancy or in anxiety regulation, an undue, nondynamic emphasis on these deficits can discourage introspection, increase the patient's sense of passivity, and reinforce efforts for external controls. Also, such an emphasis may blind patient and therapist to the psychodynamic implications of such reactions occurring in response to perceived, imagined, or symbolic losses. Attention may be directed away from the ambivalence felt toward the "lost" object and away from the regressed and conflict-laden longings for it stirred up by actual or anticipated separation.

Panic attacks are the result of a complicated chain of events, both biologic and psychologic, including conflict-specific precipitating events, nonspecific physiologic factors, and developmental and psychodynamic determinants. A wide range of effective therapeutic interventions have been demonstrated at various links in the etiologic chain of events. These include respiratory control therapy, behavior and cognitive therapies, and active and placebo pharmacotherapy. Despite undocumented claims in many psychiatric textbooks about the inefficacy of exploratory treatment, a review of the literature yields a significant and growing collection of successful case histories. For example, Bergler (1935), Wangh (1959), Rhead (1969), Schur (1971), Freeman (1988), and Rocah (1991) have provided richly detailed cases of psychoanalytic treatment of panic and agoraphobia. A psychoanalytic case of Pfeiffer (1961) includes a four-year follow-up and describes a patient with panic disorder without a significant agoraphobia. Descriptions of both short- and long-term successful psychoanalytic psychotherapies of panic with and without agoraphobia can be found in articles by Schlierf (1983), Nemiah (1984), Diamond (1985), Stoeri (1987), Baumbacher (1989), Gabbard (1990), and Milrod and Shear (1991).

Granted, one can detect a small but consistent thread of pessimism in the older literature on exploratory treatment. This is reflected in Freud's and Fenichel's oft-quoted statements about the inadequacy of interpretation alone to undo phobic avoidance and the need to induce patients to expose themselves to the feared situation. In 1958, Weinstock presented a statistical study from the American Psychoanalytic Association's Central Fact-Gathering Program that described only six of forty-six cases of completed analyses with total symptom relief. However, discussions of this study and a summary of the panel, "Phobias and Their Vicissitudes" (Ferber 1959), contain clues to what might appear to be discouraging findings. Participants were still clearly struggling to incorporate into their understanding and work the implications of preoedipal determinants, object relations considerations, and childhood trauma on symptom formation and transference manifestations. That the presence of a phobia, a symptom of "anxiety hysteria," might not imply the primacy of analyzable, oedipal-level psychopathology was in the process of being documented, as it was with hysterical symptoms (Easer and Lesser 1965, Zetzel 1968). Therefore, problems with case selection and with the management of preoedipal dependency, and idealization in the transference could be seen as major contributions to doubts of therapeutic efficacy.

CURRENT VIEWS

It is not uncommon to find in current discussions of treatment recommendations for panic patients the notion that one must decide whether the patient is suffering from a biological or psychological dysfunction, then provide the corresponding treatment modality (Cooper 1985). The need to make such a decision, however, is neither realistic nor justified, for it fails to take into account either the complexity of mind-brain interaction or the amenability of panic patients to a wide variety of interventions. Moreover, effective psychotherapy most likely produces long-term structural and functional changes in the brain (Kandel 1979). Treatment decisions should be made on the basis of a comprehensive, in-depth evaluation of the patient's presenting symptomatology, overall psychic functioning, motivation, and current circumstances. Ideally, they should reflect both long- and short-term goals so that what is offered is the most far-reaching and enduring mastery of symptoms that might be possible and reasonable to expect.

The interpretation of unconscious conflict remains the hallmark of the psychoanalytic psychotherapy of panic and agoraphobia. It is inner conflict that is stirred to a boiling point by "life events" and imbues external circumstances with imagined threats of loss and punishment. Furthermore, it is inner conflict that plays an important part in the establishment of affect dysregulation and compromised object relations and then in a vicious cycle is continually intensified by these defective psychic structures while also impinging on their functioning. Surely, considerations of deficits in biological and psychological structure will account for some aspects of the therapeutic situation and for some specific interventions, especially early on in treatment. However, an emphasis on disease or defect can undermine exploratory efforts and represent a forfeiture of therapeutic opportunity.

Older psychoanalytic conceptions of "actual neurosis" and current self psychology models, like biological models, contain notions of panic as a psychologically contentless state. Thus a patient's descriptions of his experience during a panic state are seen as representing endopsychic perceptions of the disorganization of the individual's mental apparatus and sense of self. Schur (1971) stated that in traumatic anxiety all traces of substitute gratification, the hallmark of neurotic symptom formation, disappear. Yet Wangh (1959) reported that his patient, although initially describing her attacks as having no specific content, eventually revealed specific fears concerning loss of bowel control, which expressed a variety of fantasies. In addition, Silber (1989) mentions a patient whose description of her subjective state contained derivatives of repressed memories of trauma and attempts to master them. Although some symptoms of panic represent physiological concomitants of anxiety and the consequences of the disruption of ego functioning, the thoughts and feelings of the panic state often represent the ego's continuing attempts to defend against threatening instinctual wishes and find substitute gratification for them.

A woman with an eight-year history of panic attacks and moderate agoraphobia reported that during her attacks she had a feeling of unreality and fears that she would stab her children and that she would jump out the window. During treatment, she eventually remembered several incidents of childhood sexual molestation, and did so in the same derealized state experienced during the panic attacks and the incidents. The thought of stabbing her children also echoed these incidents and her attempts to master them, expressing her rage and sense of guilt while turning from a passive sexual victim to an active, "nonsexual" abuser. In addition, the thoughts about the window coalesced memories of episodes of abuse (e.g., trying to listen through the window to kids playing) and her overwhelming excitement and fear with visual primal scene experiences.

Psychoanalytic exploration proceeds longitudinally into the past, but also laterally into other aspects of the patient's current functioning. Not only disturbances in object relations but also other neurotic symptoms are to be found as part of the symptomatology of agoraphobia and panic. In fact, one could argue that the previous case is a mixture of panic, obsessive thoughts, and dissociative symptoms. The patient's symptoms become inevitably linked to other efforts at conflict resolution.

Although unaware of any pregnancy fears, the patient had always pictured herself as a childless professional person. During college she developed some mild anxiety symptoms, food idiosyncracies, and eventually an episode of globus hystericus. Years later, the exacerbation and remission of her panic attacks bore a particular relationship to her pregnancies, while her ability to drive was related to eating rituals that were consciously designed to prevent the experience of hunger. A variety of sexual conflicts in which oral impregnation fantasies played an important role could thus be seen as an aspect of personality, a conversion symptom, a compulsive ritual, and a phobic avoidance.

MEDICATION

It is not uncommon, especially in patients with severe panic or agoraphobia, that certain early interventions are necessary to allow an exploratory process to proceed. A frequent intervention is the prescription of antipanic medication (antidepressants or benzodiazepines). These medications may be prescribed because of their ability to produce dramatic symptomatic improvement. They are also used when the patient, overwhelmed with anticipatory anxiety and the disabling effects of the symptoms, is not capable of engaging in the self-reflection necessary for exploratory work. In reducing the intensity of affects, assimilative and judgmental capacities can be called upon instead of dependence on avoidance or on a symbiotic object (Rocah 1991). In addition, the amelioration of overt symptoms can sometimes reduce the hostile dependency, and the regression therein, of the patient's relationship with his phobic partner and family. This may free the patient for opportunities for personality growth, in life and in therapy, and the establishment of a more mature therapeutic alliance. It may also interrupt a patient's preoccupation with the regressive experiences and concrete consequences of the panic attacks and allow attention to be paid to the determinants.

However, patients with panic disorder seem to be more concerned about and more apt to develop "side effects" from medication. Their tendency to overreact to even minor somatic effects of the medication is consistent with their characterization as somatisizers (King et al. 1986) and their sensitivity to the physiologic concomitants of anxiety. Paradoxically, they often fear or report that the medication will bring on the panic attacks. Here fantasies about the medication and about taking it from the doctor coincide with wishes that are an exciting cause of the panic attacks. Exploration of these reactions may allow a patient to take the prescribed medication and pave the way for continuing interpretive work.

A patient had been unable to tolerate several psychotropic medications. She reported that the initial doses of the medications produced a vague dysphoria and thoughts of impulsive sexual behavior associated with her panic attacks. After awakening from a nocturnal panic attack, she remembered a book she had read about a doctor-rapist and a movie about a psychiatrist-murderer. Along with the transference implications, this led to an exploration of her experiences of childhood surgeries, her memories of anesthesia, which she felt were the same as the dysphoric medication effect, her fears of falling asleep, and a variety of other concerns about losing control of impulses related to the trauma of the surgeries.

Successful pharmacologic intervention may be a necessary prelude to psychotherapy and help in the establishment of the therapeutic alliance. At the same time, it may reinforce pathologic defenses and represent significant gratification of regressive transference wishes. The success of medication in panic patients who are often terrified of their insides, of thinking about their internal states (Stoeri 1987), may supplement the tendency to projection and externalization already at work in their phobic symptom formations. It supports the notion of a physical illness from without and the patient's role as passive and dependent. The prescribing of medication may encourage the creation of a transference based on an idealization of the phobic partner, while the pills themselves may become a phobic companion or transitional object (Schlierf 1983). These transference developments, which often occur without medication being prescribed, impede the establishment of inner mastery. Periodic attempts to discontinue or reduce antipanic medication should be made after prolonged panic-free periods and significant reductions in phobic avoidance. Such attempts sometimes result in a return of panic attacks and almost always in a fear of their return. This may produce renewed opportunities to explore the conflicts underlying the symptoms, as well as the now more available forbidden sexual and aggressive wishes in the transference. Such efforts are most successful when a patient has expressed desires to reduce or discontinue medication, since at such times it may be said that the taking of the medication has, for the patient, become a symptomatic act, now more clearly embodying conflict-laden wishes.

Finally, it should be noted that, considering the enormous placebo effect (30 to 60 percent) in drug studies and the success of behavioral treatments that may be the equal of drug treatment, medication can sometimes be avoided without undue hardship for the patient. Panic attacks, even when acute, but of recent origin and with clear precipitants, can be ameliorated within several weeks in a dynamic psychotherapy (Milrod and Shear 1991). The calm of the therapist, the structure of a psychotherapy, with its constancy and regularity, and an early positive transference can produce significant reductions in panic. In addition, the reassurance that the patient's symptoms are of anxiety and not of a fatal illness, and that the symptoms can be understood in terms of who the patient is and the circumstances of his life, can provide considerable symptomatic relief.

FLEXIBILITY OF TECHNIQUE

A panic patient with significant destructive contact with his parents may be unable to separate emotionally and sometimes physically from his family. The family provides a continuous regressive pull and instinctual overstimulation. Besides the mutually hostile dependency, there often exists in such a family, as genetic studies would predict (Crowe 1988), a parent whose relationship to the patient significantly reflect his or her own struggles with anxiety. Such a patient is in a continuous state of crisis and seems to be transfixed on the parents as provocateurs of anxiety, rages, and impulsive actions. In such situations, consultation with the family may be necessary, as one would do in treating a child.

The analyst's task in such contacts is to defuse the family situation so as to give the patient an opportunity to engage in psychotherapy and to attempt an intrapsychic focus. Depending on the evaluation of the situation, one might refer the parents for treatment (without the patient), encourage the parents to curtail certain activities, or suggest a separation of the patient from the home. These interventions are guided by the need to create an environment for the patient that does not so continuously inflame the inner conflicts and impinge on the patient's vulnerabilities. In addition, the analyst makes suggestions that may at least halt regressive tendencies and point toward a renewal of developmental progress. It should be kept in mind that giving either family or patient the impression that suggestions imply blame of the family for the patient's problems is counterproductive, in that it serves as a reinforcement of pathologic defenses and encourages family sabotage of the therapy. The object of such interventions should be "problematic interactions," for the analyst must remain and the patient must be made aware of the complexity of these family dynamics and the patient's contribution to them.

A patient who remains highly anxious even after remission of panics is likely to telephone often and ask for advice and encouragement. Early in treatment, tolerance for these actions and wishes is more effective than interpretation. Explanations of why the analyst might not respond directly to requests for action might help a patient deal with the anger and hurt entailed in the analyst's demanding at least some tolerance of frustration. This gives the patient an opportunity to identify with the analyst and the intellectual task of the psychotherapy. Contact by phone may be quite reassuring, but such interactions eventually must be funneled back into the therapy by limiting the extent of such conversations or increasing the frequency of visits if the calls persist. The message to be communicated is that it is the process of the exploratory therapy that is ultimately curative, not the person of the analyst or the magic of contact with his voice.

A unique aspect of the transference with panic and agoraphobic patients is the treatment of the analyst as an idealized phobic partner. This idealized transference is similar to that experienced with other patients with significant developmental deficits, such as borderline or narcissistic personalities. However, here it often becomes a rather stable formation and resists disillusionment. In its midst, the therapy becomes a safe haven from conflict, which continues to be experienced intensely outside. As a patient stated, "You are the cure, they are the cause." Although this is often a powerful force in the initial reduction of symptoms and the motivation for treatment, it eventually must be undermined and analyzed as much as possible so that the patient is able to experience conflict in the transference and internalize conflict resolution. This idealization not only hides significant conflicts over aggression but also represents homosexual wishes revived as a flight from oedipal conflicts, as well as an avoidance of transference wishes toward the parent not enlisted as the phobic partner.

Likewise, phobic avoidance can become a comfortable solution for the more regressed patient. Early efforts to point out evidence of the continuing activity of conflicting wishes or even just the maladaptive nature of avoidance reinforces the patient's tendency to project and externalize. Moreover, this premature interpretive activity can represent an enactment of childhood trauma. Only over several years can such a patient begin to acknowledge an awareness of danger from within rather than from external realities and other people's wishes. Just as panic attacks reinforce the reality of inner danger situations so often do histories of impulse dyscontrol, promiscuity, and turbulent relationships reinforce the sense of danger in any awareness of forbidden wishes. However, these behaviors are often truly counterphobic activities, so that there may be opportunities to demonstrate to the patient, in the closeness and interchangeability of phobic and counterphobic symptoms, the fascination/fear duality in their phobias (Meyer and Maletic 1991). The comfortable agoraphobic, like those who insist on the spontaneity of their panic attacks, needs to deny and avoid any experiences of anxiety, since to acknowledge such anxiety might necessitate awareness of prohibited aspects of himself. It may be this denial of anxiety, and consequently, the lost opportunity for it to act as a signal of the need for defense, that is a precursor of panic in many patients (Baumbacher 1989). Therefore, the exploratory process eventually allows the acknowledgment and awareness of small modicums of anxiety and their source, which can prevent an escalation to panic states and lead to attempts at inner resolution.

TERMINATION

Termination is an especially important phase in the psychotherapy of panic-agoraphobic patients. It is only during a time of anticipation of the actual loss of the therapist forever that inner mastery can be consolidated.

During four and a half years of treatment, a patient had experienced a remission of panic attacks and a significant amelioration of her agoraphobia. From a life greatly restricted by her inability to drive on major thoroughfares or even to cross large streets by foot, she had greatly expanded the variety and range of her activities, returning to and completing college, flying on airplanes for the first time, traveling to New York City by public transportation, and greatly enjoying social activities. However, it was not until the setting of a date for termination that it was discovered that the patient was only driving away from her house, in any direction, a distance of roughly that between her house and the analyst's office. In other words, this activity still required the fantasy that she was on her way to therapy. During termination, new depths of exploration, particularly around conflicts concerning aggression, led to an expansion of the patient's ability to drive without undue anxiety.

An attempt to wean a patient from therapy by gradually reducing the frequency of sessions may be a necessary evil for the patient with greater preoedipal pathology and structural deficit. However, it reinforces the need for an external object as a moderator of anxiety and the tendency for the patient to feel that it is the absence of the therapist that causes anxiety, rather than the intensification by his absence of the individual's wishes.

CONCLUSION

Patients with panic disorder and agoraphobia may demonstrate a wide range of attendant psychopathology and personality dysfunction. The prescription of a psychoanalytic psychotherapy takes this into account in both its wide-based and in-depth approach and its modifiability in the face of obstacles created by the state of a patient's overall ego functioning. For some patients, a psychoanalytic psychotherapy (or a psychoanalysis) without significant parameters can be successful, while in others modifications in technique may be necessary as early interventions or constant ones. All in all, psychoanalytic psychotherapy can be applied with significant benefit to large numbers of patients with panic disorder and agoraphobia, offering unique opportunities for enduring change and inner mastery by increasing the ability to bear painful affects, reintegrating disowned parts of self, and allowing the development of more mature object relationships.

REFERENCES

Abraham, K. (1913). A constitutional basis of locomotor anxiety. In *Selected Papers on Psycho-Analysis*, ed. J. D. Sutherland, pp. 235–243. London: Hogarth Press, 1965.

Aronson, T. A., and Logue, C. M. (1987). On the longitudinal course of panic disorder. *Comprehensive Psychiatry* 28:344–355.

Arrindell, W., Emmelkamp, P. M. G., Monsma, A., and Brilman, A. (1983). The role of perceived parental rearing practices in the etiology of phobic disorders: a controlled study. *British Journal of Psychiatry* 143:183–187.

Barlow, D. H. (1988). *Anxiety and Its Disorders*. New York: Guilford Press.

———— (1990). Long-term outcome for patients with panic disorder treated with cognitive-behavioral therapy. *Journal of Clinical Psychiatry* 51:17–23.

Baumbacher, G. D. (1989). Signal anxiety and panic attacks. *Psychotherapy* 26:75–80.

Beck, A. T., and Emery, G. (1985). *Anxiety Disorders and Phobias*. New York: Basic Books.

Bergler, E. (1935). Psychoanalysis of a case of agoraphobia. *Psychoanalytic Review* 22:392–408.

Brehony, K. A., and Geller, E. S. (1981). Agoraphobia: appraisal of research and a proposal for an integrative model. In *Progress in Behavior Modification*, vol. 12, ed. M. Hersen, R. Eisler, and P. Miller, pp. 2–66. New York: Academic Press.

Breier, A., Charney, D. S., and Henninger, G. R. (1984). Major depression in patients with agoraphobia and panic disorder. *Archives of General Psychiatry* 41:1129–1135.

Brenner, C. (1982). *The Mind in Conflict*. New York: International Universities Press.

Busch, F. N., Cooper, A. M., Klerman, G. L., et al. (1991). Neurophysiological, cognitive-behavioral and psychoanalytic approaches to panic disorder: toward an integration. *Psychoanalytic Inquiry* 11:317–332.

Cooper, A. M. (1985). Will neurobiology influence psychoanalysis? *American Journal of Psychiatry* 142:1398.

Crowe, R. R. (1988). Family and twin studies of panic disorder and agoraphobia. In *Handbook of Anxiety*, vol. 1, ed. M. Roth, R. Noyes, Jr., and G. D. Burrows, pp. 101–113. New York: Elsevier Science Publishing.

Deutsch, H. (1929). The genesis of agoraphobia. *International Journal of Psycho-Analysis* 10:51–69.

Diamond, D. B. (1985). Panic attacks, hypochondriasis, and agoraphobia: a self psychology formulation. *American Journal of Psychotherapy* 39:114–125.

Easer, B. R., and Lesser, S. R. (1965). Hysterical personality: a re-evaluation. *Psychoanalytic Quarterly* 34:390–405.

Eaton, W. E., and Keyl, P. E. (1990). Risk factors for the onset of diagnostic interview schedule/*DSM-III* agoraphobia in a prospective, population-based study. *Archives of General Psychiatry* 47:819–824.

Faravelli, C. (1985). Life events preceding the onset of panic disorder. *Journal of Affective Disorders* 9:103–105.

Fava, G. A., Grandi, S., and Canestrari, R. (1988). Prodromal symptoms in panic disorder with agoraphobia. *American Journal of Psychiatry* 145:1564–1567.

Fenichel, O. (1934). Defense against anxiety, particularly by libidinization. *International Journal of Psycho-Analysis* 20:476–489.

Ferber, L. (1959). Phobias and their vicissitudes. *Journal of the American Psychoanalytic Association* 7:182–192.

Finlay-Jones, R., and Brown, G. W. (1981). Types of stressful life events and the onset of anxiety and depressive disorders. *Psychological Medicine* 11:803–815.

Fishman, G. (1989). Psychoanalytic psychotherapy in anxiety disorders. In *Treatment of Psychiatric Disorders*, pp. 2010–2025. Washington, DC: American Psychiatric Association Press.

Frances, A., and Dunn, P. (1975). The attachment–autonomy conflict in agoraphobia. *International Journal of Psycho-Analysis* 56:435–439.

Freeman, T. (1988). *The Psychoanalyst in Psychotherapy*. New Haven, CT: Yale University Press.

Freud, A. (1964). A psychoanalytic view of developmental psychopathology. *Journal of the Philadelphia Association for Psychoanalysis* 1:14–15.

Freud, S. (1895a). Obsessions and phobias: their psychical mechanism and their aetiology. *Standard Edition* 3:74–84.

_____ (1895b). On the grounds for detaching a particular syndrome from neurasthenia under the description "anxiety neurosis." *Standard Edition* 3:90–115.

_____ (1926). Inhibitions, symptoms and anxiety. *Standard Edition* 20:77–175.

Gabbard, G. O. (1990). *Psychodynamic Psychiatry in Clinical Practice.* Washington, DC: American Psychiatric Association Press.

Garvey, M. J., and Tuason, V. B. (1984). The relationship of panic disorder to agoraphobia. *Comprehensive Psychiatry* 25:529–531.

Glover, E. (1949). *Psycho-analysis.* London: Staples.

Gorman, J. M., Liebowitz, M. R., Fyer, J. F., and Stein, B. A. (1989). A neuroanatomical basis for panic disorder. *American Journal of Psychiatry* 146:148–161.

Greenacre, P. (1960). Considerations regarding the parent–infant relationship. In *Emotional Growth,* vol. I, pp. 199–224. New York: International Universities Press.

Hallam, R. S. (1985). *Psychological Perspectives on Panic and Agoraphobia.* London: Academic Press.

Hibbert, G. A. (1984). Ideational components of anxiety: their origin and content. *British Journal of Psychiatry* 144:618–624.

Johnson, A. M. (1941). School phobia. *American Journal of Orthopsychiatry* 11:702–711.

Kagan, J., Reznick, J. S., Snidman, N., et al. (1990). Origins of panic disorder. In *Neurobiology of Panic Disorder,* ed. J. Ballenger, pp. 71–87. New York: John Wiley.

Kandel, E. (1979). Psychotherapy and the single synapse. *New England Journal of Medicine* 301:1028–1037.

_____ (1983). From metapsychology to molecular biology: explorations into the nature of anxiety. *American Journal of Psychiatry* 140:1277–1293.

King, R., Margraf, J., Ehlers, A., et al. (1986). Panic disorder—overlap with symptoms of somatization disorder. In *Panic and Phobias,* ed. I. Hand and H. Ulrich-Wittchen, pp. 72–77. Berlin: Springer-Verlag.

Klein, D. F. (1981a). Anxiety reconceptualized. In *Anxiety: New Research and Changing Concepts,* ed. D. F. Klein and J. Rabkin, pp. 235–263. New York: Raven Press.

_____ (1981b). Discussion of *Psychoanalytic View of Anxiety,* by J. C. Nemiah. In *Anxiety: New Research and Changing Concepts,* ed. D. F. Klein and J. Rabkin. New York: Raven Press.

Kohut, H. (1971). *The Analysis of the Self.* New York: International Universities Press.

_____ (1977). *The Restoration of the Self.* New York: International Universities Press.

Lelliot, P., and Marks, I. (1988). Letters to the editor: the cause and treatment of agoraphobia. *Archives of General Psychiatry* 45:388–399.

Lelliot, P., Marks, I., McNamee, A., et al. (1989). Onset of panic disorder with agoraphobia. *Archives of General Psychiatry* 46:1000–1004.

Margraf, J., Taylor, B., Ehlers, A., et al. (1987). Panic attacks in the natural environment. *Journal of Nervous and Mental Disease* 175:558–565.

Mathews, A. M., Gelder, M. C., and Johnston, D. W. (1981). *Agoraphobia: Nature and Treatment.* New York: Guilford Press.

Meyer, J. K., and Maletic, V. (1991). The clinical and theoretical structures of adult phobias. *Psychoanalytic Inquiry* 11:333–350.

Milrod, B., and Shear, M. K. (1991). Psychodynamic treatment of panic: three case histories. *Hospital and Community Psychiatry* 42:311–312.

Nemiah, J. C. (1984). The psychodynamic view of anxiety. In *Diagnosis and Treatment of Anxiety Disorders*, ed. R. O. Pasnau, pp. 117–146. Washington, DC: American Psychiatric Association Press.

Noyes, R. Jr., Reich, J., Christiansen, J., et al. (1990). Outcome of panic disorder. *Archives of General Psychiatry* 47:809–818.

Parker, G. (1979). Reported parental characteristics of agoraphobics and social phobics. *British Journal of Psychiatry* 135:555–560.

Pfeiffer, A. Z. (1961). Follow-up study of a satisfactory analysis. *Journal of the American Psychoanalytic Association* 9:698–718.

Pollack, M. H., Otto, M. W., Rosenbaum, J. F., et al. (1990). Longitudinal course of panic disorder: findings from the Massachusetts General Hospital naturalistic study. *Journal of Clinical Psychiatry* 51:12–16.

Rappaport, E. (1959). Phobias and their vicissitudes. *Journal of the American Psychoanalytic Association* 7:182–192.

Raskin, M., Peeke, H. V. S., Dickman, W., et al. (1982). Panic and generalized anxiety disorders: developmental antecedents and precipitants. *Archives of General Psychiatry* 39:687–689.

Reich, A. (1960). Pathologic forms of self-esteem regulation. *Psychoanalytic Study of the Child* 15:215–232. New York: International Universities Press.

Rhead, C. (1969). The role of pregenital fixations in agoraphobia. *Journal of the American Psychoanalytic Association* 17:848–861.

Rocah, B. S. (1991). A clinical study of a phobic illness: the effects of traumatic scars on symptom formation and treatment. *Psychoanalytic Inquiry* 11:351–375.

Roy-Byrne, P. P., Geraci, M., and Uhde, T. W. (1986). Life events and the onset of panic disorder. *American Journal of Psychiatry* 143:1424–1427.

Schlierf, C. (1983). Transitional objects and object relationship in a case of anxiety neurosis. *International Review of Psychoanalysis* 10:319–331.

Schur, M. (1953). The ego in anxiety. In *Drives, Affects and Behavior*, ed. R. M Lowenstein, pp. 67–103. New York: International Universities Press.

————— (1971). Metapsychological aspects of phobias in adults. In *The Unconscious Today*, ed. M. Kanzer, pp. 97–118. New York: International Universities Press.

Sheehan, D. V., and Sheehan, K. H. (1983). The classification of phobic disorders. *International Journal of Psychiatric Medicine* 12:243–266.

Silber, A. (1989). Panic attacks facilitating recall and mastery: implications for psychoanalytic technique. *Journal of the American Psychoanalytic Association* 37:337–364.

Silove, D. (1986). Perceived parental characteristics and reports of early parental deprivation in agoraphobic patients. *Australian and New Zealand Journal of Psychiatry* 20:365–369.

Stoeri, J. H. (1987). Psychoanalytic psychotherapy with panic states: a case presentation. *Psychoanalytic Psychology* 4:101–113.

Tolpin, M. (1971). On the beginnings of a cohesive self: an application of the concept of transmuting internalization to the study of transitional object and signal anxiety. *Psychoanalytic Study of the Child* 26:316–354. New Haven, CT: Yale University Press.

Tyson, P. (1988). Psychic structure formation: the complementary roles of affects, drives, object relations and conflict. *Journal of the American Psychoanalytic*

Association 36:73–98.

Wangh, M. (1959). Structural determinants of phobia. *Journal of the American Psychoanalytic Association* 7:675–695.

Weiss, E. (1935). Agoraphobia and its relation to hysterical attacks and trauma. *International Journal of Psycho-Analysis* 16:59–83.

Weissman, M. M., and Merikangas, K. R. (1986). The epidemiology of anxiety and panic disorders: an update. *Journal of Clinical Psychiatry* 47:11–17.

Zetzel, E. R. (1968). The so-called good hysteric. *International Journal of Psycho-Analysis* 49:256–260.

15

Depression

Isidor Bernstein, M.D.

Psychoanalytic contributions to the study of depressive illness began with Abraham's (1911) "Notes on the Psycho-analytic Investigation and Treatment of Manic-Depressive Insanity and Allied Conditions" and Freud's (1917) paper on "Mourning and Melancholia." Later authors included Rado (1928), Gero (1936), Lewin (1950), Bibring (1953), and Jacobson (1971).

In 1946, Spitz described the infantile prototype of adult depression. He based his concept of "anaclitic depression" on the observation of hospitalized infants who lacked adequate mothering. Mahler's (1966) studies of young children extended Spitz's finding to a later period when children are involved in the process of separating from their mothers. She found "normal" children reacting to the separation process by a lowering of mood, which she termed "low key." More vulnerable children (i.e., those less able to achieve object constancy) would have more intense reactions such as clinging, weeping, rage, and panic attacks.

FACTORS CONTRIBUTING TO DEPRESSIVE NEUROSIS OR CHARACTER DISORDER

Although a genetic factor has been clearly established for bipolar disorder, the same is not true for the depressive neurosis or character disorder. One is likely to find a family history of depression involving one or more members of the patient's immediate or extended family. Here, the possibility of identification rather than a true genetic trait would be the more likely cause.

Different authors have emphasized disturbances in particular

259

phases of development as being of crucial significance in laying the groundwork for the subsequent appearance of depressive symptoms or the personality structure for the depressive character. Abraham (1911), Freud (1917), Rado (1928), and Bibring (1953) stressed the importance of oral mechanisms of incorporation and introjection in depression. Spitz's (1946) description of anaclitic depression in infants provided clinical support for the view that the events during the earliest years of development, when oral needs and gratifications predominate, are of major significance.

The most frequent cause of a depressive reaction is the loss of a loved one. This is particularly true of individuals with strong dependency needs originating in the early parent–child interactions. Such dependency intensifies the ambivalence toward the loved one. The loss (or withdrawal) of that person arouses feelings of helplessness, anger, and despair.

More recently, the role of aggression has been taken into account in understanding the forces involved in the depressive outcome (Gero 1936, Stone 1986). Because of the dependent needs, however, aggression is perceived as dangerous and the individual tries to protect the important object by turning the anger against himself. The infant or young child's methods of coping with deprivation, abandonment, or neglect may include withdrawal or self-directed aggressive behavior, such as head banging, scratching, or biting parts of his body. In latency, extreme stubbornness or other forms of negativism can also result in self-defeating behavior. The need to fail in school or sports can create tremendous stress if achievement is especially important to the individual, his family, or the social milieu. The outcome may be severe depression or even suicide.

In the oedipal phase, the boy must resolve his aggressive and competitive strivings vis-à-vis the father. If the solution he arrives at is submission to the father (and subsequently to others), his repressed aggression may be turned against himself. Repeated defeats resulting from this need to submit may culminate in a depressive outcome. In the case of the girl, her relinquishment of any rivalrous relationship with the mother may take the form of a dependent and submissive personality. At some point, this pattern may become dystonic for the girl. If the ensuing conflict ends up in a pattern of failure in any competitive situation, a depressive reaction, neurosis, or character can result.

Adolescence involves the transition from childhood to adulthood, from dependency to independence, and the establishment of the individual's identity. The combination of such tasks required of the adolescent creates a greater vulnerability to disappointments and failures due either to unfulfillable grandiose expectations or realistically impossible goals. Narcissistic injuries may be caused by a disappointing love affair, for example. Failure to gain entrance to a select college may so wound an individual's self-respect as to cause a depression. A physical defect, especially a defacing one, either congenital or as a result of an accident or injury, can cause an adolescent to suffer from such pain because of actual or expected rejection that he may withdraw into a depressed isolation. Another not uncommon event leading to depression in adolescence is the loss of a parent, sibling, or close friend.

The superego plays an important part in the way object loss or narcissistic injuries are dealt with. A major structural and dynamic force determining a depressive outcome is the type of superego that has been established. A severe, harsh, or even sadistic superego can be formed through identification with an actual or perceived harsh, punitive, or sadistic parental model. Here, the mechanisms of splitting and introjection result in the bad object being taken in to become the individual's bad self or self-representation (Bernstein 1957). Events and relationships that stimulate combinations of pain, frustration, and helplessness with consequent intense anger or rage will therefore be followed by guilt and depression in these individuals. Experiences of incest or rape can also initiate such a sequence.

VARIETIES OF DEPRESSION

Depression has been classified in a number of ways. The nosologies have this in common: There is a range from mild reactive disorder to the severe, chronic, psychotic disorder. *DSM-II* put depressive neurosis on Axis I and called it dysthymic disorder. It included affective variants with characterologic types. Dysthymia is defined as a chronic condition and is diagnosed on the basis of a history of continuous or frequent periods of depressive symptomatology of insufficient severity to justify a diagnosis of major depression.

A useful classification is based not only on symptomatic expressions but also takes into account the underlying pathology. Such an approach will differentiate between the varieties of depressive illness and will help to indicate the appropriate treatment. With that in mind, the following might be considered a psychodynamic and psychotherapeutically oriented classification:

1. Acute reactive depression
2. Persistent, recurrent depressive reaction:
   a. Depressive neurosis
   b. Depressive personality disorder
3. Severe, chronic, psychotic depression:
   a. Depressive psychosis (melancholia)
   b. Bipolar disorder, depressed

Establishing the diagnosis requires a consideration of the presenting symptoms and history, but it should also include an effort to determine the structural and dynamic aspects underlying the manifest expressions of the depressive constellation. As is true of all forms of mental illness, the pathology is the result of organic (genetic) factors, developmental failures, past and current stresses, and consequent unresolved internal conflicts leading to maladaptive solutions. Of particular importance so far as depressive illness is concerned are patterns of dealing with repeated losses, with failures of various kinds (academic, work, relationships, sexual), and with methods of coping with anger. Related to these would be the patient's major identifications, such as an identification with a depressed, abusive, punitive, or overly critical parent. The latter identifications could contribute to a harsh, sadistic superego. Also of importance would be the degree of ambivalence characterizing important relationships.

OBJECTIVES IN PSYCHOTHERAPY OF DEPRESSION

In determining the psychotherapeutic approach to be taken, it is first necessary to differentiate between simple reactive depression and the more severe and chronic forms of depressive illness. A careful history and clinical evaluation of genetic, developmental, and dynamic factors affecting the personality of the patient is required. A frequent finding is of an underlying dependent, inhibited, compulsive, or obsessional personality.

The therapist should review those factors which I have described as contributing to the depressive neurosis or character and decide which of these are accessible to work with via the therapeutic alliance. For example, guilt or self-blame and/or loss of self-esteem may be amenable to supportive and interpretive approaches to moderate the intensity of the painful feelings engendered by such patterns. Here, it would be necessary to assess the patient's ability and willingness to engage in the exploration of the origin and persistence of these trends. Such assessment could then be tested by the trial of a tactful interpretation of the least threatening or narcissistically painful issues. The patient's need to perceive the therapist as critical would have to be addressed early in the treatment.

Understanding the significance of the incident(s) precipitating the depression and the relationship to the personality structure and dynamics of the patient will enable the therapist to select more effectively the area(s) most likely to yield to psychotherapeutic intervention.

SIMPLE OR REACTIVE DEPRESSION

Grief is the normal response to loss, just as sadness is appropriate to unfortunate events. However, in a significant number of people, a more prolonged and persistent mood of depression will set in. In the simplest form of depression, this can occur in response to the death of or separation from an important loved one or respected family member or friend, setbacks in academic or work career, an unhappy love affair, or an illness or injury with disabling aftereffects.

The prototype in early childhood is the "low-key" mood described by Mahler (1966) that occurs during the process of separation-individuation. Later examples include the child's response to the birth of a sibling (including the preceding gestation period if the mother is physically or emotionally unavailable), beginning nursery school, and later, going away to camp and college. These fall into the category of reactions to separation, typically referred to as loneliness or homesickness. Recovery from such potentially painful experiences can be prompt if the basic affectionate relationship with the mother or alternative nurturing person has been reasonably consistent. Where such support has been lacking, the limited resources of the individual may render him unable to cope with the narcissistic or object-related injury. This can be in response to a single event or to a combination of two or more concomitant occurrences or to the cumulative effects of a series of such traumas. What determines the outcome? From clinical experience, it is apparent that the structure of the premorbid personality is the key to the individual's ability or lack of it to absorb the impact of the inevitable blows of life.

Mrs. A., 43, consulted me because of "depression." She connected this with her entering menopause. In addition, she told me that she was angry with her husband and children. She attributed this to their failure to live up to her expectations that they be more active, ambitious, and successful.

She was an only child. Her father had died of diabetic complications ten years ago, and her mother had died of cancer four years ago. She described her mother as being "like a doormat" in her relationship to her father. The father criticized and depreciated the patient; when she fought back, her mother wouldn't back her up. She therefore felt cheated in her relationship with her mother. She saw her father as strong, selfish, demanding, and domineering. She could see that she had become angry and critical as her father had been and didn't like this about herself.

Her father had been in business for a number of years when the business failed. Shortly after, he retired and lived on his savings and social security benefits. Mrs. A. and her husband contributed to the support of her parents. Mrs. A.'s husband had gone through a cycle similar to Mrs. A.'s father. He had been in a business that had failed but was now in a marginally successful enterprise. The family, however, was more dependent on Mrs. A.'s income from her professional work.

What had led to her depression? The patient saw herself becoming like her father and was self-critical about that. She had become nagging and demanding, causing her husband and children to react by withdrawing or reacting passively or aggressively. Consequently, she felt frustrated, hurt, angry, and unloved. The negative self-image contained an identification with the critical, demanding, and self-centered father, as well as with the masochistic, mistreated mother.

Therapy was directed at making her aware of these identifications and her defensive reactions against feelings of powerlessness by attempts to control her husband and children. As she became aware of the self-defeating results of her behavior, she made conscious efforts to control her critical and bossy behavior. It was also helpful for her to see that her criticisms of her husband and children were reflections of her own self-criticisms. These included her dissatisfaction with her physical appearance as a result of her overeating. This criticism of herself for not controlling her overeating entered into her need to criticize and attempt to control her husband's overeating. What underlay my efforts in my work with her was helping her restore some of the lowered self-esteem resulting from what she saw as her failures and those of her husband and children. The diminution of her feelings of frustration and helplessness lessened her anger at them and herself. Over a period of months, during which I saw her on a twice weekly basis, the depression gradually lifted. She became less tearful and less self-critical, and was able to be less controlling of her husband and children. When the arguments between her husband and herself diminished, he was able to seek help for himself.

It is important to distinguish the clearly reactive depressive reaction from the more chronic depressive neurosis or illness (Stone 1986). Simple sadness or sorrow due to bereavement, disappointment, or rejection may be resolved by the individual himself if he is able to provide or secure comforting libidinal or narcissistic supplies from within or from important others. When these are not available or forthcoming, recovery may be prolonged. The following case illustrates the need for therapy when the individual seems to recover but then suffers a relapse.

A 66-year-old man was referred by his sister-in-law because of her concern about his lack of motivation and interest. He confirmed his appointment and appeared on time. He spoke slowly, in a low tone and with some hesitation. His wife had died one and a half years ago. He had devoted a great deal of time and effort to care for her during the terminal stages of cancer. He thought he had gone through the process of mourning and had adjusted to his loss. In fact, he had begun seeing a woman friend who had become a widow about two years ago, and they were talking of living together. He enjoyed the relationship with this woman but had not accepted her proposal.

He had been employed as a salesman for an advertising agency but did not go back to work after his wife's death. However, he did arrange to work at home, making telephone calls to his old clients, and thereby obtaining business for his firm. For the past two months he had become increasingly less motivated to work or socialize. He felt there was no purpose to his going on. Although he asked himself questions about what he should do, he had done nothing to implement his answers. In fact, he felt rather hopeless. He had had thoughts of suicide but had done nothing to harm himself. Upon my questioning him regarding his feelings, he stated that he had pain of a physical nature, that is, pain extending from the midline of his chest to his abdomen.

I reviewed with him his wife's terminal illness. She had not wanted to be hospitalized and undergo chemotherapy, but both he and their daughter persuaded his wife to go ahead with that treatment. The doctors had advised them that the chemotherapy might either help or make things worse. Unfortunately, it turned out to be the latter. She became sicker and subsequently died. I indicated to him that he had apparently not resolved all of his feelings regarding the loss of his wife and that I felt it would be helpful for him to continue discussing this with me. He agreed but was concerned about the cost. I discussed this with him and arranged for a low fee in keeping with his circumstances. We set up a twice-a-week schedule.

It was apparent from his account that he blamed himself for having pressured his wife to undergo chemotherapy and that he attributed her subsequent death to the adverse effects of the medication. His unconscious anger at her abandonment of him through her death was shifted to anger at himself for having contributed to the fatal outcome. The suicidal thoughts could be understood as a product of his self-directed anger. There may also have been a fantasy of joining her in death.

Treatment was directed to making him aware of the fact that he continued to blame himself for his wife's death as a consequence of a fantasy of being more powerful than he actually was. I could show him that this attempt to see himself as powerful was a defense against feelings of helplessness in the face of the irreversible course of her disease.

The underlying personality structure of this man was that of an active, aggressive type, used to dealing with situations in an active way. He was not inclined to introspection, so only a limited amount of insight could be expected. However, he was able to accept my interpretations based on my formulations. From his account of patterns of dealing with situations occurring in school, work, and family relationships, I could point out to him how he had dealt with these in an active way. It was then possible to have him see that he felt guilty because he attributed his wife's death to his actively pressuring her to accept chemotherapy. His mood gradually improved, so it seems reasonable to assume that the interpretations had relieved some of the guilt causing his depression. He then directed his attention to deepening his relationship with his woman friend and making plans with her for his future. At that point, he decided to terminate treatment.

Because of the brevity of the treatment, it was not possible to explore his unconscious anger at his wife for having left him through her death. The prognosis was therefore guarded. About six months later, he wrote to me to pay part of the balance of his bill and told me that he still had times when he was struggling with his problems, but that overall he was managing better than he had been.

More severe reactions resulting in depressive neurosis or depressive personality require further explanation. Here, the history usually reveals earlier difficulties regarding separation and establishment of independence (Mahler 1966). In some cases, this is due to an earlier lack of maternal or parental empathy or support. Deprivation of physical and/or libidinal availability of the mother or maternal surrogate may impact on the child's feeling of self-worth. This may lay the groundwork for recurrent feelings of worthlessness precipitated by the inevitable disappointments, failures, and rejections that occur in the normal course of everyday living. Similarly, a child who is constantly criticized by one parent without receiving a balancing modicum of praise from that parent or the other parent will be predisposed to depressive reactions and neuroses. What is encompassed here are the various forms of deprivation or abuse that result from loss or absence of parental nurturing over an extended period of time.

Mr. B., a 40-year-old man, was referred for treatment because of continued depressed feelings. These had followed the hospitalization of an older sibling toward whom he had had long-standing ambivalent feelings. The patient tried to be helpful in the situation, but his brother responded with derogatory remarks. The combination of hostility and guilt on the part of Mr. B. reactivated earlier fantasies of revenge for mistreatment by the older brother. The impotent rage then found expression in self-destructive behavior, namely, excessive drinking and psychosomatic reactions.

The patient's mother had been a curiously unempathic woman who would ignore her child's needs for closeness and reassurance at times of stress. He was able to gain her attention through physical distress, for example, food sensitivities resulting in eating problems. His unhappiness due to her usual unavailability was expressed through a sad expression that was commented on during the time he was growing up. The additional attention he received as a result of the various physiological disturbances evoked resentment and hostility from Mr. B.'s older brother, who persecuted him in a number of annoying ways. Mr. B. attempted to reduce the brother's hostility by concealing his own superior academic achievements. This method of coping with his brother's envy was carried over to later personal and business dealings. The result was that it limited Mr. B.'s success. The impact on his self-esteem contributed to Mr. B.'s depressed mood.

Therapy was first directed toward the masochistic self-sacrificing behavior. Since he isolated the earlier origins of the more current masochistic pattern, it was necessary to show him how they were connected. For example, he would allow himself to be defrauded by neglecting to follow up on outstanding debts. As he became more assertive in this regard, his somatic symptoms became more marked. This, in turn, had to be linked with the early relationship with the mother. Mr. B. had used this as a substitute for a more directly competitive relationship with both his brother and his father. The more forbidden unconscious death wishes accounted for Mr. B.'s feelings of guilt, which were aroused when his father became ill and died and recurred with the illness of his brother. The self-blame and self-punishment could be understood as the consequences of a harsh superego reaction to the infantile competitive and murderous wishes. Progress in therapy was slow because any improvement would stir up a defensive negative therapeutic reaction. This would require working through in order to consolidate the hard-won gains.

Mr. B. was discharged from treatment after he had established an apparently comfortable state. He remained vulnerable to subsequent recurrences of his neuroses whenever someone close to him would fall ill. This required an additional period of treatment, but of shorter duration than the original course.

UNIPOLAR AND BIPOLAR DISORDER

In these conditions, both biological and psychological factors need to be considered. Treatment consists of both pharmacological and psychological modalities.

Mr. C., 22, was referred for continuation of therapy after having been discharged from a hospital. He had been hospitalized because of bizarre behavior, hyperactivity, poor concentration, hallucinations, and depression. He was first diagnosed as having a psychotic disorder; this was subsequently changed to bipolar disorder, manic with psychotic features. He was given lithium and improved sufficiently, so that he was able to live independently and work on a regular basis. During his manic phase he had become involved in a brush with the law that resulted in a two-year probation requiring him to continue psychiatric treatment.

When I saw him, he was dressed in working clothes and spoke like an uneducated backwoodsman, despite his having been graduated from a high school in the Northeast. He talked in a loud voice and complained angrily about having left the Appalachian area, where he had had friends and had been happy. He had come home at the insistence of his mother.

Mr. C. told me that he was adopted and knew nothing about his natural mother. His adoptive family consisted of his parents, a younger sister, and a younger brother. He stated that they all had problems, and their interaction resulted in a noisy and contentious household. The adoptive parents had been divorced when he was 12 years old, and the father had left a year later. The patient began drinking beer and whiskey at that time. He described a great deal of violence in his home caused by the father abusing the mother and the patient. After the father moved away and married another woman, the patient had no further contact with him.

The patient left home when he was 14 years old and lived with another family in a different state for about a year. He then joined his adoptive grandparents in Florida. While there, he continued his education, achieving a straight A average. He spent about six months of the year with his grandparents and then rejoined his adoptive family for the remaining six months of the year.

When he was 17, Mr. C. rejoined his mother and siblings. It was then that he developed a religious mania with some delusional trends. He enlisted in the army, where his bizarre behavior was first attributed to alcoholism. He was hospitalized and then discharged from the army. He went to live with an aunt in another state. At the age of 18, during a religious holiday, he felt overwhelmed with guilt and self-hatred and attempted suicide. He was hospitalized, given lithium, and discharged. A year later, again on a religious holiday, he became delusional with manic behavior and was hospitalized once more. After his release, he lived with his adoptive grandparents for a short time and then returned home. He became depressed; for some unexplained reason, he was not taking his medication. In a confused state, he got into an argument and was picked up by the police and taken to a state hospital. From there, he went to a halfway house. He returned to the New York area and was referred to me for continuation of therapy.

Mr. C. was having a difficult time adjusting to being at home. There were arguments with his mother, who was a controlling and domineering person. He argued with her about the way she was treating his "spoiled" younger brother. To prevent escalation of his anger, which had precipitated decompensation in the past, I had several interviews with the mother to counsel her. She had been pressuring him to resume his education, and he did not wish to do that. I suggested that he find some routine and undemanding work that would help to diminish the amount of time that he had at home and to establish a routine that would help to stabilize the situation. They both accepted this plan.

Therapy was, at first, on a twice-a-week schedule. The home situation improved, and Mr. C. settled into the daily routine fairly comfortably.

Since he was an adopted child, there was no available family history for bipolar disorder. Although he had thought about making inquiries, he had not attempted to obtain information from the adoption agency. The main focus in therapy was dealing with his anger and fear of losing control. The fact that he was forced to continue psychotherapy was one source of resentment. That was directed more at the authorities, particularly his probation officer, and his mother. Since a recurring pattern of reacting to pressure was mounting rage, I allowed him to reduce the frequency of his visits with the proviso that we would resume more frequent appointments if he became more upset.

There is no doubt that the biological element of the bipolar disorder is active in this patient. The principal dynamics involve the unresolved rage at the abandoning biological parents and the adoptive father. Added to this was the anger at the domineering, controlling, and critical mother. Mr. C. attempted to reverse the experience of having been abandoned by turning to an adoptive family of his own choosing, that is, his grandparents or the army, and then abandoning them. His fear of being overwhelmed by his murderous rage led him to escape into a psychotic religious mania and when that failed, to suicide. With these dynamics in mind, therapy was oriented to lessen both internal and external pressures contributing to the intense anger this man was experiencing.

DEPRESSION IN CHILDREN AND ADOLESCENTS

Until fairly recently, depression in children and adolescents was largely unrecognized. Even though Freud and early analytic writers stressed the oral determinants for depression, the actual occurrence of depression in infancy and childhood was not noted. After Spitz's (1946) research on infants suffering from what he termed *anaclitic depression* or hospitalism, more attention was given to the effects of various types of deprivation on infants and children. Difficulty occurred in recognizing depression in children and adolescents, even though suicide in adolescents is not uncommon.

Diagnosing depression in such populations can be difficult. Preverbal and nonverbal children will express dysphoria through somatic channels or via such behavior as withdrawing, sleep difficulties, excessive fatigue, or loss of appetite. Sadness, tearfulness, or weeping are clearer indications of unhappiness; persistence of such reactions should alert the clinician to the presence of a more pervasive affective disorder. Poznanski et al. (1985) classified the symptoms of depressed children into two categories: (1) essential symptoms consisting of verbalized dysphoria, pervasive anhedonia, nonverbal dysphoria, and lowered self-esteem; (2) qualifying symptoms, including sleep difficulties, excessive fatigue, cognitive impairment, psychomotor disturbances, appetite change, social withdrawal, and somatic complaints.

Don, 17, the son of Greek parents, was brought to treatment because his parents had become concerned when he told his father that his life was "all messed up" and that he felt like committing suicide. This comment was made during a discussion concerning Don's poor academic performance. He had been retained in the fifth grade and again in the sixth grade, so that he was now in a class with students two years his junior. His parents were convinced that Don could do better if he would work harder. This idea was reinforced by comments from Don's teachers. Don, however, told his parents that he was unable to apply himself to his studies and that he hated school. He had proposed switching to an alternative route to obtain a high school equivalency diploma, but they were opposed to this idea. Don's reaction to their pressure was that he needed "more room, more space." In fact, he spent much of his spare time away from his home; he had long talks with an aunt who lived nearby. Don felt that she was more understanding. He also spent a good deal of time at the home of a friend whose parents regarded him as another son, even giving him an allowance.

Don's father was a middle-aged factory worker who had been on the same job for many years. He worked hard and evidently expected the same of his two sons. He suffered from moderate hypertension, which was controlled with medication. His wife was ten years younger; she worked as a domestic to contribute to the family income. She was in good health, but a short time before the interview with me she had been hospitalized briefly because of metrorrhagia. During her illness, the father became involved with another woman. When his wife later learned about this, she became very angry and threatened to leave him. Don's father broke down into tears and begged his wife for forgiveness. When Don asked his father why he had been crying, the father confided in him. Don told his mother that he had lost a great deal of respect for his father, that he thought about it a great deal, and that it added to his difficulty in concentrating on his studies.

Don's past history was essentially noncontributory.

Don himself had requested an opportunity to talk to a psychiatrist and was anxious to tell me about his problems. He was a nice-looking, heavyset young man. As reported by his mother, he repeated to me that he needed "space" because he felt controlled by his parents. He didn't like the school that he was in and didn't like being in a class with 14-year-olds (the same age as his younger brother). He wanted to be a writer and believed that he could accomplish this by taking courses leading to a high school equivalency diploma. He would then enter college, where he could pursue his studies with people his own age.

He informed me that he didn't get along well with his brother, who "bugged" him and who, he felt, was favored by their parents. Don became so angry with him one time that he lost his temper and hit his brother. He admitted that he had a "short fuse."

Don felt that he could not get his parents to hear what he had to say. He wanted me to tell them what he had told me. I asked him what in particular he wanted me to tell them and informed him that I would tell them nothing more than that about our discussion. He wanted them to know that he hated the school he was in and wanted to pursue the alternative that he had in mind. I agreed that I would tell them that when I saw them.

This young man's depressive reaction and suicidal threat were partly a result of suppressed rage at his parents' insistence that he remain in school. He saw this as their insensitivity to his needs and their interest instead that he fulfill their expectations. In addition, the fact that he could not gain their approval caused him to feel that he was a disappointment to them and therefore not a good son. The poor self-image was added to by his poor academic performance and his having to be in classes at the same level as his younger brother.

Treatment was directed at enabling him to express his feelings of frustration and anger, to connect this with revengeful fantasies of abandoning his family and turning to more accepting relatives and friends as he was in the process of acting out. The guilt, loss of self-esteem, and self-directed anger could then be shown to him to cause his depressed mood and suicidal thoughts.

COUNTERTRANSFERENCE PROBLEMS

A depressed patient's mournful countenance, repetitive complaints, preoccupation with himself, and direct or indirect suicidal threats impose a significant burden on a therapist. The therapist may react by sharing the patient's discouraged outlook, feelings of emptiness, and repressed anger. In an effort to counter such feelings, the therapist may withdraw, prescribing medication or advising hospitalization before seeing how the patient responds to the emotional support and interpretive interventions provided by psychotherapy.

It is, of course, important not to dismiss suicidal threats. Tactful questioning regarding any preparation for suicide, such as the accumulation of potentially lethal amounts of medications, is in order. Where family members are concerned and available, they may be questioned regarding the availability of drugs or weapons that could be used. Patients who have made actual suicidal attempts may require direct supervision by a family member during the initial phase of therapy and during periods of intensification of symptoms.

CONCLUSION

Psychoanalytic understanding of the genetic and developmental origin of depressive disorders enables the therapist to formulate a series of structural and dynamic configurations that can be applied to the various clinical types that he will encounter in his practice. This provides him with the means to create an effective treatment plan that will be appropriate to the specific needs of his patients. The availability of such effective psychotherapy expands the range of therapeutic modalities beyond the limits of psychotropic medication.

REFERENCES

Abraham, K. (1911). Notes on the psycho-analytic investigation and treatment of manic-depressive insanity and allied conditions. In *Selected Papers*, trans. D. Bryan, and A. Strachey, pp. 137–156. New York: Basic Books.

Bernstein, I. (1957). The role of narcissism in moral masochism. *Psychoanalytic Quarterly* 26:358–377.

Bibring, E. (1953). The mechanism of depression. In *Affective Disorders*, ed. P. Greenacre, pp. 13–48. New York: International Universities Press.

Freud, S. (1917). Mourning and melancholia. *Standard Edition* 14:243–258.

Gero, G. (1936). The construction of depression. *International Journal of Psycho-Analysis*. 17:423–461.

Jacobson, E. (1971). *Depression*. New York: International Universities Press.

Lewin, B. D. (1950). *The Psychoanalysis of Elation*. New York: Norton.

Mahler, M. S. (1966). Notes on the development of basic moods: the depressive affect. In *Psychoanalysis—A General Psychology*, ed. R. M. Loewenstein, L. M. Newman, M. Schur, and A. J. Solnit, pp. 152–168. New York: International Universities Press.

Poznanski, K., Mokros, H. B., Grossman, J., and Freeman, L. Diagnostic criteria in childhood depression (1985). *American Journal of Psychiatry* 142:1168–1173.

Rado, S. (1928). The problem of melancholia. *International Journal of Psycho-Analysis* 9:301–317.

Spitz, R. A. (1946). Anaclitic depression: an inquiry into the genesis of psychiatric conditions in early childhood. *Psychoanalytic Study of the Child*, 2:313–342. New York: International Universities Press.

Stone, L. (1986). Psychoanalytic observations on the pathology of depressive illness: selected spheres of ambiguity or disagreement. *Journal of the American Psychoanalytic Association* 34:329–362.

16

Borderline Patients

Warren H. Goodman, M.D.

DIAGNOSTIC AND DYNAMIC CONSIDERATIONS

The diagnosis and treatment of borderline patients has oversaturated the psychiatric literature over the past fifteen to twenty years. This has been due to the frequency with which such patients are encountered in clinical practice and the particularly vexing problems they raise in connection with management and treatment, which are encountered not only with borderline patients, but with other patients who fall into related diagnostic categories. The advent of self psychology and the popularization of object relations theory associated with the British school of psychoanalysis, as well as the so-called widening scope of mainstream classical psychoanalysis, are probably all developments that have contributed to greater focus on borderline patients. The incorporation of the borderline diagnosis and the schizotypal diagnosis within *DSM-III* and *DSM-III-R* has done much to legitimize and concretize this diagnostic entity, which probably more accurately reflects a heterogeneous group of disorders.

It is probably true that the majority of dynamically oriented psychotherapists do not adhere rigidly to the guidelines of *DSM-III-R* when thinking about borderline patients but have a more general concept in mind, that is, that group of patients with severely compromised ego functions. The compromised ego functions, in turn, produce clinical pictures of extreme volatility and instability, leading to chaotic transferences and consequent serious challenges to the conventional dynamic psychotherapeutic framework. These challenges intrigue therapists, as they seem to call into play recent conceptualizations of the psychotherapeutic dyad, transference–countertransference configurations, and clinical implications of the discoveries concerning infant and childhood development for the phenomenology of ego regression.

There are some typical therapeutic issues that are common to the psychotherapeutic encounter with borderline patients, although these themes are certainly not exclusive to them. They include (1) separation anxiety and general considerations of separation-individuation; (2) problems in reality testing; (3) manifestations of contradictory self and object representations producing the so-called phenomenon of splitting; (4) identity issues as seen, for instance, in the as-if personality; (5) problems of low self-esteem; (6) problems with the harsh punitive superego and intractable guilt (both conscious and unconscious), along with related problems of moral masochism; (7) difficulties with impulse control; (8) the consequences of child abuse (both physical and sexual); (9) chronic dependency; (10) social isolation; (11) underachievement; (12) sadomasochistic interpersonal relationships; and (13) problems with narcissism. These issues do not necessarily constitute the totality of the experience with the broadly defined borderline group, nor are they encountered exclusively with borderline patients.

Approaches to the solutions of these problems as they are promulgated in the literature vary considerably, from extremely supportive techniques to highly abstinent, expressive, and exploratory formats. It would seem that the ideal approach would not be encumbered ideologically but rather would recognize individual characteristics of each seriously troubled patient. From the side of the patient, the relative strengths and weaknesses of the various ego functions, the degree of vulnerability to regression, the previous course and history of such regressions, experiences with previous therapeutic encounters, the degree of psychological mindedness, the capacity for development of a working alliance, intelligence, and the level of motivation are among the factors that need to be considered. From the side of the therapist, clinical experience, capacity to deal with countertransference, frustration tolerance, theoretical and clinical training, and psychodynamic orientation are all factors that could influence the degree to which a given therapy is either supportive or expressive/exploratory. The results of these various factors will determine the final approach. Ideally, this approach will not remain static, but will change as the underlying factors influencing both patient and therapist change during the course of therapy. The concentration on the aforementioned problematic therapeutic issues will also shift over the course of the treatment, as one or another of them comes more sharply into focus.

There are certain common characteristics that should be kept in mind. These personality disorders are long in developing, whether the major contributions have been constitutional or developmental or a result of intrafamilial dynamics, history of trauma, and so on. Therefore, it follows that the therapies of these conditions, other than for crisis interventions (which do occur with volatile patients), are largely protracted encounters lasting for many months or even years. This degree of involvement, as well as the agenda of work that has to be accomplished, requires an extended duration of therapy.

It should also be remembered that unequivocally successful outcomes of one-time psychotherapies with borderline patients is not a modal phenomenon. Anecdotal reports seem to vary along a spectrum from significant to minimal success. Definitive studies have yet to be done, but it would appear that greater success is achieved after multiple therapeutic experiences. The level of success seems to vary in a linear way with the level of ego strength of the patient. It behooves the therapist who attempts to work with borderline patients to maintain modest expectations while being on the alert for the flagging of his own therapeutic zeal.

The presence in the literature on these patients of a plethora of treatment approaches suggests that there are factors that produce positive change that may be misidentified by the authors. These factors may well reside in commonalities of attitude and technique that may not be related in any linear way to the specific theoretical orientations espoused.

THE THERAPEUTIC AND WORKING ALLIANCE

It should be mentioned that, throughout the course of any treatment with a borderline patient, the status of the therapeutic or working alliance is, at best, problematic. As we shall see, the initial efforts in the therapeutic interaction are devoted to developing some rudimentary alliance with the patient. The illusion of cooperation can be ruptured at any time by a real or perceived loss of empathy with the patient, which can promote regression. The alliance problem is further compounded by the fact that many borderline patients, because of their limited ego resources, are frequently unable to devote sufficient monetary assets to their therapies and, as a result, are probably seen with inadequate frequency. The problem surfaces during regressed periods, when sufficient upsurges of psychotic or self-destructive symptomatology warrant hospitalization. It is at such times that the alliance is sorely strained and the patient often winds up transferring to another therapist. This is a particular problem for those therapists who are largely engaged in office practice and have minimal hospital affiliation. The negative transferential feelings generated by the hospitalization experience and the disappointments and angers that may have precipitated the hospitalization become insurmountable in terms of reestablishing the therapeutic relationship.

The effort to establish some semblance of a therapeutic or working alliance is hindered by the fact that only a rudimentary observing ego may be available, and the therapeutic split between the observing and the experiencing ego may not be well defined. Furthermore, the sense of reality and the relationship to reality are impaired, and on occasion reality testing itself is compromised. This has implications for the capacity of the patient to differentiate the therapist as a separate individual and may create problems in establishing object constancy, even if reality testing considerations are not germane. Because of these difficulties, the borderline patient, more so than the neurotic patient, cannot appreciate the therapist as a real individual whose role is to help resolve the presenting difficulties in cooperation with the patient.

As has been mentioned, the treatment of the borderline patient is intrinsically protracted. During the opening phase a relationship must be developed that includes the construction of a therapeutic alliance. This is followed by the commencement of an ongoing process of internalization of various ego strengths through contact with the therapist and the strengthening of ego functions by the use of clarification, observation, confrontation, and interpretation. The process of internalization is contributed to by both nonverbal and verbal means, that is, by the therapeutic stance of the therapist, his helping function, his capacity to sustain the angry onslaughts of the patient, and his judicious use of verbal interventions that promote growth, sharpen the observing ego, yet spare the patient's narcissism in order to avoid an upsurge of destructive negative transferential acting out. Since we are talking of a protracted treatment, it is ironic that so many of these patients are treated on a weekly basis. Many patients have limited economic resources (a function, to a large extent, of their limited ego strength) and are therefore treated in clinic situations where there are frequent changes in therapists, reifying their fears of abandonment on a repetitive basis. Many patients who are treated in outpatient settings are seen in psychiatric training facilities and free-standing clinics, and therefore experience interruptions in their treatment because of the reality of academic progression. Obviously, these interruptions have to be deleterious to the development of rudimentary basic trust in subsequent therapeutic experiences.

BASIC CATEGORIES OF TREATMENT

The modalities of treatment can be sorted into three basic categories. The largest number are in supportive treatment, in which the patient is seen no more than once a week. Reality issues are addressed, for the most part, with a view toward augmenting the patient's capacity to deal with realistic situations and adapt to day-to-day living. Techniques are predominantly those of reality testing, clarification, observation, and confrontation. Interpretation is used less frequently, although it may be appropriate to further the rather sharply delimited goals. It is used to make the patient conscious of what he is not aware of in the here and now and usually extratransferentially and without recourse to invoking the past or primary objects. Regression is avoided; when it does occur, it is dealt with by verbal interventions geared to restoring the patient's equilibrium, such as by reality testing and supportive interventions. Mild positive transference is not interpreted, and negative transference is interpreted only when it promotes destructive acting out or threatens the ongoing integrity of the therapeutic alliance. Ideally, this supportive modality is suited for the group of difficult patients who have the most limited ego strengths, are the most regressed and maladaptive, and possess the least psychological mindedness.

The second broad modality of treatment of the borderline patient is intensive or exploratory psychotherapy, in which, in addition to clarification and observation and the occasional use of reality testing and supportive reassurance, there is frequent use of interpretations. The interpretations include explanations of transference as it is allowed to emerge in the therapeutic situation in the context of promoting a moderate and somewhat controlled regression. The frequency can be two to three times a week (Kernberg [1975] advocated a three-times-a-week encounter). Therapy with this modality is conducted face to face.

Obviously, the subgroup of patients for which this modality is suited includes those with higher-level ego functioning, lower anxiety levels, greater frustration tolerance, more solid reality orientation, and a concomitant capacity to develop an observing ego and a realistic enough perception of the therapist to promote a reasonable working alliance for extended periods of time. There must be a mutual confidence on the part of the therapist and patient in the patient's capacity to withstand moderate regression, to possess sufficient ability to conceptualize the "as if" qualities of transference feelings and interpretations, and to differentiate the therapist from past primary objects. Generally speaking, this patient subpopulation does not have a history of intercurrent hospitalization for serious psychotic regressions. In an ideal situation, a supportively treated patient who is able to sustain protracted contact with the same therapist over a period of time within the modality may gradually, through subtle changes in the technique of the therapist and with a more interpretive handling of the transference, be transformed into a patient who may be able to be treated in the intensive/exploratory modality. It often occurs that the improvement in ego strengths is accompanied by a better adaptive mode, so that socioeconomic impediments to greater frequency of treatments will have been removed.

The third modality is classical analysis, although one has to use that term with certain qualifications. Those patients appropriate for this modality obviously possess the highest level of ego strength. They also possess keen psychological mindedness and a capacity to maintain an alliance through the trials and tribulations of intense transference experiences.

There are those who might argue that the patients described here may not even fall into the borderline category, but I would submit that they could well have started out as borderline and continue to behave that way during stressful periods. In any event, the fine texture of the so-called classical analysis that they undergo would be quite different from the classical analysis of the neurotic. There would be interventions of greater frequency, which would be intuitively provided by the analyst in deference to a patient's greater sensitivity to sensory deprivation. There might be a greater sprinkling of quasi-supportive verbalizations on the part of the therapist. There would probably be a greater readiness on the part of the therapist to interpret potentially destructive negative transference and a greater vigilance in anticipating its emergence.

Perusal of the literature in which reports of such analyses are provided seems to reveal much more frequent use of parameters, such as setting time limits on the treatment, or other behavioral manipulations, such as threatening premature termination of the treatment. Scrutiny of process material from such analyses also reveals a greater frequency of interventions that approach reality testing or grossly supportive self-esteem building comments, which may very well be effective therapeutic techniques but are nevertheless at great variance with classical analytic technique as used with neurotics. Admittedly, given these departures from classical technique, this modality is more abstinent, more promoting of regression, and more geared to developing transference neuroses than the previous two modalities and deserves a separate categorization. It is not yet clear what percentage of patients in the borderline category successfully benefit from this approach.

THE PROBLEMS OF AGGRESSION AND REGRESSION

The earliest phase of treatment with the borderline patient, irrespective of the modality undertaken, will revolve around an attempt to form some semblance of an alliance. The difficulty encountered is that the patient has had a prehistory of unsatisfactory relationships with people from early childhood on and very likely a series of therapeutic encounters that have ended on a sour note. In order for the patient to develop rudimentary basic trust, cognizance must be taken of his expectation of rejection on the one hand, and his fear of engulfment on the other. The therapist must anticipate the patient's aggression rushing to the fore in a negative interpersonal interaction, which manifests itself in various acting-out behaviors, including missing sessions, verbalizing diatribes against the therapist, entering into self-destructive relationships, and even manipulating through suicide.

The confrontation of the patient with his self-defeating behavior is critical, as are observations and clarifications that convey to him the therapist's awareness of the patient's nihilistic rage and fear of retaliation and his consequent distancing behavior and inevitable feelings of terrible aloneness. This can be taken up in the context of the fear of the burgeoning relationship with the new therapist and in observations about fears of other close relationships. At this stage, limit setting may be indicated, but it should always be accompanied by careful explanation of how this contingency is exercised only to enhance the patient's ultimate self-interest.

Suicidal threats, especially by the borderline patient who is also manifestly depressed, should be taken quite seriously. While the therapist should be ever mindful of the manipulative valence of such threats, it is important that he be sensitive to the patient's feeling of aloneness and repeated experiences of real or symbolic object loss. This may require the therapist to make himself more available as a real object to the patient. Availability by phone, written communication, and irregular or extra hours may be necessary. Empathic and sympathetic interventions that reveal the therapist's awareness of the depth of the patient's pain and isolation are critical. Eventually, the therapist's empathy, reliability, steadfastness, and capacity to contain and withstand the patient's aggressive onslaught will constitute the nucleus around which a therapeutic alliance can be forged.

Closely related to the issue of careful diagnosis is the problem of regression. Perusal of the literature reveals that many therapists purport to do extremely abstinent forms of therapy and analysis with what appear to be extremely compromised patients, some of whom, to my reading, cannot be distinguished from ambulatory schizophrenics. In the course of these analytic therapies, the authors frankly record the depth of serious and, in some cases, protracted psychotic regressions that are intercurrent during extended therapeutic encounters. Implicit in the writings is that the regression per se is therapeutically central to a favorable outcome. While it is true that in classical psychoanalysis a comprehensive transference interpretation necessarily presumes the presence of an intense transference and therefore a considerable level of regression, it must be remembered that this observation was made in relation to hypothetically healthier patients with relatively intact egos. Nevertheless, there appears to exist in certain quarters a kind of magical belief, highly romanticized, that the patient (regardless of level of ego strength) who is allowed to regress, or indeed, whose regression is promoted in the therapeutic situation, will somehow inevitably reconstitute on a higher level of functioning on the basis of the insight he attained during the regression.

Knight (1953), working with institutionalized borderline patients, albeit in an open hospital setting, recognized that the use of a too classical or abstinent technique could lead to serious psychotic regressions in patients and advocated careful evaluation of ego functions before allowing regression to take place in therapy. Zetzel (1971) cautioned against frequency of contact for fear of developing intense transferences that could not be resolved. Although there has been a definite movement away from that conservative approach over the years to a more adventurous psychotherapeutic intervention, these caveats should be kept in mind. At the other end of the spectrum are a number of analysts of the British school who have undertaken rather abstinent analytic interventions with very regressed patients.

In my opinion, there should be an inverse linear relationship between the degree of ego compromise and the level of regression allowed within the psychotherapy. Certain of these regressions seem to come out of the blue, totally unbidden, although retrospective reflection often reveals the empathic flaw, intercurrent event, or unrecognized transference vicissitude that may have precipitated the regression. These regressions are particularly pernicious in that they can be long-lasting, can extend outside the therapeutic situation into the patient's everyday life, and can severely compromise functioning even to the point of institutionalization. The result can be a rupture of the therapeutic alliance, as well as a serious and possibly protracted interference with the patient's quality of life and interpersonal relationships.

The therapist must be thoroughly aware of his countertransference rescue fantasies, which may prompt his encouragement of such regressions to take place in the service of remaking his patient in the tradition of a Pygmalion. Regression should always be measured and controlled. The impact on the patient should be reasonably predictable on the basis of careful ongoing experience with the patient in therapy and after a thorough evaluation of the patient's ego strengths and weaknesses and therapeutic and personal history.

COUNTERTRANSFERENCE ISSUES

Since we have alluded to countertransference, it would be helpful to elaborate on the various problems of countertransference that are either specific to treatment of borderline patients or more poignantly experienced with them. As noted, there is a rescue fantasy that can be a part of the therapist's conscious or unconscious attitude in relation to the seriously afflicted patient. For the most part, however, the therapist has to be wary of the development of strong reactions to the ubiquitous and intense aggression communicated overtly and covertly by the patient.

The countertransference problem could manifest itself in overt or subtle retaliation. It is very easy to become annoyed with a patient and withdraw from or break off communication, which invariably is experienced as a rejection and can precipitate regression. The acting-out therapist can even be overtly insulting or perhaps inadvertently short, curt, and cool, all of which can have untoward effects. It is important to be aware that while the patient is acting out, he is also testing the therapist's responses. As is well known, borderline patients have a particular sensitivity that allows them to intuit the therapist's psychological weak spots. They can make the therapist feel defensive and possibly promote the kind of retaliation alluded to earlier. This intuition probably evolves from their hypervigilance to slights and from their porous self-boundaries that allow them to be uncannily empathic with all kinds of uncomfortable emotions on the part of the people with whom they develop relatively close relationships. Their anticipation of pain in interpersonal relationships (derived from their traumatized life histories) arms them with a negative predisposition toward other individuals, the therapist being no exception, which allows them to use these intuitions to inflict pain. These phenomena are alluded to in the literature as devaluation and projective identification.

On the other side of the coin is the phenomenon of idealization, in which the other individual, including the therapist, can be defensively elevated to a lofty position and can become the object of potential primitive wish fulfillment to compensate for feelings of extreme deprivation and low self-esteem. This can promote narcissistic responses in the vulnerable therapist. As in all instances of countertransference with its potential for subtle and gross enactment, the therapist is best protected from its consequences if he has sufficient insight into his own conflicts and vulnerabilities to become alert to his own mounting anger or the various defenses against it.

The subject of countertransference leads to the general issue of patient–therapist fit. There are obviously certain patients who do well with a given therapist, yet who have a history of having aborted previous therapies. No doubt, preparatory work in previous therapies may make an impact on the situation; however, it is very likely that certain indefinables about the complementarity of conflicts and areas of vulnerability rooted in the life history and development of both therapist and patient are at the basis for such a good fit. There are certain therapists who have a particular ability to deal with very regressed patients, and there are those whose tolerance for such patients is very low but who work quite well with higher-level borderlines and are able to titrate gratification without fostering dependency. The permutations and combinations are legion, and each therapist should have such an awareness during the evaluation period of the potential for a good match. In general, a "good enough" therapist must have a high level of frustration and anxiety tolerance to treat borderline patients, and must be able to become aware of his own psychological vulnerabilities in anticipation of transference storms that can call forth potentially destructive countertransferences. A relatively stable, quiescent, and gratifying personal and professional life is optimally desirable to treat these patients, since they provide so much stress. It is also advisable to limit the number of such difficult patients because of their trying demands.

CLINICAL EXAMPLES

Some of the points made in the previous discussion can be illustrated with a few case vignettes.

Now in her mid-thirties, Ms. M. had been married very briefly in her early twenties and had decided to terminate the marriage because her husband was "conventional" and restricted her aspirations to have a career. This was very negatively received by her very conventional parents, but the patient persevered.

After fifteen years of being single, a period marked by a few close relationships, she felt very unwanted and unlovable. This was exacerbated by an episode in which her father chose not to leave his business to her, but rather to sell it to a younger man who was an employee of his. This verified her feelings of being an unwanted and undesirable female. The father's decision came at a time when the patient had suffered from debilitating infectious illness, from she which she subsequently recovered. Nevertheless, she felt that her father deemed her too fragile and too incompetent by virtue of her femininity and vulnerability to illness to carry on the family business.

She became depressed at that point, and her therapist hospitalized her briefly after she made a suicidal threat. The therapist was told by the staff of the hospital that the rapport with the patient was broken. With that, the ill-fated therapy, which had lasted several years, came to an end. The patient was referred to me upon discharge.

Therapy initially consisted of a protracted period during which basic trust and an alliance had to be developed, since the patient felt betrayed by her family, especially her father, and her previous therapist. She had become demoralized about occupational reverses and experiences of being rejected in relationships with men and made suicidal threats.

The therapeutic approach included making myself available to her as a real object by allowing between-session phone calls or extra sessions, expressing concern, and conveying empathic interventions regarding her plight. Concomitantly, there were discussions indicating that while she had the power to manipulate and control the therapy and that there was ultimately nothing I could do about preventing her suicide, she would in essence sabotage the therapy and end the relationship, if not her life. Gradually, the suicidal threats dropped away. With encouragement, the patient sought additional close personal relationships and improved her status by going on to more challenging jobs after obtaining an advanced degree on a part-time basis.

The case illustrates that suicidality has to be taken very seriously, especially in a borderline patient with a history of intercurrent major depression. It should be noted that in this particular case antide-pressant medications of various kinds were used at times of critical outbreaks of depression, all of which were reactive to a very specific disappointment. Augmenting the corrosive effect on the patient's self-esteem caused by the father's rejection of her as a business heir was the mother's ongoing negative comparison of her with her older brother and older sister and petty critical evaluations of her choice in clothes, hairdo, and makeup. These ongoing denigrations during her adult years, as seen in therapy, echoed the more insidious undermining of her self-esteem, which took place during the patient's childhood years. Supportive interventions concerning her low self-esteem were frequent and constituted a significant part of the work that took place on a thrice weekly basis over a number of years. Putting her mother's and father's critical and derisive atti-tudes into perspective, contrasted with her realistic accomplishment and interpersonal acceptance by peers and colleagues, stabilized her greatly.

The case of Mr. C. illustrates the prominence of identity confu-sion and dependency in certain borderline patients, as well as severe separation anxiety.

Mr. C. was born of a mixed marriage in which his father converted to the religion of his mother. As a child, the patient was always terrified to be away from his parents. As he approached late adolescence, he developed a tendency to cross-dress. He rationalized that if he were female, he would have been loved by his parents, as he felt his older sister was. He attended a nearby college, which allowed him to remain at home. His parents then decided to move farther away, so he left school. He was unable to serve in the military because of a severe separation anxiety. His emotional distress was significant enough to gain him a deferment. He was able to get training in a technical field and worked for a large corporation.

It became clear in therapy that his cross-dressing had to do with his need to use his mother as a soothing object in effigy, which took the form of a very concrete identification with her by dressing in women's clothing. His fear of loss and separation and feelings of unworthiness of being loved extended to his social relationships with women. When he married, he converted to his wife's religion, which was different from either of his parents' religions. By conforming in this way, he felt that he could then maintain the love of his wife, even though his parents disapproved of her. She, however, was actually very devoted to him.

The patient was given to severe feelings of panic when he would go on vacation or when he would have to in any way leave his accustomed environment. Any changes in locale in relation to his job, even though he worked for the same company for many years, would engender similar intense feelings of anxiety.

It appeared that his parents were both emotionally cold and distant from him and had only responded to him during childhood when he was in some physical or emotional distress. Unfortunately, he would use similar mechanisms to gain attention from his wife. He would lament the fact that he could not relate closely to his three daughters, with the exception of his youngest daughter, who had developed a severe psychosomatic illness during late adolescence. The identification with her as the sick and needy one was quite clear.

The patient was stabilized in a supportive psychotherapy in which the constancy and availability of the therapist was of critical importance. He developed an intense attachment, but as his problems with separation and his irrational fears of rejection and separation were discussed on an ongoing basis, he could gradually tolerate vacations and weekend separations from the therapist. His understanding of his use of cross-dressing as a kind of supportive soothing object mitigated some of the very intense shame about his behavior and raised his self-esteem. His chronic distrust of his wife as someone who would ultimately reject him was called into question in the light of actual experience during the marriage, and he was able to become more open with her. After several years he bought a country house, where he could relax with his family. This resulted in his giving up certain night jobs that he had taken ostensibly to make additional money, but basically to avoid intimacy with his family. The fear of engulfment, which was the obverse of his fear of separation, had necessitated that kind of orientation for many years. After several years of treatment, the patient was considerably less guilty and less masochistic in terms of his lifestyle, was able to enjoy himself, suffered less anxiety, and tolerated separations much more adaptively.

Mr. F. was a middle-aged man who had been in treatment all of his adult life with several different therapists, about whom he spoke derisively. He began therapy with me after the recent death of his previous therapist, a man he admired for his earthy strength. He aspired to being very much like this rugged therapist, who would go hunting and fishing and do masculine things. The patient related how he began to wear leather jackets and ride a motorcycle, thinking he was emulating his therapist. Ironically, when the patient had to be hospitalized for a gall bladder operation, the previous therapist visited him in the hospital and charged him for the visit. The patient was furious. Sometime later, when the previous therapist was hospitalized for a myocardial infarction, which was the ultimate cause of the therapist's demise, the patient visited him in the hospital and inadvertently gave him a book entitled *To an Early Grave*. His intense repressed hostility toward the previous therapist could only be appreciated retrospectively.

At the time he began treatment with me, the patient was working for his father, a very successful business man whom the patient envied. Nevertheless, the father was closer and more caring than the patient's mother, who, like the father, was of advanced age but who was very cold to the patient when he was a child. She was a narcissistic woman preoccupied with her doll collection. The successful father was also very narcissistic and was involved in many self-aggrandizing community activities. The patient complained bitterly that the father would dominate him in the business and did not give him sufficient opportunity for freedom of judgment.

At one point, the patient had a dream in which he inherited a farmer's farm and farmhouse. A major source of the patient's hostility clarified after he realized that his own name meant "farmer" in the language of his ethnic origin, and the oedipal significance of this awareness struck him.

The patient's appreciation of his competitive and acquisitive desires with respect to his father's power and the love of his mother helped him put his hypercritical attitude toward his father into perspective and enabled him to accept the warmth and support that his father was capable of giving him. This was especially helpful since the patient had replicated his father's lifestyle by marrying a severely dysfunctional woman who was of no support to him whatsoever and was a tremendous emotional and financial drain. He was stabilized to the point where he could feel more self-confident and successful in his father's business. He was able to increase his social involvement as an individual, since his wife was self-confined to their house with multiple psychosomatic illnesses.

This case illustrates that, within the matrix of a highly supportive treatment, interpretations of dream material can be utilized, even in an oedipal context, to achieve a specific strategic supportive goal.

Ms. F., a medical student, came to treatment through a very convoluted mode of referral after having been in therapy since early adolescence with multiple therapists. Either she would leave treatment or the therapists would interrupt the program because they felt that they could not work with her. The patient was extremely derisive, angry, aloof, and contemptuous. She described in pithy terms her encounters with her various therapists, many of whom were known to me. All of the descriptions were quite critical, but when describing personal characteristics of these various people there was always a certain kernel of truth.

Needless to say, when the patient began therapy she almost immediately began to be derisive and devaluing of me, comparing me unfavorably with several of the previous therapists. Gradually, her previous therapist, who concluded that he could no longer work with her, was most idealized.

An attempt was made to probe the possible antecedent models for this tendency to split. This led to a long diatribe about the shortcomings of her mother, who was a professional woman. The patient was the youngest child and only girl among four siblings, all of whom were quite academically successful. Her father was also a rather successful professional man.

It became clear that the patient would necessarily sabotage the potentially close relationship with me because of her ultimate fear of abandonment and rejection. After about six months, she decided that she could no longer work with me and requested a referral, despite the fact that her anticipated fear of rejection by me had been interpreted to her. This was not sufficient to contain her anxiety. The fact that she requested a referral directly from me indicated some element of positive regard, and I made a referral to another therapist. She stayed with him for over a year, until she found that certain transient health problems that he had were indicative that she might be abandoned again. She sought consultation and went on to yet another therapist. Her tenures of treatment seem to be increasing in duration.

The supervision of a resident's case in which the presenting symptom was bulimia revealed yet another expression of a similar dynamic connected with separation anxiety. The patient in question came from a broken home, and the central issue of loss of control emerged as the focus of the therapy. The displacement of concerns regarding control emanated from the fear of the loss of significant objects. Indeed, she had lost her father, by divorce, at a very early age. She had subsequently lost her mother through illness and death during adolescence. These conflicts were displaced onto her capacity to control her appetite. In this instance, interpretation was successful in modifying the patient's symptomatology. The patient continues to improve in ongoing treatment.

Another case treated by a psychiatric resident demonstrated chronic suicidality. The patient was a male homosexual who had AIDS. He had procrastinated many months before starting AZT therapy, during which time he continued compulsively promiscuous homosexual activity. The patient was at first confronted with a certain amount of limit setting in the therapy, which seemed to quiet his self-destructive behavior for a time, but he insidiously began to sabotage the treatment by missing sessions and denying the importance and relevance of the treatment. He eventually broke off treatment in an attempt to proceed with his self-destructive lifestyle. The patient was not in treatment long enough to clarify the antecedents for this behavior, but what did emerge was that he was in a business with his father and brother, and had always been the ineffectual black sheep of the family in the eyes of his parents and sibling. His acting out was, to some extent, a retroflexion of his aggression toward them and an attempt to demonstrate that he could be more contemptuous, demeaning, and destructive of himself than his family.

Another case seen in supervision was that of a young mother who physically abused her two children and was remanded by the courts. Interestingly, there was no history of her having experienced abuse at the hands of either of her parents. It emerged that she had bouts of episodic dyscontrol, related to a chronic intermittent affective disorder, which responded to tricyclic antidepressants. Nevertheless, there were many characterological issues in the borderline realm related to her tendency to split, her volatility, and her shallow interpersonal relationships and paranoid orientation. Obviously, this affective disorder compromised her developing object relations, to the point where serious characterological difficulties evolved.

CONCLUSION

There are many manifestations of psychopathology that are collectively seen as borderline and require specific and disparate therapeutic tactics. I have attempted to demonstrate that while many patients can be beyond the reach of immediate and dramatically successful therapeutic efforts, over a period of time, with ongoing and serial therapies, inroads can be made into the various elements of their psychopathology. Generally speaking, a flexible therapeutic approach that focuses on conflict resolution while taking into account the degree of ego strengths and weaknesses can lead to helpful therapeutic intervention over time and justifies dedicated psychotherapeutic efforts.

REFERENCES

Kernberg, O. (1975). *Borderline Conditions and Pathological Narcissism.* New York: Jason Aronson.
Knight, R. (1953). Borderline status. *Bulletin of the Menninger Clinic* 17:1–12.
Zetzel, E. (1971). A developmental approach to the borderline patient. *American Journal of Psychiatry* 128:867–871.

17

The Narcissistic Personality

Martin H. Blum, M.D.

By 1900, with the publication of "The Interpretation of Dreams," Freud had created the framework for the understanding of the transference object. Operating at the behest of the censorship, he stated, the mobile energies of the primary system made possible defensive condensation and displacement: the transfer of childhood wishes in modified form onto more acceptable substitutes from current perception, thereby keeping the earlier wishes in repression. Using this model, he could trace, in his analysis of the "Dream of the Botanical Monograph," the line that led from his childhood incestuous and masturbatory wishes to his sexual urgency at the time of his engagement, and then to the very act of writing the dream-book (Freud 1900). Also in 1900 (although he delayed publication for five years), Freud wrote the case history of Dora to show the identity of structure that united the dream, the neurosis, and the analytic situation. The figure of the analyst himself became the preeminent example of the transference object (Freud 1905).

However, within the decade, Freud was already describing clinical material that could not be fitted within this framework. In the autumn of 1909 he undertook the analysis of an idealizing homosexual who, he commented to Jung, seemed to have Leonardo da Vinci's constitution without his genius. What he observed in this patient was that there was an attraction to women that could not be distinguished from the normal case, but that on each occasion, the patient "transferred" his excitation onto a male object. This was outside the usual expectation that such transferences onto an object should lead, analytically, to one of the primal figures of childhood, since the beloved boys were clearly substitutive figures and revivals of the patient himself in childhood. Freud surmised the existence of a three-step process. At first, there had been an intense erotic

attachment to the mother. This had been repressed, and an identification with her had been substituted. In this state, the patient
loved himself as his mother had loved him. Finally, the patient used
extraneous figures (the beloved boys) as objects onto whom he
could transfer the feelings about himself that were acquired through
the identification (Freud 1910).

Thus, coincident with his first description of the mechanism of
narcissistic object choice, Freud brought into play the importance of
the mechanism of identification. He noted that identification can
serve as the kind of psychic structure he was later to describe as a
differentiating grade in the ego: an object representation that has
ceased to pattern motor impulses into the outer world, but instead
has become part of a reflexive process that redirects impulse back
upon the self. A generalized form of this mechanism was to be
announced as the theory of the superego fourteen years later,
underscoring the close links between narcissism and the superego
(Freud 1923).

Before this occurred, however, Freud generalized what he had
discovered about the choice of an object along the path of narcissism.
In 1914 he declared that the love relation with the self was a universal
stage in human development and remained the permanent foundation for all object relationships that arose from it and could return to
it (in secondary form) under adverse conditions (Freud 1914). From
1914 on, the analyst had to accept that the examination of the transference object could as readily lead back to self representations as to
object representations (and, in most cases, to both).

NARCISSISTIC SEXUALITY

The sense in which Freud had invoked the concept of narcissism
(the conditions governing overt sexual behavior) was the common
reference of the term around the turn of the century, having been
used in this way by both Nacke and Havelock Ellis (Freud 1914).
Such cases are still present in analytic practice and offer a high road
to the understanding of the subject. I shall illustrate this with some
examples from my own experience.

Vignette 1.

A young academic was obligated to take a shower before he could have
intercourse with his wife. This was because he got his erection from

looking at his mirror image while toweling himself. He spoke often of his envy that women could cause erections without effort and of his contempt for men foolish enough to let themselves be excited by women.

Significantly, this patient's father and stepfather had both died acutely and unexpectedly in the weeks in which his sister and stepsister had been born. His fears of exertion were all anticipations of death. He was terrified that becoming a man was fatal. When he looked in the mirror, he identified with his mother, a powerful figure who had outlived her husbands. The patient was terrified of becoming addicted to intercourse as a substitute for the affection he had not gotten from his depressed mother. He feared that he would regress, have premature ejaculations, and lose bowel control at the moment of orgasm. His mother had always impressed him because she could go out all day in a boat without having to urinate.

Vignette 2.

A professional woman in her late twenties revealed that, in order to be orgastic, she had to become aroused by looking at her nude image in a full-length mirror while her husband caressed her invisibly from behind. In a related dream, she was lying on the analytic couch while her double, clad in a sheer peignoir, walked about the room. She said to the analyst (who, in the dream, was also her brother), "You think it's you who's exciting me, but it's her."

The patient's angry denials that men could arouse her were a defense against fears that she would lose her initiative, her independence, and her invulnerability to rejection. However, to be frigid was to be like her mother, whose rejection of sexuality had been the subject of frequent, frightening family arguments when she was growing up. She was terrified of her hunger for contact, the by-product of her mother's severe depression, which had lasted until her early adolescence. By taking herself as her own object, she simultaneously solved all these problems.

During latency, the patient's brother had been her partner in much quasi-incestuous play. When she looked in the mirror, she felt identified with him. This had the meaning both of obtaining power over him by exciting him (the mirror image was seen as feminine) and of becoming him in a way that dated to adolescence, when she indulged in erotic daydreams of being him and making love to a voluptuous secretary. During intercourse, she had the feeling that her vagina grasped the penis as if it were a dildo and that she then used it to penetrate her husband.

Both of these cases exactly exemplify Freud's formula of a former object relationship being replaced by an identification with the object, and the image of the self in that relationship being sent out into the world to become the source of erotic arousal. What these cases add to that formula is that, in both instances, the entire mechanism makes possible a real object relationship that would otherwise be destroyed by the forces the narcissism defends against. They are merely extreme examples of the general proposition that object relations, on inspection, prove to have their basis in narcissistic mechanisms. It is in this form, not as an alternative to, but as a foundation of object relations, that narcissistic mechanisms are most commonly met with in clinical practice.

PATHOGENESIS

Narcissistic mechanisms tend to be called into play when there is a need for protection against the object hunger, depression, and rage that would be elicited by an object relationship. The childhood of these patients is always marked by extremely painful interactions with parents who are not prepared to treat the child as a separate individual with a psychological life of its own. Rather than finding the personality features of the child as they develop and greeting the emergence of new traits and abilities with pleasure, these parents can only relate to the child insofar as it serves to maintain their own self-esteem. The role assigned to the child may evolve with time, but its center is always in the parents, never in the child. All parental behavior that appears to gratify and care for the child is actually motivated by a desire to maintain the parental self-image.

The child's need for recognition and acceptance soon leads it to discover that it will receive these needed emotional nutrients only when, and to the degree that, some preexisting expectation in the mind of the parents is being fulfilled. These expectations have no relation to the child's own needs, capacities, and achievements, but are regulated solely by the parental picture of the child that is needed as an external part of a narcissistic defense. This distorting influence operates universally through all the stages of development and leaves its imprint on all of them.

At any point in the developmental process, the emergence of

attitudes or traits that are irrelevant or antithetical to the parental needs is met with denial, attack, or emotional withdrawal. The personality of the child cannot develop as an instrument for modulating and gratifying inner impulses, but must serve as a scanning mechanism directed at that portion of the environment comprised of the parental expectations. Watching replaces inner perception as the primary regulator of behavior, with consequent heightening of voyeuristic-exhibitionistic tendencies.

Such a child lives in a state of perpetually compromised self-esteem, never knowing if he is lovable or good until told so from the outside. The parents' indifference to or rejection of the child's personality gives rise to continual insecurity and severe separation anxiety, since the child is systematically punished for any attempt to establish independent well-being. Value depends solely on reinforcing the self-representation of the object. This heightens the dependence on the object and drives the child toward the creation of a sham personality, based on the perception of projected parental fantasies, which raises the level of received parental narcissistic interest. Identification with the adult who is pleased that the child possesses narcissistically valuable traits forms the first kernel of a self–self relationship, which offers some degree of autonomy.

Additionally, the constant hostility to which the child is subjected at every failure to fulfill expectations leads to a heightened tendency toward identification with the aggressor. The child compensates for his experiences of pain and humiliation by playing at being the victimizer and learns to hate and withdraw from his own personality, just as the parents do. This mode of self–self relationship will almost always result in the projection outward of the despised self-representation. It is impossible to integrate this kernel with the one derived from fulfillment of the parental expectations. The developing split in the child's psychic apparatus mirrors the split in the environment.

Alongside the child's need to preserve well-being and establish autonomy, there runs a second thread. The child inevitably becomes aware of the fragility of the parental psychological balance and of the degree to which playing the assigned role is necessary to maintain the intactness of each parent. Often it is an issue of protecting a parent from serious decompensation. Under these circumstances, the child becomes the psychological parent of its parent, acting to hold the parent intact by offering the needed narcissistic supplies that will keep the parent operative. In this way, submission to the object is wedded to caring for the object.

The brutal assaults on a sense of self-worth that the child sustains promotes the development of compensatory fantasies that deny the trauma. In these fantasies, the child becomes the cold, rejecting figure, the magnetic exhibitor who reduces the audience to fascinated, needy, and contemptible enthrallment. The child is demanding, self-centered, and frustrating. This collection of fantasies is the core of the ego ideal and the nucleus of the potential grandiose self. Since they are partially based on identification with the aggressor, they also serve as superego precursors. Throughout development these images will be projected out onto objects and then reintrojected with consequent constant blurring of the difference between self and object. At the end of this process, the child will be prepared to treat others as if they were merely external manifestations of fantasy images necessary to the maintenance of his own self-esteem.

DEPRESSIVE AFFECT

Depressive affect is generated when there is a sense of inability to close the gap between the real self and those aspects of the ego ideal that are necessary for the maintenance of self-esteem. The child who is raised as an external part of the parents' own self-esteem maintenance will have especially severe problems in avoiding depressive affect. On the one hand, the value of the real self is badly impaired. It is often realistically deficient because of the unsuitability of the rearing environment to help realistic maturation. At the same time, it is the target of introjected hatred derived from the parental attitudes toward any manifestations of the real self. The ego ideals have also undergone a distortion, which makes them harder to achieve. The fantasy images of the self are based on either identification with the aggressor, and are therefore difficult to enact in a consensual relationship, or scenarios of submissively winning the love and approval of a cold, rejecting, and egocentric object. The reaction formations against these ideals, sham reciprocity, and sham self-assertion, however utilitarian, do not serve to elevate the mood. The result is frequently a state of mild, blank depression marked by a sense of emptiness, loneliness, meaninglessness, and a lack of gusto and enjoyment.

Compounding these problems is the failure to internalize an idealized "inner presence" with which to establish an inner relationship that will maintain self-esteem. Optimally, an individual can generate self-esteem by following the dictates of conscience and thereby eliciting the approval of the superego. This function of the superego is like that of an internalized imaginary companion. No one is ever entirely alone who is "right" in the eyes of conscience. This provides independence from the approval of the object world. Failure to internalize such a function leaves the individual vulnerable to fluctuations in the level of external admiration and acceptance. This vulnerability is reduced by identification with elements from the ego ideal.

Vignette 3.

Freud was troubled with indiscretion, boastfulness, procrastination, and inability to focus his efforts, a condition he blamed on the weakness and laxity of his father. In his dream of "Non Vixit," he acquired the blazing blue eyes of his mentor, the stern, disciplined North German Protestant Brucke (Freud 1900). From then on, he told Jones, whenever he was tempted to take the easy way out, he would have a quasi-hallucination of two blue eyes staring at him, and he would be invigorated to make the effort to do the right thing (Jones 1953).

THE NARCISSISTIC SELF: RIGID OSCILLATION

The lives of narcissistic personalities are often marked by a rigid oscillation between two organizations of the self, marked by an identification with either the grandiose or the submissive ego ideal. These oscillations are often played out in successive relationships.

Vignette 4.

A man in his early thirties had spent several years in adoration of a spoiled, self-centered, and demanding woman from a socially prominent family. He had felt proud that she criticized his taste and his manners, and felt happy that she was an "ice princess" like his mother. When she left him for another man, he took up with a woman from a different religion that he thought inferior. He regarded her as overweight and blowsy and compared her to a farm animal. A particularly important part of their relationship was his anger whenever she appeared "too" cheerful. He would pick on her until she started to cry, then feel a wave of tenderness toward her as he comforted and consoled her.

Even when this patient was playing the grandiose role, it was not his desire to inflict pain on a separate object. By making the woman cry, he converted her into the crying child he used to be, identified with her, then switched to the role of the comforting and loving figure that he had sought. This is like the end of a beating fantasy in which, after the beating has been administered, the child is loved very much.

Vignette 5.

A woman had spent several years as the mistress of a prominent businessman with an invalid wife. She catered his parties, bought birthday presents for his children, and opened his country homes. As soon as he became free, he dropped her. She then took up with an investment banker. She would wheedle him into pinning up her hems for her, laughing to herself that she had him crawling on his hands and knees before her, then cajole him into saying that he had enjoyed the experience. As soon as he said this, she no longer felt derisive and contemptuous, but "melting" and affectionate.

The experience of fusion as a culmination of submissive relations has been noted frequently, especially by Annie Reich (1940, 1953, 1960). It is also present in grandiose relations. In the first case, the experience is one of ecstatic reunion with one's ego ideals. In the latter, it is a tender reunion with one's capacity to love. This was first noted by Rousseau, who stated that the act of crying in empathic union with another's pain is so delicious that we are willing to injure to enjoy it.

The oscillation between the two forms of narcissistic personality organization may also occur within a single relationship. In many cases, there is a submissive acquiescence to maltreatment by a demanding, egocentric other until some boundary line is crossed and the formerly injured party becomes entitled, grandiose, and belittling for a period before again lapsing into the more usual behavior. Such patterns are illustrative of the usefulness of grievance collection in proving love-worthiness, building self-esteem, and acquiring entitlement.

DYNAMICS OF THE NARCISSISTIC SELF

The core problem of the narcissistic personality is that the failure to internalize self-esteem regulation, the debased images of the real self, and the distorted ego ideals combine to generate depressive affect. The core dynamic is the elevation of self-esteem by magical transformation of the self through identification with one of the fantasy images in the ego ideal. Patients enact fragments of alternate personalities as a way of avoiding the impact of unpleasant and depression-producing realities. As they shift from one fantasy image to another, their personalities become disparate and discontinuous. They appear to have the quality of "as if" personalities, having no structure of their own and changing into different people according to the circumstances. Much of their life is spent in such role enactment.

Vignette 6.

A high school girl had achieved notoriety in her hometown by her enactment of the role of an argumentative suffragette who condemned heterosexuality as political imprisonment for women. On entrance to a leading women's college, she found herself surrounded by others with identical attitudes. She was no longer singular. She became severely depressed, took to her bed, and lay in a stupor for thirty-six hours. On arising, she found that her personality had been transformed. Henceforth, she was soft-voiced and continuously seductive in her manner. She immediately set about the seduction of the most prestigious of her professors.

Closely allied to this role enactment is the continuous exercise of manipulative pressure to induce the object to accept the assigned complementary role. It should be remembered that object relations in these personalities tend to be subsidiary to the needs of defense. In cases of doubt about the ego ideal that is being enacted, valuable information can be obtained by assessing the nature of the behavior into which the object is being pressured. In all cases, this will be a role that represents the complement of the one the patient is enacting, the other part of the original self–self relation. It is particularly important to recognize that much of what is called masochistic provocation is actually a manipulative attempt to evoke angry, grandiose actions from the object and represents neither a wish to suffer nor an occasion for the therapist to disparage the object.

TREATMENT

The strongest technical resource of the therapist lies in a comprehensive grasp of the dynamics and the natural history of the syndrome under treatment. The therapist's vision of the course that the patient takes in treatment is an essential ingredient of treatment technique since, as Loewald (1960) has pointed out, much of the mutative tension arises from the therapist's continuous transmission of an image of what is possible for the patient. Thus the view of where the patient is going acts as a powerful, unspoken intervention.

The two factors that most quickly disqualify a therapist are attitudes of therapeutic perfectionism that discount movement on the part of the patient as insufficient, and an emotional aversion to the personality formations that emerge in the treatment of narcissistic personalities. If the therapist is dismayed by the very things that make the patient proud, there will emerge a tendency toward reality testing, setting limits, or vigorous and premature interpretations of acting out. Such therapeutic aggressiveness will block the natural development of the case. It can result in a sterile therapeutic relationship in which the patient relates to the therapist via a sham personality that is actually a defense against the emergence of narcissistic traits.

To avoid such dilemmas, the therapist must be prepared to see the patient become progressively more self-centered, dominating, exhibitionistic, and, in a word, overtly narcissistic. Attention must be focused on the problems of the patient (which are usually self-esteem maintenance), not on deviations from a hypothetical normality.

When, as is commonly the case, narcissistic masochism is used as a defense against identification with aggressivized ego ideals, the undoing of the defense will result in the identification becoming open and manifest. Treatment need not stop there, but it must go through that phase. The goal of the first phase of treatment is the emergence of the overt grandiose self. This first phase may be divided into two subsections: early treatment and the period of negative therapeutic reaction. Of course, any division of treatment into phases is arbitrary, as they tend to overlap. Furthermore, there are always clinical relapses to contend with.

The first phase of treatment involves establishing a relationship with the patient. This poses special difficulty since, because of his rigid defenses, the patient can only establish pseudo-relations along self-esteem-maintenance lines. Therefore, there can be no real treatment alliance, if this is defined as the patient's willingness and ability to form a rational, secondary process identification with the therapist as therapist. Instead, the patient encounters initial difficulties in relating to anyone who functions as an independent individual and not as a complementary aspect of his own self-representation. There can be little trust in the therapist, and therapeutic errors at any time are met with silence, withdrawal, or attack. Attempts by the therapist to form any type of object relationship are reacted to as if they were threatening encroachments to be fended off. Since, in ordinary technique, it is the therapist's interpretive activity that establishes the therapeutic object relationship, it is precisely premature interpretive activity that is antitherapeutic in these cases. The patient tends to react to interpretations as if they were criticisms. The hurt and shame he feels for being "criticized" far outweigh whatever beneficial effects the interpretation itself might have had. Similar strictures apply to any interventions that demonstrate the therapist's superior wisdom, psychological acuity, or claim to help the patient. When the therapist takes the lead or acts as someone who can give something to the patient, there is bound to be a reaction of fear, humiliation, and narcissistic rage. Even so simple an intervention as asking a question may be reacted to as a criticism of what the patient has already said, a labeling of the previous material as incomplete and unsatisfying to the therapist.

For precisely these reasons, it is extremely inadvisable to do any form of supportive therapy with narcissistic personalities. The whole basis of supportive therapy is the claim that the therapist is in a position to lend a prosthetic ego to the patient. This immediately establishes the therapist's claim to be superior to the patient and stands as a constant affront to the patient's attempts at self-esteem elevation. A narcissistic patient reacts to any and all supportive maneuvers as humiliations, which he is afraid to identify for fear of wounding and angering the therapist. This silent resentment builds up between the therapist and patient until the relationship becomes entirely sterilized or else breaks up in a series of destructive escapes from the therapist's influence. A narcissistic patient who has had previous contact with supportive therapists rarely has anything good to say about the prior treatment.

Between interpretation and support lies clarification. The therapist must accurately understand and verbalize the nature of the patient's interactions with others and with himself, the desired response of the other to those manipulations, and the feeling that such desired responses would elicit. Each such pattern of action and desired reaction defines an ego-ideal fragment. Put another way, while the therapeutic relation is dominated by the patient's need for rigid defense, the therapist should look forward to the ego ideal that the patient is attempting to enact, not backward to the impelling drives. The ability to see where the patient is trying to go and to understand ways in which these goals are striven for becomes the backbone of the therapeutic relationship. The first job of the therapist is to bind the patient to the figure of the therapist and to the treatment, and it is this sort of psychological tact manifested as empathic clarification that will do the binding.

Early material frequently includes incidents of being exploited, abused, denigrated, and ignored. It is a profound therapeutic error to utilize these complaints as an excuse for advocating separation from the persecuting object or as a pretext for discussing the patient's own hostility. What is being sought is a certificate of entitlement, a self-reassurance that better treatment is merited, an enhancement of value. If the material is initially grandiose, though it rarely is, the goal remains the same. It is recognition that forges enough of a union between therapist and patient to permit the beginning exploration of the nature of the object. Little by little, the patient will explain the qualities of the object that serve to maintain the self-esteem and why only objects of this type are exciting and interesting. If this exploration is carried out in an atmosphere of sustaining empathy, the patient will begin to acknowledge the nature of the ego ideal and to confess to moments in which it has been enacted.

Vignette 7.

After some time in treatment, a male patient confessed that whenever he urinated, he deliberately wet the bathroom floor because it gave him a feeling of superiority to think of his wife cleaning it up.

Vignette 8.

After some time in treatment, a woman revealed that whenever she was well dressed, she imagined a photograph being taken of her and placed in an album that contained pictures of every time she had looked good. The existence of this album gave her a feeling of self-confidence.

As these elements of grandiosity begin to emerge, along with their affects of excitement, the first negative therapeutic reactions begin. Every apparent move toward independence, self-assertiveness, or competence based on the enactment of grandiose ego ideals becomes an occasion for heightened anxiety and threatening depression. Fears of loss of the object, retaliatory attack, and humiliation become paramount. This gives the treatment an oscillatory quality. Moments of excited self-admiration with associated mirror transferencelike relations will be followed by episodes of depression or anxiety and return to previous modes of self-organization. If the appropriate response to the emergence of the grandiose self is one of tactful clarification, the appropriate response to the negative therapeutic reaction is accurate interpretation. At these times, it is important to interpret the relapse as a response to the negative affects aroused by the emerging grandiosity.

As the clinical surface becomes more confused, it is important for the therapist to remain aware, at all times, of where the grandiosity is. If it has been assigned to an object in the patient's life or to the therapist, the response is interpretation. If it is self-assigned and enacted, then the response is clarification. Optimally, this procedure leads to gradual unification of the fragments of grandiosity that begin to be enacted more systematically. With fewer relapses, the patient now begins to excite his own admiration and interest and to become proud of himself. The therapist is gradually relegated to the role of a listener to tales of the patient's (usually realistic) adventures and accomplishments.

Vignette 9.

As her grandiose self emerged, a woman in her twenties purchased an extremely low-cut dress and wore it to the theater and to concerts. Buoyed by the incredulous and admiring attention she attracted, she extricated herself from a severely masochistic relationship, learned to drive a car, took up painting again, and got a better job.

At this point, the first elements of genuine object relations become visible in the therapeutic field. These are sometimes preceded by the emergence of idealizing transferencelike relations. These may appear as admiring statements about the therapist's wisdom, which are contrasted with self-denigrating assessments of the patient's helplessness and inability to cope. Alternatively, the therapist may be depicted as cruel, callous, exploitative, indifferent, or frightening. It is not the positive or negative affect that determines the idealization. Such transferencelike relations must be interpreted as all idealizations are interpreted, or else the patient will develop a sticky, dependent pseudo-transference that will immobilize the therapy and keep the patient clinging to the therapist in helpless subjugation.

Not all patients are capable of giving up their rigid, defense-oriented mode of object relations. In general, it is easier to aid these patients in the sphere of work than in the sphere of love. The setting of the goals of treatment must take into account the magnitude of the developmental trauma, the resources of the personality, and the flexibility available at this point in the patient's life. In cases of such severe magnitude, we must not disdain partial improvements.

CONCLUSION

Clinical work with narcissistic personality disorders amply confirms Freud's prediction that the study of the ego is dependent on the study of the narcissistic neuroses (Freud 1914). In them we see writ large the very fabric of the human mind. No child can escape some degree of the treatment which, in excess, provides the pathogenetic background of these pathological conditions. Hence, no patient can fail, to some degree, to demonstrate the grandiose and submissive patterns I have described. Defense against depressive affect is a central preoccupation for all patients. Most anger contains a large component of narcissistic rage. Above all, the study of the ways in which therapists can make healing contact with the more narcissistically damaged patient sheds revealing light on the mechanisms of that empathic rapport that is the necessary substratum of every therapeutic relationship.

REFERENCES

Freud, S. (1900). The interpretation of dreams. *Standard Edition* 4, 5:1–625.

⸺ (1905). Fragment of an analysis of a case of hysteria. *Standard Edition* 7:7–122.

⸺ (1910). Leonardo da Vinci and a memory of his childhood. *Standard Edition* 11:63–137.

⸺ (1914). On narcissism: an introduction. *Standard Edition* 14:73–102.

⸺ (1923). The ego and the id. *Standard Edition* 19:12–66.

Jones, E. (1953). *The Life and Work of Sigmund Freud*, vol. I. New York: Basic Books.

Loewald, H. (1960). On the therapeutic action of psychoanalysis. *International Journal of Psycho-Analysis* 41:16–33.

Reich, A. (1940). The psychoanalysis of extreme submissiveness in women. *Psychoanalytic Quarterly* 9:470–480.

⸺ (1953). Narcissistic object choice in women. *Journal of the American Psychoanalytic Association* 1:22–44.

⸺ (1960). Pathologic forms of self-esteem regulation. *Psychoanalytic Study of the Child* 15:215–232. New York: International Universities Press.

18

The Treatment of Eating Disorders

Melvin A. Scharfman, M.D.

During the past decade there has been a dramatic increase in the incidence of eating disorders, to the point where one can almost speak of epidemic proportions. This increase has occurred primarily among adolescent and young adult women, historically the overwhelmingly most frequent population in terms of incidence. There is also a considerable overrepresentation of occurrence in the middle and upper social classes. In my own experience, during the first twenty or so years of my practice I recall three or four young women who presented eating disorders. By contrast, in the past six years I have had at least three young women in treatment at any given time. This increased incidence has brought with it the opportunity to learn a great deal more about eating disorders. The number of scientific publications on the subject has increased at a rate that is almost as rapid as the increase in incidence of the illness.

DIAGNOSTIC CONSIDERATIONS

Some of the possible reasons for this increase will be discussed later on, but I would like to turn first to a consideration of what eating disorders are in terms of diagnostic groupings, then review some of the literature in this area, consider the various treatment modalities available at this time, and finally present some clinical experience of my own to suggest some factors in evaluating the modality of treatment.

Let me begin with the *DSM-III* criteria that are listed under disturbances of infancy, childhood, or adolescence.

1. An intense fear of becoming obese that does not diminish as weight progresses.
2. A disturbance in body image, (e.g., claiming to "feel fat" even when emaciated).
3. A weight loss of at least 25 percent of original body weight or, if under 18, a weight loss of original body weight plus projected weight gain expected from growth charts combined to equal 25 percent.
4. Refusal to maintain body weight over a minimal normal weight for age and height.
5. No known physical illnesses that would account for the weight loss.

One would have to make several clarifying comments and additions to these diagnostic criteria. The self-inflicted weight loss is often brought about by a rejection of a mature sex-specific body shape where there is no other major underlying physical illness or external restriction on food. Patients have a preoccupying and persistent dread of becoming fat. They manipulate to maintain low body weight by either dietary restraint, self-induced vomiting, use of purgatives, or excessive exercise. Their disturbances in body image lead to perceptual distortions of their bodily dimensions and often to an extreme distaste of many bodily functions. In addition, amenorrhea and a number of other behavioral and psychological sequelae of starvation occur in a majority of cases in which the condition continues over a period of time.

The ways in which weight loss is brought about and maintained have led some to suggest subcategories of anorexics, namely, restrictors, or those who maintain a relatively continued pattern of severe dietary restriction, and bulimics, those who experience periodic episodes of binge eating followed by some kind of self-induced purging.

These considerations of what constitute the basic descriptive aspects of someone categorized as anorexic have changed over the years (e.g., with the inclusion of the bulimic type), but they remain essentially of limited application. Anorexia seems to be far less a disease or even a specific symptom complex, but rather a variety of symptoms that vary considerably from patient to patient. What was earlier described as the typical form of anorexia can now be seen as just one form in which this disturbance presents. Indeed, there appear to be anorexics who show essentially a neurotic structure and others who show a borderline personality organization. Still others appear to have disturbances in their self system or have a so-called false self. Finally, anorexia may occur in patients who are overtly psychotic.

HISTORICAL BACKGROUND OF THE DISORDER

One of the earliest historical descriptions of anorexia was by Richard Morton (1694), who, in writing about tubercular disease, described what he called the state of nervous atrophy. This was characterized by decreased appetite, amenorrhea, food evasion, emaciation, and hyperactivity. He attributed the cause of this disturbance to a malfunction of the central nervous system. His clinical descriptions could apply to many of the patients we see today. In 1874, Gull first coined the term *anorexia nervosa*, also giving excellent clinical descriptions. He noted its typical onset during adolescence, occurring mostly in females, and began to consider a significant psychological component. He also was well aware of the influence of the prolonged starvation and the patient's general metabolic functioning and of the need for active intervention under professional supervision.

At almost the same time, Lasegue (1873) described "anorexia hysterique," relating to it to a fixed belief that food is injurious to the body and must be avoided. He also noted some psychological features, including self-doubt, the need for approval, and the family's role in the development of this particular problem. To quote from his description:

> A young girl, between fifteen and twenty years of age, suffers from some emotion which she avows or conceals. Generally it relates to some real or imaginary marriage project, to a violence done to some sympathy, or to some more or less conscious desire. At other times, only conjectures can be offered concerning the occasional cause, whether that the girl has an interest in adopting the mutism so common in the hysterical, or that the primary cause really escapes her. . . .
> The repugnance for food continues slowly progressive, meal after meal is discontinued . . . things may be thus prolonged during weeks

or months without the general health seeming to be unfavorably influenced, the tongue being clean and moist and thirst entirely absent . . . Another ascertained fact is, that so far from muscular power being diminished, this abstinence tends to increase the aptitude for movement. The patient feels more light and active, rides on horseback, receives and pays visits, and is able to pursue a fatiguing life in the world without perceiving the lassitude she would at other times have complained of.

If the situation has undergone no change as regards the anorexia and refusal of food, the mental condition of the patient is brought out more prominently, while the dispositions of those surrounding her undergo modification as the disease becomes prolonged. If the physician had promised rapid amendment, or if he has suspected a bad disposition on the part of his patient, he has long since lost all moral authority.

The family has but two methods at its service which it always exhausts — entreaties and menaces, and which both serve as a touchstone. The delicacies of the table are multiplied in the hope of stimulating the appetite; but the more the solicitude increases, the more the appetite diminishes. The patient disdainfully tastes the new viands, and after having thus shown her willingness, holds herself absolved from any obligation to do more. She is besought, as a favor and as a sovereign proof of affection, to consent to add even an additional mouthful of what she has taken; but this excess of insistence begets an excess of resistance. [pp. 145–149]

These contributions introduced the idea of psychological factors playing the central role in the etiology of the illness. This was somewhat reversed by Simmonds (1914), when he associated the clinical picture with pituitary atrophy. For the next twenty or thirty years anorexia was considered a medical illness. It was not until psychoanalytic thinking began to become more integrated with psychiatric theory and practice that anorexia nervosa was again considered to be related to psychological conflict. In various fragments of clinical practice and the existing theory, it was an easy step to describe anorexia as being related to unconscious conflicts that involved fears of oral sadistic impulses often connected with fellatio fantasies, fears of oral impregnation, or other unconscious conflicts. The most consistent psychoanalytically related studies of anorexia were contributed by Bruch (1973). From one perspective, she took much more of what we would now consider a developmental approach; that is, she saw anorexia as coming from a failure of early parent–child interaction, with a subsequent failure on the child's part to develop an appropriate independent psychological identity.

Briefly, Bruch first differentiated primary anorexia nervosa from other nonspecific psychologically determined weight loss problems that could occur in such illnesses as hysteria, depression, and schizophrenia. She pointed out that many cases in the older literature represented atypical forms rather than primary anorexia nervosa and described the increased incidence in recent years as an increase in primary anorexia nervosa. While she concurred in the kind of descriptions given above, she added that anorexic patients have an inaccuracy in identifying bodily and emotional states and a pervasive sense of ineffectiveness. She also pointed out that these patients do not suffer from loss of appetite, but instead are almost totally preoccupied with food and eating. She described anorexics as being uncertain in identifying hunger and as using eating as a pseudo-solution of many personality difficulties and problems of living. She described such patients as having disturbances in their psychological development, with deficits in self-identity and autonomy, in addition to disturbances in sexual maturation and gender identity. She described the condition as being closer to the borderline state than to neurosis.

Bruch described particular sociocultural aspects. Generally speaking, anorexics were good children, gratifying to their parents, successful, and raised in stable, even privileged, homes with upwardly mobile parents. She described the initial onset of the illness as being a personality change, in which these previously compliant girls become negativistic, angry, and distrustful, rejecting help and care that is offered, claiming not to need help, and insisting on their right to eat what they want to and to be as thin as they want to be. She emphasized that they do not see their own severe emaciation and don't consider their weight loss abnormal or ugly. In fact, they take pride in a skeletonlike appearance. They feel dissociated from their own bodies, as something separate from their psychological selves or as a possession of their parents.

Having grown up markedly dependent and feeling essentially ineffective, anorexics are not prepared to deal with the onset of adolescence. They have an impaired sense of autonomy and are unable to make decisions about their future. They begin to engage in a struggle for autonomy by trying to be effective in controlling their own body in at least one area, namely, by maintaining discipline over their eating. Bruch described their defiance as essentially a defense against feelings of being powerless and ineffective if they give in to their parents, and a defense against not having a solid sense of their own core identity or a feeling of autonomy. They attempt to define a sense of self, but in a way that can only lead to failure and further isolation and helplessness.

Bruch saw great similarities among most of the patients she described. Their disturbances in bodily sensation, their ways of describing hunger, their eating behavior, and their hyperactivity were all similar. The patients also shared the fact that they were not sick but felt they were doing something constructive. Interestingly, up until the 1970s, most such patients said they had never known of anyone else who had such a condition and felt they were finding their own solution. Bruch noted that now more and more patients had heard about such a disturbance, read about it, or saw it in a friend at school. That is, she saw what she called an increasing group of "me too" girls who competed with each other, yet at the same time, clung to each other in groups.

In addition, Bruch presented the first good description of a kind of cognitive disturbance, pointing out that many of these girls failed to enter fully the stage of formal operations with its accompanying ability to perform abstract thinking and evaluation, the kind of thinking so characteristic of adolescents. In these patients, she found such ability deficient or absent. In its place was the kind of early childhood thinking characterized by egocentricity and by preconceptual and concrete operations.

One of Bruch's major contributions was to emphasize the role of the family. She pointed out that the anorexic is cared for materially, psychologically, and culturally, yet somehow there is an accompanying neglect of the expression of needs, wants, and feelings. She described such mother–infant pairs as being characterized by inappropriate responses on the part of the mother, so that the interaction, which the child needs to develop a sense of body identity with accurate perceptions and conceptual awareness of her own functions, is impaired. The mother is unable to "read" the child, to respond appropriately to the individual needs, but rather reacts according to her own needs. The result is a failure in the child's separation from the parent. The child remains tied to the mother, deprived of developing her own autonomy and decision-making ability. She is overly obedient and overly conforming. In other terms, Bruch described a disturbance in the self system and in the sense of self-esteem as the central problem in the anorexic.

Following Bruch's pioneering contributions, a host of other psychoanalytically oriented contributions to anorexia have appeared in recent years. Many of these have attempted to add the object-relations perspective to the earlier psychoanalytic understanding, drawing on Mahler's contributions. One of those who contributed from this perspective, Masterson (1977), discussed anorexia from an object-relations perspective, considering the anorexic as having encountered difficulty in separation-individuation with corresponding ego deficits and distorted self and object representation. He described split introjects, namely, a maternal introject that is critical, hostile, and withholding whenever the anorexic attempts to separate, and another maternal introject that is responsive and rewarding to the anorexic's more regressive, clinging behavior. Corresponding to these split object relationships are split self representations. To attempt autonomy is to be inadequate, guilty, empty, and generally bad, whereas to remain attached to the mother is rewarded. Not surprisingly, this perspective considers that there are borderlinelike features operating in the anorexic.

Sours (1980) extended classic psychoanalytic understanding somewhat further. He also stressed difficulty in separation-individuation with poor selfobject differentiation, difficulties in self and object constancy, poor self-esteem and ego deficits. More specifically, he elaborated on some of the ego deficits in terms of the difficulties these patients have in access to their own affects, memories, and fantasies. They suffer from a kind of ego impoverishment related to the nutritional impoverishment, but also to difficulties in forming a therapeutic alliance. He stressed the development of a therapeutic alliance through understanding and interpretation of the atypical development of their ego functions in self and object representations. He interpreted the relatively primitive defenses of the patient—denial, negation, disavowal, splitting, and omnipotence—while attempting to maintain an analytic stance.

Other contributors have attempted to apply Kohut's (1966, 1971) perspective of self psychology to understanding the treatment of the anorexic. Goodsitt (1969), in particular, suggested an understanding of the patient as deriving from a deficit in the early maternal caretaking experience that results in failed development of self. In his perspective, such a patient failed to internalize an empathic mother and therefore cannot successfully separate. She is unable to regulate her own sense of well-being, is unable to feel secure, to comfort herself, to feel cohesive, or to learn to regulate her own tension or self-esteem. His therapeutic technique, following Kohut, is to suggest that the therapist allow himself to be utilized as a selfobject by the patient, that is, to understand that the patient is having a disturbance of a narcissistic kind. Given an empathic response by the therapist as selfobject, the patient's archaic grandiosity and idealization appear and can eventually be converted into a more cohesive self, with better self-esteem and healthier goals and ideals. When the therapist fails in that role, the patient will feel helpless and ineffective, overwhelmed, unworthy, incomplete, and empty. Life without an empathic selfobject is boring, mechanical, and unproductive. Goodsitt describes anorexia nervosa as a disorder of the self, essentially a developmental deficit, and feels that such understanding must be added to the object relations contributions for the therapist to be able to treat the anorexic successfully.

While there are far too many other contributions to mention, I must return to where we began in this historical review, that is, to biology. A number of different biological or psychopharmacological theories have appeared in recent years with their own modality of treatment, namely, the use of psychopharmacological agents, for the most part antidepressants of the tricyclic type. These theories postulate disturbances in hypothalamic functioning in terms of catecholamine and opioid receptive systems, which are normally involved in the regulation of natural eating. Whether such disturbances in neuroregulators occur regularly and whether they are primary or secondary to nutritional deficits cannot yet be determined. At this point, one must say that the use of such medication is largely on an empirical basis. It seems more related in terms of its success to the presence of depressive symptomatology in the anorexic.

THE CHOICE OF THERAPEUTIC MODALITY

Having briefly surveyed some of the contributions to understanding anorexia, it becomes clear that there is an interplay of multiple predisposing and pathogenic factors that may contribute in varying degrees to the presenting symptomatology. At this point in our knowledge, our therapeutic stance will largely be indicated by our understanding of the relevant degree of significance of each of these factors, and the potential therapist has much to choose from if he is to go beyond the boundaries of any single theoretical persuasion.

In trying to give at least some guidelines for consideration of treatment modality, I will be focusing on those patients for whom outpatient treatment is possible. It is not that I think that inpatient treatment is not appropriate in some cases, but that decision at this point in time is largely made upon assessing the medical status of the individual patient or the feeling that the patient could not be treated within an extremely chaotic home situation, where persistent parental intrusion undermines the therapeutic process. There are, of course, some researchers who feel that an anorexic should always be treated on an inpatient basis, regardless of her medical condition, because the family always colludes in maintaining the patient's illness, even if they are involved in a therapeutic effort themselves. Practically speaking, the vast majority of anorexic patients are treated on an outpatient basis.

Therapists are still left to choose from a wide variety of treatment modalities. Individual therapy ranges from a supportive, noninterpretive, educational, and behavior-modifying technique to classical psychoanalysis. Those who view the patient as having borderline psychopathology can choose from a confrontative, interpretive modality of treatment or a more supportive, noninterpretive modality, recognizing that these patients are not really capable of engaging in any exploratory therapy. Those who advocate somewhat more of a psychoanalytic approach can choose from classical conflict theory models, which stress defense interpretation and understanding of the transference, or models that emphasize a holding environment with mirroring techniques leading to the development of self-object transferences, the appearance of archaic grandiose self representations, and the eventual internalization without interpretations of defenses or drives. Still others, based on their understanding of a disturbance in the family situation, particularly in the mother–child relationship, can choose family therapy as the prime modality of treatment (Yager 1981).

Given this menu of treatment choices, how does a therapist decide on the optimal treatment for a patient? This is no easy matter, and I can only share with you some of my own impressions. The focus will be on individual psychotherapy of an exploratory nature, modified where necessary.

The choice of modality of treatment depends on more than a descriptive diagnostic assessment. It requires an in-depth structural and dynamic assessment of the particular patient as well. If eating disorders are symptomatic expressions of conflict, it is necessary to know the nature of some of the core conflicts. Symptoms may be expressions of more phallic oedipal conflict, or largely conflict-related to separation-individuation problems. In other cases, there may be a regression from phallic oedipal conflict to preoedipal conflict. Such regression may be primarily drive regression or may involve ego and superego functions. Still others have developmental maturational failures of the kind described earlier, with limited ego autonomy, poor sense of self, some difficulty in self-object representations and so on. This means that a comprehensive evaluation of both structural and dynamic aspects is essential. The inclusion of all the factors described in the section on assessment will allow for an informed choice on the preferred modality of treatment. I will try to illustrate this by presenting three clinical vignettes.

CLINICAL EXAMPLE: NEUROTIC CORE

Laura was 18 when I first saw her in consultation. She had come home toward the end of the first semester from the rather prestigious college she attended. She said she had not been happy at school and had probably chosen the wrong college. She minimized her parents' primary concern in agreeing to her taking a leave of absence, namely, that she had lost more than 20 pounds over three and a half months.

An attractive young woman, about 5' 7", she had weighed about 125 pounds when she left for school. After arriving there, she began to feel fat. At first, she rationalized that it was a good time to go on a diet, since she really didn't like the food at school anyway. Within a few weeks, she lost interest in food and began to lose weight more rapidly. When she tried to eat in social situations (because she felt it would be embarrassing if she didn't), she began to feel nauseous and would go to the bathroom and throw up what she had eaten. She was not alarmed by this weight loss, but was aware that she felt it was getting out of her control, that she no longer could eat. After several months, she failed to get her menstrual period, but she told me this had happened several times in previous years. Her unhappiness at school had increased. She felt uncomfortable with the social life, was doing reasonably well academically, but was uninterested in her courses and felt uncertain about what she wanted to do with her life. All these factors suggested to her that maybe she should take a leave of absence.

Laura was born and grew up in the suburbs. She was the middle child of three, having a brother who was two and a half years older, now a junior in college, and another who was two and a half years younger, attending the same high school she had attended. Her family was well-to-do. Her father was a successful corporate lawyer, her mother an attractive, intelligent woman who had graduated college. For the most part, her mother had been a housewife, somewhat active in local charitable organizations, but basically a homebody.

Laura had done well in school and had a group of friends she was quite close to in the neighborhood, but no one with whom she was especially close. She said she had never really had a boyfriend, although boys had expressed interest in her. She tended to dismiss most of these boys as being either "jocks," who didn't have any brains, or "nerds." Besides, they were too young and not very sophisticated.

Somewhat talented both intellectually and artistically, she had devoted a number of years to modern dance and had performed with school and local groups. However, she had no ambitions to pursue this as a career.

She knew that her father hoped she would go to law school and join his firm. He had been somewhat disappointed when his older son had decided to major in engineering. She and her father were very close, and she felt she had much more in common with him than she had with her mother. Her father had always been warm and affectionate to her, her mother much less so. At times, as she moved into her teens, she became uncomfortable that her father was too affectionate. If he complimented her appearance or some academic achievement, she felt embarrassed. She was particularly embarrassed when he watched a dance performance. She thought that perhaps she was too close to him and that this had something to do with her difficulty in getting closer to young men. She would like to meet a young man who was bright and who would be interested in her as a person, interested in her mind.

She had always felt distaste when some of the girls she knew had begun to speak about beginning sexual experiences. The second weekend she was at school, her roommate had a boyfriend visit. That night, the couple had returned to the room after she had gone to bed. She awakened during the night and realized that they were having sex. She left the room and the next day asked for a change of room assignment. She found the other girl's behavior disgusting. She said she couldn't understand why sex was a necessary part of a relationship. Why couldn't a man and woman just be friends?

Even in this brief bit of what was the initial presenting picture, it became clear that Laura was involved in a number of neurotic conflicts centering on her inability to accept her sexuality, her ambivalent feelings about men resulting from unresolved oedipal issues, and her intensely competitive attitude toward her brother. There are, of course, many other factors involved, but it was clear that she did not have any difficulties in separation-individuation, although the presenting occurrence of difficulty at going off to college could suggest that. For her, college felt more connected to fears of sexuality than fears of being alone. There was no history of other impulsive behavior. Unlike some other patients, there was a relatively clear precipitant for the onset of the symptoms. Her interpersonal relationships were quite differentiated and were developmentally appropriate, except for the difficulty in intimacy with men. While mildly depressed and troubled by her withdrawal from school, there was no suicidal ideation or severe depressive symptomatology. She related quite well, was verbal, certainly seemed capable of introspection, and, in fact, was psychologically minded. While she was not terribly troubled by the weight loss, this was not total indifference. Rather, she was aware something was wrong with the whole pattern of her life and of uncertainty about her goals. She responded quite well to an early comment about her attempts to please her father and went on to indicate that this was part of what she wanted to find out about herself. What did she really want for herself? Somehow she didn't think it would be law.

This young woman, I felt, was one of the small group of anorexics who could be in psychoanalysis. Certainly, she was capable of participating in and using an exploratory insight-oriented treatment. In fact, she decided she wanted to enter analysis and made arrangements to transfer to a local university. Having agreed to begin analysis, Laura then spent the initial period of time trying to demonstrate that she was really not worth the time and effort. There were other patients who certainly must be more interesting than she was, and I would be far more interested in them. This began to focus on those occasions when she saw a particular male patient whose hours preceded hers several days a week. In her fantasy, he was a young doctor I would like and would help to become successful and happy. She could connect this to her feelings about her parents' having preferred her older brother to her. Eventually, her younger brother also appeared in her thoughts as someone who had a preferred status. She was the disappointment. At the same time, she imagined that I would be more interested in her if she were a young psychiatrist who wanted to become a psychoanalyst. It was pointed out to her how much she wanted to please me, just as she had always sought to please her father, but also how she had carried over the anticipation of being disappointed because of a preference for a son.

Laura went through a variety of material centered on various memories that confirmed for her not only that her father preferred boys, but that her mother also had a strong preference for her sons. Her own competitiveness and resentment of her brothers became clearer to her. Throughout her childhood she had sought to win her father's attention, following her initial disappointment in her mother when her younger brother was born. She had done this by becoming a kind of tomboy, being very active in swimming, tennis, and other sports. Her father admired her performance in all of these, and she enjoyed that. It was only in relation to her father watching her perform when she danced that she became very uncomfortable, particularly following puberty. It was now clear that it was also safer to seek attention from her father through her masculine strivings than it was to have him respond to her as a young woman. Much of this was paralleled in the transference. When this was pointed out to her, there began a subtle change in her manner of relating as well as in her dress, all in the direction of presenting herself more as an attractive young woman. Her fears of acknowledging any sexual wishes of her own became much clearer to her. There was clearly a great deal of oedipal guilt involved, but this was also very much connected to her envy and resentment of men. Underlying this phallic envy, the envy of her brother nursing at the mother's breast appeared as we reconstructed some of her early observations of her mother with the new baby. She had strong wishes to suck at and swallow the breast-penis. One of the first aversions she had had when her weight loss started centered on an intense distaste for milk and milk products and a wish to avoid them. She became aware through a series of memories about visiting a farm that she had observed cows being milked and had also observed animals having intercourse. She was startled when she realized the connection she had made between milk and semen and then found it all very funny. Following this, all of her difficulties with food intake began to change.

Material shifted to her relationship with her mother, and more of maternal transference appeared for a while. She and her mother became friends and were much closer emotionally. As the analysis proceeded, oedipal themes again became dominant. In the transference, as well as in the other material, there was a well-organized transference neurosis that was gradually worked through.

Without going into more detail about the analysis, Laura had an excellent clinical result. Not only was she symptom-free, but she underwent a number of characterological changes in becoming much more comfortable with herself as a woman, and much freer in making her own choices in life about career and relationships.

In my experience, Laura represents the smallest group of anorexic patients, but also the group with the best overall outcome. On the other hand, a large number of patients unable to undertake psychoanalysis do very well in analytically oriented psychotherapy of an exploratory type if they are assessed as having a basically neurotic or neurotic character structure and intact ego functions. For them, it is the treatment of choice.

CLINICAL EXAMPLE: NARCISSISTIC PERSONALITY

Turning to another kind of patient, let me briefly describe Roberta. She was 16 when she came for treatment because of a progressive loss of weight over a two-year period. Five feet four inches, she now weighed a little over 90 pounds. Her facial features were just short of being beautiful, and she was always very well dressed. Yet she attempted to hide her body, wearing pants and high-necked blouses with long sleeves. She spoke in a relaxed, seemingly friendly manner, but could tell me very little about herself or the people around her. Her weight loss troubled her slightly, not because of the loss itself, but because she had developed the pattern of inducing regurgitation after she ate. This was to help her achieve a perfect figure. She wanted everything about her to be perfect and was embarrassed about her pattern of vomiting. She kept this as a secret because it was disgusting.

In many areas of her life she appeared to be just what she wanted to be— that is, perfect. Her parents had given a history that described her as always well behaved, easy to handle, and a pleasure to have around. She had been independent at an early age, by which the mother meant she was able to take care of herself. She chose her own clothes from early childhood on. She was always concerned with looking pretty. She was a good girl who presented no problems for the mother. One example of this was how easily she had taken to a caretaker who was brought in when the mother developed some complication following the birth of her second child when Roberta was 2. Roberta never fussed, never seemed to express any jealousy toward the baby, and never made demands on the mother: "She was always a little lady." She did well at school, seemed to get along well with friends, and had few problems. Other than frequent vague somatic complaints, she had been physically well.

Both parents repeatedly told me what a pleasure she was. They had none of the aggravation their friends had with their own teenagers. Roberta was not rebellious, never provoked, and didn't struggle over parental limitations. She was never demanding, except that she always liked to look well. This, however, did not bother her parents, particularly her mother, who placed a great premium on appearance. Both parents, in fact, presented as overly perfect people. Her father was a reasonably successful businessman who had a number of friends of his own as well as mutual friends. He liked playing golf with his male friends, which relaxed him after he worked so hard. The mother was an attractive, well-dressed woman who spent much of her time with female friends playing cards, going to matinees, and otherwise entertaining herself. She was particularly pleased that her children required so little time. Neither one had any idea whatsoever that Roberta could have any problems. When they gradually became aware of her continuing weight loss, they decided to bring her for consultation. Roberta herself, in typical fashion, had raised no objections when consultation was suggested.

During the initial interviews, Roberta had no wish to talk about her troubles with food or about her weight loss. It made her uncomfortable to think that in any area she could be less than perfect. She was willing to talk, but stayed on the most superficial level. She was only vaguely aware of her lack of knowledge of her own feelings. It was much later on in treatment that she could describe herself as a "plastic person" or a "china doll." She came to treatment, really, because of her wish to become perfect, unaware of the fact that she always felt she had to be perfect in some attempt to get more of a response from her mother. She had separated prematurely and developed a false sense of self that was autonomous and independent, but at the cost of sacrificing her affect. Anger, jealousy, and frustration were feelings she was not aware she ever had. Progressively she had developed an idealized self that emphasized control and good performance. To be needy was bad. To show feelings was bad. Her self-esteem depended on continuing praise, largely over her appearance and over being a good girl. She was intolerant of criticism of any kind. In treatment, which I decided would be supportive, nondirective, and noninterpretive for a while, she developed a fairly typical idealizing transference. My comments were always just right, my house was beautiful, my life must be perfect. She used cues, such as seeing some of the college stickers on my own children's cars when they were home, to confirm that they were perfect. Having helped them be perfect, I could help her be perfect.

Like most such patients with narcissistic disturbances, Roberta had very little awareness of any inner life. What she could describe in the way of fantasies were all searches for approval or looking for a response from an audience. She gave up her symptoms in order to please me, although they recurred whenever there was an interruption in the treatment. The enormous degree of impoverishment underneath this surface image of a well-functioning young woman was quite dramatic.

Treatment extended over a long time, never really focusing on the eating disturbance. Only very gradually was it possible to make Roberta aware of her own feelings of not being her own person and of her underlying rage against her mother. She clearly saw herself as having no choice but to be an extension of her mother. Her mother had wanted her to be a perfect controlled child, and she had sacrificed much of herself to respond to that need, always feeling that it was the only way she could ever really get any approval from her mother. When Roberta began to try to function independently, she became critical of her mother and her mother's lifestyle. After some time, her mother went into her own therapy.

Roberta herself has done quite well. Gradually, it has become possible to interpret to her in selected areas and to begin to widen her awareness of her inner life. She has a long way to go, but it appears that she will be able to get through the narcissistic shell that had so crippled her life. I am certain that some would suggest that Roberta could be treated in a family therapy situation. I am sure that symptomatically she would have gotten similar relief, but that, of course, was not the goal of treatment. While a certain amount of loosening up of her character constrictions might have occurred in such a setting, I myself doubt that they would be as extensive. I saw Roberta as someone who had to undergo some degree of structural modification if she were ever to be able to lead an independent, satisfying life. She herself said not too long ago, "First, I let you get through that wall around me, now I let other people do that, too. Sometimes it really hurts, but it's the only way I've ever really felt happy, really enjoyed myself or really felt love."

Roberta presented a kind of preoedipal pathology that results in a narcissistic consolidation, but with a fragmentation of self that results in what Winnicott refers to as a "false self." She has been able to go a little farther than some such patients, but it was a slow process in the context of a holding environment, and a long time before any real interpretive work could be done.

CLINICAL EXAMPLE: BORDERLINE PERSONALITY

I would like to turn to another kind of preoedipal pathology presenting with an eating disorder, but one much more compatible with an underlying assessment of a borderline personality.

Joan was a little over 16 when I first saw her. She came from a middle-class family, although she looked more like a member of a motorcycle gang. She came to the interview angrily, having apparently been fighting with her mother just prior to the interview. She was immediately abusive when she entered the office, telling me that she didn't need a shrink, this is all bullshit, her mother needs a shrink. She immediately assumed that I, like any other adult, would be critical and unaccepting of her: "Don't stare at me just 'cause you don't like my clothes," and "You think I'm a freak. Do I look skinny to you? I like it this way." After telling her that I understood that she didn't want to be here, that it wasn't me that made her come, she calmed down a little. I suggested that maybe as long as she was here, we could talk about whatever she wanted to talk about.

First, she told me that she wanted to set some things straight. She didn't have any eating problem. She wasn't skinny. She looked in the mirror and liked what she saw. She was even a little too fat. She could get fat because she liked to "pig out" and the only way to avoid that was to purge herself. She did this by vomiting, using laxatives, and at times, diuretics. She just wanted to lose weight to feel good. Her mother was a "fat slob," and she certainly didn't want to be like her.

Joan had very few qualms about telling me some of her other functioning, doing so exhibitionistically. She had been sexually active since she was 14 and had had a rather large number of partners. She did it because it felt good. She always liked having a guy, but it bugged her mother: "It would kill her if she knew some of what I'd done." She also told me she had used drugs starting at 13 by smoking marijuana. She had since taken uppers and downers, ranging from Quaaludes to barbiturates. Most recently, she had tried using cocaine. She also did all of these things because they made her feel good. Her functioning in school was barely passing, with frequent truancy, but she considered school a waste of time anyway. She only wanted to do what she wanted to do when she wanted to do it.

After a while, I wondered why she had to run after so many things to make her feel good. Were there times when she felt bad? She laughed and said, "You mean, when I feel like I'm shit? That's what she wants me to be, a big round ball of shit."

It became apparent during the consultation that Joan's inner life was chaotic and dominated by impulses. She had a symbiotic, intensely ambivalent tie to her mother, hating the part of her that ever felt she needed her mother. Life for her was an alternation between a good fairy and a wicked witch, polarizations, both of the way she saw her mother and the way she saw herself. She not only had distortions of her own body image, but literally felt that what might happen to her body would affect her mother more than it affected her. She had primitive defenses in addition to splitting, namely, denial and projection. There was an underlying anaclitic depression that she struggled against with overt defiance and provocative rage. She found it difficult to trust anyone. Her alternation between binging and purging paralleled her search for a good object and her spitting it out.

While Joan was never fully able to describe her inner feelings or body sensations, it was clear that she wasn't always sure that they belonged to her. Her pervasive depression had led her into a number of areas of self-destructive behavior, of which her anorexic bulimic pattern was only one. There were times when I first started seeing her that hospitalization was under serious consideration as her weight loss approached a dangerous level. Fortunately, she took this as an indication of my concern and caring and gained enough weight so that we could continue working on an outpatient basis.

As with any borderline patient, the treatment was difficult and frustrating. Joan had very little sense of basic trust or object constancy. She constantly tested me to see whether I could tolerate her rage, her seductiveness, or her dependency. She would see me only if I had no contact with her parents, and I had to refer them to a colleague.

In treating such a young woman, there is very little opportunity for careful, well thought out interpretations. The need for some help in achieving impulse control makes it impossible for such a patient to tolerate too much deprivation. Help in managing life situations and ego support are necessary if some degree of therapeutic alliance is allowed to form. Such a patient can gradually look at the distorted picture she has of herself and of the world. Impulsivity makes interpretation very difficult. Some degree of ego support and growth are first necessary. Joan was only able to first recognize that she herself felt out of control. Such a patients needs to know that the therapist will help her control herself. It is for this reason that with such a patient, therapists consider the use of medication, hospitalization, or other adjuncts to therapy along cognitive or behavioral modification lines. While these were not necessary in this particular case, they sometimes are.

Certainly, in some anorexics interpretation is not enough, and a more classical, nondirective, interpretive psychotherapy is not likely to be successful. This is true for the more disturbed borderline patients, all of whom require some time before interpretation can be used effectively. Most borderline patients respond well to a mixture of supportive and interpretive approaches. The mix varies according to the clinical assessment of the therapist as treatment proceeds.

CONCLUSION

There has been increasing diagnostic specification in terms of classifying eating disorders. There has also been a proliferation of treatment techniques without adequately discussing the basis for one or another kind of treatment. This chapter is a beginning in suggesting that the treatment of an eating disorder is very much dependent upon the type of underlying psychopathology. Central to this thesis is the need for a careful, complete assessment of all aspects of a patient's functioning and an initial psychodynamic formulation. The nature of the treatment should be largely dependent on the dynamic evaluation of the individual patient, with the therapist flexible enough to be prepared to use any of a variety of techniques or to refer the patient to someone who may be more skilled in the application of those techniques. Several brief clinical descriptions of three very different kinds of young women, all of whom present with eating disorders, have been presented to suggest how the initial evaluation influenced the choice of treatment modality.

REFERENCES

Bruch, H. (1973). *Eating Disorders: Obesity, Anorexia Nervosa and the Person Within*. New York: Basic Books.

Diagnostic and Statistical Manual of Mental Disorders. (1980). 3rd ed., p. 67. American Psychiatric Association: Washington, DC.

Goodsitt, A. (1969). Narcissistic disturbances in anorexia nervosa. In *Adolescent Psychiatry*, vol. 5, ed. S. C. Feinstein and P. L. Giovacchini, pp. 304–313. New York: Jason Aronson.

Gull, W. W. (1874). Anorexia nervosa. *Transactions of the Clinical Society of London*, vol. 7, pp. 22–28.

Kohut, H. (1966). Forms and transformations of narcissism. *Journal of the American Psychoanalytic Association* 14:243–272.

——— (1971). *The Analysis of the Self*. New York: International Universities Press.

Lasegue, C. (1873). On hysterical anorexia. In *Evolution of Psychosomatic Concepts*, ed. M. R. Kaufman and M. Heiman, pp. 141–155. New York: International Universities Press, 1964.

Masterson, J. F. (1977). Primary anorexia nervosa in the borderline adolescent: an object relations view. In *Borderline Personality Disorders*, ed. P. Hartocollis, pp. 475–495. New York: International Universities Press.

Morton, R. (1694). *Phthisiologia: Or a Treatise of Consumptions*. London: Smith and Walford.

Simmonds, M. (1914). Uber hypophysisschwund mit todichem ausgang. *Deutsche Medizinische Wochenschrift* 40:322–340.

Sours, J. A. (1980). *Starving to Death in a Sea of Objects: The Anorexia Nervosa Syndrome*. New York: Jason Aronson.

Yager, J. (1981). Anorexia nervosa and the family. In *Family Therapy and Major Psychopathology*, ed. M. Lansky, pp. 249–280. New York: Grune & Stratton.

19

Psychosomatic Disorders

Stanley Grossman, M.D.

DIAGNOSTIC CONSIDERATIONS

The classical psychosomatic conditions include the original seven by Alexander (1950) but have been expanded to cover such disorders as coronary artery disease, angina, irritable bowel and esophageal reflux-tetany syndromes, gout, and migraines. While the original hypothesis suggested that emotional conflict was etiological, later considerations, which I will discuss below, imply more "loop" models. *DSM-III-R* (1987) is more general, taking the more atheoretical position that psychosomatic disorder exists when any psychological factors affect any physical condition. Thus conflict or stress may contribute to the initiation or exacerbation, and, I believe, to the predisposition, of a broad spectrum of physical disorders. We now tend to think that psychological factors are contributors to the onset of disease in the context of a biological predisposition and that the physical condition, once established, activates emotional conflicts, which then may appear psychogenic in origin.

Two cases will be presented to illustrate these disorders with demonstrable physical changes—ulcerative colitis and bowel motility. The discussion will not include the gastrointestinal changes seen in anxiety disorder that are nonspecific and part of a generalized autonomic arousal without a specific target organ. The cases I will describe were chosen because dynamic psychotherapy was the treatment of choice. First, I will discuss some of the historical perspectives of psychoanalytic theory as it applies to the development of these disorders and to their treatment.

OVERVIEW OF PSYCHOANALYTIC THEORY OF ETIOLOGY AND TREATMENT

In his description of the Dora case, Freud (1905) interpreted the patient's "tussis nervosa" as caused by an unconscious forbidden fantasy to be like her rival, expressed symbolically in somatic reaction. The patient in the so-called Wolf man case (Freud 1918) had diarrhea and a fear of rectal bleeding, which was interpreted as a wish-fear to be like the mother (menstrual flow).

This was the model for many years. Up until the early 1960s, when psychoanalysis was at its zenith, the interpretation by Freud was applied to many disorders, including psychosis and psychosomatic disorders. However, we were limited by our state of theory, both psychological and biological. We knew more about psychodynamics regarding conflict and symbolic meanings than we did about the ego, the superego, object relations, and the complex structure of conflict. For example, Mahler's (1968) systematic studies of childhood development were not yet available, and Kernberg's (1975) and Kohut's (1971) works on the borderline and narcissistic disorders were still to come. Thus we attempted to interpret the meaning of physical symptoms as primarily symbolic expressions of warded-off anxiety stemming from unconscious conflict. Therapeutically, id interpretations were made with the goal to make the unconscious conscious. Physical symptoms were thus seen as psychological constructs with a physical facade that could be interpreted away. This characterized Sperling's (1946, 1952) early work with children, in which she recognized the importance of the mother–child interaction. Sperling differentiated the goals of supportive psychotherapy, in which a dependent transference was not to be resolved. The patient may have remissions but occasionally returns for treatment under stress. She contrasted this with psychoanalysis, in which the transference is resolved and the patient theoretically is "cured."

Weinstock (1962) surveyed analysts who reported several cases with long-term symptom relief from ulcerative colitis when treated with psychoanalysis or psychoanalytic psychotherapy. Currently, there are some analysts who feel that analysis is possible and have good anecdotal results, such as 8- to 25-year remissions of asthmatics (personal communication with Dr. Lawrence Deutsch, 1991). Dr. Deutsch believes that physical symptoms represent a communication of conflict that is not verbalized and that, with interpretation, are resolved in fairly short order. The analyst then considers the underlying character or psychological equivalents such as phobias or depression. As Sperling (1946) stated, the symptom is a somatic dramatization of a psychological conflict and symptom. My view is that the symbolic expressions of conflicts we do see are frequently secondary to the physical symptoms. When interpreted, they can relieve the physical symptoms. For example, in the context of a particular personality, the illness revives old issues with a parent (struggle over toilet training) and is an expression of those conflicts.

In the 1950s and 1960s more sophisticated genetic and developmental factors were found to be crucial. Alexander's (1950) work, which was later elaborated by Engel (1977), emphasized a more complex bio-psycho-social approach to psychosomatic disease. For example, it was felt that in peptic ulcer, the "oral" conflict in a biologically predisposed individual (having high serum pepsinogen) was activated under the stress of a perception of a meaningful loss, and that those two elements are closely linked. Thus the level of pepsinogen, a genetic marker, could be predicted by psychological testing. Based on this, ulcer disease predictions, such as those by Weiner and colleagues (1957), in their classic army study, could be done with high reliability. Mirsky (1958) discovered and hypothesized that high pepsinogen at birth stimulated a predisposition and development of oral traits and temperament, which in turn made certain demands for a fit with a responsive mother. If the oral demands for gratification were too high, then a predisposition to ulcer formation arose, ready to be activated later in life. This led Engel (1975) to a somato-psycho-somatic formulation of disease onset. However, Alexander's (1950) psychological formulations were based mainly on zonal conflicts (oral, anal). Thus in ulcerative colitis, there was a repressed need to give, to fulfill an obligation, which, when combined with resentment and a feeling of hopelessness about the ability to fulfill that need, led to a psychophysiological regression and chronic autonomic stimulation of the bowel. That obligation or duty would be fulfilled in childhood by giving stool (Beschrung), a gift, which, when combined with a biological predisposition, led to ulcerative colitis.

Alexander was clinically astute, but it was not clear whether the diarrhea, as in irritable bowel disorder, stirs this conflict up secondarily. In fact, bleeding may be the primary symptom, confounding his theory. Alexander and colleagues (1968) presented case material in a research study illustrative of different personalities and conflicts that he felt were disease specific. The case interviews were deleted of medical data and analysts were able to predict which disease the patient had, much greater than chance. Engel (1955) did retrospective studies on ulcerative colitis patients and found them to be premorbidly dependent personalities, with obsessive-compulsive features, supporting Alexander's theories.

As our model of the mind became more sophisticated, so did our psychosomatic speculations. Schur's (1955) classic work on somatization teased out the crucial elements in the pathogenesis of psychosomatic disorders. Stress (anxiety) worked specifically on defenses, and other ego functions that failed, leading to regressive resomatization of emotions, in turn leading to physiological discharge. Conversely, restoration of secondary process or verbalization led to desomatization. Schur astutely noted that the basic character of many patients was borderline. He realized that interpretive efforts and some shoring up of defenses and ego function were needed.

Schur hints at the borderline aspect of unstable affects and object relations, as well as difficulties in processing psychological data. Robbins (1990), in a paper on schizophrenia and primitive personalities, agrees with Nemiah and Sifneos (1970) on the ego defect of alexithymia. The defect is in registering and processing emotions, associated with poor affect and object representations (defect vs. conflict). According to the researchers, this may lead to marked anxiety and regression in psychotherapy and analysis, when defenses against painful feelings are loosened. Robbins feels that these genetic weaknesses predisposing toward schizophrenia are masked in early childhood, and that until the patient leaves home he is protected by a pathological family structure. This is quite similar to a psychosomatic patient. The patient, as McDougall (1982) stated, may become object addicted, experiencing a permanent need for an external (tranquilizing) object. Interestingly, psychoendocrine and neurophysiological correlates of alterations in emotional (ego) defenses and the effects of object relations were expanded upon from the 1960s on.

LATER PSYCHOBIOLOGICAL FINDINGS

Sachar et al. (1963) showed in schizophrenics and later in depressives that defensive failure or strain (i.e., talking about loss) leads to marked cortisol elevations, which has pathogenic effects on various organ systems, and that when delusional (defensive) formation takes place, cortisol levels return to normal. This was elaborated on later by Hofer et al. (1972), who showed that cortisol levels could be predicted in parents of dying children in a similar fashion. Wardedoff grief (the defense) showed decreased cortisol levels found in comparison to overt grieving. Earlier, Katz et al. (1970) had shown that women who were markedly distressed and pessimistic before breast biopsy showed markedly increased cortisol production when compared to the more hopeful pre-op patients. Tennes (1982) showed increased steroids in the most distressed infants separated from their mothers and had higher resting levels than calmer infants.

Depression and anxiety thus directly affect organ systems, including the neuroendocrine. Engel (1955) discussed the effects of these stressors not only in psychosomatic patients but in patients who develop any physical disease. Real or imagined loss, especially loss of the "key object," as Engel stated in his studies on ulcerative colitis, is pathogenic. Engel spoke of the "giving up–given up" complex preceding the onset of physical disease. This state seemed to represent both an acute and a chronic unresolved bereavement (as described by Hofer [1984] later).

These mind–body interfaces have been further elaborated upon in the past twenty years, but there are still many unanswered questions. For example, one wonders why illness and death occur more frequently when a spouse dies (Parkes 1972), or why ulcerative colitis occurs more frequently with stress of separation. What psychophysiological complexes are responsible for irregular heart beats and death? Are there psychological predictors of high serum cholesterol? Do patients who develop bowel disorder have abnormal hyperactive gut reactions at birth? How are the two related?

In a presentation to the American Heart Association, Redford Williams reported that teenagers who scored high on hostility scales had higher levels of cholesterol and low-density lipoproteins in adulthood; this may be the pathogenic component in the type A personality. At the same conference, Doctor Mara Julius reported that easygoing law and medical students in a prospective study had a 4 percent death rate by age 50 versus a 20 percent rate for a high-hostility group. These psychological factors may have been preceded by biological markers present before adolescence.

Some recent work showed an animal model for ankylosing spondylitis with associated colitis that was connected with the complex protein HLAB-27. Humans with ankylosing spondylitis have a significantly higher titer of this protein than does the normal population. Ulcerative colitis is frequently associated with spondylitic changes in humans. The somatopsychic-somatic hypothesis of Engel (1975) had postulated an early genetic marker of an antigen or protein attached to the cells of the infant's colon that remains dormant until, under the stress of not good enough mothering or actual separation, it leads to an autoimmune reaction to the person's own body tissues and then to colitis. A recent presentation before the American Psychosomatic Society by McCarthy (1991) indicates the usefulness of cancer chemotherapeutic agents aimed at these anti-gen–antibody complexes. McCarthy also discussed the current theory of a bacterial infection "causing" peptic ulcer. This same bacterial infection may play a similar role in ulcerative colitis, producing a subsequent autoimmune response. As time goes on, psychobiological data may fill in the gaps and confirm or refine some of these hypotheses.

CURRENT PSYCHOBIOLOGICAL CORRELATIONS

It became clearer that further integration of an object relations, developmental ego psychological-conflict model, as well as a psy-choneuroendocrine model, had to be shaped. A big step was taken by Hofer (1984) in a series of studies. Hofer showed that rat pups separated at 2 weeks developed specific behavioral and physiolog-ical responses within forty-eight hours: increased behavioral activ-ity, an initial increased heart rate, and gut motility. If the mother was reintroduced, the behavior calmed down, but if milk was not provided, the cardiac rate remained the same. Only the mother's milk (via a later detailed gut–brain cardiac nerve pathway) regulated the rate. Hofer later found more sustained cardiac rate changes—an increase, then a decrease, then a slower return to normal in two weeks. He discovered that this acute phase of separation, which was analogous to the "protest phase" of Bowlby (1969), was followed by a more chronic phase (Bowlby's [1973] phase of despair) with irregular sleep, REM disruption, decreased cardiac rate, de-creased growth hormone, increased irregular heartbeat, and de-creased T cell count. This seems to bear close resemblance to the changes found in humans. Hofer postulated that the mother initially acts as a psychobiological regulator; her functions are later psychi-cally internalized at specific developmental stages, and then become self-regulated. We can speculate that borderlines and narcissistic personalities do not internalize effectively; subsequently, they de-velop an intense need for real objects. As Schur (1955) mentioned, this personality is frequently associated with psychosomatic disor-ders.

Neuropsychological correlates of the above are being discovered. Skinner (1988) traced the brain frontal-cortical connections with the autonomic nervous system, especially the cardiac accelerator nerve, offering a theoretical basis for the benefit of various therapies in reconditioning organ systems. In his study on pigs, induced ventricular fibrillation was followed by recovery. Unless the nerve fibers were cut or blocked by beta blockers, the pigs given further stimulation died. Skinner postulated that learning or anxiety can decrease or increase cardiac activity. In other words, psychological intervention can modify the frontal cortical projections and transmitters. In fact, squid axon cells change in "learning" (Kandel 1983), and decreased norepinephrine synapse sensitivity occurs with psychotherapy (Hoffman et al. 1982). One can speculate that psychotherapy may lead to more soothing good internalized objects and self-representations, which then help maintain mental and biological stability. This new learning by way of conflict resolution or supportive therapy may be mediated by the neuroendocrine pathways.

All this led Hofer (1984) and Taylor (1987) to postulate that psychosomatic disease is a product of psychobiological dysregulation. A need for objects is necessary in early development for healthy regulation and in pathological cases for dysregulation. Taylor, utilizing Winnicott's transitional object and Kohut's selfobject hypotheses, found that the slow internalization of objects is crucial biologically and psychologically, and barring this internalization, "external self-objects" are forever necessary. There is much evidence of the relationship between object closeness and biological change. An example is roommates developing similar menstrual cycles (McClintock 1971, 1978).

A 15-year-old patient of mine who was depressed finally complained to her mother about "not being listened to." Her mother said, "You must have PMS. It's funny, my menstrual cycle started at 12 too. After one year, we synchronized together, then this past year we moved emotionally further and further apart, so that our cycles are opposites now. You know, people who are close get the same cycles." This is suggestive evidence for object closeness and physiological synchronization. These dyadic and group phenomena are fascinating. We know something of group formation: that psychological identification takes place; that if the individual shifts to another group, his biology changes. Here is some evidence that biological identification also occurs. Schwartz (1984) found that treating a depressed patient did not alter the dextramethasone test reaction even after the depression was relieved. It did not change until the patient was able to reestablish a significant relationship with a woman. Narcissistic individuals do have more labile vasomotor systems when feeling alienated from objects. They do not have the "warm glow" associated with healthy exhibitionism. They respond to preverbal aspects of objects as borderlines do. They feel an immediate warmth or coldness and react physiologically. They become exquisitely sensitive to temperature and sound and light changes. The tone of someone's voice means more to them than the content. They may literally feel chilled and turn off.

Weiner (1989) elaborated on the biological forerunners of disease, such as a hyperactive cough reflex and bronchospasm found in future asthmatics, or excessive reaction to food by the gut found in patients with irritable bowel syndrome (Snape and Cohen 1979). Weiner held that the mother is the major regulator and that her loss initiates the disease process. However, even with the mother present, there seems to be a basic defect in the individual's feedback mechanisms. The person is easily angered and hard to calm down. He exhibits a lack of satiation by eating, or a lack of knowing when exercise or dieting is enough. We have to do more research on psychological conflict and the role of fantasy in physical disease and how psychotherapy results in physiological changes.

I will now attempt to outline my ideas on how, despite the lack of a one-to-one relationship between perceived stress and somatic reaction, psychotherapy seems to work well in relieving symptoms of the disease and helping with adjustments to them. Later, I will describe one case in more detail.

OVERVIEW OF PSYCHOANALYTIC PSYCHOTHERAPY OF PSYCHOSOMATIC PATIENTS

There are many viewpoints about the individual psychotherapeutic approach to psychosomatic disorders. I will deal mainly with the psychoanalytic psychotherapeutic mode, which usually involves twice weekly face-to-face treatment, utilizing a dynamic understanding of personality development and symptom formation with resolution of anxiety and symptoms. My thesis is that the core personality of many psychosomatic patients includes dependent, compulsive, narcissistic, and borderline features. The primary case will attempt to illustrate the importance of object relations and pathological mourning in the onset of ulcerative colitis. The role of conflict in the incomplete mourning will be highlighted.

Karasu (1979) reviewed the therapeutic approaches and outcomes of various treatment philosophies. He was mainly critical of the lack of controlled studies. However, some studies have been done that indicate the value of psychoanalytic psychotherapy. One study by Karush and colleagues (1969, 1977) followed fifty-seven controls and thirty ulcerative colitis patients in analysis or psychotherapy for a period of thirty years. The therapeutic group did slightly worse in the first year, both symptomatically and proctoscopically; the treatment group, especially patients in psychoanalytic psychotherapy or analysis, did significantly better than the controls. The more psychologically integrated patients, where there was a precipitating event and where the symptom represented or accompanied a strong affect, did best. The less differentiated, more dependent, or schizophrenic patients did less well, their disease tended to be more progressive, and they came to surgery more often. Interestingly, this group had difficulty in verbalizing feelings, could not establish a warm therapeutic alliance, and were unable to see psychological events as meaningful.

The Alexithymic Concept

This brings to mind the alexithymic concept of Sifneos (1973) and Krystal (1983), who described primary and secondary alexithymia. The former is predominant in psychosomatic disorders, while the latter is present in severe chronic or life-threatening illnesses and post-traumatic stress syndromes. In a limited study, Smith (1983) found that 30 percent of general medical patients exhibited alexithymia.

Unfortunately, these authors tended to discourage insight-oriented, transference-defense interpretive therapy, feeling that this worsened patients' conditions. Their view is that solely supportive techniques are indicated. Psychosomatic patients had little access to feeling and verbalizing emotions. The authors held that this indicated a primary neurological deficit. My own experience indicates that there are some psychosomatic patients and others with primarily psychological disorders who are not psychologically minded. There is little curiosity about their inner life, they tend to deny, externalize, and show some ego weakness, such as pervasive anxiety, poor object and affect constancy, poor body-image constancy, and lack of fantasy elaboration. They are stimulus-response bound, describing emotions in vague physical terms, such as "up-tight." They also fear eruption of emotions, describing ideational, emotional, and physical "cascading" when upset (Knapp 1968).

Alexithymia: Defect or Defense?

My experience has been that it is true that some patients cannot engage in therapy. However, as I will describe in some detail, many of these so-called ego defects are defensive in nature, reversible, and can be dealt with by interpretation and clarification, utilizing dreams and childhood material with recall of emotionally charged events and some modification of the personality. For example, a patient of mine with ulcerative colitis cried whenever she felt "upset." She gradually was able to fractionate specific affects, linked to specific earlier events with a good therapeutic outcome. I would agree with Hogan (1990) that the massive denial can be pessimistically sub-sumed as alexithymia, or else attempted to be dealt with as in any psychoanalytic treatment. I would also agree that countertransfer-ence feelings of helplessness and anxiety about the severity of the physical condition are frequently present. For example, the severity of each case of ulcerative colitis and Crohn's disease (a variant mainly involving the small bowel) varies. In my experience, most cases are helped in reducing the severity and recurrence of the episodes. There are many cases that are recurring or chronic and unremitting, with some yielding only to surgery. The organic substrate remains even after successful treatments and may be activated by recurrent severe conflict situations.

Taylor's *Psychosomatic Medicine and Contemporary Psychoanalysis* (1987) has an excellent review of the history of psychosomatic concepts, including alexithymia. Briefly, Taylor feels that alex-ithymia is a nonspecific disturbance in the processing and expres-sion of emotion resulting in a subjective life that is different than the normal or neurotic disorders. Patients under stress are more likely to abuse food, alcohol, and drugs, and will experience vague and almost indescribable physical distress due to autonomic instability, or they will develop psychosomatic disorders. This is in agreement with the Harvard University study of graduates who develop somatization phenomena (Vaillant 1978).

How Theoretical Perspectives Affect the Therapeutic Approach

As I stated before, one's theoretical perspective as to the pathogen-esis of psychosomatic disorder dictates one's psychotherapeutic or nonpsychotherapeutic approach. Sperling (1946, 1952) felt that a psychosomatic disorder was basically a conversion phenomenon that could be interpreted away. The symptoms represented symbolic expression in somatic language of unconscious conflicts, fantasies, and affects (mainly depression). Deutsch (personal communication 1991) suggests that there is a biological anlage to asthma and ulcerative colitis, which even after a "cure" can be reactivated by a major stress. He also states that this anlage in ulcerative colitis may later manifest itself in colon cancer.

Less optimistic is Reiser (1978), who feels that the basic psychosomatic process is too deep to be touched by interpretation. However, one can take the patient into psychoanalytic treatment for the usual indications, such as character pathology. However in 1985, Reiser convincingly illustrated how interpretation was mutative in an acute panic reaction that supposedly had a biological etiology.

Schur (1955) was cautiously optimistic about treatment and described the complexities of one patient with eczema who was treated in psychoanalysis. The patient's basic character was that of a borderline, with all of the usual difficult transference storms. One of Schur's goals was to enable the patient to express emotions in a controlled way, with a minimum of somatization responses. He felt that just encouraging the patient to express his anger in a displaced form was not therapeutic, but the anger had to be traced back to its childhood roots with some resolution of the transference. Schur's concepts of the borderline, with the problem of nonspecific and specific ego weaknesses and defenses and object relations, presaged Kernberg. He also emphasized the preoedipal elements; for example, the skin was the primary contact with the mother and served as a conduit for many emotions. Rage at the mother was expressed by scratching the skin.

The followers of Alexander (1950) would conjure up a specific conflict when a patient with a psychosomatic disease presented himself. Treatment would proceed in an analytic way by interpreting the conflict, not the symptom itself. Because of the cessation of chronic autonomic stimulation, the symptom would abate.

CASE ILLUSTRATIONS

Mr. M., a 30-year-old married biology teacher, was in weekly analysis because of anxiety and diarrhea with mucous. Gastrointestinal studies were negative, except for a mild duodenal inflammation. A diagnosis of mucous colitis was made, and the patient was referred for psychotherapy. The following treatment summary is quite condensed.

Mr. M. presented as a highly intellectual but anxious individual. Six months prior to my seeing him, he had had a viral infection with several loose stools. This lingered through the school year. He developed acute anxiety in class, believing he had nothing to say, and would be compelled to leave the class and go to the bathroom. He felt ashamed and gradually withdrew from his wife and friends.

He presented as a compulsive personality needing to fill every minute productively. He worked seven days a week; prior to the illness, he lost a weekend job, which made him anxious. He also had a tendency to be obsessive; for example, when buying a car, he determined the paint on a Canadian make of a standard model was better.

His early history revealed that he was an obedient child who always produced for his mother. He recalled that his mother had raved over his early toilet training. He defended against this wish to passively please by getting everyone to depend upon him.

I pointed out that his diarrhea and anxiety connected with the idea of needing to produce. Over a few sessions I realized that the patient saw everyone, including me, as a demanding mother, demanding perfection for approval. He tried to please everyone by producing a stool instead of words. He resented having to please and realized that he unconsciously held back from talking in class, as in therapy, as an expression of conflict. A few sessions dealt with his defending against conflicted-compliant wishes. His symptoms abated and he returned to work.

One can speculate that the transference led to an internalization of a more benign (less demanding) maternal imago. One can further speculate that these more stable internalized object representations will serve as stable biological regulators.

I will now detail a case of ulcerative colitis treated by psychoanalytic psychotherapy.

Initial Presentation

The patient, a married woman in her fifties with three married children, presented with bleeding, cramps, and diarrhea. She had been treated by her gastroenterologist with cortisone enemas and asulfadiene, without relief. At the time, she was an assistant to the director of a health care facility.

The patient talked of her symptoms with appropriate concern and revealed a feeling of sadness and hopelessness. She was worried that her husband was upset over her avoiding his sexual advances. This was her second marriage of fifteen years. Her previous marriage had ended in divorce, precipitated by her husband's having an affair, and she had reacted with anger and depression. This had led to her first treatment for two years, which had helped her reestablish dating, albeit with sadistic men. She felt "fortunate" in finding a husband, a prominent academician, who treated her well. They enjoyed their marriage until five years ago. At that time, her stepson had moved into the house, soon after they had moved from another state. She became increasingly irritable toward both her husband and stepson and vaguely recognized a feeling of jealousy. She also felt that her relationship with her husband was compromised but that any expression of this would lead to further anxiety about his loving her. It was at this time that her gastrointestinal symptoms began. One can speculate that the imagined loss of her husband led to dysregulation of her bowel function.

The patient's family history revealed that her brother (a year older than she) had died at 19 during World War II of shrapnel wounds ("to the gut"—initially her fantasy, but later confirmed). She has four older sisters. Another sister had died ten days before her mother had given birth to her older brother. Her father had died thirty years ago, at age 77, from natural causes, and her mother at 87, twenty years ago, also from natural causes. One of her sisters had Crohn's disease (a variation of ulcerative colitis) but was successfully treated with surgery many years ago.

Her father had retired from his business in his forties. She described him as a compulsive collector, controlling the patient and infantilizing her mother. The patient was close to him in an ambivalent way, secretly enjoying his preference for her but feeling she was just a substitute for her brother and dead sister. Her father was frequently depressed and constantly implored her to deal with his partner, a brother. Following her first year at college, he "forced" her to write a biography of her brother, who had recently died. During this time, she was depressed and called or came home frequently. Her father never got over his son's death.

Her mother was described as beautiful, but cold and infantile, preferring the patient's sisters and brother. After the father's death, the mother depended more on the patient and developed a warmer relationship. The patient was chronically enraged at her mother, who, after her divorce, had accused the patient of not being a good cook. The patient blamed her mother for never teaching her, although during treatment memories emerged of their cooking together.

As a child, the patient felt like a victim. Memories were recalled of her feeling alone, sitting on the porch, and crying and feeling "tuned out." Her sisters treated her like Cinderella, dressing her for contests (child star lookalike). She had felt that she had to go along with this. She recalled with much affect that her sisters had misled her about her birthday, telling her she was 5 when she was really 4 ½ and not revealing her true age until she was 8. She remembers feeling "upset," but had said nothing. Her sisters had done this ostensibly because "she loved learning and wanted to go to school early."

The patient was close to her brother but envied his social contacts and was jealous of his being preferred by her parents. She dated his friends. She recalled being anxious about being left alone with her brother when her parents went out, having vague fears that he would come into her room. A recurrent memory in treatment associated with increasing anger was that of his teasing her, running around the dining room table, and then of her hitting him with a wood map.

Just prior to her brother's death, her elder sister's husband had shown her a letter from her brother who stated his anxiety about being killed. Her brother-in-law had said, "Don't tell your parents." She didn't. She now felt that magically, if she had, she might have saved him.

Initial Interviews

Initial interviews were telling. The patient appeared distressed, eager to talk, and was animated. As she told me about her brother, tears ran down her face. She put a hand to her face and said, "I must be crying!" I reminded her that she was talking about her brother's death. She responded, "Oh, that must be it. I just feel upset." Tears became a global expression of sadness, anger, and anxiety. In treatment over the next six years, she was gradually able to recognize and fractionate out the specific affects.

I saw her as mainly an obsessive-compulsive character, with a psychosomatic disease and a pathological grief reaction, who used denial, repression, isolation, and a defensive globalization of feelings. One could label this alexithymia.

Course of Treatment

The patient came twice weekly for six years. I used a psychoanalytic psychotherapeutic approach with interpretation and clarification.

The patient was intelligent, motivated, and had some insight that an "upset" precipitated, and later aggravated, her symptoms. After about a year, her gastrointestinal symptoms disappeared, only to reappear after the summer vacation during her final year of treatment and again during the final months of the termination phase of treatment. Interestingly, she developed an occasional cough, which was diagnosed as obstructive pulmonary disease by a pulmonologist, based on a mild decrease in pulmonary capacity. She was placed on various medications, which she has since decreased without worsening of her symptoms. Her coughing (without wheezing) seems to be precipitated by choked-off emotions. The onset seemed to overlap the disappearance of the colitic symptoms. Her pulmonary function studies have returned to normal.

Therapy

The patient began by talking about her distress at her job. She felt trapped and criticized by a cold female boss who was never satisfied with her work. Episodes of bleeding occurred frequently during the first several months of treatment and she seemed puzzled. I connected her feeling stuck in many previous (masochistic) relationships with people whom she could neither please nor leave. She thought of her mother, father, and husband. She recalled being excited after her divorce about dating a man whom she never could figure out, who would call her at the last minute to make or break a date.

Intellectually, she recognized that she had to have and remain in suffering relationships, yet she felt like the victim. Her ideal was to be able to endure painful feelings, and she slowly began to associate to her brother's suffering and death.

During her first treatment, her therapist had told her she felt depressed because of her guilty realized wish to see her brother killed in the war. She had reacted to this interpretation with puzzlement and anxiety.

She did wonder about resentment toward men, recalling her anger at her brother for teasing her. She remembered how her mother had told her that "men were special and that she was smart enough to marry a special man, a professor or a doctor." At this point, she developed cramping and bleeding. I said that although she described this blandly, she must have strong feelings about this, especially in the face of her accomplishments. She cried, and in an annoyed voice she blamed her mother for not teaching her to cook and for scolding her for not being able to hold onto a husband. I commented that her tears were angry ones. "I don't know who I am, what I am, or what I'm worth," she said.

This theme, especially in comparison to her husband's position, gradually evoked feelings of envy: "I feel good when my husband admires my pretty clothes and is proud to have me on his arm." This connected with her resentment when she made her husband doubt himself by not responding to his sexual advances. In turn, this evoked tremendous guilt and fear of loss of love. I interpreted that her guilt may be related to her envy and anger at her husband, which she expressed by withholding.

She suddenly thought of her sisters' dressing her as a child star and her submitting so as to gratify their needs. Again, she sounded angry but felt little emotion. I mentioned how the material sounded anger-provoking and how she was feeling so little. She admitted that she was annoyed by people manipulating her; she then had an increase in cramps and pain. I commented that her annoyance must be frightening, since she had to turn it on herself. She had an affectively charged image of a "bloody explosion," and recalled recently finding a letter that described how her brother was killed by shrapnel in the abdomen in the Battle of the Bulge. She cried and said she felt sad.

This work continued over a period of months. Her symptoms fluctuated, and she was characterized by self-punitive behavior of a nonsomatic nature.

Transference Consolidation and the Role of Early Trauma

A major resistance emerged after a year. The patient's physical symptoms abated for the next four and a half years. She began to feel "tuned out" to her feelings, as she did in childhood. I mentioned that perhaps she was avoiding feelings about her brother (whose name was the same as mine). She realized she needed me, but resented it: "As if a woman needs a man!" Anxiety dreams emerged of her brother in a shadowy room. Gradually, a memory from age 7 appeared of playing in bed with her brother. She suddenly recognized her fear of entering my office with me, hesitating at the door as I turned on the lights.

A theme suggestive of an early seduction emerged, "as if it were in the shadows." At age 3 or 4, while at the beach, she apparently was molested under the boardwalk. This memory emerged with greater clarity, in the images of shooting stars and bright lights, as her repression gradually lifted. This is typical of early sexual overstimulation, seduction, or primal scene. This probably was a screen memory for seduction by her brother, since many memories were elicited (e.g., reading a sex book as well as playing in bed with him). The more exact reconstruction was not possible, but some convincing genetic links were made in relation to me in the transference.

She dreamed that her brother called her: "He says we have three children; I thought I have to switch my therapy appointment." She wondered for the first time about me and asked if I had children. She noticed other patients and was curious whether I found them interesting. She expressed anxiety to be with me. Gradually, she began dealing with her need to see herself as forced by me, her brother, and her father to defend against her own wishes to be with us. The forcing was not interpreted at a deep sexual level associated with rape fantasies. Her conflicted incestuous sexual feelings interrupted the mourning process. To miss her brother was forbidden and tinged with envy. She had to tune out. Some of her wishes to be with me were connected with maternal longings to be cared for.

The Mourning Process as Therapeutic

This led to a resumption of the mourning process for her father and brother, with appropriate crying and sadness and with a cessation of the colitis. The patient was able to experience missing her husband when he went on business trips. At first she said that "it was like a sore ache inside. Funny, like I describe my bowel. Why can't I get over my brother's death?" I interpreted that she never could get her feelings out about her brother, father, or husband because she was frightened of her depression, as she was in college after her brother's death. She cried for three days, having images of herself as evil. She recalled the exact moment she was told of her brother's death: "I cried then, but I didn't feel it. I feel sad now."

She was able to connect the affects of mourning, anger, and guilt after persistent interpretation of her use of repression, isolation, somatization, and denial. Warm memories of father emerged as well as sadness over his death at age 77, when she was in her 30s. She was also able to feel the "loss" of her old neighborhood when she moved just prior to the onset of her symptoms. "Tuned out" was a defensive globalization. The memories were affectively linked and gradually relinquished, as in normal mourning: "I feel like my bleeding is crying inside. I can cry on the outside without feeling ashamed or guilty. I don't have to hurt myself."

Overview of Therapeutic Changes and Termination

Over the past five years many personality changes have been effected. The patient has become happier with her husband, friends, and co-workers. She is more assertive and is now the successful head of a health agency. However, she experiences feelings of being treated as older than she is and of resenting co-workers who make demands that she doesn't think she can fulfill. This has been worked through with some childhood reconstructions. Most important, she has begun to tolerate and process her emotions. She is able to tolerate co-workers' squabbles and is available to help them without fostering excessive dependence.

There was a brief recurrence prior to termination when angry mourning feelings about being abandoned by me were discussed. She was in a car accident that briefly reactivated her physical symptoms (associating to fear of leaving, guilt regarding her brother). The accident was an unconscious wish to join her brother in death.

The obstructive pulmonary disease has not been a problem. The onset seemed related to recognition of phobic concerns about her husband's business trips, with a gradual awareness of choked angry feelings at him, her parents, and me for abandoning her. The patient now feels that she is more her own person as a woman, and does not need to be a man to be successful or assertive. Instead of saying that she must be angry, she now *feels* anger.

Termination was difficult, she had to prove she could be independent, and her connected unconscious fantasy that she could or did kill her envied brother was worked through to a degree. Interestingly, her colitis briefly recurred. However, she was able to achieve almost instantaneous relief using cortisone enemas.

CONCLUSION

This patient could have been diagnosed as alexithymic and given supportive therapy. Psychoanalytic psychotherapy produced symptomatic relief and some characterologic and structural changes (e.g., she became more assertive, had a better sense of identity, accepted and dealt with emotions, and developed healthier relations). The patient was able to free associate, report dreams, use the transference to some extent, and make sense of her childhood. The mourning process was fostered and worked through. The conflicts that had stalled this process seemed pathogenic in the development of ulcerative colitis. The role of early sexual overstimulation may have also been pathogenic in the development of the patient's defensive style and somatization. All this points to the need to carefully evaluate concepts such as mourning and alexithymia, and put them in a psychodynamic framework.

I have tried to illustrate the efficacy of psychoanalytic psychotherapy in the treatment of psychosomatic disorder. However, additional elements to our classical concept of psychotherapy seemed important in producing therapeutic change.

For example, drive-defense compromise formations, involving dependency conflicts, were mainly dealt with by interpretation in the transference. However, developmental and object relations concepts also seemed quite important. Thus, dependency involved more than conflicts over oral gratification. It also seemed to serve as the vehicle for internalization of aspects of the therapist and early parental figures necessary for biological homeostasis. Conflict resolution went hand in hand with a more realistic integration of the patient's self and object images.

Along these lines, early seduction as well as (an) unavailable primary object(s) are probably etiological in the defective internalization of a protective, soothing, and encouraging parental imago. This may be a predisposing element in the development of psychosomatic disorders. The working through of these issues seemed crucial in the treatment of my patient.

Finally, it behooves us to understand current neurobiological and developmental concepts that have tended to confirm the validity and explain the efficacy of our psychotherapeutic work. Mutual exchange with these researchers will be useful to all.

REFERENCES

Alexander, F. (1950). *Psychosomatic Medicine.* New York: W. W. Norton.

Alexander, F., French T. M., and Pollock, G. H. (1968). *Psychosomatic Specificity: Experimental Study and Results,* vol. 1. Chicago: University of Chicago Press.

Bowlby, J. (1969). *Attachment and Loss: Attachment,* vol. 1. New York: Basic Books.

———— (1973). *Attachment and Loss: Separation,* vol. 2. New York: Basic Books.

Diagnostic and Statistical Manual of Mental Disorders. (1987). 3rd ed.-rev. Washington, DC: American Psychiatric Association.

Engel, G. (1955). Studies of ulcerative colitis III: the nature of the psychologic processes. *American Journal of Medicine* 19:231–256.

———— (1975). Psychological aspects of gastro-intestinal disorders. In *American Handbook of Psychiatry,* vol. 4, ed. M. F. Reiser, pp. 653–692. New York: Basic Books.

———— (1977). The need for a new medical model: a challenge for bio-medicine. *Science* 196:129–136.

Freud, S. (1905). Fragment of an analysis of a case of hysteria. *Standard Edition* 7:3–122.

———— (1918). From the history of an infantile neurosis. *Standard Edition* 17:3–122.

Hofer, M. A. (1984). Relationship as regulator: a psychobiological perspective on bereavement. *Psychosomatic Medicine* 46:183–196.

Hofer, M. A., Wolff, C. T., Friedman, S. B., and Mason, J. W. (1972). A psychoendocrine study of bereavement. Part II. Observations of the process of mourning in relation to adrenocortical functioning. *Psychosomatic Medicine* 34:492–504.

Hoffman, J. W., Benson, H., Arns, P. A., et al. (1982). Reduced sympathetic neuron system response. *Science* 215:190–192.

Hogan, C. (1990). Treatment of patients with psychosomatic symptoms. In *On Beginning an Analysis*, ed. T. Jacobs and A. Rothstein, pp. 229–242. New York: International Universities Press.

Kandel, E. R. (1983). From metapsychology to molecular biology: explorations into the nature of anxiety. *American Journal of Psychiatry* 140:1277–1293.

Karasu, T. B. (1979). Psychotherapy of the medically ill. *American Journal of Psychiatry* 136:1–11.

Karush, A., Daniels, G. E., O'Connor, J. F., and Stern L. O. (1977). *Psychotherapy in Ulcerative Colitis.* Philadelphia: W. B. Saunders.

Karush, A., O'Connor, J. F., Daniels, G. E., and Flood, D. (1969). The response to psychotherapy in chronic ulcerative colitis. *Psychosomatic Medicine* 31:201–226.

Katz, J., Weiner, H., Gallagher, T. F., and Hellmar, L. (1970). Stress, distress and ego defenses: psychoendocrine responses to impending breast tumor biopsy. *Archives of General Psychiatry* 23:131–142.

Kernberg, O. (1975). *Borderline Conditions and Pathological Narcissism.* New York: Jason Aronson.

Knapp, P. H. (1968). Acute bronchial asthma: psychoanalytic observations on fantasy, emotional arousal, and partial discharge. *Psychosomatic Medicine* 22:88–105.

Kohut, H. (1971). *The Analysis of the Self.* New York: International Universities Press.

Krystal, H. (1983). Alexithymia and the effectiveness of psychoanalytic treatment. *International Journal of Psychoanalytic Psychotherapy* 9:353–378.

Mahler, M. S. (1968). *On Human Symbiosis and the Vicissitudes of Individuation.* New York: International Universities Press.

McCarthy, D. (1991). *An update of gastrointestinal disorders.* Paper presented at the annual meeting of the American Psychosomatic Society. Santa Fe, N.M., April.

McClintock, M. K. (1971). Menstrual synchronization and suppression. *Nature* 229:244–245.

——— (1978). Estrus synchrony, its mediation by airborne chemical communications. *Hormones and Behavior* 10:264–276.

McDougall, J. (1982). Alexithymia, psychosomatosis, and psychosis. *International Journal of Psycho-Analysis* 9:379–388.

Mirsky, I. A. (1958). Physiologic, psychologic and social determinants in etiology of duodenal ulcers. *American Journal of Digestive Diseases* 3:285–314.

Nemiah, J., and Sifneos, P. (1970). Affect and fantasy in patients with psychosomatic disorders. In *Modern Trends in Psychosomatic Medicine*, vol. 2, ed. O. Hill, pp. 26–34. London: Butterworth.

Parkes, M. (1972). *Bereavement Studies of Grief in Adult Life.* New York: International Universities Press.

Reiser, M. F. (1978). Psychoanalysis in patients with psychosomatic disorders. In *Psychotherapeutics in Medicine*, ed. T. B. Karasu and R. I. Steinmuller, pp. 63–74. New York: Grune & Stratton.

——— (1985). Converging sectors of psychoanalysis and neurobiology: mutual challenge and opportunity. *Journal of the American Psychoanalytic Association.* 33:11–34.

Robbins, M. (1990). Disturbance of affect representation in primitive personalities. Unpublished.

Sachar, E., Mason, J. W., Kollmer, H., and Artiss, K. (1963). Psychoendocrine aspects of acute schizophrenic reactions. *Psychosomatic Medicine* 25:510–537.

Schur, M. (1955). Comments on the metapsychology of somatization. *Psychoanalytic Study of the Child* 10:110–164. New York: International Universities Press.

Schwartz, L. S. (1984). Case report: normalization of dextramethasone suppression test associated with social support system improvement. *Psychiatric Journal of the University of Ottawa* 9:45–46.

Sifneos, P. (1973). The prevalence of "alexithymic" characteristics in psychosomatic patients. *Psychotherapeutics in Psychosomatic Medicine* 26:65–70.

Skinner, J. E. (1988). Brain involvement in cardiovascular disorders. In *Behavioural Medicine in Cardiovascular Disorders*, ed. T. Elbert et al., pp. 229–249. New York: Wiley.

Smith, G. R. (1983). Alexithymia in medical patients referred to a consultation-liaison service. *American Journal of Psychiatry* 140:99–101.

Snape, W., and Cohen, S. (1979). How colonic motility differs in normal subjects and patients with irritable bowel syndrome. *Practical Gastroenterology* 3:21–25.

Sperling, M. (1946). Psychoanalytic study of ulcerative colitis in children. *Psychoanalytic Quarterly* 15:302–329.

—————— (1952). Psychotherapeutic techniques in psychosomatic medicine. In *Specialized Techniques in Psychotherapy*, ed. G. Bychowski and J. L. Despert, pp. 279–301. New York: Basic Books.

Taylor, G. J. (1987). *Psychosomatic Medicine and Contemporary Psychoanalysis*. New York: International Universities Press.

Tennes, K. (1982). The role of hormones in mother–infant transactions. In *The Development of Attachment and Affiliative Systems*, ed. R. N. Emde and R. J. Harmon, pp. 75–80. New York: Plenum.

Vaillant, G. E. (1978). Natural history of male psychological health: what kind of men do not get psychosomatic illness? *Psychosomatic Medicine* 40:420–430.

Weiner, H. (1989). The dynamics of the organism. *Psychosomatic Medicine* 51:608–635.

Weiner, H., Reiser, M. F., Thaler, M., and Mirsky, I. A. (1957). Etiology of duodenal ulcer: relation of specific psychological characteristics to rate of gastric secretion (serum pepsinogen). *Psychosomatic Medicine* 19:1–10.

Weinstock, H. (1962). Successful treatment of ulcerative colitis by psychoanalysts: a survey of 28 cases with follow-up. *Journal of Psychosomatic Research* 6:243–249.

20

Psychotherapy With Older Adults

Arthur M. Schwartz, M.D., and
Jules Glenn, M.D.

INTRODUCTION

Although in some societies the elderly are treated with respect and possess even more prestige than the young, this is generally not true in our society. Here, the elderly are frequently pushed aside; they are looked upon as burdens, are forced to retire, and are susceptible to physical and emotional attacks. Their frailties are emphasized and their strengths minimized. That this generalization is not universally true, however, is apparent in that our former President was over 70 and our current President is over 60.

It is difficult to set an age at which a patient can be considered elderly. The degree of cognitive and physical failure and difficulties in adapting due to "old age" varies greatly. Some 60-year-olds are frail and inflexible; many 70-year-olds are spry and vigorous. It is therefore with trepidation that we arbitrarily select patients over the age of 60 as the focus of this chapter.

Generally, it is at age 60 that the problems associated with aging become more prominent. Numerous threats of loss and actual loss become realities starting at this time. After age 60 loss becomes more important year by year. The losses include those in the mental, physical, and personal arenas. For many older people, memory, especially short-term memory, may become less sharp. Although experience and knowledge frequently make such cognitive difficulties less important, the individual may note these losses and worry about them. Jokes about "old-timers' disease" reveal the individual's inner concern. Mental flexibility and adaptiveness may limit the individual, especially when job demands or loss of a job place the patient in a difficult position. He may find his finances limited, his areas of sublimation lessened, and his ability to control his life decreased. Sadness or even depression about these and other losses may further interfere with adaptiveness.

Physical changes may also become a problem. The older person is more likely to become ill and even find himself faced with death. On a less dangerous level, he will note that he is weaker, less coordinated, and less capable of using his body well. His walk may become stiff and halting. His sexual interest and prowess may diminish, even as he wishes that he were younger and more potent. His self-esteem may suffer as he fails to live up to his ideals and wishes.

Also important are the repeated losses of friends and family, even very close family, to death and distancing. The older person may find himself isolated when he can no longer take care of himself and his children do not wish to take him in. Further, diminution or loss of visual or auditory perceptions may result in failure to experience contact with those about him. Individuals may experience the threat of death and disease as losses of bodily functions and parts, as well as losses of objects.

The various losses will inevitably create feelings of sadness, anxiety, and even serious depression. Furthermore, old conflicts dealt with adaptively in the past may not be contained as successfully, as the hierarchy of defenses alters with age. Anxiety and other symptoms may appear.

Many patients may be treated through dynamic psychotherapy. Through the therapist's interpretations the patient's hierarchy of defenses may be altered so that greater adaptation results. Psychoanalysis is usually not the therapy of choice because of limited flexibility of the patient as well as temporal considerations; it may not be sensible for a patient with a limited life expectancy to engage in a treatment that may take a long time. Psychoanalytically informed noninterpretive interventions may be required as the chief means of therapy or to supplement interpretations. The patient may need to feel the therapist's approval of him, his willingness to support the patient's need for control, and even the therapist's affection. The therapist may use countertransference as a very important vehicle for achieving a cure or improvement. The therapist's empathy for patients and love of his parents transferred to older patients can be used adaptively in therapy. Of course, a therapist's unconscious or conscious hatred for his own parents may be displaced to older patients with disastrous results. Identification with an older patient who is ill and may die may result in the therapist's dropping or avoiding the patient.

Medication may supplement other treatments. When it becomes the sole means of help, though, the human element is diminished and effectiveness is lessened. Medication includes drugs that diminish depression (e.g., tricyclic antidepressants, MAO antidepressants, and lithium), drugs that relieve anxiety (e.g., benzodiazapines and Buspar), and antipsychotic drugs (e.g., Thorazine and Mellaril). Patients with serious illnesses, including those who are close to death, may require drugs specific to the disease or analgesics. The therapist may find it helpful or necessary to deal with relatives and medical personnel who may be upset and find it difficult to deal with the patient's condition.

Old age is a period of ease of regression, partly because of organic brain changes, partly because of the pressure of anxiety and depressive affect based on factors mentioned above. Decreased ability to achieve mature sexual gratification, for example, may facilitate a search for regressive pleasures. Ego regression includes increased use of more primitive defenses and difficulties in evaluating reality. Drive regression includes increased oral and anal modes of gratification. As the older person becomes dependent on his children, a reversal of generations occurs. The mature older person pictures his children as his parents, and the children see themselves as the parents of their parents. The older person's resentment toward his parents displaced onto his children may become accentuated.

CLINICAL EXAMPLES

Given the variety of problems the aged face, one cannot expect that a single treatment plan would apply to all. In the clinical examples that follow, a number of modalities are used ranging from psychoanalysis to psychoanalytically oriented interpretive therapy, to support afforded to the individual undergoing treatment, to support of the family and encouragement of environmental changes, to the use of medication. Many cases require several approaches flexibly applied.

A Depressed Woman

Mrs. Z., 70, wanted treatment for feelings of sadness and periods of crying. She often berated herself and those about her. Her unhappiness started when her husband of forty years left her for a woman in her early forties. A series of unfortunate events led him to separate from the patient and then start divorce proceedings.

A year prior to that, Mrs. Z. had sustained a chest injury when the taxi she was riding in collided with another car. During hospitalization she had fallen and broken her hip, requiring further hospitalization. One leg became shorter than the other, resulting in difficulty walking and chronic back pain. Mrs. Z. became a semi-invalid who complained continuously about her condition. Her husband soon found he couldn't stand her moaning and groaning and decided to leave her.

Although her psychiatrist had decided that her depression was appropriate to the circumstances, not endogenous, and that it required once-a-week psychotherapy rather than medication, she felt miserable nevertheless. She appealed to her husband not to leave her, to no avail. She begged her son, who was a psychologist, and her daughter, who was a lawyer, to halt her husband's desertion of her. Her children objected to their father's behavior and told him so, but they still saw him and had dinner with him. Mrs. Z. became furious at her children. She started to cling to them, to call them frequently, to cry and complain to them. When they suggested that she be calm, that she find other interests and socialize more, she stubbornly refused. She felt they too were deserting her. When her husband initiated divorce proceedings, she decided to attack him by revealing to the Internal Revenue Service what she considered to be his illegal financial dealings.

Mrs. Z.'s therapist pointed out the self-destructive, even masochistic, nature of her behavior. She was an intelligent, perceptive woman, attached to her therapist, and could see that what he said was true. She altered her plans to call the IRS but continued to badger her children; she remained markedly and regressively dependent on them.

Her therapist interpreted suicidal fantasies that appeared in a similar way. Mrs. Z. would hurt herself, but ironically she would solve her husband's and his girlfriend's problems if she killed herself.

As this story revealed itself, Mrs. Z. talked about her childhood. Her parents were poor but hard-working. Both of them held jobs with long hours in order to make ends meet. As a result, Mrs. Z. as a child hardly saw them. She felt that she grew up without a mother. Although unaware of her resentment toward her parents, she vowed not to deprive her own children as she had been deprived. She sacrificed herself for her children and was proud of their professional and personal achievements, which she enjoyed vicariously. She was especially resentful of her children's disloyalty, since she felt that she had given up so much for them. Similarly, she became a devoted caretaker of her parents when they grew old and frail.

Over many sessions, her therapist gradually showed her, and she agreed, that she wanted her children to be good parents to her. She experienced her children and her husband as the bad parents of her childhood; she displaced resentment, which she was unaware of as a child, from her parents to them. She felt entitled now, but not as a child.

A consequence of this displaced fury was that Mrs. Z. did not achieve the love she wished. Instead, she drove her family away from her, as when she threatened not to talk to her daughter if the daughter spoke to her father. Her behavior was self-damaging. She would hurt herself more than she would hurt her children, a punishment for her own aggression and a masochistic gratification.

As Mrs. Z. acquired these insights, she felt that she could control her life better. Her depression diminished markedly. She behaved more adaptively with her children and enjoyed their closeness. Still angry at her husband, she could use her aggressive feelings wisely to fight for her legal rights as a divorced woman.

The Psychoanalysis of an Older Patient

Psychoanalysis is generally not used with the elderly, partly because a patient's advanced age seems to preclude prolonged therapy intended to alter dynamics rather than simply provide support. However, a case reported in the psychoanalytic literature shows that such intensive treatment can be undertaken successfully (Sandler 1984).

Sandler's presentation of her patient, Mrs. A., in a rather elegant manner makes the patient's chronological age, 69, fade into the background. Nevertheless, the patient's depressive symptoms turn out to result from her inability "to cope with internal stresses and conflicts aroused in her by the process of aging" (p. 489).

Mrs. A. was analyzed four times a week using the couch. The analysis depended primarily on interpretations of the patient's feelings of loss. It was apparent that Sandler's warm feelings for Mrs. A., her positive countertransference, helped the patient mobilize her own feelings yet also distracted her. Sandler enjoyed her patient's feelings about her past life so much that for a while she did not realize that the stories helped the patient to avoid her current difficulties. Sandler soon had to deal with her own countertransference as she reacted to her analysand's controlling attitudes and need to manipulate her. Control became a central issue.

An excellent teacher, Mrs. A. had arranged to continue working as an adviser at a private school after the usual retirement age of 60. When the headmaster, a friend, decided to leave, Mrs. A. quit, despite assurances by his replacement that she could continue. The headmaster's sudden departure without telling Mrs. A. ahead of time was a serious blow to her self-esteem.

After Sandler's Easter vacation, the patient's enthusiastic engagement in the analysis stopped. Mrs. A.'s anger, silence, detachment, and control dominated the treatment. Sandler interpreted a dream about vacations as an indication of the patient's need for control as a way of avoiding feelings of abandonment, helplessness, and anxiety, based on past experiences of loss. Mrs. A. confirmed and expanded the interpretation through painful memories of her anger at abandonment in childhood by the parents she loved. She became "an ideal, all-giving, all-wise and omnipotent grownup" (p. 483) to avoid disturbing feelings.

After about two years of analysis, Mrs. A., now symptom-free, more relaxed, and less perfectionistic, talked of leaving for Australia with her husband to visit a cousin she had been fond of as a child. With the help of Sandler's interpretive comments, Mrs. A. recognized a resurgence of sexual feelings and guilt about being unfaithful to her husband and her analyst. Relieved, she was able to end the analysis successfully.

Sandler concludes that "as an effort at psychoanalytic archaeology the work would have to be regarded as far from successful. On the other hand, if we consider Mrs. A.'s problem as having been due to a failure to make an adequate psychological transition from one developmental level to another, we can be more than satisfied" (p. 485).

Psychotherapy Years After a Successful Analysis

Very often patients who are eager to engage in insight-oriented therapy have benefited from psychoanalysis or analytically oriented treatment in the past. Their successful experiences convince them that similar help will again be available. Such was the case with Mrs. L.

This 60-year-old woman returned to her analyst five years after her analysis had terminated. During her first treatment, she had accomplished a great deal. Sexual inhibitions had been overcome, as had anxiety, depressive affect, and periods of rage. She had completed college, received a Ph.D in philosophy, and now taught at a local university.

Mrs. L. returned to her analyst because manifestations of rage had emerged once more. While driving her 85-year-old stepmother, she had found herself using insufficient caution. Her car struck another car in front of her, but luckily no one was hurt. Her therapist thought that a period of twice-a-week therapy could help.

Mrs. L.'s mother had died of a brain tumor when the patient was 22 months old. After a period of living with her father and his mother and sharing a room with him, Mrs. L. had been upset to learn that her father was planning to remarry. Her stepmother was unusually mean; she openly insulted both her husband and the patient, chastising her for poor schoolwork. Mrs. L. was a sad child who could not concentrate at school and did poorly. Her father reacted to his wife by staying away from home a great deal, running his business, and playing cards and golf. Mrs. L. felt that he did not protect her from her stepmother.

During the analysis her unconscious fury at her biological mother, who had died and left her, her father, who did not protect her, and her stepmother, who had threatened her, emerged. Positive and negative oedipal feelings became conscious. When her father had died, he left Mrs. L. a token amount of money; the bulk of his estate went to his wife. Mrs. L. realized her attachment to him, her love for him; she recalled as a child seeing his penis. Her fury at her stepmother arose in part because she took the patient's father away from her. The fury was also a part of a sadomasochistic relationship with her stepmother, a relationship that included affectionate feelings and defenses against them. The analytic work included interpretations of transferences from the patient's parents.

The issues outlined above reappeared in the psychotherapy. Mrs. L. felt that her therapist was attacking her repeatedly, but then realized this was not true. She did not feel angry at him for this, but was angry at her husband and stepmother. These displacements were repeatedly interpreted by the therapist. When away from her therapist, Mrs. L. would not feel his criticism; instead, she would be depressed and her anger at her husband would intensify. The transferences could be traced once more to her interactions with her parents. She needed them and loved them, was furious at them for their neglect and desertion, and was depressed at her loss of them.

Her desire for union had become obvious during her analysis, when she associated cunnilingus and fellatio with "long-distance intercourse," union with her dead mother who was far away. Now these desires, which had been repressed, became even clearer as she and her therapist repeatedly discussed an extremely engrossing novel she had read, *The White Hotel* by

D. M. Thomas. In this book, an analysand of Freud's had an affair, which was vividly described, with a son of Freud. Years after the analysis, which included symptoms of pain that were premonitions of her death, the Nazis actually killed the analysand. In a final section of the novel, Freud's former analysand is in heaven. She meets ancient and dead philosophers, such as Plato and Aristotle, and her mother, at whose breast she nurses.

Mrs. L.'s repeated discussion of *The White Hotel* clarified her attachment to her therapist and enabled her to detach herself from him. Mrs. L. accepted the interpretations of her attachment to the analyst as a continuation of those for her mother. The emphasis was on her love for and hatred of her mother, which could be gratified by union with her mother in heaven or her therapist in celestial treatment. Her return of symptoms, for which she had to reenter therapy, could keep her tied to her former analyst. Eventually, she could mourn and become independent.

For the most part, this treatment bore the characteristics of a successful analytically oriented therapy of a younger person. The patient's conflicts were analyzed and the patient, a remarkably perceptive woman, benefited from insight. Age did play a role, for as the patient became older, her longing to die and be with her mother grew. She was nearer to that blissful state when she started the therapy at 60. She unconsciously tried to hasten the process by causing an auto accident in which she and her stepmother would die. The fury behind this wish was important, but the reunion played a huge role.

Progressive Organic Brain Disease

The patients discussed thus far have benefited from psychoanalysis or psychotherapy without the complicating presence of organic changes or the immediate threat of death. In these cases, medication was not necessary. More seriously disturbed patients react emotionally to cerebral damage. Such patients make many demands on the therapist's time. In addition to formal sessions, the therapist must deal with family and other caretakers. He gets little immediate (and often long-term) gratification, especially if the patient's course is downhill despite his interventions. Goals are often modest. The therapist hopes to stem or slow regression without making the patient insensible to his or her surroundings. Perhaps, he hopes, he can help the patient spend more time with his or her family with less strife and with less suffering.

At this point, we would like to describe Mrs. G., an 81-year-old woman with progressive organic brain disease. Regressive elements could merely be slowed for a time, but never really stopped. The patient had been living with her married daughter for the past eleven years, since the death of her husband. The daughter called to make an appointment.

When Mrs. G. arrived for the consultation, the psychiatrist asked her whether she could tell him why she was brought to see him and what she thought the trouble was. She said, "I used to go with my husband to business every morning. I would ride in the car with him and I was good at figures. What caused me to be this way? I have ear trouble, used to see so many doctors, saw a GYN man. He said I lost five pounds and I had a hysterectomy eight years ago, haven't had a vacation in eleven years. I have a companion, that woman in the waiting room. I think at times she finds me difficult. I have no friends; I live with my daughter; food annoys me and my sleeping is poor."

Although there were signs of organic brain damage, the main issue at this time was the patient's depression. Hence, the psychiatrist started her on the antidepressant Imipramine at a small dose, 10 mg twice a day. He also told her that from what she had been saying, he felt that she missed her husband and wished very hard that the old days were back, those times when her husband was running the business and she was helping out by being good with figures. Since this was around the anniversary of her husband's death, the feelings of missing him were much stronger. In addition, he gave her another appointment and mentioned that they would have further opportunity to speak about her life and to especially try to understand her feelings about missing her husband.

The rest of the session was spent gathering history and completing a mental status examination. The patient had impairment in recent and in old memory, which was not severe.

For the next appointment, Mrs. G. came with her daughter. She said that she was frightened because she knew that they were late and she was afraid that the therapist would throw her out. Indeed, her family was talking about hospitalizing her (i.e., throwing her out). The psychiatrist learned that from the family, but also from the patient, who said that the very thought made her feel extremely edgy. Mrs. G. did not verbalize very much by herself and had to be encouraged to speak.

The therapist's interpretations and clarifications to the patient focused on the anniversary of her husband's death. The patient expressed wishes to die and be united with her husband at that time (Jones 1951). Her family complained that she was making "noise," which consisted of complaints, shouting, and being difficult to manage around the house. This was Mrs. G.'s way of letting people know how much she missed her husband. The psychiatrist consciously tried to take her husband's place by being, as it were, the boss. He offered guidance to the companion who was staying with Mrs. G. in the daytime hours, while her daughter was working (doing the same type of work, by the way, that the patient had done). In addition to the Imipramine, the therapist prescribed a small amount of Haldol (0.25 mg twice a day) to help reduce the patient's agitation. By the next session, this symptom had disappeared; Mrs. G. felt calm. Patient and therapist were able to talk together more easily.

During the time she wasn't in the office, the therapist engaged in numerous phone calls with Mrs. G.'s daughter and son-in-law. It became clear that the daughter's threat or talk of hospitalization was being felt by the patient as an abandonment. The therapist explained to the daughter that her mother's agitation and outbursts of temper were quite natural in that she felt she was being threatened with being sent away.

At this point, the therapist left for a previously planned four-day vacation. He gave the patient and her family the name of a covering psychiatrist, whom they decided to see. This doctor changed the medication. He cut the Imipramine and increased the Haldol. The patient became annoyed and angry with her original psychiatrist for leaving her and seemingly giving the wrong medication. The patient became even more aware of her therapist's absence since his regimen was abandoned.

With her therapist's return, Mrs. G., although angry, became somewhat calmer. After a while, though, her impulse control diminished. She became more boisterous and attacked her caretakers physically. The companion who stayed with the patient during the daylight hours when the family was not home was proving to be inadequate. The therapist discussed with the patient the possibility of sending her to a well-run nursing home—not a hospital—where he would continue to see her and be the physician in charge. She was agreeable to that, and the transfer was arranged.

With the help of Haldol, Imipramine, and twice-weekly psychotherapy, the patient achieved a greater degree of stability for a while. Eventually, organic changes became more pronounced. Multiple cerebral infarcts developed. Transitory episodes of weakness and paralysis of the limbs and aphasia appeared as the patient became more difficult to manage. She had to be transferred to a hospital, where her difficult behavior could be dealt with. The organic changes continued relentlessly. Soon after she entered the hospital, Mrs. G. could no longer recognize her family or therapist.

Dealing with a patient who is dying drains the therapist considerably. He must call on his inner strength and wisdom especially as he manages a patient he becomes attached to and expects to lose and for whom he must mourn.

Medication and Psychotherapy

Patients with less serious disturbances may require medication as well as psychotherapy. Mr. D., 62 years old and never married, was such a patient. A rather extreme physical deformity made him short in stature and hunchbacked. Burdened with a severe limp, he walked extremely slowly. He became aware of his appearance in puberty when other children made fun of him. He remembered talk of rickets in his family, which consisted of his mother, father, and a sister.

In his initial interview, his very next memory was of losing his parents. His family, who were Jewish, had lived in Vienna prior to World War II. He recalled that at age 16, he and his 18-year-old sister said goodbye to their parents, who remained in Vienna, while the two escaped to America with the help of a gentile friend. They never saw their parents again. Learning years later that his father and mother had not survived the Holocaust, Mr. D. began to repeat the prayer for the dead at appropriate religious holidays. He continued this until his own death from cerebral infarcts several years after he started therapy for a depression.

His first depression at age 34 occurred after he formed a business partnership that lasted twenty-eight years. Through his treatment with electroconvulsive therapy and psychotherapy, he remained symptom-free until a few weeks before the consultation, when the business was about to be taken over by a much larger firm. Mr. D. felt that he and his partner were about to be taken in by the other firm. He said, "Our partnership is finished. We are being swallowed by the larger organization." He became so upset that he moved in temporarily with his partner and his partner's wife.

As psychotherapy began, it became apparent that the beginning and the end of the partnership had precipitated depressions for similar reasons. Both were experienced as separations. Mr. D. remembered the loss of his parents and felt sad at the thought. Difficulty breathing at night, which required oxygen, was associated with his parents, who were gassed in a concentration camp. When his therapist connected these feelings, Mr. D. objected. "You sound very farfetched," he said. Nevertheless, his therapist's persistence in showing him the powerful impact of the loss of his parents (he had to go to temple even now to pray for them) and his upset at losing his older clients to younger people from the new firm helped him begin to see that this was true. In response, Mr. D. placed his hand over his sternum and said, "This is where I feel the heaviness."

Mr. D. added to the history. He described himself as giving and generous. Although he and his partner had had disagreements, there was never a serious argument. He recalled that he had known his partner's wife first and had actually introduced them. Talking about his romantic life, he said that he could never expose himself to a woman because of his deformities. He became more and more depressed as he harped on the ugliness of his body. Because he suspected a bipolar element to the disturbance, his therapist gave him Imipramine and supplemented it with lithium.

Mr. D. began to feel better—"like my old self," he said. He became interested in the world again and wanted to do everything. He started to become manic as he became somewhat forward with women in the office, something he had never done before. His phallic urges intensified (see Abraham 1911, Fenichel 1945, Loeb and Loeb 1987).

As therapy continued, Mr. D. accepted interpretations connecting his loss of parents and his later depressions. He recalled that, as a teenager in Austria, he had wanted very much to become a physician, an identification with his father who had been in the medical corps during World War I. Also, now that he was planning to return to his own apartment, he described his envy of his partner's full family life. He said that he could not allow himself to think about having a woman who would love him. At this point he again recalled his realizing at the age of 5 that he was deformed and couldn't run like other kids.

When his therapist suggested that a fear of women was even more important than his deformity in causing his trouble, he retorted, "I have now heard the most stupid remark in my whole life. You should see this body. A woman couldn't look." He was becoming more assertive and able to display his hostility more freely. Soon he confirmed his therapist's suggestion. His deformity appeared to be experienced as a castration, possibly a defense against wishes that arose in the oedipal period. Mr. D. said that his secretary, whose husband had died, had asked him to dinner; he tried to discount the therapist's statement that she knew about his deformity but wanted to go out with him anyway.

Mr. D.'s depression had disappeared by the beginning of the therapist's summer break. He was now taking lithium but not Imipramine. After the break, Mr. D. was depressed again. The business merger was not working, he said. As he and his therapist continued their work together, his therapist showed him his reaction to the loss of the therapist during the summer and its revival of feelings connected with the loss of his parents. Mr. D. admitted that over the summer he had had his first fight with his partner's wife—he felt that she treated him like a child. As he discussed his feelings toward women, his defensive emphasis on his deformity, his castration fears, and his envy, his depression lifted; no medication was necessary.

Unfortunately, in the midst of the work, Mr. D. suffered a massive cerebral vascular accident, from which he never regained consciousness. He died a few days later.

DISCUSSION

The patients under discussion had a variety of personality structures and varying degrees of biological and psychological impairment. Berezin (1972) emphasized the personality rather than the chronological age of each patient. According to him, aging can change preexisting behaviors and produce new behaviors, but personality remains relatively stable. Healthy adaptive personality characteristics are as durable as pathological traits. Often the character traits are accentuated as the individual has to cope with the demands of aging. Sandler (1984) looked at old age as a new developmental stage that requires new adaptations.

In many patients, control becomes an important need as they try to maintain mastery over their changing environment, their changing bodies, and their recurring losses (Goldfarb, 1953a,b, Goldfarb and Sheps 1953). Older people invariably experience loss and react to it with sadness or depression. They erect defenses against these affects, as well as against anxiety and shame. Their bodily failures may be experienced as castration. Their loss of friends and loved ones may alert them to their own vulnerability and remind them of early deprivations or desertions. Sexual desires may be muted but are not gone; sexual conflicts of childhood continue into old age. Aside from diminished libido due to physical changes, the lack of external stimulation and the inhibiting influence of depression may lessen sexual drives.

Regressive propensities are prominent as people grow old. When conflicts or circumstances make mature genital gratification difficult or impossible, pregenital pleasures may be sought consciously or unconsciously. Hence, older people become concerned about their bowel habits and regularity, or concentrate on nutritional interests. Older people who are being taken care of by others, including their children, may become angry if this care is not forthcoming. These wishes have a realistic base when the elderly are unable to care for themselves because they suffer cognitive deficits or become ill and require help. Organic brain disease will often produce regression in the sense that mature and adaptive thinking diminishes or becomes impossible.

The therapist has numerous ways of dealing with his patients' difficulties. We have seen that many patients who are psychological minded and flexible will benefit from interpretations, while others will require more support, guidance, and environmental alteration to help them cope with the aging process and environmental influences. Certainly, the attitude of the therapist is pivotal. Bar-chilon (1958) emphasized the role of countertransference cures. He considered countertransference to be the single most important factor in therapy with the elderly. He used the term broadly to cover the variety of emotional reactions to the elderly in general and to specific patients in particular. Hence, useful empathy, affection, optimism, and stimulation are included in the therapeutic counter-transferences. The therapist's enthusiasm, appreciation, admira-tion, and sympathy may be vital, as it was in the residents Barchillon supervised.

There is a danger that the patient's failure to live up to the doctor's unrealistic expectations will lead to disillusionment and depression. The therapist must give up some of his feelings of omniscience and not be overly ambitious in regard to the patient's capacity for improvement. Rather than aim for marked and unrealistic structural change, the therapist should be happy to improve the patient's affective state, mostly depression, to lessen hypochondriasis, and to reduce anhedonia to a degree. Through his attitudes and sometimes his exhortations, he must try to convince the elderly patient that life and living are better than the nothingness of death.

Myers (1986) was impressed with the intensity of his own countertransference reactions that evolved during treatment. These, he said, "may be a function of unresolved conflicts about one's own prior analyst [or] . . . one's parents" (p. 41). Using his own dreams as illustrations, Myers recognized that he, a younger person treating an older one, had a strong wish to rescue the patient, a continuation of his own desires to save his father. Displacements from the therapist's parents to his patient may be useful or may hinder the work. Arlow (1986), in discussing Myers's paper, noted that age has a profound impact as an organizer of life, but that what constitutes "older" is quite relative. The psychotherapist's emotional reactions, including countertransference, may interfere with his work (Cola-russo and Nemiroff 1987). Arlow cautioned that a younger therapist may feel like a usurper in attempting to heal an older patient. He may also resent his own now elderly parents and, through displace-ment, attack his patient, an example of transference. Or he may respond to his elderly patient's transference to him with antagonism to the patient, whom he equates with his parents, an example of countertransference in the strict sense of the term (Glenn this volume; Aronson 1986).

As a result of guilt for his feelings toward his patient or through identification with an ailing, deficient, or dying elderly person, the therapist's personal fear of injury may be aroused. The therapist may defensively or aggressively deprecate his frail older patients whose mental capacities may be inferior to his (Kahana 1980). The dying patient presents a particularly potent problem. The therapist may want to avoid him, not think about him, indeed let him die without help (Eissler 1955, Schwartz 1977).

Because the elderly may arouse strong feelings, the therapist may avoid treating them. He may do this directly by refusing to see such patients, or he may discourage patients from continuing to see him by making such remarks as "What do you expect? You're getting older."

Butler and Lewis (1977) suggest additional reasons for the avoidance of older patients: (1) Older patients encourage therapists to think about their own age. (2) Feelings of helplessness and anticipated therapeutic impotence occur in therapists of patients with progressive organic brain disease. (3) Therapists may fear that a patient will die during the course of the treatment, a not unrealistic possibility when a patient is, say, 75 years old. Therapists may thus want to avoid the pain of mourning for a person he becomes close to. (4) Therapists may feel that they are wasting their time with the elderly and that they are not being "cost efficient." (5) Analysts may recall Freud's belief that the elderly are insufficiently flexible and therefore not suitable for psychoanalysis; they may interpret this to mean that such patients cannot be helped by psychotherapy as well. (6) Finally, therapists may fear that their colleagues will make fun of them for treating "crocks."

Certain therapeutic principles can be derived from the literature on the treatment of the older patient and from the cases described here.

1. Flexibility in attitude toward the elderly is essential. One must not lump them together as if they all have the same traits. As with younger patients, one must assess each patient and determine the optimal treatment. Some will do best with analytically oriented psychotherapy or psychoanalysis; others will require personal support from the therapist and the environment. Indeed, the therapist often will have to deal with the family and other physicians of the patient. The therapist accustomed to taking a neutral position may find himself surprised and challenged when he has to argue with physicians caring for his hospitalized patient about their reluctance to give adequate analgesics to a patient in pain, for instance (Schwartz 1977).

The therapist's flexibility will include a willingness to shift gears—

to provide medication, like antidepressants, to visit the patient in the hospital or at home when necessary, and to interpret conflicts to a patient whose psychotherapy is primarily supportive. The therapist will be sympathetic to the patient's reality difficulties, then encouraging and optimistic about the patient's future prospects, thus generating interest and excitement. Cath (1973) wondered whether a therapist can help a patient overcome a sense of depletion of the self by working together with a patient in such a way as to reinfuse the general instinctual loss from which the elderly person frequently suffers. Cath felt that a balance can be struck between external and internal depleting forces and restorative forces derived from the organism, the mind, and the external world, including society.

2. Control is often a central issue. The therapist may interfere with the patient's need for control by grabbing it from him. Instead, he should encourage the patient's sense of control through interpretation, as in Sandler's (1984) case, through actual encouragement to hold onto the reins of life, or through restraint in interpreting desperate needs for control.

3. As we have seen, the therapist must deal with his own emotions. He should understand and, if necessary, control his own transferences, countertransferences, and identifications when they interfere with his work. He should use his emotions to help him understand the patient and to provide the patient with sustenance, encouragement, and a desire for life and pleasure.

4. Sexual issues may be very important. Elderly patients may find themselves unable to enjoy sex because of bodily changes. For example, thinning of the vaginal epithelium may result in dyspareunia. Under a gynecologist's care, this can be dealt with by local applications or oral ingestion of such hormones as estrogen. Estrogen's harmful effects in producing malignancies has to be assessed and a decision made with the patient as to what is best for her well-being.

Medication may cause impotence. The dose of beta blockers for hypertension may have to be titrated so that the patient's illness is under control and his sexuality improved.

When a patient has a sexual partner, accommodations have to be made regarding sexual desires, since the elderly generally are sexually excited less often than younger people. The therapist may help a patient with these adjustments through interpretation or advice. Similarly, interpretation or advice may help a patient overcome inhibitions about getting satisfaction through masturbation when intercourse is not available.

5. The therapist must be alert to the other effects of medication and be ready to discontinue or diminish usage when deleterious effects occur. Such effects include confusion, which has to be differentiated from mental aberrations due to organic cerebral damage.

CONCLUSION

Treatment of the elderly has to be based on careful evaluation of the individuals under care. Therapies include psychoanalysis, psychoanalytically oriented psychotherapy, and analytically informed supportive therapy, which may involve environmental manipulation as well as medication. As individual traits are taken into account, the therapist must be flexible. His emotional reactions to his patients (including countertransference) are important therapeutic tools but may interfere with therapy.

REFERENCES

Abraham, K. (1911). Manic-depressive insanity. In *Selected Papers of Karl Abraham*, ed. J. Strachey, pp. 137–157. New York: Basic Books, 1953.

Arlow, J. A. (1986). Discussion of paper by W. Myers. *Bulletin of the Association for Psychoanalytic Medicine* 26:45–46.

Aronson, M. J. (1986). Transference and countertransference in the treatment of difficult character disorders. In *Between Analyst and Patient*, ed. H. Myers, pp. 13–32. New York: The Analytic Press.

Barchilon, J. (1958). On countertransference "cures." *Journal of the American Psychoanalytic Association* 6:222–236.

Berezin, M. A. (1972). Psychodynamic considerations of aging and aged: an overview. *American Journal of Psychiatry* 128:1483–1491.

Butler, R. N., and Lewis, M. I. (1977). Aging and mental health. In *Positive Psychosocial Approach*, ed. N. L. Mullins and L. Brunngraber, pp. 270–291. St. Louis: C. V. Mosby.

Cath, S. A. (1973). Psychoanalytic concepts of creativity and aging. *Journal of Geriatric Psychiatry* 6:155–159.

Colarusso, C. A., and Nemiroff, R. A. (1987). Clinical implications of adult developmental theory. *American Journal of Psychiatry* 144:1263–1270.

Eissler, K. R. (1955). *The Psychiatrist and the Dying Patient*. New York: International Universities Press.

Fenichel, O. (1945). *The Psychoanalytic Theory of Neurosis*. New York: W. W. Norton.

Goldfarb, A. (1953a). The orientation of staff in a home for the aged. *Mental Hygiene* 37:76–83.

———— (1953b). Recommendations for psychiatric care in a home for the aged. *Journal of Gerontology* 7:343–347.

Goldfarb, A., and Sheps, J. (1953). Promoting understanding of aged patients. *Social Casework*. December, pp. 1–8.

Jones, E. (1951). Dying together. In *Essays on Applied Psychoanalysis*, pp. 9–21. London: Hogarth Press.

Kahana, R. J. (1980). Psychotherapy with the elderly. In *Specialized Techniques in Individual Psychotherapy*, ed. by T. B. Karasu and L. Bellak, pp. 314–336. New York: Brunner/Mazel.

Loeb, F., and Loeb, L. (1987). Psychoanalytic observations on the effect of lithium on manic attacks. *Journal of the American Psychoanalytic Association* 35:877–902.

Myers, W. A. (1986). Transference and countertransference issues in treatment involving older patients and younger therapists. *Bulletin of the Association for Psychoanalytic Medicine* 26:41–47.

Nemiroff, R. A., and Colarusso, C. A. (1985). *The Race Against Time: Psychotherapy and Psychoanalysis in the Second Half of Life*. New York: Plenum.

Sandler, A. (1984). Problems of development and adaptation in an elderly patient. *Psychoanalytic Study of the Child* 39:471–489. New Haven, CT: Yale University Press.

Schwartz, A. M. (1977). Psychotherapy with the dying patient. *American Journal of Psychotherapy* 31:19–35.

Thomas, D. M. (1981). *The White Hotel*. New York: Viking.

INDEX